DID YOU KNOW?

DID YOU KNOW?

PaRragon

Bath • New York • Cologne • Melbourne • Delhi
Hong Kong • Shenzhen • Singapore • Amsterdam

This edition published by Parragon Books Ltd in 2014
and distributed by

Parragon Inc.
440 Park Avenue South, 13th Floor
New York, NY 10016
www.parragon.com

ISBN 978-1-4723-7751-7

Printed in China

Contents

INTRODUCTION

FACTS ARE ALL around us. Sometimes it seems there are too many facts for our brains to absorb. This book helps your brain by making the facts interesting and easy to understand.
There are two different ways that the facts are presented:
1. In the first half of the book as facts in panels.
2. In the second half as questions and answers.

Fact Panels

Hundreds of key facts are provided in the fact panels. Each key fact has a bullet point (·) to help you find it.

Captions also provide additional vital information.

Questions and Answers

One of the best ways of presenting information is in the form of asking questions and then giving the answers. This book does this as well as providing short quizzes to test how well you remember the facts.

Categories

The book is also broken down into different categories such as animals, science, plants, space, etc. to help you find the information you want quickly.

Superb illustrations throughout the book provide visual information to add to your factfinding.

How to use this book

THIS BOOK has many features to help you look up things or just enjoy browsing from page to page. There are several illustrations on almost every page.

The Factfinder has helpful introductory text at the beginning of each section.

The Factfinder section is packed with fascinating factboxes like this one.

Planet Earth

THIRD PLANET OUT FROM THE SUN, our Earth looks from a dista like a great round blue jewel hanging in the darkness of space. It is blue because three-quarters of its rocky surface is drowned under ocean waters which shimmer in the light of the Sun. No other plane this much water on its surface. Here and there, its rocky surface pokes up abo the water to form half a dozen large continents and thousands of smaller islan The very ends of the world are glistening white – the permanent polar ice cap

FACTS: Earth measurements

- The size of the Earth
  Modern measurements show the distance round the Earth is 40,024km at the equator. The Earth's diameter at the equator is 12,758km – slightly larger than its diameter pole to pole, by 43km.

- The weight of the Earth
  The Earth weighs 6,000 trillion trillion tonnes.

- The angle of the Earth
  The Earth tilts over at an angle of 23.45°.

  ▽ Satellites have allowed the Earth to be measured more accurately then ever before. Satellites can detect movements of the continents of just a few millimetres or small variations in the height of the sea's surface.

△ The Earth looks round, but it is not a perf Because it spins faster at the equator than is actually shaped more like a tangerine, bur at the equator and flattened at the poles. S used to describe its shape as an oblate sphe (flattened ball). Now satellite measurement detected other slight irregularities, so they geoid, which simply means Earth-shaped.

98

There are many photographs throughout the book.

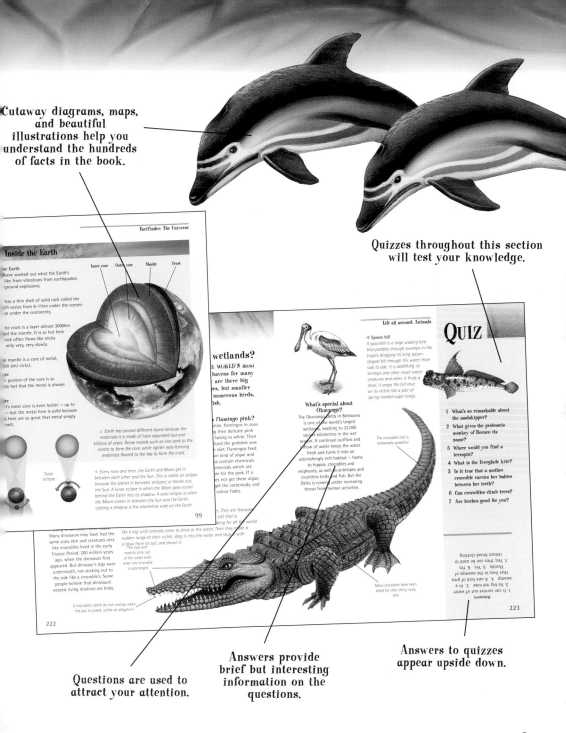

Cutaway diagrams, maps, and beautiful illustrations help you understand the hundreds of facts in the book.

Quizzes throughout this section will test your knowledge.

Questions are used to attract your attention.

Answers provide brief but interesting information on the questions.

Answers to quizzes appear upside down.

Factfinder: The Universe

Inside the Earth

...e Earth
...have worked out what the Earth's ...like from vibrations from earthquakes ...ground explosions.

...has a thin shell of solid rock called the ...ch varies from 6-11km under the oceans ...m under the continents.

...he crust is a layer almost 3000km ...ed the mantle. It is so hot here ...ock often flows like sticky ...only very, very slowly.

...e mantle is a core of metal, ...un and nickel.

...re ...r portion of the core is so ...ly hot that the metal is always

...re ...'s inner core is even hotter – up to ... – but the metal here is solid because ... here are so great that metal simply ...melt.

Inner core   Outer core   Mantle   Crust

◁ Earth has several different layers because the materials it is made of have separated out over billions of years. Dense metals such as iron sank to the centre to form the core, while lighter rock-forming materials floated to the top to form the crust.

Solar eclipse

◁ Every now and then, the Earth and Moon get in between each other and the Sun. This is called an eclipse because the planet in between 'eclipses', or blocks out, the Sun. A lunar eclipse is when the Moon goes round behind the Earth into its shadow. A solar eclipse is when the Moon comes in between the Sun and the Earth, casting a shadow a few kilometres wide on the Earth.

99

...wetlands?
...E WORLD'S most ...havens for many ...are there big ...rs, but smaller ...numerous birds, ...ish.

...flamingo pink? ...hile, flamingos in zoos ...ng their delicate pink ...fading to white. Then ...lized the problem was ...r diet. Flamingos feed ...in kind of algae and ...e contain chemicals ...tenoids which are ...le for the pink. If a ...es not get these algae, ...get the cartenoids, and ...colour fades.

...s. They are fearsom... ...tail that is ...king for all th...

...like a log, until animals come to drink at the water. Then they make a sudden lunge at their victim, drag it into the water and stun it with a blow from its tail, and drown it.

The eyes and nostrils stick out of the water even when the crocodile is submerged

Many dinosaurs may have had the same scaly skin and creatures very like crocodiles lived in the early Triassic Period, 200 million years ago, when the dinosaurs first appeared. But dinosaur's legs were underneath, not sticking out to the side like a crocodile's. Some people believe that dinosaurs' nearest living relatives are birds.

A crocodile's teeth do not overlap when the jaw is closed, unlike an alligator's

222

Life all around: Animals

◁ Spoon bill
A spoonbill is a large wading bird that paddles through swamps in the tropics dragging its long spoon-shaped bill through the water from side to side. It is searching for shrimps and other small water creatures and when it finds a meal, it snaps the bill shut on its victim like a pair of spring-loaded sugar tongs.

What's special about Okavango?
The Okavango Delta in Botswana is one of the world's largest wetlands, swelling to 22,000 square kilometres in the wet season. A continual outflow and inflow of water keeps the water fresh and turns it into an astonishingly rich habitat – home to hippos, crocodiles and elephants, as well as antelopes and countless birds and fish. But the Delta is coming under increasing threat from human activities.

The crocodile's tail is immensely powerful

Many crocodiles have been killed for their shiny, scaly skin

QUIZ

1   What's so remarkable about the mudskipper?

2   What gives the proboscis monkey of Borneo its name?

3   Where would you find a terrapin?

4   What is the Everglade kite?

5   Is it true that a mother crocodile carries her babies between her teeth?

6   Can crocodiles climb trees?

7   Are leeches good for you?

Answers
1. It can survive out of water 2. Its big red nose 3. In a swamp 4. A rare bird of prey that lives in the swamps of Florida 5. Yes 6. Yes 7. Yes, they can be used to reduce blood clotting

223

9

Amazing Factfinder

This is an atom. It is so tiny that two billion would fit on the dot on the top of this "i."

This is what a silicon chip looks like from about 8 inches away. It is about 1/8 inch long.

This is what a butterfly looks like from about 3 feet away. It is about 3/4 inch across.

This is what a lion looks like from about 33 feet away. It is about 10 feet long.

INSIDE THIS SECTION there is a huge array of facts about everything from the smallest thing in the Universe to the biggest. The tiniest things in the Universe, like atoms, are so small you can only see them under the most powerful microscopes. The very tiniest are particles called quarks, so small that billions of them would fit inside an atom. The biggest things, like stars and galaxies, are so big you can only see them all when they are very far away. The very biggest is a wall of galaxies in space called the Great Wall, over a billion light-years long. In between come all kinds of things, from insects and the little electronic chips that make computers to larger animals like lions and us humans, and from great mountains and rivers to entire continents and the world.

MEASUREMENTS

1,000 picometers = 1 nanometer
1,000 nanometers = 1 micrometer
1,000 micrometers = 1 millimeter
10 millimeters = 1 centimeter = 3/10 inch
2.5 centimeters = 1 inch
12 inches = 1 foot
5,280 feet = 1 mile
5.878 trillion miles = 1 light-year

This is what our galaxy, the Milky Way, looks like from two million light-years away–that is, about 12 billion billion miles. It is about 100,000 light-years (about 600 million billion miles) across.

SMALL THINGS & BIG THINGS

SMALL THINGS

• A Cesium atom measues only 0.00000002 inch across.
• The smallest known living thing is a tiny microbe called *Nanoarchaeum equitans* with a diameter of just 400 nanometers.

BIG THINGS

• The largest galaxy is probably at the centere of the Abell 2029 galaxy cluster in the constellation of Virgo, thought to be 5.6 million light-years across.
• The largest structure made by living things is the coral Great Barrier Reef, off Queensland in Australia. It is over 1,860 miles long.

This is what the Sun looks like from about 87 million miles away. It is about 808,000 miles across.

This is what the Earth looks like from 62,000 miles away. The Earth is around 8,000 miles across.

This is what mountains like the Matterhorn in the Alps look like from about 6 miles away. It is about 14,692 feet high

11

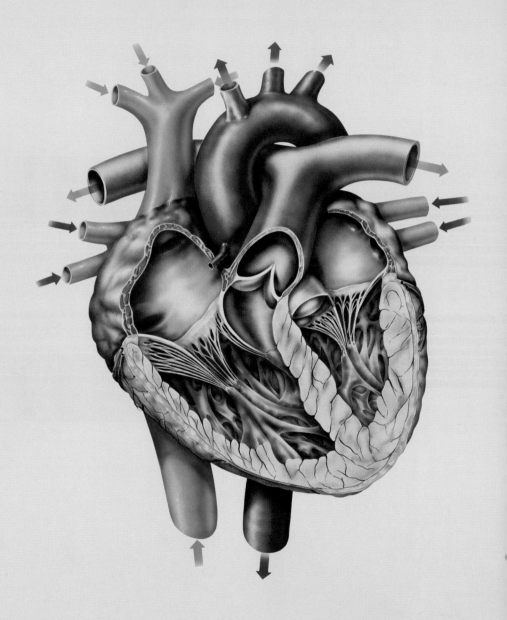

PEOPLE

Heart and blood

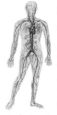

THE HEART IS ONE OF THE BODY'S MARVELS, pumping blood around the body ceaselessly. Every second of the day, even as you sleep, the heart's powerful muscles are contracting to send a jet of blood shooting through the body's intricate network of blood vessels. Blood flows right around the body and back to the heart, creating a complete circulation to every part of the body. Without it, you would quickly die. Blood carries the oxygen, nutrients, and chemicals that every body cell needs to survive, and washes away all the waste products, including carbon dioxide.

FACTS: About blood

- **What is blood?**
  It is a complex mix of cells and platelets in a clear yellowish fluid called plasma. Washed along in the plasma too are salts, hormones, fats, and sugars.

- **Red blood cells**
  The most numerous blood cells are button-shaped "red" blood cells, which are like rafts that ferry oxygen around the body, held on board by a protein called hemoglobin.

- **White blood cells**
  Big "white" blood cells play a vital role in the body's defense against disease. White blood cells called neutrophils swallow invaders. Lymphocytes help identify them.

- **Platelets**
  Tiny cell fragments called platelets help plug leaks such as cuts.

▶ *Blood is a mix of red cells (erythrocytes), white cells (leucocytes) and tiny platelets in plasma.*

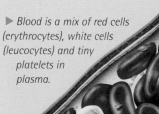

FACTS: About circulation

- **Arteries**
  Blood flows out from the heart through large blood vessels called arteries, which branch into smaller arterioles and then into tiny capillaries.

- **Veins**
  Blood flows back to the heart through small venules that join to form larger veins. The load of oxygen makes blood redder in the arteries than in the veins.

- **Double circulation**
  There are two systems of circulation in the body, each pumped by a different half of the heart.

- **Sides of the heart**
  The left of the heart drives the "systemic" circulation, which carries oxygen-rich blood from the lungs around the body. The right half of the heart drives the "pulmonary" circulation, which drives blood through the lungs to the left side of the heart.

- **Pulse**
  The pumping of the heart sends regular shock waves through the circulation, detectable as a pulse. To feel your pulse, lay two fingers gently on the inside of your wrist. Counting the number of pulses per minute tells you how fast your heart is beating.

DATA: Blood & heart

- **RACING BLOOD**
  Blood flows through the arteries at 1m a second.

- **BLOOD VESSELS**
  There are 37,000 miles of capillaries in the body.

- **HEART RATE**
  The heart beats an average of 80 times a minute.

▲ This doctor is checking his patient's risk of suffering from "coronary heart disease." In this disease, the supply of blood to the heart muscle is restricted in some way—and may be cut off altogether, causing a heart attack, in which the heart stops beating.

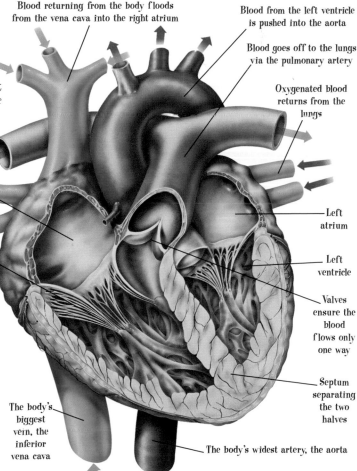

Blood returning from the body floods from the vena cava into the right atrium

Blood from the left ventricle is pushed into the aorta

Blood goes off to the lungs via the pulmonary artery

Oxygenated blood returns from the lungs

Blood returning from the body gathers in the right atrium

Blood from the right ventricle is pushed into the pulmonary artery

Left atrium

Left ventricle

Valves ensure the blood flows only one way

Septum separating the two halves

The body's biggest vein, the inferior vena cava

The body's widest artery, the aorta

▶ The heart is not just one pump but two, separated by a thick wall of muscle called the septum. Blood from the veins flows into each half of the heart from the top, flooding the "atrium," the first of the two chambers. This is a small reservoir where blood builds up before entering the second chamber, or "ventricle." The ventricle has extra thick, muscular walls that squeeze the blood out and send it shooting through the arteries.

Lungs

IF YOU STOPPED BREATHING for more than a minute or two, you would quickly die. Breathing provides your blood with the oxygen from the air that is vital to the survival of every cell in your body. Just as fire burns only if there is plenty of oxygen, so body cells need oxygen from the blood to break down the food they also get from the blood. Without oxygen, brain cells live only a few minutes—which is why the brain is quickly damaged if the heart stops pumping blood. When cells break down food, oxygen joins with carbon in the food to make carbon dioxide, which you breathe out.

FACTS: About breathing

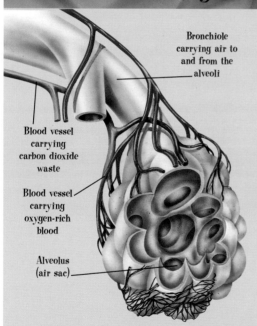

Bronchiole carrying air to and from the alveoli

Blood vessel carrying carbon dioxide waste

Blood vessel carrying oxygen-rich blood

Alveolus (air sac)

▲ At the end of every airway in the lung, there are clusters of tiny air sacs called alveoli—over 300 million altogether. This is where oxygen is transferred into the blood. The "blue" blood vessels carry carbon dioxide to the alveoli ready for breathing out. The "red" vessels carry fresh oxygen to the rest of the body.

- **Nose and throat**
  Normally, you breathe air in through your nose—although you can also breathe through your mouth. Air then flows down through your throat through a tube—called the pharynx at the top, the larynx in the middle, and the trachea (or windpipe) at the bottom.

- **Two lungs**
  The trachea pipes air into your lungs, the two spongy grayish-pink bags in your chest. Lungs transfer oxygen from the air into the blood.

- **Airways**
  The lungs are like hollow trees with hundreds of branching airways called bronchioles.

- **Air sacs**
  Around the end of each bronchiole are clusters of air sacs, or "alveoli," like bunches of grapes.

- **Air to blood**
  When you breathe in, oxygen from the air passes through the thin walls of the alveoli into the tiny blood vessels wrapped around them.

- **Blood to air**
  Unwanted carbon dioxide passes from the blood through the alveoli walls into the lungs—and so goes out of the body as you breathe out.

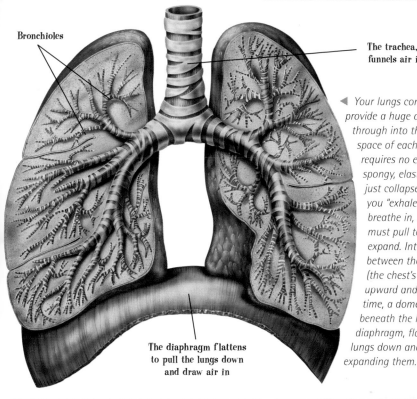

Bronchioles

The trachea, or windpipe, funnels air into the lungs

◄ Your lungs contain miles of airways to provide a huge area for oxygen to seep through into the blood in the short space of each breath. Breathing out requires no effort, because the spongy, elastic material of the lungs just collapses like a balloon when you "exhale" (breathe out). But to breathe in, muscles in the chest must pull to make the lungs expand. Intercostal muscles between the ribs lift the ribcage (the chest's framework of bone) upward and outward. At the same time, a domed sheet of muscle beneath the lung, called the diaphragm, flattens out, pulling the lungs down and further expanding them.

The diaphragm flattens to pull the lungs down and draw air in

DATA: Breathing

- **BREATHS IN A LIFETIME**
  The average person will take over 600 million breaths during their lifetime.

- **LUNG AREA**
  Opened out and laid flat, the lungs would cover an area the size of a tennis court.

- **LUNG CAPACITY**
  On average, we breathe in and out roughly a quart of air every ten seconds or so.

- **LENGTH OF AIRWAYS**
  The branching of the bronchioles means that altogether there are probably over 1,500 miles of airways in the lungs!

FACTS: Respiration

- **What is respiration?**
  Respiration means not only breathing but also the conversion of sugar to energy in body cells. This conversion is called burning, because it creates heat.

- **Aerobic respiration**
  Aerobic respiration occurs when muscle cells burn sugar with oxygen. Anaerobic respiration occurs when they burn sugar without oxygen.

There is not enough time during a sprint to boost the oxygen supply to the muscles, so they work anaerobically. Only on longer runs do they begin to work aerobically.

Muscles

EVERY MOVE YOU MAKE–running, dancing, smiling, and everything else–depends on muscles. You even need muscles to sit still: without them, you would slump like a rag doll. Muscles are bundles of fibers that tense and relax to move different parts of the body. There are two kinds: muscles: those that you can control, called voluntary muscles, and those that you can't, called involuntary muscles. Most voluntary muscles are "skeletal muscles," muscles that move parts of your body when you want them to. Involuntary muscles are those like your heart and the muscles around your digestive system, which work automatically.

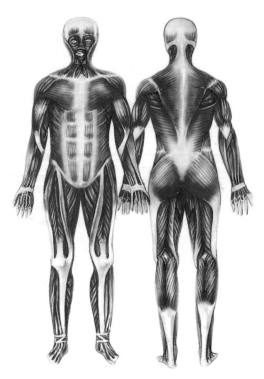

▲ *The body is covered with an almost complete sheath of skeletal muscle pairs, making up 40 percent of the body's weight. There are more than 600 in all, the largest of which is the gluteus maximus in the buttocks. In theory, you can control each muscle pair individually. But most work in combinations so well-established by habit that they always work together.*

FACTS: About muscles

- **Muscle pairs**
  Muscles work by getting shorter, pulling two points together, then relaxing. So most muscles come in pairs: one to pull, the other to pull it back. Typically, there is a "flexor" to bend or flex a joint, and an "extensor" to straighten it again.

- **Muscle fibers**
  Muscles are bundles of fiber-like cells. Some contain just a few hundred, others a quarter of a million or more.

- **Striped strands**
  Most skeletal muscle fibers are made of thin strands called myofibrils. All along the myofibrils are dark and light stripes called striations, which are actually two alternating substances—actin and myosin.

FACTS: About muscles and exercise

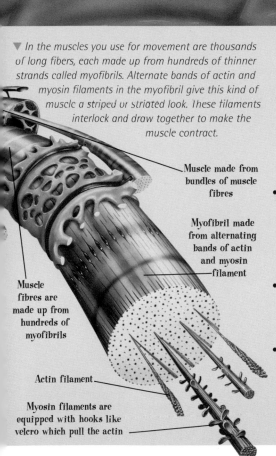

- **Red muscle and white muscle**
Slow-twitch "red" muscle fibers are good for prolonged gentle movements. "White" fibers are for short, powerful bursts. Fast-twitch red ones work for both.

◀ *Athletes train to develop big muscles, big lungs, and a strong heart.*

- **Oxygen boost**
When muscles work hard they need more oxygen to burn sugar. So when you run your breathing gets faster and deeper, and your heart pumps faster and harder to boost blood supply. A fit person develops bigger lungs and a strong heart. If you're unfit, a long run makes you pant and your heart beat fast.

▼ *In the muscles you use for movement are thousands of long fibers, each made up from hundreds of thinner strands called myofibrils. Alternate bands of actin and myosin filaments in the myofibril give this kind of muscle a striped or striated look. These filaments interlock and draw together to make the muscle contract.*

▶ *In the upper arm, the biceps, at the front, is the flexor muscle that contracts (and swells) to bend the arm. The triceps, at the back, is the extensor that contracts to straighten the arm out again.*

Muscle made from bundles of muscle fibres

Myofibril made from alternating bands of actin and myosin filament

Muscle fibres are made up from hundreds of myofibrils

Actin filament

Myosin filaments are equipped with hooks like velcro which pull the actin

- **How muscles contract**
In the muscle fibers, filaments of actin and myosin interlock. When the brain sends the muscle a message to contract, little buds on each myosin filament twist sharply, pulling on actin filaments and contracting.

- **Shortening power**
There are millions of actin and myosin filaments in each muscle. When they pull together, they can shorten the muscle by almost half its length.

- **Smooth muscle**
Not all muscles are striated. Muscles called smooth muscles contract blood vessels to control blood flow to the digestive system to push food through. The heart is powered by "cardiac" muscle, which beats automatically, though its rate may vary.

Bones

YOUR BODY IS SUPPORTED by a strong frame called the skeleton. The skeleton not only provides an anchor for muscles, but makes a mount for skin and other tissues, and protects the heart, brain, and other organs. It is made of over 200 bones, linked by a rubbery substance called cartilage. Bones are very tough and light because their outside is made from a mixture of hard minerals such as calcium, and stringy, elastic collagen. Inside the tough, dry casing, there are holes, called lacunae, full of living cells called osteocytes, which are bathed in blood-just like every other cell in the body.

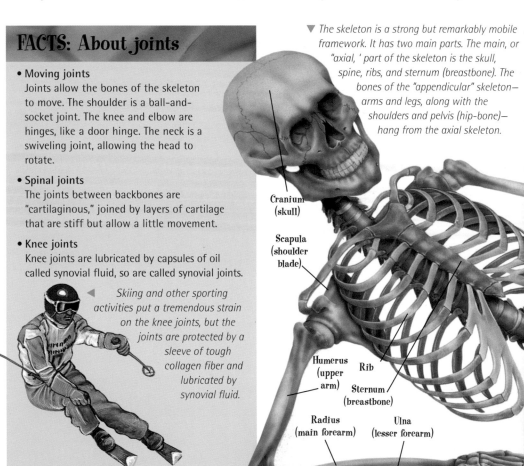

FACTS: About joints

- **Moving joints**
  Joints allow the bones of the skeleton to move. The shoulder is a ball-and-socket joint. The knee and elbow are hinges, like a door hinge. The neck is a swiveling joint, allowing the head to rotate.

- **Spinal joints**
  The joints between backbones are "cartilaginous," joined by layers of cartilage that are stiff but allow a little movement.

- **Knee joints**
  Knee joints are lubricated by capsules of oil called synovial fluid, so are called synovial joints.

▼ The skeleton is a strong but remarkably mobile framework. It has two main parts. The main, or "axial, ' part of the skeleton is the skull, spine, ribs, and sternum (breastbone). The bones of the "appendicular" skeleton—arms and legs, along with the shoulders and pelvis (hip-bone)—hang from the axial skeleton.

◄ Skiing and other sporting activities put a tremendous strain on the knee joints, but the joints are protected by a sleeve of tough collagen fiber and lubricated by synovial fluid.

Cranium (skull)

Scapula (shoulder blade)

Humerus (upper arm)

Rib

Sternum (breastbone)

Radius (main forearm)

Ulna (lesser forearm)

FACTS: About bones

- **Fusing bones**
  Babies have over 300 bones, but many fuse together as they grow, so adults have only 206.

- **Strong bones**
  Weight for weight, bone is five times stronger than steel.

- **Long and short bones**
  The longest, strongest bone is the thigh bone, or femur. The smallest is the stirrup in the middle ear.

- **Bone make-up**
  Bone is made up from a network of collagen (protein) fibers filled with calcium and phosphate.

- **Bone breakers**
  Fresh bone material is constantly being made in cells called osteoblasts. Old bone is broken down by osteoclasts.

- **Bone marrow**
  In the hollow center of the breastbone, ribs, and hips is soft, spongy red "marrow" where red and white blood cells are created. All your bones have this red marrow when you are born, but as you grow older, the marrow of long bones such as the legs and arms turns yellow.

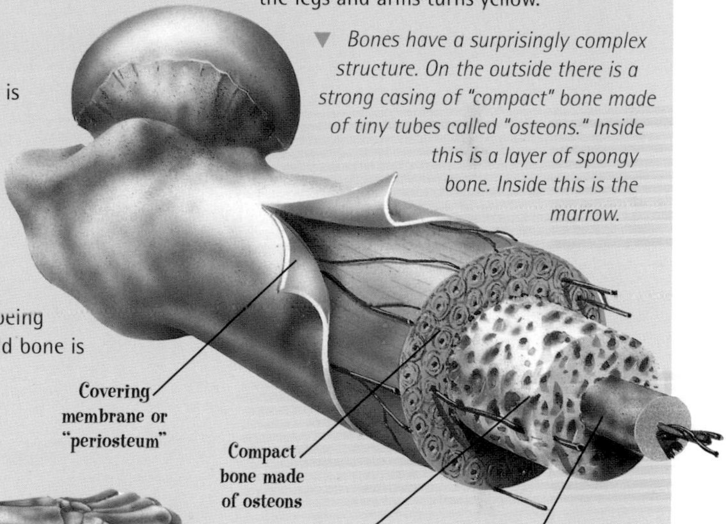

▼ *Bones have a surprisingly complex structure. On the outside there is a strong casing of "compact" bone made of tiny tubes called "osteons." Inside this is a layer of spongy bone. Inside this is the marrow.*

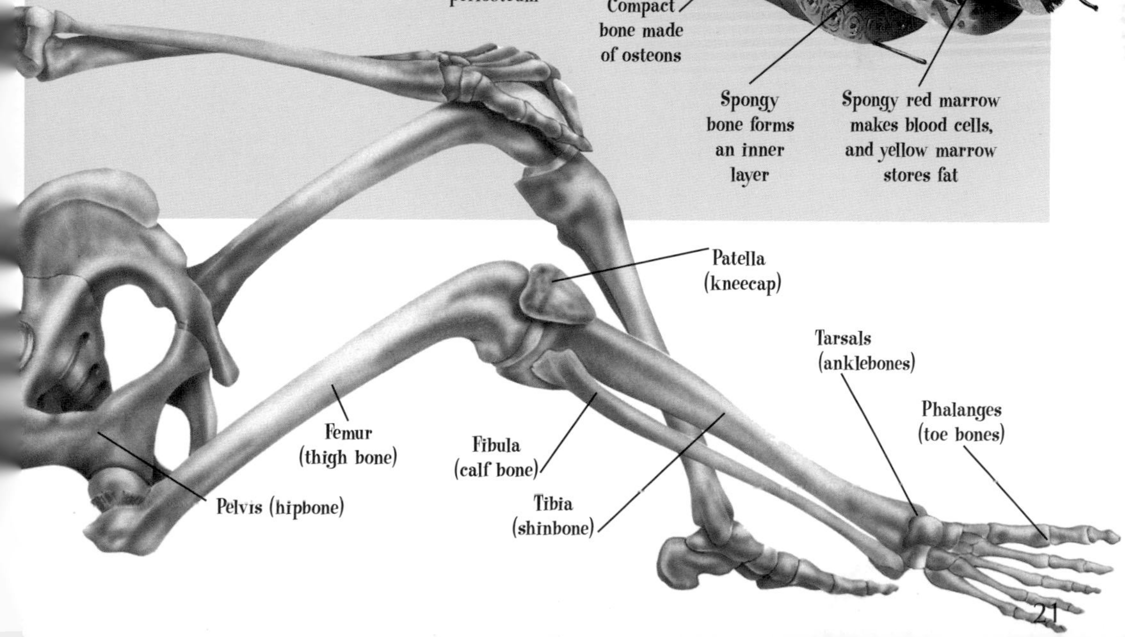

Covering membrane or "periosteum"

Compact bone made of osteons

Spongy bone forms an inner layer

Spongy red marrow makes blood cells, and yellow marrow stores fat

Patella (kneecap)

Tarsals (anklebones)

Phalanges (toe bones)

Femur (thigh bone)

Fibula (calf bone)

Pelvis (hipbone)

Tibia (shinbone)

Senses

OUR SENSES TELL US what is going on in the world around us. Even when we are asleep, our senses are picking up sensations, some from inside the body, some from outside, and feeding them to the brain via the nerves, which are like the body's telephone wires. We have five main senses to tell us what is going on in the outside world–sight from our eyes, hearing from our ears, smell from our nose, taste from our tongue, and touch from most of our skin. Besides this, there are internal senses such as pain, and the balance organs in the ear, which tell you whether you are standing upright, or moving fast.

FACTS: About sight

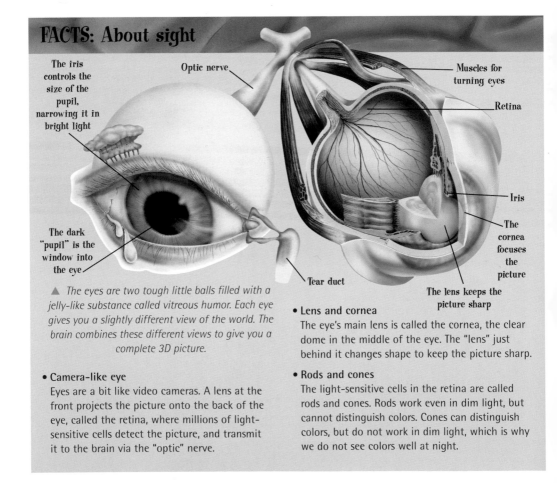

The iris controls the size of the pupil, narrowing it in bright light

Optic nerve

Muscles for turning eyes

Retina

The dark "pupil" is the window into the eye

Iris

The cornea focuses the picture

Tear duct

The lens keeps the picture sharp

▲ The eyes are two tough little balls filled with a jelly-like substance called vitreous humor. Each eye gives you a slightly different view of the world. The brain combines these different views to give you a complete 3D picture.

• **Camera-like eye**
Eyes are a bit like video cameras. A lens at the front projects the picture onto the back of the eye, called the retina, where millions of light-sensitive cells detect the picture, and transmit it to the brain via the "optic" nerve.

• **Lens and cornea**
The eye's main lens is called the cornea, the clear dome in the middle of the eye. The "lens" just behind it changes shape to keep the picture sharp.

• **Rods and cones**
The light-sensitive cells in the retina are called rods and cones. Rods work even in dim light, but cannot distinguish colors. Cones can distinguish colors, but do not work in dim light, which is why we do not see colors well at night.

22

"Umami" (savory)

Bitter

Sour

Sweet

Salty

◀ Smell relies on a small patch of "olfactory" nerves inside the top of your nose that react to minute traces of chemicals in the air. Taste is a mixture of sensations, including smell. But your tongue has five main different kinds of taste receptors, called taste buds. They react to sweet, salty, bitter, sour, and savory tastes in food. Although all parts of the tongue can detect these five tastes, different parts are more sensitive to each flavor.

▼ There are touch receptors all over the body, embedded in the skin. They react to four kinds of feeling—a light touch, steady pressure, heat and cold, and pain. Receptors called Meissner's corpuscles are responsible for light touch. Merkel's discs pick up steady pressure.

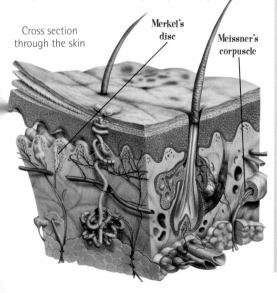

Cross section through the skin

Merkel's disc

Meissner's corpuscle

FACTS: About hearing

▼ The flap of skin on the outside of your head is only one part of the ear, called the outer ear. It just funnels sound down a canal called the ear canal into your head. The real workings of the ear are inside your head. Here are the bones of the middle ear and the curly tube of the inner ear.

Ossicles

Stapes

Eardrum Incus Cochlea

Ear canal Malleus

- **The middle ear**
  The middle ear is the ear's amplifier. Sound entering the middle ear hits a taut wall of skin called the eardrum, shaking it rapidly. As it shakes, it rattles three tiny bones, or "ossicles," called the malleus (hammer), the incus (anvil), and the stapes (stirrup).

- **The inner ear**
  The inner ear is mainly a curly tube full of fluid, called the cochlea. As the ossicles rattle, they knock against this tube, making waves in the fluid. Minute detector hairs move in response to these waves and, as they move, they send signals along nerves to the brain.

- **Two ears**
  Because we have two ears, we can detect where a sound is coming from—by the minute differences in loudness between each ear.

The nerves and brain

INSIDE YOUR HEAD IS THE MOST amazingly complex known structure in the universe: the human brain. It looks like a huge, soggy gray walnut with a wrinkled surface. It is split into two halves and weighs on average about 3.3 pounds. But within this soggy mass are billions of intricately interconnected nerve cells. The chemical and electrical impulses continually shooting through your brain cells produce all your thoughts and control nearly all your actions–and record every sensation–by signals sent back and forth along the remarkable network of nerves that link your body to the brain like the wires in a computer.

FACTS: About the brain

- **Brain damage**
  Brain cells depend on oxygen in the blood. If the supply is cut off for even a few seconds, a person loses consciousness. If it is cut off any longer, cells die and the brain becomes damaged.

- **Parts of the brain**
  The layout of the brain reflects the way it evolved. As it grew out from the primitive brain stem at the top of the spine, it became more complex, developing first into the hindbrain, and then the complicated cerebrum.

- **The center of the brain**
  The core of the brain includes the thalamus and midbrain and controls basic functions such as breathing and heart rate. The hypothalamus here controls hunger and sleeping. Around the thalamus is the limbic system, which influences your emotions.

- **The cerebrum**
  The huge wrinkles of the cerebrum wrap around the core of the brain. This is where you think and complex tasks such as memory, speech, and conscious control of movement go on. All the folds allow a huge number of nerve cells to be squeezed inside the skull.

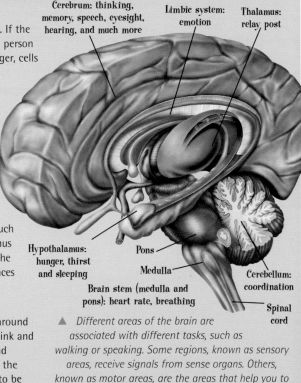

Cerebrum: thinking, memory, speech, eyesight, hearing, and much more

Limbic system: emotion

Thalamus: relay post

Hypothalamus: hunger, thirst and sleeping

Pons

Medulla

Brain stem (medulla and pons): heart rate, breathing

Cerebellum: coordination

Spinal cord

▲ *Different areas of the brain are associated with different tasks, such as walking or speaking. Some regions, known as sensory areas, receive signals from sense organs. Others, known as motor areas, are the areas that help you to control muscles and enable you to move.*

FACTS: About nerve cells

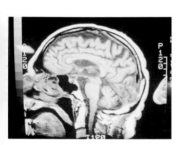

▼ Nerve cells receive signals from other nerve cells through tiny branches called dendrites and send them out along a thin, winding tail, or axon. At the far end of the axon the signal is sent on to other cells across tiny gaps called synapses.

Axon
Synapse
Nucleus
Dendrite
Axon of another nerve cell

- **Nerve cells**
  Nerve cells, or "neurons," are long-lived, but when they die, they are not replaced by others.

- **Multi link**
  The nervous system is a network of long strings of nerve cells linked together like beads on a string.

- **Neurotransmitters**
  Nerve signals are sent across synapses, the gaps between nerves, by shots of chemicals called neurotransmitters. Different receptors pick up different neurotransmitters.

◀ Brain scans show scientists what is going on inside a living brain, and so they now know a great deal about the way the brain works. This has helped them identify, for instance, which areas are active when you are speaking.

DATA: Nerve facts

- **NERVE SPEED**
  The fastest nerve signals travel at 394 feet per second.
- **NERVE LENGTH**
  Axons vary from 0.04 inch to 3 feet long.
- **BRAIN CONNECTIONS**
  There are 100 billion cells in your brain, each connected to as many as 25,000 others.

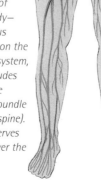

▶ The network of nerves in the body—called the nervous system—focuses on the central nervous system, or CNS. This includes the brain and the spinal cord (the bundle of nerves in the spine). From the CNS, nerves branch out all over the body.

New life

LIKE MOST HUMANS, your life probably began when your mother and father made love. Inside men's bodies are "reproductive organs" that are always making millions of tiny cells called sperm, which resemble tiny tadpoles. Inside women's bodies are reproductive organs that release an egg into their uterus (womb) at a certain time every month. Your life began when your mother and father made love at the right time, so that one of your father's sperm worked its way into an egg and fertilized it. The fertilized egg grew gradually inside your mother's uterus until, at last, after nine months or so, you were born.

FACTS: About reproductive organs

- **Puberty**
  You are born with reproductive or sexual organs, but they only develop in the right way for you to have children once you reach the age of puberty – typically 11–13 years. At puberty, chemicals called sex hormones flood through your body, stimulating the changes that turn boys into men and girls into women.

- **Puberty in boys**
  When a boy reaches puberty, his testicles grow and begin to produce sperm. At the same time, he begins to grow pubic hair and hair on his chin.

- **Puberty in girls**
  When a girl reaches puberty, she begins to grow breasts and her monthly periods, or menstruation, start. She, too, grows pubic hair.

- **Menstruation**
  Menstruation is the monthly cycle of changes in a woman's body that prepares her for having a baby. Every four weeks, her ovary releases an egg so that it slides down the Fallopian tube and into her uterus. If the egg is not then fertilized, the lining of the uterus breaks down and blood flows out of the woman's vagina.

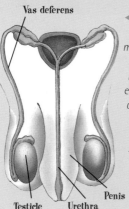

Vas deferens

Testicle   Urethra   Penis

◄ In a man's reproductive organs, the sperm is made in the two testes, or testicles. When making love, the man's erect penis is inserted into a woman's vagina. When the penis is stimulated enough, a liquid called semen carries the sperm from the testes out through the end of the penis into the vagina.

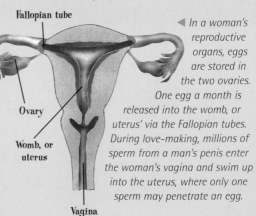

Fallopian tube

Ovary

Womb, or uterus

Vagina

◄ In a woman's reproductive organs, eggs are stored in the two ovaries. One egg a month is released into the womb, or uterus' via the Fallopian tubes. During love-making, millions of sperm from a man's penis enter the woman's vagina and swim up into the uterus, where only one sperm may penetrate an egg.

FACTS: About pregnancy

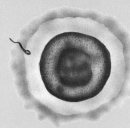

▲ *The moment a sperm enters an egg and fertilizes it is called conception. This is the moment a pregnancy begins. A baby is born about nine months later.*

- **Embryo to fetus**
  During the first eight weeks of pregnancy, while internal organs are developing, the new life is called an embryo. After that it is called a fetus.

- **Life line**
  The fetus is supplied with oxygen and food via a tube called the umbilical cord. This links the fetus to the placenta, a spongy organ on the lining of the uterus.

DATA: Ova and embryos

- **FERTILE PERIOD**
  An egg, or ovum, can only be fertilized in the 12-24 hours after it is released (called ovulation).

- **GROWING LIFE**
  At four weeks, an embryo is no bigger than a grain of rice, but once it becomes a fetus it grows rapidly. At 20 weeks, a fetus is 10 inches long.

The umbilical cord carries the blood supply from the mother that gives the fetus oxygen and food

The placenta is shed after the birth and follows the baby out

After delevoping in the uterus for nine months, the baby turns head down, ready to be born

Cervix, known together with the vagina as the birth canal

In the safety of the mother's uterus, the new human life grows from just a few cells to an embryo, then a fetus, to become a baby in nine months, growing larger and more recognizably human by the day. Throughout this time, it is kept warm and cushioned from the outside world inside a bag or sac of fluid called amniotic fluid. When it is ready to be born, the cervix, or neck of the uterus begins to expand, so that the baby can be pushed out through the vagina and into the world.

27

Food and waste

BEFORE YOUR BODY CAN USE any of the food you eat, the food must be broken down into simple chemical molecules. This is called digestion. It begins the moment you put food in your mouth and chew it until it is soft. It continues as you swallow the food and it is pushed down the long tube through your body called the alimentary canal, or digestive tract. A barrage of chemicals and squeezing muscles assault the food all the way through its journey until most is ready to be absorbed through the walls of the intestines and carried to the rest of the body in the blood. Food that cannot be digested leaves the body through the anus.

FACTS: About waste disposal

- **Cleaning the blood**
  Toxic chemicals and excess water often build up. It is the task of the kidneys to filter these out of the blood and concentrate them into urine.

- **Kidney**
  The kidneys are two bean-shaped organs in the middle of the back. As they filter blood, they regulate body fluid and salt levels and control blood acidity. They filter approximately 7 quarts of blood an hour.

- **Ureter and bladder**
  The ureters are the tubes that pipe urine continually from the kidneys to the bladder, a bag where urine builds up until you are able to empty it. The bladder can hold up to half a quart of urine.

- **Urethra**
  When you urinate, urine from the bladder drains out of the body through the urethra. This is 8 inches long in men, but just 1.5 inches long in women.

- **Urine**
  Urine is 95 percent water but contains the poison urea, which is made in the liver.

  ▶ *The kidneys, ureters, bladder, and urethra together make up the urinary system, the body's liquid waste disposal system. Urine is all that is left after valuable ingredients are retrieved by the kidneys from the blood.*

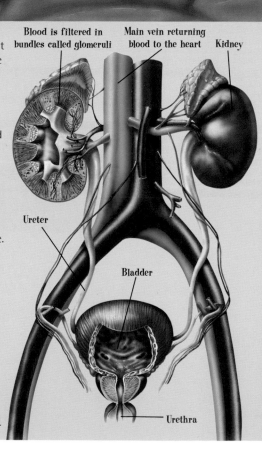

Blood is filtered in bundles called glomeruli

Main vein returning blood to the heart

Kidney

Ureter

Bladder

Urethra

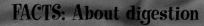

FACTS: About digestion

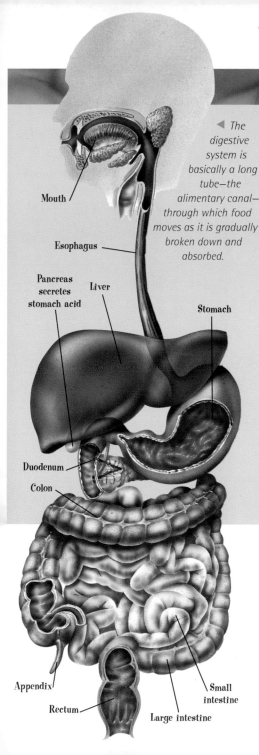

◀ The digestive system is basically a long tube—the alimentary canal—through which food moves as it is gradually broken down and absorbed.

Mouth

Esophagus

Pancreas secretes stomach acid

Liver

Stomach

Duodenum

Colon

Appendix

Rectum

Small intestine

Large intestine

- **The stomach**
  Food spends about six hours in the stomach. Here it is churned up by the muscles of the stomach wall and attacked by "gastric" juices, including hydrochloric acid and powerful enzymes, secreted by glands in the stomach wall.

- **Stomach gate**
  Food is held in the stomach by a ring of muscle called the pyloric sphincter until it is partly digested.

- **Food names**
  A lump of swallowed food is called a bolus. Once partly digested by the stomach, it is called chyme.

- **Small intestine**
  From the stomach, food goes into the tube called the small intestine, where it is absorbed into the blood. Food undigested here passes into the large intestine, or bowel, where waste is turned solid.

- **Rippling muscles**
  Food is moved through digestion by ripples of the muscles in the wall of the digestive tract. Muscles extend in front of the bolus or chyme and contract behind it to push it along. This is called peristalsis.

- **Liver**
  The liver has many functions, including turning digested food into blood proteins.

DATA: Digestion

- **A LONG JOURNEY**
  Your intestones are folded over so many times that they are six times as long as you are tall–up to 33 feet.

- **FOOD IN THE BODY**
  Food takes an average of 24 hours to pass all the way through the alimentary canal.

The healthy body

THE HUMAN BODY IS REMARKABLY GOOD at taking care of itself and has a wide range of mechanisms to help it adjust to different circumstances. But to stay healthy, it needs the right food and regular exercise. Most of the food we eat is fuel burned by the body for energy. But the body also needs small quantities of foods, such as proteins, which are needed to repair cells and build new ones. It also needs minute traces of chemicals that it cannot make for itself: vitamins and minerals. A healthy diet is one that includes all of these foods in just the right balance and quantity.

FACTS: About diet

- **Foods**
  There are three main kinds of food—carbohydrates, fats, and proteins—as well as vitamins, minerals, water, and fiber.

- **Carbohydrates**
  Carbohydrates are foods such as sugars and starches, which are found in abundance in foods such as bread, rice, potatoes, and sweet things. Along with fats, they are the body's main source of energy.

◀ *You need a balanced diet to get the carbohydrates, fats, and protein you need, plus vitamins and minerals, and the fiber needed to take food through the digestive system. A good diet might include fresh fruit and vegetables, brown bread, fish, eggs, cheese, and liver.*

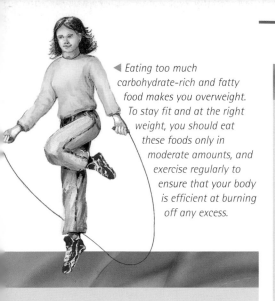

◀ Eating too much carbohydrate-rich and fatty food makes you overweight. To stay fit and at the right weight, you should eat these foods only in moderate amounts, and exercise regularly to ensure that your body is efficient at burning off any excess.

FACTS: Vitamins & minerals

- **Vitamins**
Vitamins are chemicals vital for life, and are found in foods. There are 13 major vitamins: A, C, D, E, K, and 8 varieties of B. Each has a range of tasks in the body. Vitamin C (in fruit like oranges) helps fight infection and keep gums and teeth healthy. Vitamin A (in foods like carrots, green vegetables, and milk) helps keep skin and bones healthy.

- **Essential minerals**
Essential minerals include small amounts of salt, calcium for bones, iron for red blood cells, and tiny traces of minerals such as iodine.

▲ Vitamins are mostly fairly simple chemicals, such as folic acid (one of the B vitamins), but they are vital for life. This picture shows a vitamin crystal in close-up.

- **Fats**
Fats are greasy foods that won't dissolve in water. Some are solid, such as meat fat and cheese. Others, such as corn oil, are liquid. Fats are not only used by the body as energy stores but are a source of vitamins D and E.

- **Too much fat**
Too much fat not only makes you fat. Too much "saturated" fat—mainly animal fat such as butter—can boost the risk of heart disease.

- **Essential acids**
The body needs 20 "amino acids" to build into protein to make and repair cells. The body can make 12 of these; the other eight it must get from protein in food. These are the "essential amino acids."

- **Protein**
Protein in fish and meat has all the amino acids the body needs. Fruit and vegetables have only some of them, which is why vegetarians must choose the right mixture.

- **Protein sources**
Beans and nuts are the most protein-rich foods. The protein content in: soybean flour is 40%; peanuts 28%; cheese 25%; raw meat 23%; raw fish 15%; eggs 12%; bread 8%; rice 6%.

 # DATA: Food

- **FOOD NEEDS**
On average, people need around 2,000 calories of energy food a day, depending on how active they are.

- **FOOD INTAKE**
It is estimated that people in the United States eat an average of around 2,700 calories a day. In Ethiopia, people may have to survive on less than 500 calories a day.

Sickness and disease

EVERY NOW AND THEN, people succumb to sickness and disease. Most diseases, fortunately, are minor and the victim usually recovers quickly, thanks to the body's remarkable defense system, called the immune system. Sickness is caused either by an internal failure of one of the body's mechanisms–or by invading microbes or germs. This is where the immune system comes in. The body's immune system not only identifies the germs, but fights them with an array of chemical and biological weapons, including formidable "immune cells." Only the very worst diseases defeat the body's immune system.

FACTS: About the immune system

- **The lymphatic system**
  Lymph is a clear fluid that drains from cells into the bloodstream via a network of capillaries, called the lymph system. Immune cells patrol all through the blood, but are concentrated in the lymph system.

- **Inflame response**
  Some germs set off an inflame response. This attacks all germs the same way, increasing blood flow and bringing a flood of cells called neutrophils into play.

- **Antibodies**
  Antibodies are labels that attach to germs and show killer cells which cells to kill.

- **Killer cells**
  Among the many kinds of immune cells, two kinds of white blood cell are the most important: killer 'T' cells, which engulf germs, and B lymphocytes, which identify invaders and make antibodies.

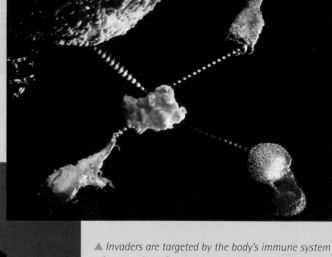

▲ *Invaders are targeted by the body's immune system in a number of ways to ensure they are beaten off.*

◀ *Vaccination is designed to trigger the body to make antibodies against a disease.*

FACTS: About germs

◄ People infected with the HIV virus often succumb to the deadly disease AIDS. This virus is deadly because it attacks the body's immune system and renders it ineffective.

• **Infection**
Many germs cause infection, when bacteria, viruses, or fungi multiply within your body. As they multiply they either damage cells directly, as viruses do, or may release harmful toxins.

• **Fever and inflammation**
Infection activates the immune system. Many of the symptoms you feel—fever, weakness, inflammation—are actually side effects of the immune system's struggle.

• **Bacteria and viruses**
Viruses are very tiny and can only multiply by entering other cells—such as your body's cells—and taking them over. Bacteria are much bigger and are tiny one-celled organisms.

DATA: Immune cells

• **ANTIBODY NUMBERS**
There are thousands of different antibodies in the blood, each targeted against a particular "antigen" (invader).

• **GIANT EATER**
A single "macrophage" (giant eater) T cell can eat up to 100 bacteria.

▼ Unlike viruses, bacteria can multiply outside the body and can be grown in dishes of protein to create "cultures." By growing cultures, scientists can test antibiotic drugs on them and see which are the most effective at killing them off.

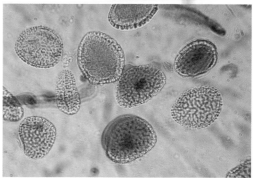

▲ A common form of allergy is hay fever. In the summer, grasses and other plants release pollen. When this is inhaled, it can cause allergic reactions in some people, like streaming eyes and sneezing.

What's wrong?

BEFORE YOU CAN BE TREATED for any illness or injury, the doctor has to decide just what is wrong. This is called diagnosis. The most important clues for a diagnosis are usually the symptoms–that is, all the signs that something may be wrong–a cough, a rash, a pain in your side, and so on. The doctor may also find clues in the story of events that led up to the illness, called the history. The illness or injury can often be identified from the symptoms and history alone. If not, you may have to undergo various tests or have pictures taken of your insides with X-rays or scanners.

FACTS: Looking for clues

- **History**
  Most visits to the doctor begin with the history. While you tell the doctor your symptoms, he or she asks you other questions about the course of events, takes notes, and begins to form an idea about the nature of the problem.

- **The examination**
  The doctor may then go on to look at and listen to the appropriate parts of your body where he thinks there may be further clues. This is called the physical examination. A doctor may look at your eyes with a device called an opthalmoscope, for instance, or tap on your tummy to hear if the taps vibrate through your internal organs normally. He may also check your temperature or blood pressure.

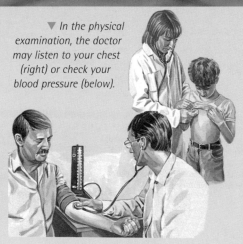

▼ In the physical examination, the doctor may listen to your chest (right) or check your blood pressure (below).

- **Listening to the chest**
  The doctor can tell a great deal just by listening to your chest using a stethoscope. A stethoscope is a simple listening tube. The tight membrane picks up slight sounds inside your body, and the tube transmits them to the doctor's ears. Stethoscopes are particularly important for any problems connected with your breathing or heart.

  ◀ Athletes continually monitor their bodies–whether they are ill or not–to check that they are achieving peak performance.

FACTS: About CT and other scans

- **CT scans**
  CT, or Computerized Tomography, scans use computers to build up a series of pictures showing slices through the body.

- **How CT works**
  Inside a CT scanner, an X-ray gun rotates around the patient, firing as it goes. Light detectors on the far side pick up the rays. A computer analyzes what happened to each ray as it passed through the patient's body to build up a detailed picture.

- **MRI scans**
  MRI, or Magnetic Resonance Imaging, uses a powerful magnet to line up all the protons (tiny atomic particles) in a patient's body. A brief pulse of radio waves then knocks them briefly out of alignment. As they snap back into alignment afterward, they send out little radio signals themselves. The scanner picks up all these billions of tiny signals to give a detailed picture of the body inside.

▼ *CT scans are especially good at showing deep inside the brain and have revolutionized the treatment of head injuries.*

The X-ray gun rotates round the porthole firing low dose X-ray beams

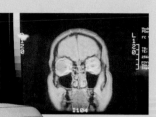

◀ *For a CT scan, the patient lies on a moving bed and slides into a porthole in the scanner.*

FACTS: About X-rays

- **X-rays**
  X-rays are a simple and effective way of taking a black and white picture of the inside of your body.

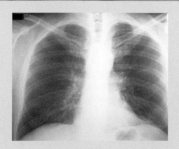

▶ *This is an X-ray of someone's chest. The rib cage shows up clearly as pale, curved bars.*

- **X-rays**
  X-rays are a bit like light, but they are made from waves too short to see—and they can pass straight through certain tissues in your body to turn photographic film black. Tissues that block their path show up white on film.

Treatments and cures

YOUR BODY HAS ITS OWN RANGE OF defenses against illness, called the immune system, and it can fight off many diseases unaided if you are fairly fit. But doctors have many treatments to help when the immune system cannot cope. Some are so effective that many illnesses that were once inevitably fatal, such as tuberculosis, can often now be treated with drugs. Many diseases can be prevented by vaccination programs, which make the most of the body's immune system. Bacteria, viruses, and other germs which cause illness can also be kept at bay by proper hygiene.

FACTS: About drugs

- **Antibiotics**
  Many illnesses that are caused by bacteria can be treated with drugs called antibiotics. These were originally made from molds and fungi, but are now made synthetically. They include penicillin and tetracycline.

- **How drugs are made**
  In the past, drugs mostly came from natural substances. Now most are made in the laboratory or designed on computers. A few drugs are made by manipulating the genes of living organisms so that they produce the drug. Insulin, for example, can be made in the pancreas of pigs or oxen, although it is increasingly also made synthetically now.

◄ *The range of different drugs a doctor has to treat illnesses is now enormous. Most come as pills that can be swallowed, but a few are injected directly into the blood with a needle.*

FACTS: About vaccination

▶ *This is the germ that causes the terrible disease AIDS, magnified tens of thousands of times. The germ is a virus that attacks the body's immune system. Doctors are looking for a vaccine against it.*

▼ *Most children have vaccinations at regular intervals as they grow up, against diseases such as diphtheria, whooping cough, and tetanus.*

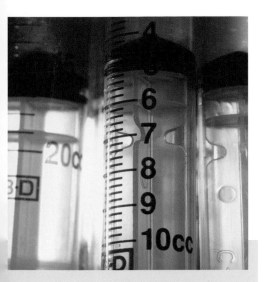

▲ Many vaccines are made by genetic engineering — that is, by altering the genes of the germ to make it harmless. These are called live attenuated organisms

- **Disease protection**
  You can be protected from some diseases by immunization or vaccination.

- **Passive immunization**
  For immediate, short-lived protection from an infection, you might be injected with blood from someone who has already survived the disease. The blood contains tiny proteins called antibodies that defend your body against the invading germ.

- **Active immunization**
  For long-term protection, you may be injected with a killed or mild version of the germ. Your body then makes its own antibodies against the germ and so is resistant to further infection.

- **Killing diseases**
  Many previously common diseases—diphtheria, polio, measles, and whooping cough—are now quite rare thanks to mass vaccination of children. Smallpox is now very rare indeed.

▶ The way ordinary hospitals and doctors treat illnesses is based on science and is called conventional medicine. But there are many alternative approaches. Some are based on traditional methods passed down from generation to generation over thousands of years. Many people in Africa go to a healer. Other alternatives include herbal medicine which uses herbs as treatments, and Chinese acupuncture, which uses needle pricks in carefully chosen places.

▼ When people are ill, proper care may be as important as the right medicines. If you are only mildly ill, your family or friends can look after you. In the hospital, you may be tended to by nurses, who make sure you are taking medicines correctly and provide the right food and fluids.

37

Body repairs

SOMETIMES, WHEN YOUR BODY cannot heal itself, or when treatment with drugs is inappropriate, the only solution may be to cut it open and physically repair it, just as you would a broken-down car. This is called surgery. Surgeons might cut open your body to remove a diseased or wrongly functioning organ, such as your appendix, or mend a broken bone. They might also, if you are very ill, take out an organ from your body and replace it with a healthy organ from another person (maybe from someone who has died). This is called a transplant.

FACTS: About surgery

- **Local anesthetic**
  A minor operation is generally done under a local anesthetic. This means a drug is applied to the skin or injected to numb any feeling in just the area being operated on.

- **General anesthetic**
  Major operations are done under a general anesthetic. This means the patient is given a drug by injection or breathes a gas that makes him or her unconscious for the entire operation. You would need a general anesthetic to have an organ transplant, or to have your appendix removed.

▲ In a heart transplant, a diseased heart is cut out and replaced with a healthy heart from someone who has died.

- **Organ transplants**
  All these parts of the body may be transplanted: kidney; cornea of the eye; the heart; the lungs; the liver; and the pancreas.

- **Transplanted organs**
  After a transplant, the body's immune system may reject the new organ as foreign. So the patient is given drugs to suppress the immune system.

◀ Major surgery involves a team of people working together in a specially equipped room called an operating room. The team is headed by the surgeon but also includes other personnel, such as anesthetists and nurses.

FACTS: About implants and prosthetics

- **Implants**
  Sometimes, damaged or diseased parts of the inside of the body such as the hip bone may be replaced by purpose-made parts made of materials such as metal and nylon. These are called implants.

- **Pacemakers**
  People with heart problems, for instance, may be given a pacemaker, a tiny electronic device that sends out electrical signals to the heart muscles to keep the heart beating steadily.

- **Prosthetics**
  Prosthetics are artificial parts attached to the outside of the body. Someone who has lost an arm, for instance, may be given an artificial one, complete with hinged elbow and movable fingers.

▶ *Implants have to be made of tough, non-corrosive material. This illustration shows parts of the body that may be replaced by parts made of the metal titanium—the same tough, shiny metal that is often used in aircraft.*

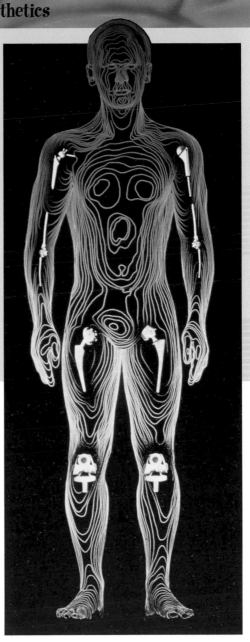

▼ *Using a microscope, a microsurgeon can carry out operations on a minute scale—to connect fine blood vessels in the eye, or rejoin minute nerves and tendons severed in an injury.*

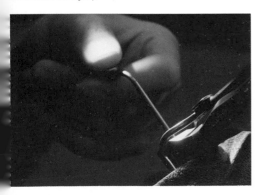

ANIMALS

Small mammals

MAMMALS COME IN ALL SHAPES AND SIZES and live in a huge variety of places, from the frozen arctic wastes to the hottest desert. Like fish, birds, amphibians, and reptiles, they are "vertebrates"-animals with backbones. This really means they have a bony skeleton inside their bodies, which makes a strong frame for hanging everything on. Besides a backbone, mammals usually have two pairs of limbs, a skull to hold the brain, eyes, ears, and a nose-and then a heart, lungs and other organs inside the ribs.

FACTS: About mammals

- **Warm-blooded**
  Mammals are said to be endothermic (warm-blooded) and reptiles exothermic (cold-blooded). This doesn't mean reptiles' blood is necessarily colder. It just means that mammals are able to keep their blood and bodies equally warm all the time—which is why they can survive in so many different places.

- **Babies**
  All mammals begin life as a tiny egg inside their mother's body. But most young mammals develop inside their mother's body until they are born as babies. Very few baby mammals can cope by themselves when they are born and most need looking after by their parents for a while. Human babies need looking after for many years.

- **Mammals that lay eggs**
  A few mammals living in Australia called monotremes lay eggs rather than have babies. These include the duck-billed platypus.

◀ The badger is one of over 5,400 known species of mammal around the world.

- **Milk-power**
  Unlike other animals, mother mammals feed their babies on milk until they are old enough to cope with solid foods. Milk gives all the fat and protein the baby needs to grow.

- **Milk on tap**
  The more babies a mother mammal tends to have, the more pairs of nipples she has. Humans have just one pair, but pigs have seven pairs.

- **Big and small**
  The biggest mammal is the blue whale, which is 100 feet long and weighs 200 tons; the smallest is the Etruscan shrew, which is less than 2 inches long and weighs only 0.05 ounce.

- **Fur coats**
  All mammals have a fur coat, even if it is just made up of a few strands, as with humans, rhinos, and whales. Fur keeps the animal warm by trapping a layer of insulating air. Seals have special oily, water-repelling fur and a layer of thick fat called blubber to keep them warm in polar oceans.

- **Clever creatures**
  Compared to other animals, much more of a mammal's brain is cerebrum, the part of the brain devoted to intelligent behavior. In humans and apes, the proportion is biggest of all.

▲ Porcupines are small mammals covered with incredibly long spines, which protect them from predators. When threatened, they rustle or rattle their spines—or even run backward into the enemy, spines pointing.

FACTS: About rodents

- **Rodents**
  There are over 2,270 species of rodent, including rats, mice, rabbits, and guinea pigs.

- **Front teeth**
  All rodents have two pairs of ever-growing, razor-sharp front teeth, or incisors, for gnawing.

▲ Weasels are among the most effective of all small predators— they are both agile and strong.

◀ Squirrels have fur-lined cheek pouches that they use for storing food.

▶ Beavers are the biggest of all rodents, except for the South American capybara. They live in water and use their sharp teeth to gnaw through trees to get wood to dam streams. They build their homes, called lodges, in the pond created behind this dam.

The inside of the beaver's lodge is above water level, but it is reached by an underwater entrance

Beavers have two very sharp teeth for gnawing

Beavers' big flat tails and webbed back feet make them good swimmers

Large mammals

SOME MAMMALS ARE TINY, but the big mammals are the biggest living things in the world. The biggest of all the mammals on land are elephants, which can grow up to 13 feet tall–as high as a double-decker bus – and weigh 7.7 tons, which is as much as a big truck. Not that much smaller are two other creatures of tropical Africa and Asia, the rhinoceros and hippopotamus. All of these big mammals are herbivores, which means they eat plants. So, too, are the many medium-sized animals, such as buffaloes and horses.

FACTS: About elephants

- **Long nose**
  An elephant's most remarkable feature is its long trunk, or "proboscis," which it uses for breathing, smelling, pulling down branches, picking up objects, making trumpeting noises, and sucking up water.

- **Long life**
  Elephants live longer than all mammals other than humans, surviving to the age of 86 in captivity.

- **Big ears**
  When an elephant holds its ears back flat, it is either relaxed or feeling intimidated by another. A dominant or aggressive bull (male elephant) often sticks its ears out.

- **Big teeth**
  Elephants have two giant teeth, called tusks, which they use for digging or fending off enemies. Bulls sometimes lock tusks and wrestle with their trunks to see who's strongest.

- **Keeping cool**
  To cool off in the heat, elephants stretch out or flap their ears. They also cover themselves with mud or spray themselves with dust or water. Coating their skin like this also helps condition their skin and provide a protective layer.

- **Herds**
  Elephants live in herds, ranging from four to 30 members, led by a mature cow, or "matriarch." The rest of a herd is generally made up of several females and their young, as well as a few young bulls. Adult males tend to move off and live on their own or in all-male groups.

Tusks curve as they grow

▶ Elephants in Africa are much bigger than those found in Asia, with an African bull measuring up to 13 feet tall and weighing 7.7 tons.

▲ Rhinos such as this Indian rhinoceros have thick, hairless skin that is arranged like protective armor, folding at the neck, shoulders, and legs to allow movement. Some species of rhino also have one horn; some have two. These horns are actually made of densely compacted hair, or "keratin."

The African elephant has much bigger ears than an Indian elephant and a sloping forehead instead of a domed one

▼ Horses belong to a group of mammals called ungulates, or hooved mammals. As with pigs, cattle, and camels, claws have been replaced with hooves. Each foot of a horse has one toe with a toenail, which is the hoof. They are very fast runners, using just the tip of this toe as they move.

FACTS: About herbivores

- **Grazers and browsers**
  Herbivores that eat grasses are called "grazers," while those that eat leaves, bark, and the buds of trees and bushes are called "browsers." Some animals only eat one kind of plant, but most will actually eat a variety, depending on whatever is available.

- **Steady eating**
  Because plants are not as nutritious as meat, most herbivores need to spend large amounts of time eating—unlike carnivores, which feed only occasionally. An elephant, for example, usually feeds for at least 18 hours every day.

▶ The takin (right) is a herbivore that lives in Central Asia. It looks a bit like a goat, but with shorter horns and a stockier body covered with dense brown hair.

DATA: Large mammals

- **THE BIGGEST ANIMALS**
  Rhinos and hippos are the second-heaviest land mammals after elephants. An African white rhinoceros weighs up to 4 tons.

- **AN ELEPHANT'S DIET**
  Elephants eat up to 440 pounds of food per day. They also drink about 50 gallons of water a day.

- **HORSE BREEDS**
  There are over 300 breeds of domestic horse.

Big cats

LIONS, TIGERS, JAGUARS, PUMAS, AND LEOPARDS are kinds of big cats that are found all over the world except the South Pacific. Although they have the same basic body structure as pet cats, they are very different in other ways. They vary in size considerably, from the big tiger to the tiny wild cat, but big cats are usually much bigger and stronger than pet cats, and they roar and grunt rather than meow, and purr. All are deadly hunters, slinking up on their prey and then pouncing on it. Their sharp claws, powerful jaws, and fangs inflict terrible wounds on victims.

FACTS: About tigers

- **Very big cat**
  Tigers are the largest of the big cats in the wild, with huge heads and growing 8 feet long. The long tail adds almost another 3 feet.

- **Disguising stripes**
  Tigers are instantly recognizable by their stripes. But in the forest areas of South Asia where they live, their black stripes on a gold background act as camouflage. Their chins and stomachs are snowy white.

- **Head hunter**
  Tigers prey on large animals such as deer, buffalo, antelopes, and wild pigs, hunting mainly at night. But it takes a tiger a lot of effort to make a kill; nine out of ten times, the victim will actually get away.

- **Endangered tigers**
  Hunters killing tigers for their skins and farmers clearing the forest for land have decimated tiger numbers. They are now restricted to special reserves in Asia, mainly in India and Sumatra.

- **Lone males**
  Tigers have their own ranges, but a male's may include that of some females. They meet only to mate.

- **Young tigers**
  Two to four tiger cubs are born at a time and live with their mother for 3 years as they learn to survive.

▶ *Tigers are solitary creatures, living alone most of their lives. To keep other tigers out of their territory, they leave urine samples and scratch marks on trees.*

FACTS: About lions

A male can be up to around 10 feet long from his nose to the tip of his tail. Males also have a mane, which gets darker as they get older. Females have no mane and are also a bit smaller.

- **King of the beasts**
  Lions are majestic big cats once found all over South Asia but now found mainly on the grasslands of Africa. They are the only truly social cats, living together in groups called prides. The adult male lion is instantly recognizable by the big mane that covers its head.

- **What lions eat**
  Lions feed on wildebeest, zebras, and antelopes—occasionally giraffes. They have big side teeth and short, strong jaws for eating flesh.

- **Lions on the hunt**
  It is usually the female that hunts, alone or in pairs, although the males are the first to eat once the prey has been caught. The hunting lionesses stealthily approach a victim, then make a short dash and pounce on it quickly. If they don't succeed in their short dash, they give up and wait for another opportunity. Only one in four hunts leads to a kill.

- **A quiet life**
  A lion spends 18 hours a day sleeping, since the meat it eats is so nutritious. It eats one solid meal and then goes without food for the next few days.

Among the many smaller big cats is the margay, which lives in the forests of South and Central America and preys on small mammals and birds. The margay is solitary, has good reflexes, keen eyesight and is an excellent climber. However, it has been hunted for its coat and as a result is now quite rare.

With its spotted coat, the jaguar is one of the most beautiful of the big cats. It lives in South American forests, usually near water, and hunts peccaries, capybaras, and fish. It looks a bit like the leopard of Africa and Asia, but these have black blotches or rings, whereas jaguars have spots with rings around them.

47

Monkeys and apes

HUMANS, APES, MONKEYS, AND LEMURS all belong to a group of animals called primates. Most of them, except humans, live in places where there are trees, and they have hands with fingers and feet with toes for gripping branches. The apes are our closest relatives in the animal world and have similar long arms, and fingers and toes for gripping. Monkeys have long arms too, but they are usually much smaller, and they have a tail for helping them balance as they swing through the trees. They live all over the world in warm regions.

FACTS: About lemurs and langurs

- **What are lemurs?**
  Lemurs are nocturnal animals with big, staring eyes. They have soft, thick fur and bushy tails, which they use to intimidate other animals, signal to other lemurs, and wave scent around (from glands in their bottoms!).

- **Where lemurs live**
  Nearly all lemurs live in forests on the island of Madagascar off the east coast of Africa. They tend to live mostly in trees.

- **Kinds of lemur**
  There are around 100 species of lemur (inlcuding sub-species). Some are brightly colored, such as the ring-tailed lemur, which has black and white rings all the way down its tail.

- **Tiny primates**
  Lemurs are all quite small—the biggest is only as big as a large house cat, while the smallest, the lesser mouse lemur, grows to only 5 inches.

- **Langurs**
  Langurs are small monkeys that live in the forests of Southeast Asia and mainly eat leaves.

  ▷ *Like other langurs, the Hanuman langur has a strong stomach that can cope with the toughest leaves.*

◁ *Monkeys are divided into those of the Old World and the New World. Old World monkeys, such as the baboon (left), live in the warmer parts of Africa and Asia. They tend to be larger than New World monkeys but do not have prehensile tails (tails that grip). Their backsides are usually bare and their nostrils are close together.*

◁ *New World monkeys live in Central and South American forests. Many, such as the spider monkey (left), have prehensile tails to help them climb and hang from branches, keeping their legs and arms free for holding food. Their noses are also much wider than those of Old World monkeys, and their nostrils face outward.*

FACTS: About apes

- **Fellow apes**
  Apes are so closely related to humans that some zoologists divide apes into three kinds—lesser apes (gibbons and siamangs), great apes (orangutans, gorillas, and chimpanzees), and humans. None has a tail.

- **Great apes and lesser apes**
  Great apes are almost human-shaped, though they tend to have longer arms, big, protruding jaws—and, of course, are covered with fur. They are often very smart, too, especially chimpanzees. Lesser apes are smaller and less intelligent, but they can be very agile climbers indeed.

- **Chimpanzees**
  Chimps are humans' closest relative and the most intelligent of the apes. They communicate with varied vocal sounds, gestures, and facial expressions. They also use tools such as sticks to get food.

- **Gibbons**
  Gibbons are agile apes that live in Southeast Asian forests and swing swiftly from branch to branch—up to 10 feet in a single swing.

- **Orangutan**
  Orang utan is Malay for "person of the forest." They live in the rain forests of Borneo and Sumatra and look like hairy old men.

▼ *Gorillas are the biggest of the apes. A big male can be 5.5 feet tall. They look ferocious, but are among the gentlest of creatures. They eat only berries and leaves, and the male only becomes aggressive when a rival male intrudes on his group—even then he only beats his chest and roars.*

Adult males are called silverbacks because they have gray hairs on their backs

The gentle gorilla only roars like this when his family is threatened

Pandas, bears, & dogs

ALL BIG CARNIVOROUS (MEAT-EATING) ANIMALS are essentially either cats or dogs. Cats are very obviously cats, but the dogs include bears as well as the more obviously dog-like creatures, such as wolves, foxes, jackals, and coyotes. To a zoologist, a bear is somewhat like a big dog without a tail. Both bears and dogs are mostly hunters that eat meat, but unlike cats, bears especially will also eat other things if food is scarce. Surprisingly, although pandas look like bears, they are actually more closely related to raccoons.

FACTS: About wolves, foxes, and jackals

- **Big dogs**
  The dog family is a group of around 35 species including wolves, foxes, wild dogs, domestic dogs, jackals, and coyotes. All dogs have long legs, long narrow muzzles, and pointy canine teeth for eating flesh. They all also have a very good sense of smell.

- **Wolf packs**
  To hunt animals bigger than themselves such as moose, deer, caribou, or musk oxen, wolves hunt together in packs. Wolf packs use smell to trace their prey, then try to isolate a weak animal within the herd and run it down.

- **Top dogs**
  The eldest male and female in a pack maintain a strict hierarchy. Any wolf that tries to challenge their dominance is subdued or even expelled from the pack altogether. A pack may consist of 7–20 wolves.

◄ The red fox is very adaptable and is often found living in cities, surviving by raiding garbage dumps.

- **Foxes**
  Foxes are clever hunters that prowl at night, alone or in pairs. They catch and eat rats, mice, and rabbits, but they will also willingly eat whatever is available, such as fruit, birds, and even human food scraps.

- **Jackals**
  Jackals live in Africa and Asia and look like small wolves. They hunt alone, not in packs, killing rats, mice, and birds. They only meet up when there is a chance of getting in on the leftovers from the kill of a lion or a leopard—their deadliest enemies.

◄ Wolves once lived all over Europe and North America, but they have now been all but exterminated in Europe and live only in remote areas of North America.

50

FACTS: About bears

- **Where bears live**
  Bears live mostly in the northern hemisphere, in all kinds of environments. Only the spectacled bear lives in South America.

- **Brown bears**
  Many brown bears are called "grizzly" because of the white fur on their shoulders.

- **Polar bears**
  White polar bears live in the Arctic and are the only bears that live on meat alone.

▲ *Brown bears such as this Himalayan bear hibernate. They put on weight during the autumn and then retreat to a den for winter.*

▼ *The giant panda is one of the rarest animals, living only in the mountainous forests of central China, where its food, a certain kind of bamboo, grows. The bamboo is not very nutritious, so pandas spend 10–12 hours a day eating. They rarely have cubs, so the birth of a panda is special.*

Pandas have a pad on their forepaws, called a sixth finger, to help them grip bamboo shoots as they chew

DATA: Pandas, bears, and dogs

- **THE BIGGEST BEAR**
  The largest bear is the Kodiak, a type of brown bear from Alaska, which measures up to 8 feet and weighs up to 1,700 pounds.

- **THE LITTLEST BEAR**
  The smallest of the bears is the sun bear of the Southeast Asian rain forests. It is only about 4.5 feet tall and 60 pounds in weight.

- **WOLF RANGE**
  One wolf pack may inhabit a huge territory-up to 380 square miles. They also cover great distances when hunting for food.

- **PANDA FOOD**
  Because bamboo has such a low nutritional value, pandas may eat up to 85 pounds of stems and leaves in a single day.

Sea mammals

MAMMALS ARE WARM-BLOODED CREATURES that breathe air and raise their young on milk. Most are land animals, but they are remarkably adaptable, and a few kinds spend all their lives in the sea, swimming around with the ease of a fish and only coming up for air occasionally. There are two main kinds of sea mammal. There are seals, sea lions, walruses, and sea cows, which mostly live in cold places and have both fur and a thick layer of fat called blubber to keep them warm. Then there are whales, dolphins, and porpoises, which have no fur, only blubber.

FACTS: About whales, dolphins, and porpoises

- **Cetaceans**
Whales, dolphins, and porpoises are together known as cetaceans. Many are very gentle and intelligent creatures.

- **Breathing**
Whales can stay underwater for hours, but they must eventually come up for air and spout out water from a blowhole on top.

- **Schools**
Dolphins live in groups called schools up to 300 strong.

- **Dolphin talk**
Dolphins keep in touch by clicks, barks, chattering sounds, screams, and moans, each of which seem to have a meaning that scientists do not understand. They find their way with sounds too high for the human ear to hear.

- **Whale sound**
Whales use booming sounds to keep in touch. Finback whales can hear each other even when they are over 500 miles apart.

Playful leaps, somersaults, and spins help knit groups of dolphins together

▲ Dolphins are very friendly, playful, and intelligent creatures. They form strong social relationships, with close mother-child bonds. Mating pairs seem to stay together for life.

- **Toothed and toothless whales**
Some whales, such as the sperm and killer whales, have teeth and eat large fish. Others, like the humpback and blue whales, have no teeth. Instead, they have special comb-like sieves in their mouths called baleens. They feed by straining tiny, shrimp-like creatures called krill through the baleen.

FACTS: About seals, sea lions, and walruses

- **Going ashore**
  Seals, sea lions, and walruses are agile swimmers, but unlike whales and dolphins, they can live on land—although once ashore, they tend to waddle.

- **Breeding grounds**
  In spring and summer, thousands of seals crowd together on the shore to breed in vast colonies.

- **Seals and sea lions**
  Seals and sea lions look similar, but while seals have only ear openings, sea lions, like most land mammals, have ear flaps. Sea lions can also move their back flippers under their body to help them move around on land, unlike seals.

- **Seal meals**
  Seals and sea lions feed mainly on fish, but also eat shellfish. Crabeater seals feed mainly on krill, while bearded seals eat mainly clams.

- **Walruses**
  Walruses are big creatures, a little like overgrown seals, growing up to 10 feet long, but they have massive tusks and face whiskers.

- **Leopard**
  The most ferocious seal is the Antarctic leopard, which grows to 13 feet and feeds on penguins.

▼ *Seals spend most of their lives in the sea, but come ashore to give birth. They stay on land for several weeks in colonies called rookeries, feeding their young milk. Every now and then, hunters will cull (kill) the young pups while they are still ashore—both for their fur and to keep down numbers. Many believe this is cruel. Others say it is necessary.*

▶ *Sea cows—dugongs and manatees—are plant-eating seals that live in warm coastal waters. Dugongs live around Africa and Asia. Manatees live in coastal rivers in the southeastern United States, the West Indies, and northern South America. They greet one another with muzzle-to-muzzle kisses.*

Manatee

53

Pets

PEOPLE HAVE KEPT ANIMALS for many thousands of years–sometimes to help with particular tasks, sometimes as companions, sometimes simply to look at and admire. Dogs were first tamed around 10,000 years ago to help with hunting, and since then many other animals have been adopted as pets–cats, birds, hamsters, guinea pigs, horses, and many others. There are more pet owners now than ever before, with hundreds of millions of animals living in homes around the world–including over half a billion cats!

FACTS: About cats

- **Egyptian cats**
  The Ancient Egyptians tamed wild African bushcats to catch mice 3,500 years ago. Later, the Egyptians thought cats sacred.

- **Rough tongues**
  Cats' tongues are covered with bristles, which help them lap up liquids and foods and groom themselves, as with a comb.

- **Catnaps**
  Cats spend a lot of time sleeping—in short naps. But they can be awake and ready for action in an instant.

- **Cat litter**
  Most female cats are ready to be mothers by 10 months old—though many are neutered by their owners to stop them from breeding. Female cats are pregnant for 9 weeks and give birth to a litter of 2–5 kittens.

◀ There are many different breeds of cat, from common tabbies and tortoiseshells to valuable pedigree Siamese and Persian cats.

Dogs

There are over 150 different breeds of domestic dogs, but all are descended from the wolf, and, even though tame, they retain many wolf-like traits—body language, guarding territory, hiding bones, and so on.

▲ Many pets were originally working dogs, like the collie. Originally from Scotland, collies make wonderful sheepdogs. They are fast runners, quick learners, and have an amazing sense of smell. They can even locate a sheep lost in the snow.

▶ Some pets were originally hunting dogs, like terriers. Great diggers, with strong teeth and jaws, terriers were once used to dig out rats, rabbits, and badgers from the ground, and their name comes from the Latin terra, for "earth."

▲ *Hamsters only live for two or three years. Golden hamsters (above)—the small variety kept as pets—all descend from a single wild litter found in Syria in 1930.*

▲ *Many pet dogs come from hunters and gun dogs, such as setters, pointers, and retrievers. When a red setter (above) spots a game bird, it crouches slightly and freezes, pointing its nose to the bird for the hunter.*

▼ *St. Bernards are among the many dogs used to help in emergencies. They were once trained at the monastery of the Great St. Bernard Pass in Switzerland to rescue people who got lost in the surrounding mountains.*

FACTS: About fish

- **Tropical fish**
  Small tropical fish such as butterfly fish, angel fish, and guppies are kept for their bright colors. But they are used to warm water, so they must be kept in heated tanks.

- **Deadly fish**
  Some people like to keep piranhas from the Amazon. They have sharp teeth and are voracious flesh eaters, and are able to attack in a mass and eat large animals.

▶ *Descended from dull-coloured carp, goldfish were carefully bred by the Chinese and Japanese and are now the most popular of all pet fish.*

DATA: Pets

- **BIGGEST DOG**
  The tallest breed of dog, on average, is the Irish wolfhound–43 inches to its shoulder.

- **HEAVIEST DOG**
  The heaviest dog is the St. Bernard–200 pounds.

- **SMALLEST DOG**
  The smallest dog is the miniature Yorkshire terrier–under 17 ounces.

- **OLD CAT**
  Cats may live up to the age of 20.

- **TINY FISH**
  The smallest known fish is *paedocypris progenita*, measuring just 0.3 inch long.

Farm animals

BACON, HAMBURGERS, SHOES, BUTTER, wool sweaters, milk, and many other things are provided by animals kept on farms–including cattle, sheep, pigs, and hens. All these animals are descended from wild animals, but they were domesticated–made tame–many thousands of years ago to give us a steady supply of meat, milk, eggs, fur, wool, and leather. Since then, farmers have created many hundreds of breeds of each animal, such as Herefordshire cows and Merino sheep, to create a more meaty animal, or one that gives better milk or wool.

FACTS: About cows

- **What are cows?**
  Cows, or cattle, are descended from the wild auroch tamed 9,000 years ago. Male cattle are bulls; females cows; and young cattle calves.

- **Dairy cow**
  Females are raised for milk, butter, and cheese and are called dairy cows. They give birth to a calf each year, and after the birth provide milk twice a day for 10 months.

- **Beef breeds**
  Male cattle are raised for meat. Cattle also provide leather, glue and droppings for fertilizer. Beef breeds are rounder and heftier than dairy cows.

- **Chewing the cud**
  Cows chew their cud. They have four stomachs, and after swallowing food they bring it back up into their mouths for further chewing.

▲ *Goats are kept for meat, milk, skins, and wool. Goats' milk is very good for people who are allergic to richer cows' milk, while Angora and Kashmir goats provide very fine wool. Goats are often kept in rocky mountain areas because they are agile and have strong enough jaws and stomachs to live off coarse vegetation.*

▼ *Pigs are kept for meat—pork, bacon, and ham—and leather. Their hairs are also used to make artists' brushes. The domestic pig is descended from the European wild boar, which is much hairier and darker than the domestic pig, and also has tusks. Most pigs are now raised on factory farms, where they are fed on special diets that help them grow rapidly.*

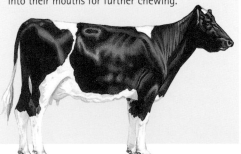

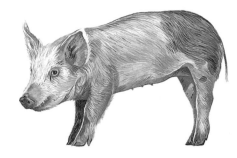

FACTS: About poultry

On a few farms, hens may scratch around for insects and seeds in the farmyard and lay their eggs in a small hut called a coop. These are called free-range hens.

- **Fowl**
Ducks, geese, turkeys, and chickens are all called poultry and are bred in captivity to be eaten or to provide eggs, meat, and feathers.

- **Old hens**
Chickens have been domesticated since the 5th century B.C. and there are over 100 different varieties. Females are called hens; males are called cocks or roosters.

Turkeys are a type of pheasant. There are several different species, but they all descend from the native wild turkey of North America.

- **Egg laying**
Hens lay one or two eggs a day. To keep them laying, the eggs must be taken every day. If not, the hens wait until they have a small collection, then sit on them, keeping them warm for about 20 days until chicks hatch.

- **Battery hens**
Very few hens are free range. In Europe and North America, most are crowded into rows of small boxes called batteries inside a heated building where they are fed and watered, and waste and eggs are collected automatically.

- **Turkey tail**
Male turkeys have 14–18 feathers in their tails, and when courting females they spread these feathers out and raise them above their backs. All species of turkey have a "wattle" of bare, floppy skin that hangs down from their head and neck.

- **Turkish turkeys**
The name turkey may have come from the mistaken idea that the bird came from Turkey.

DATA: Farm animals

- **COW BREEDS**
There are over 800 different breeds of cattle.

- **MILLIONS OF SHEEP**
It is estimated that there are over 1 billion sheep in the world and around 1,000 different breeds.

- **MILK PRODUCTION**
Cows produce around 4 gallons of milk a day, or 1,600 gallons a year.

- **TURKEY EGGS**
Turkey hens lay just 100-120 eggs in a year- chickens can lay three times that number.

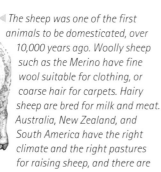

The sheep was one of the first animals to be domesticated, over 10,000 years ago. Woolly sheep such as the Merino have fine wool suitable for clothing, or coarse hair for carpets. Hairy sheep are bred for milk and meat. Australia, New Zealand, and South America have the right climate and the right pastures for raising sheep, and there are vast sheep farms or "stations" here.

Tropical birds

THE TROPICS ARE HOME TO some of the world's most beautiful and spectacular birds. In the rain forests in particular, there is a huge variety of colorful birds, because color is a real asset in finding a mate. In Indonesia and Australia there are birds of paradise and lyre birds with magnificent tail feathers. In South America there are the brilliantly colored cotingas and huge-beaked toucans. Then there are parrots, such as macaws and budgerigars, as well as big birds like flamingoes and hornbills, and tiny birds such as hummingbirds.

FACTS: About weaver birds

- **Home makers**
  Weaver birds are small birds that live in the tropics of Africa and Asia. They get their name because many weave elaborate nests.

- **Nest weaving**
  Using their bills and feet, they make pouch-shaped nests from plant fibers, which they suspend from tree branches, away from predators. The entrance is usually a funnel with a hole at the end, just big enough for the weaver but small enough to keep other unfriendly animals out.

- **The biggest bird nests**
  Sociable weaver birds of South Africa build big nests containing enough separate cavities for hundreds of pairs of birds under one communal roof. Each has its own entrance tunnel, complete with grass stems pointing downward over it to help keep enemies out.

▲ Pelicans are fish-eating birds with special pouched bills, which they use to scoop up fish from the water. These pouches can hold up to two or three times as much as their stomachs.

▶ The nest of the village weaver is begun by the male bird. When he has found a female willing to move in, she finishes the inside of the nest. The male then leaves her to lay her eggs while he goes off to start another nest.

▶ Like all bee-eaters, the carmine bee-eater has a long tail—the streamers are up to 4.7 inches. Their long, downward-pointing, curved bills are perfect for catching bees on the wing. They rub the bee against a branch to remove the sting. Carmine bee-eaters of Africa often ride on the backs of other birds such as ostriches and storks, as well as grazing mammals such as antelopes and cattle, in order to pick up insects disturbed by their feet.

▶ *The Paradise whydah lives in Africa. The male has perhaps the most spectacular tail feathers of any bird, four times as long as its body. When in flight, the whydah holds two short upper tail feathers upright while the longer ones dangle down. To attract a female, it flies above her so that the long feathers wave up and down in an attractive way!*

The tail feathers of a breeding male can be as long as 11 inches

◀ *The hoatzin is a large ungainly bird that lives in the forests of northern South America. It is an awkward flier so tends to glide from tree to tree. The young have two hooked claws on their wings to help them move about.*

FACTS: About parrots and cockatoos

- **Bill for nuts**
  Parrots are colorful birds of the tropics with curved bills for eating fruit and seeds, and cracking nuts.

- **Parrot feet**
  Parrot feet have two toes pointing forward and two backward, allowing them to grip onto branches and hold food.

- **Three species**
  There are three groups of parrots—true parrots, cockatoos, and New Zealand parrots—making over 370 different species altogether. The largest is the hyacinth macaw (39 inches bill to tail). The smallest is the tiny buff-faced pygmy parrot (3.3 inches).

- **Mimic**
  Some parrots, such as the African gray parrot, can imitate the human voice.

▲ *Like all parrots, the scarlet macaw can be incredibly noisy, with a raucous, rasping caw.*

◀ *Male Andean cock-of-the-rocks are famous for their color and their spectacular courtship routines.*

DATA: Tropical birds

- **BIGGEST NEST**
  A South African sociable weaver bird nest can be up to 13 feet deep and 24.5 feet long.

- **OLDEST BIRDS**
  Parrots are the longest-living order of birds, and a Major Mitchell's Cockatoo called "Cookie" has lived to be over 80 years old in a zoo.

Temperate birds

BIRDS IN TEMPERATE REGIONS may not be as colorful and spectacular as those of the tropics, but there is an enormous range and variety. There are town and garden birds such as the sparrow, the magpie, and the pigeon. There are woodland birds such as the nuthatch and the nightjar. There are birds that live near water, too–freshwater birds such as ducks and swans, waders such as curlews and redshanks, and seabirds such as gulls and puffins. Then there are the magnificent birds of prey such as eagles, kestrels, hawks, and falcons, and the night-hunting owls.

FACTS: About water birds

▶ Like many birds of wetlands, the sandhill crane has become endangered by the destruction of its habitat.

▶ Like many birds, the redstart feeds on insects, and has a wide beak for catching them in flight. It was originally a woodland bird, but has adapted well to environmental changes.

◀ The waxwing gets its name from the waxy red tips on some of its wing feathers. Like many seed- and fruit-eating birds, it has a short, pincer-like beak for cracking seeds.

- **Waders**
  Wading birds, such as curlews and plovers, have long legs for wading through the water and long bills for probing around in the mud to look for food.

- **Waterfowl**
  Waterfowl, such as ducks, geese, and swans, have webbed feet for swimming and long, flexible necks for reaching into the water.

- **Seabirds**
  Many seabirds are very good divers and roam the open sea looking for food. They often lay their eggs in nesting grounds high up on the cliffs so that they are kept safely out of the reach of predators.

▲ Common pheasants, like this Monal pheasant, came originally from Asia, but they have adapted well to other partys of the world. They are now the most widespread of all game birds, and are favored by hunters.

DATA: Temperate birds

- **ANCIENT BIRD**
  The oldest known bird was a Siberian red crane that died in 1988, aged 82.

- **SHARPEST EYES**
  The keen-eyed peregrine falcon can spot a pigeon at 5 miles away.

▲ *Jays are seed-eating birds that like acorns, which they bury for winter food. But they sometimes steal nestlings and eggs from the nests of other birds.*

▼ *The pigeons that swarm over many city squares are all descended from domestic pigeons, which came in turn from the wild rock dove. They are called "feral" because they were once tame and are now wild.*

FACTS: About birds of prey

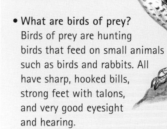

▶ *The peregrine falcon can plummet at speeds of 125 mph when diving down on prey.*

- **What are birds of prey?**
  Birds of prey are hunting birds that feed on small animals such as birds and rabbits. All have sharp, hooked bills, strong feet with talons, and very good eyesight and hearing.

- **Different quarry**
  Different birds specialize in hunting different things: honey buzzards eat bees and have talons shaped for digging out nests; eagles have large talons for snatching up rabbits and squirrels; harriers eat snakes and other reptiles; ospreys specialize in catching fish such as salmon.

- **Birds under threat**
  Many birds of prey have been endangered by hunting, egg collecting, and game keepers and pigeon breeders who want to stop the birds of prey killing game birds and pigeons.

▶ *Owls hunt at night and have large, round eyes to see well in poor light, but their hearing is also so sharp that they can catch prey in the pitch dark by sound alone.*

REPTILES ARE SCALY-SKINNED CREATURES such as crocodiles, lizards, and snakes. They are sometimes said to be cold-blooded. But their blood is not cold; it can be as warm as a mammal's. Mammals get their warmth by eating. Reptiles can survive on very little food, but they depend on the Sun for warmth and must continually shuttle between warm and cold places to stay at the right temperature. They may spend hours basking in the Sun, gaining enough energy to go hunting for food. But they depend on the Sun for warmth, so they cannot live in cold places.

FACTS: About snakes

- **What are snakes?**
  Snakes are thin, limbless reptiles that live mostly in warm regions. They are predators, but with no limbs; they kill their prey with poison or by constricting (squeezing) them to death.

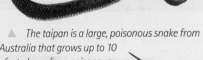

▲ The taipan is a large, poisonous snake from Australia that grows up to 10 feet—large for a poisonous snake. It is from the same family as the cobra—the elapids—all of which have venom in their front fangs.

- **Tongue scent**
  Snakes have no ears, but sense their prey from sound vibrations on the ground. They also use their tongues to smell with and only use their eyes when close to things, as their eyesight is poor.

- **Snakes with bite**
  Many snakes are venomous—that is, they have a poisonous bite. Those with fangs in the front of their mouths, such as vipers and rattlesnakes, are more dangerous than back-fanged snakes—because back-fanged snakes must get a victim fully into their mouths to bite.

▼Like all vipers, the Gaboon viper has long fangs in the front of its mouth that hinge back into the mouth when not in use. The fangs are hollow and act as "syringes"—injecting venom straight into the victim when the snake bites.

- **Big squeeze**
  Boas and pythons kill large victims by constriction. The snake coils itself around its victim. Each time the trapped animal breathes out, the snake tightens its hold until its prey finally suffocates.

▲ Geckos can climb up walls and even run across ceilings because they have feet like suction cups. Their toes are flat with pads underneath them, and these pads are covered with hundreds of tiny hooks that can grip onto flat surfaces.

FACTS: About alligators

- **Crocodiles v. alligators**
  Crocodiles and alligators are large reptiles that live in warm rivers and swamps. Crocodiles have thinner snouts and a fourth tooth on the lower jaw that is visible when the mouth is shut.

- **Floating predators**
  Alligators and crocodiles are predators that lurk under the surface with just their eyes and nostrils above the water, and they can take prey by surprise by springing out suddenly.

▼ The alligator of the Florida Everglades is now a protected animal because it was once endangered by hunters wanting its skin.

▲ Turtles and tortoises are together known as chelonians, and all live inside an armored shell of bony plates. On their back is a domed "carapace," and underneath is a flat "plastron." Some can pull their arms, legs, and head right in. They are slow moving, but withdrawing inside their shell protects them.

➤ The frilled-necked lizard of Australia may not be very big, but it makes up for its lack of size with its enormous frill. Normally, the frill hangs limp, but it spreads out up to 10 inches whenever the lizard is threatened, making it look three times as large and twice as dangerous.

▼ Iguanas like the Madagascan iguana (below) are large, tropical lizards. The marine iguanas of the Galapagos are one of the very few lizards that live in the sea. They can stay under the water for up to an hour.

Amphibians

AMPHIBIANS ARE CREATURES such as frogs, toads, newts, and salamanders that live part of their lives on land and part in the water. Most begin life by hatching in water from big clusters of eggs called spawn. At this stage, they are more like fish, but they soon grow legs and develop lungs for breathing air. Before long, they are ready to climb ashore, where most will spend the majority their adult lives. Even so, amphibians rarely stray very far from water and must return there in order to lay their eggs, which would dry out on land.

FACTS: About frogs and toads

- **Skin breathers**
  Most frogs breathe partly through their skin and so need to keep damp all the time. They are very good swimmers and, except for tree frogs, spend most of their time in or near water.

- **High jumpers**
  Neither frogs nor toads have tails as adults, but they have long, strong back legs for jumping.

- **Biggest frog**
  The largest frog is the goliath from West Africa, which measures up to 31.5 inches when stretched out and weighs up to 6.6 pounds. The smallest are found in Papua New Guinea and average just 0.3 inch long.

▲ *Tree frogs of tropical rain forests take advantage of other moisture sources to live in the trees far from water.*

- **Flying frog**
  Flying frogs are tree frogs that can glide through the air. They have sticky discs on their fingers for gripping onto branches, and their hands and feet are webbed to act as airbrakes.

- **Warty toad**
  Generally, toads have drier, wartier skin than frogs and have shorter hind legs that are better for walking than jumping, unlike a frog's. Toads are also less active than frogs.

▲ *Poison arrow frogs of the Amazon are brightly colored to warn that their sweat glands contain a deadly poison—which Indians used to smear on their arrows.*

- **Baby swallower**
  The male Darwin's frog of Chile swallows the spawn left by the female and keeps it in his throat until it hatches as little tadpoles.

FACTS: About newts and salamanders

- **Lizard look-alikes**
Newts and salamanders look a little like lizards, but unlike lizards, which are reptiles, these are amphibians and begin life in water. Newts live in temperate climates and hibernate during the winter under logs and stones. Salamanders live in warmer areas and so do not need to hibernate.

- **Giant salamander**
The biggest salamander of all is the Chinese giant salamander, which grows up to 6 feet long.

- **Colored newts**
Many male newts have bright colors and special markings during their mating season to attract females. The crested newt has a bright orange or yellow belly as well as a bumpy crest down the length of its back.

▷ *Newts are the most water-loving of all the amphibians, spending much of their lives in ponds.*

- **Egg-wrapping**
To protect their eggs from predators, female newts wrap each egg in a leaf with their feet.

- **Fire salamander**
Fire salamanders got their name because they shelter underneath logs, and so, when in the past logs were burned on fires, salamanders hiding underneath would come rushing out of the fire.

1. The fertilized eggs of a frog are called spawn. Each of the blobs in spawn is an egg containing an embryo, protected in a bag of jelly

2. The eggs hatch in water after a week or so into fish-like tadpoles that swim around, breathe through gills, and grow rapidly

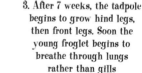

3. After 7 weeks, the tadpole begins to grow hind legs, then front legs. Soon the young froglet begins to breathe through lungs rather than gills

▷ As they grow from eggs to adults, all amphibians, like the frog, go through a series of dramatic changes, called a metamorphosis. Each creature has its own special way of developing. But the sequence shown here for the frog is fairly typical.

4. The froglet's legs continue growing and its tail shortens. After 14 weeks, the frog is an adult and leaves the water

65

Insects

INSECTS MAY BE TINY, but they are by far the most numerous of all creatures. There are nearly a million known species, and they are found almost everywhere. Ants scurry along the ground. Bees buzz around hives. Butterflies flutter over flowers. Insects are very varied in look, but all have six legs and a body divided into three sections–head, thorax, and abdomen. They also have two compound eyes with anything from six to 30,000 lenses and a variety of other sensors such as antennae (feelers), which they can use to hear, taste, and smell.

FACTS: About butterflies, moths, and caterpillars

- **Butterflies and moths**
  Butterflies and moths are both part of a big group of insects called Lepidoptera, which means "scaly wings," because their wings are covered with tiny, dust-like scales.

- **What's the difference?**
  Butterflies are usually brightly colored and fly during the day. They have thin, hairless bodies and a pair of clubbed antennae. Moths tend to be drabber, because they rest during the day—on trees and dead leaves—and so must be camouflaged. They have plump, hairy bodies and straight antennae.

- **Caterpillars**
  Butterflies and moths begin life as an egg and then hatch as long, thin caterpillars, which eat leaves voraciously for a month.

Butterflies like the red admiral can migrate astonishing distances, as far as many birds— even crossing oceans, with the help of the wind.

- **Chrysalis and cocoon**
  When the caterpillar is ready, it spins a cocoon of silk around itself or creates a hard shell called a chrysalis. Inside, it becomes a pupa, grows wings, and, amazingly, changes to an adult butterfly or moth before emerging.

- **Nectar seeker**
  Most butterflies feed, if at all, only on nectar, the sweet juice of flowers, and so spend their brief lives fluttering from bloom to bloom.

Caterpillars are fat and slow-moving, and so are very vulnerable to predators. But the Puss Moth caterpillar can scare smaller enemies by rearing up, waving its tail, and squirting formic acid.

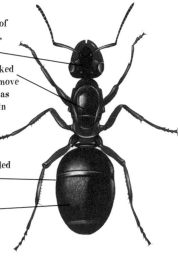

The head consists of mouth parts, eyes, and antennae

The thorax is packed with muscles that move the legs, as well as housing the main body organs

Insects breathe through holes in their sides called spiracles

The abdomen holds all the insect's digestive organs and its sex organs

Insects look very different from other animals. Not only are their bodies split into three sections, but they have no bones. Instead, they have a rigid shell or "exoskeleton," made of a tough substance called chitin.

FACTS: About bees

- **Bee hive**
  Bees live together in large numbers in hives or nests. In each colony there is one queen, many female workers, and a few drones (males).

- **Queen bee**
  Only the queen can lay eggs—up to 1,000 a day. Drones exist only to mate with the queen, after which they die.

- **Worker bee**
  Workers collect pollen and nectar from flowers and bring it to the nest. Pollen is fed to larvae and nectar is used for honey.

▶ *A honeybee's main protection is the sting in its tail. Its bright yellow and black stripes are a warning.*

Termites are insects that live in huge colonies in the tropics. Together, they build huge mounds to live in out of dust and saliva, complete with air conditioning. Some termite mounds can be 9 m tall.

◀ *Dragonflies are large, fast-flying insects that can dart at up to 37 mph. Their four wings move independently of one another and make a rattling sound. They can also fly backward.*

 # DATA: Insects

- **LONGEST INSECT**
  The world's longest insect is a stick insect from Borneo that is over 10 inches long.

- **SMALLEST INSECT**
  The world's smallest is the fairy fly, just 8 one-thousands of an inch long!

- **AN ANT'S STRENGTH**
  An ant can lift 50 times its own weight – that is like you lifting a lorry!

PLANTS

Plants

THERE ARE OVER 4,000,000 different kinds of plant, ranging from tiny plankton that are barely visible under a microscope to giant trees hundreds of feet tall, the world's largest living things. They grow almost everywhere—on land and in the sea, on plains and on mountaintops, even in deserts and snowy wastes. Indeed, 40 percent of the world's land is covered by trees and grass. What makes plants very different from animals is that they do not move around and have no need of senses (or a brain) because they can make their own food from sunlight.

FACTS: About stems

- **The plant stem**
  The stem supports the plant's flowers and leaves. It is also a pipe to take water, minerals, and food up and down between the roots and the leaves. Water goes up from the roots via tubes called xylem. Food goes down from the leaves in tubes called phloem.

- **Woody and herbaceous**
  Many plants have stems that are green and flexible. They are called herbaceous plants, because many are herbs such as parsley. Woody plants such as trees have stiff stems or trunks covered with bark.

  ▶*Bamboo is an unusual plant. It is a kind of grass and starts off with a soft, bendy, herbaceous stem. But as it grows, very rapidly, the stem becomes hard, tough and woody.*

FACTS: About leaves

- **Sun traps**
  Leaves are a plant's solar cells and catch the light to make the food the plant needs to grow. Most are broad and flat to catch as much sun as possible.

- **Stalk and blade**
  Each leaf is attached to the stem by a small stalk called a petiole. The flat part of the leaf is called the blade.

- **Simple and compound**
  Some leaves, such as maple leaves, are called simple leaves because they only have one blade. Other leaves, such as those of the walnut and willow, are called compound because they have a number of blades on the same stalk.

- **Biggest leaves**
  The biggest leaves belong to the raffia palm tree, which can grow up to 65 feet long.
  ▶*The lines on leaves are veins, which not only provide a frame to support the leaf, but carry water in and the food the leaf makes out.*

70

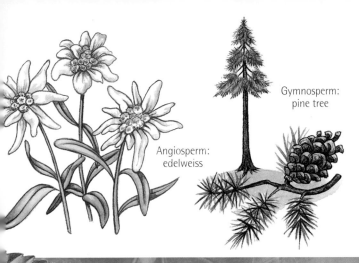

Angiosperm: edelweiss

Gymnosperm: pine tree

◀ The first plants to grow on land were plants such as fungi and lichen, which grow from tiny cells called spores. However, most plants today grow from seeds, not spores. Unlike the more primitive spore-making plants, seed-making plants have stems, leaves, and often roots and flowers. Seed-making plants are divided into gymnosperms, which have cones, and angiosperms, which bear flowers.

FACTS: About photosynthesis

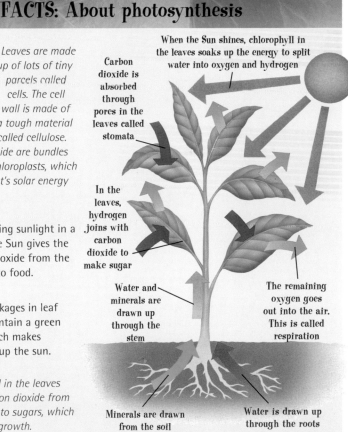

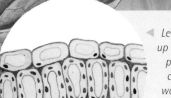

◀ Leaves are made up of lots of tiny parcels called cells. The cell wall is made of a tough material called cellulose. Inside are bundles called chloroplasts, which are the plant's solar energy converters.

- **Food making**
  Plants make their food by absorbing sunlight in a process called photosynthesis. The Sun gives the plant energy to change carbon dioxide from the air, and hydrogen from water, into food.

- **Green packages**
  Photosynthesis occurs in tiny packages in leaf cells called chloroplasts. These contain a green substance called chlorophyll, which makes leaves green. It is this that soaks up the sun.

▶ In photosynthesis, chlorophyll in the leaves uses the Sun's energy to turn carbon dioxide from the air and hydrogen from water into sugars, which the plant uses as fuel for growth.

Carbon dioxide is absorbed through pores in the leaves called stomata

When the Sun shines, chlorophyll in the leaves soaks up the energy to split water into oxygen and hydrogen

In the leaves, hydrogen joins with carbon dioxide to make sugar

Water and minerals are drawn up through the stem

The remaining oxygen goes out into the air. This is called respiration

Minerals are drawn from the soil

Water is drawn up through the roots

Roots and bulbs

THE GREEN AND COLORFUL PARTS of a plant are the leaves and flowers you see above the ground–but there is more to a plant beneath the surface. This is where the plant's roots are, growing down into soil or water. Roots not only hold the plant in place, anchoring it in the soil, but also draw up the water and minerals that the plant needs to grow. In some plants, such as beetroot, the roots also act as a food store. Sometimes, new plants can grow, or plants that die back can regrow, from the parts below the ground, which form bulbs, corms, rhizomes, and tubers.

FACTS: About roots

▲ *Root vegetables are vegetables that grow underground. But not all of them are really roots. Carrots and beets are true roots, but potatoes are tubers, which are underground stems, and onions are bulbs, which are underground leaves.*

• **Growing plant**
When a plant begins to grow, the seed sends out a single primary root. This quickly branches out into secondary roots. The tips of these are protected by a root cap as they probe through the soil.

• **Taproots**
Some plants have just one very large root, with only a few very fine roots sprouting off it. The large root is called a taproot.

• **Fibrous roots**
Some plants, such as grasses, have lots of fine roots spreading out in a dense mat. These are called fibrous roots. Some rye grasses grow up to 7,500 miles of roots in just a cubic yard of soil.

• **Root hairs**
Every root has very fine "root hairs" branching off it. These hairs are very good at soaking up water and minerals from the soil.

• **Parasitic roots**
Parasitic plants are unable to take up water and minerals from the soil themselves. Instead they draw their food from other plants. Mistletoe, for instance, wraps its roots around apple trees.

• **Climbing roots**
Some climbing plants, like ivy, not only have roots underground, but on the stem too. These stem roots serve mainly to hold the plant onto trees, walls, and fences.

• **Deepest roots**
The roots of a wild fig tree in Transvaal, South Africa, go down 400 feet into the ground. An elm tree seen growing in Largs, Scotland, had roots 360 feet deep.

FACTS: About bulbs, corms, rhizomes, and tubers

- **New from old**
  Some plants only grow once from a seed. But many perennials can die back and then grow anew again and again from parts of a root or stem. This is called vegetative propagation.

- **Rhizomes**
  Plants such as irises sprout from thick stems called rhizomes that grow sideways beneath the ground.

- **Tubers**
  Sometimes, the end of a rhizome swells into lumps called tubers. Potatoes are tubers.

- **Corms**
  Flowers such as crocuses grow from the bulbous base to their stem, called a corm.

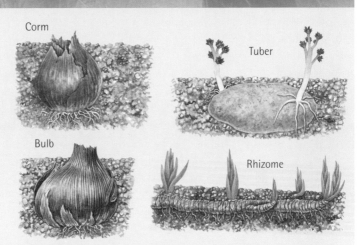

Corm

Tuber

Bulb

Rhizome

▲ To survive the winter, many plants die back to leave nothing visible above the ground. But the plant stays alive in the form of a corm, tuber, bulb, or rhizome. All of these are "storage organs," providing food to sustain the plant through the winter and to feed new shoots when they re-emerge the following spring.

- **Bulbs**
  Bulbs, such as onions, look like corms, but they are actually made of leaf parts rather than the stem, which is why the onion has layers.

- **Food stores**
  Plants such as lupins grow in a ring around the outside of an old stem as the stem gets older and grows wider.

FACTS: About runners and suckers

◀ Strawberry plants are plants that spread by growing runners—that is, long stems that creep over the ground. Here and there along the stem it puts down new roots and a new plant grows.

Strawberry runners

- **Creeping stems**
  Some plants, such as roses, propagate (grow new plants) not from seeds or bulbs, corms, rhizomes, or tubers, but from long thin stems that creep over the ground (runners) or under it (suckers).

- **Buried leaves**
  With some plants, like begonias, new plants can grow from broken leaves that get embedded in the soil.

Flowers, seeds, & fruits

MOST OF THE WORLD'S PLANTS are flowers. Not only garden and wild flowers, but many trees and every herb, shrub, grain, fruit, and vegetable is a flowering plant, or "angiosperm." The blooms may not all be as big and beautiful as those of a rose, but all flowering plants have flowers, and all serve a purpose. Flowers are not just for show–they are sexual, and contain male parts, which make the pollen to fertilize the eggs, or "ovules," made by female parts. Only when pollen and ovules come together can flowers create the fruits and seeds from which new plants will grow.

FACTS: About seeds and fruits

- **Seeds**
  Seeds are the tiny packages from which new plants grow. A hard shell, or "kernel," holds not only the new plant in embryo, but all the food it needs to nourish it.

- **What is a fruit?**
  When scientists talk of fruit, they don't just mean apples and pears, but the part of a flower that protects the seed as it ripens and helps spread it. A flower's eggs grow inside its ovaries. Once the eggs are fertilized and turned into seeds, the ovary swells around it into a fruit.

- **Juicy fruits**
  Fruits are often juicy and sweet when ripe so that animals are tempted to eat them. The seeds are then spread in the animals' droppings.

  ◄ *The pips inside each grape are seeds from which new grape vines might grow.*

◄ *Even though they are often very small, like this bottlebrush of Australia, most trees have flowers.*

- **Plums and cherries**
  Fruits such as plums are called "drupes." They have a fleshy outside and a hard kernel or stone inside protecting the seeds. The stone may be too big for animals to swallow, so they eat just the flesh, but the seeds still get spread.

- **False fruits**
  Some fruits are called false fruits because they are made from more than just the ovary of the flower. Apples and pears, for example, have the ovary as their core, but their fleshy parts are actually swollen stalk.

- **Legumes**
  Peas, beans, and other legumes are soft, dry fruits held in a case called a pod.

▶ Poppies are "annuals" and flower, scatter their seeds, and die in just one year. Buds appear in early summer, then open up as it gets warmer, releasing a flower that is fully grown by midsummer. Once pollinated, their petals wither and fall off, leaving a seed capsule. By fall, the capsule has dried and developed holes, and the ripe seeds can be shaken out by the wind.

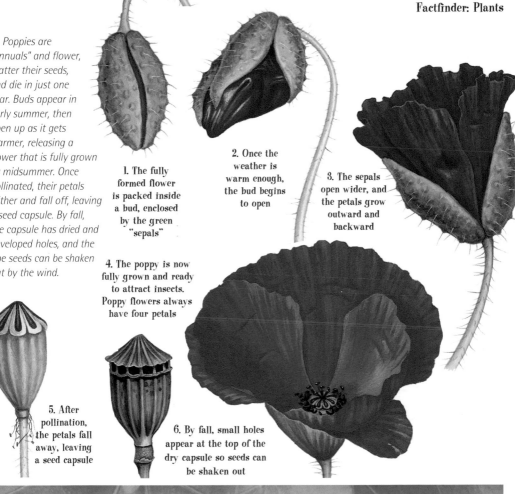

1. The fully formed flower is packed inside a bud, enclosed by the green "sepals"

2. Once the weather is warm enough, the bud begins to open

3. The sepals open wider, and the petals grow outward and backward

4. The poppy is now fully grown and ready to attract insects. Poppy flowers always have four petals

5. After pollination, the petals fall away, leaving a seed capsule

6. By fall, small holes appear at the top of the dry capsule so seeds can be shaken out

FACTS: About spreading plants

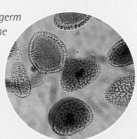

▶ Pollen are the male germ cells that must reach the eggs to fertilize them. They are microscopically small, and some are spread by sticking to the legs and bodies of insects drawn to the flower's nectar.

• Scattered far and wide
Plants can't move, but they can spread their pollen and seeds over a wide area. Only a few seeds will grow, so plants usually produce large numbers to ensure their survival.

• Seed spreading
Some seeds are so tiny that they are easily carried by the wind. Others have hooks or hairs on them so that they catch on the fur of passing animals.

Garden & wildflowers

ALL FLOWERS WERE WILD ONCE, but through history gardeners have adapted them to the garden by selecting seeds and grafting plants together to bring out particular qualities. Their efforts have created a huge range of beautiful new plants, including roses, carnations, chrysanthemums, tulips, and many more. There are now hundreds of thousands of kinds of garden flowers, while wildflowers are becoming rare as human activity restricts the places where they can grow. Many wildflowers, such as the lady's slipper orchid, are now in danger of becoming extinct.

FACTS: Garden flowers

- **Big and bold**
  On the whole, garden flowers have much bigger flowers in bolder colors than their wild cousins. The wild dog rose has tiny pale pink or white blooms. Garden roses have big blooms in strong colors, from deep red to blue.

- **Cut flowers**
  Once cut flowers could only be bought in the right season. Now they are grown in warm places all year round, such as Colombia, and flown in chilled conditions to bring them fresh to local shops in under two days.

  ▽ An enormous range of cut flowers can now be delivered all year round.

FACTS: Wild flowers

▷ The edelweiss survives because it can grow at very high altitude in the Alps, sprouting out from cracks in the rocks. This is because its leaves and blooms are covered with a coat of woolly hairs that protect it from the cold.

- **Meadows and woodlands**
  Every kind of place has its own kind of wild flower. On heathlands, flowers such as bell-heather, gorse, and scarlet pimpernel grow. In meadows, tiny buttercups, daisies, clover, and ragged robin grow in the grass. In woodlands, flowers like bluebells, primroses, and celandines grow. By the sea, sea campion and thrift grow on the rocks, and birdsfoot trefoil on grassy clifftops.

- **Protected flowers**
  Some wildflowers are now so rare that the few survivors must be protected by law. This is true of many orchids.

FACTS: About perennials & biennials

- **Annuals**
  Annuals are plants, such as delphiniums, that grow from seeds, flower, disperse their seeds, and die in a single growing season.

- **Biennials**
  Biennials live for two years. In the first, the plant grows leaves on a bulb or taproot that sustains it with food through the winter. It flowers in the second summer.

- **Perennials**
  Perennials such as wallflowers and chrysanthemums live several years, surviving through the winter on underground food stores such as bulbs.

- **Ephemerals**
  Ephemerals such as groundsel are short-lived plants that grow from seed, bloom, and die within a few weeks.

▲ *The giant sunflower is a perennial. It is a native of Peru but is now grown in many places, both for its big yellow flowers and for its seeds which give cooking oil.*

▼ *Flowers probably evolved their colorful blooms and beautiful scents to attract the insects they rely on for pollination. But the efforts of gardeners over the centuries have added many new and often spectacular blooms to those created by natural evolution, including roses, tulips, delphiniums, and many more. Many of these new flowers no longer rely on insects for pollination, but are pollinated by humans.*

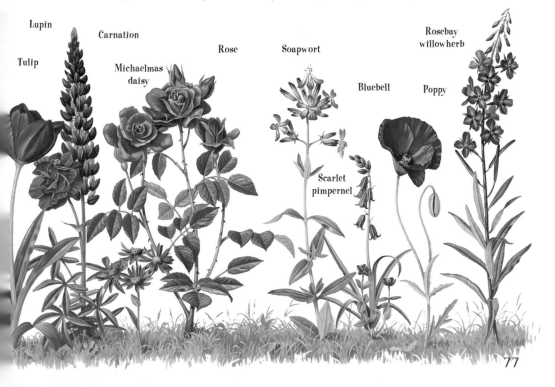

Lupin

Carnation

Rose

Soapwort

Rosebay willowherb

Tulip

Michaelmas daisy

Bluebell

Poppy

Scarlet pimpernel

How trees grow

ALTHOUGH SOME DWARF WILLOWS grow just a few inches high, trees are generally the largest of all plants. Indeed, the giant redwood tree is the biggest of all living things. Trees can grow big because they don't have soft, green "herbaceous" stems like other plants; they have stiff, brown, woody stems, covered with protective bark, that can grow tall and support an enormous weight of leaves. With most trees, there is a single, thick central stem—the trunk—and leaves and side branches grow far enough above the ground that they are well out of the reach of most browsing animals.

FACTS: About tree trunks

▲ Slicing through a tree's trunk can reveal a lot about its history—its age, the rate at which it has grown, and the conditions it has faced over the years.

• Inside the trunk
The center of a trunk is the dead "heartwood." The living part is the middle—the "sapwood" and the "cambium". Outside is a protective layer of bark.

• Tree rings
Each ring inside the trunk represents a year's growth. Rings close together indicate slow growth; rings far apart indicate rapid growth.

FACTS: About seeds

• Seed production
Because only a small portion of their seeds survive, most trees produce thousands each year.

• Seed dispersal
The seeds of many trees are dispersed by wind, so are shaped to become airborne easily—maple tree seeds are encased in a pair of flat wings, while willow seeds are shaped like tiny parachutes.

▼ Many trees have seeds that are spread by the wind. The eucalyptus trees of Australia are among the many that have long helicopter-like wings on which they can flutter long distances before they land.

▶ *Timber is either hardwood, from broad-leaved trees, or softwood, from conifers. Softwood trees are much faster growing (about 33 feet every 30 years) and are grown in huge numbers on plantations in places like the Rocky Mountains in the United States and Canada (right). Because they grow faster, these trees provide softer wood. Softwoods are mostly used for making cheap furniture, paper, and for building. Hardwoods are used for more expensive furniture and shipbuilding.*

◀ *Cedars have smooth, upright cones that are made up of lots of closely packed scales, each attached to two seeds. Over a few years these scales gradually break off the cones and fall to the ground, taking their seeds with them.*

- **Seed cones**
  The seeds of conifers develop inside hard, protective cones until they are ready.

- **Catkins**
  Oak trees produce male flowers called catkins— long clusters that hang from the branches and release pollen into the air. When the pollen lands on the ovaries of female flowers and fertilizes them, the ovaries develop into acorns.

- **Nuts and berries**
  Some trees have seeds growing inside soft, fleshy fruits, such as berries. Others have them growing inside hard shells, such as acorns and walnuts.

DATA: Trees

- **THE BIGGEST TREE**
  In the world is "General Sherman," a giant sequoia in California–290 feet tall and 82 feet round.

- **THE FASTEST-GROWING TREES**
  The Foxglove tree can grow 20 feet in its first year and up to 12 inches in just three weeks.

- **THE LONGEST-LIVING TREE**
  The oldest surviving tree was a bristlecone pine in Nevada, that had lived for 5,100 years.

- **THE LONGEST LIVING SPECIES**
  The oldest surviving species of tree is thought to be the maidenhair tree of China, which first appeared over 160 million years ago.

Deciduous trees

DECIDUOUS TREES are trees that lose their leaves at some time during the year, usually to cut down their need for water. In cool regions, they lose them in winter because water is hard to come by when groundwater is frozen. In warm regions, they lose them in the summer, when the soil dries out quickly. All deciduous trees are flowering plants and have broad, flat leaves, which is why they are also known as broad-leaved trees–although there are also evergreen broad-leaved trees. Broad-leaved trees include deciduous trees such as ash and chestnut, evergreen trees such as holly, and palm trees.

FACTS: About palm trees

- Long leaves
  Palm trees have thick, tough leaves that help them survive in hot places. There are about 2,800 species, some with leaves as long as 40 feet and as wide as 8 feet.

- No branches
  Palms have no branches. The leaves grow directly out from the trunk.

  ▶ *The leaves, stems, and fruit of palm trees provide lots of useful products, ranging from baskets, furniture, food, oil, and even soap.*

▼ *In spring, the buds of new leaves shoot on the trees, and slowly open. Flowers appear on the tree, too, and fruit trees blossom. Because plenty of sunlight can still filter down to the ground through the thin canopy of leaves, woodland flowers such as bluebells bloom beneath the trees.*

▼ *In summer, the leaves on the trees are fully grown, providing a sheltered home for a wide variety of different animals and plants. The dense foliage keeps the woodland beneath at an even temperature—nights are warmer, and days are cooler here than out in the open.*

FACTS: About deciduous trees

- **Tree life**
  Oaks and other trees can live up to 500 years. Some elms, which reproduce from suckers, never really die at all because the trees are constantly renewing themselves, creating a whole grove of their offshoots.

- **Fallen trees**
  Every now and then, trees die and fall over. As they crash to the floor, they open up the woodland floor to the sky, creating a glade where new trees and other plants thrive.

▲ *Deciduous forests once covered the whole of Europe and eastern North America, but now only fragments of these remain.*

- **Oak trees**
  There are around 600 species of oak tree, some deciduous, some evergreen. But all grow from acorns.

- **Dutch elm disease**
  Elm trees were once common in northern Europe, but many have been killed by Dutch elm disease—a fungus whose spores are spread by beetles that live in the bark.

- **Coppicing**
  Many woodlands have long been managed by foresters. Trees such as willows are cut off at the trunk or "coppiced." The new straight shoots that grow from the top make "withies," which are good for basketmaking.

▼ *By fall, the days are getting colder and there is less water available. To survive, the trees must prepare to lose their leaves. The chlorophyll that makes the leaves green starts to break down, and sugars in the leaves gradually turn them brown, red, or orange.*

▼ *As winter approaches, the trees get ready to close down altogether. The leaves that changed color in fall start to drop off, leaving the trees bare and dormant. During this time, though, winter buds develop, containing new leaves that will burst open the following spring.*

Conifers and cycads

CONIFERS, AND THEIR TROPICAL RELATIVES cycads and gingkos, are among the oldest of all kinds of plants. They first appeared over 300 million years ago, long before the age of dinosaurs. Conifers, cycads, and gingkos are all called gymnosperms, and make their seeds in cones. Conifers are tall, mostly evergreen trees that generally grow in cool and mountainous regions. A few cypresses are the only tropical conifers. Cycads, however, are tropical trees that look like stubby palm trees. Gingkos, or maidenhair, trees are tall trees with fan-shaped leaves that grow only in eastern China.

FACTS: About coniferous forests

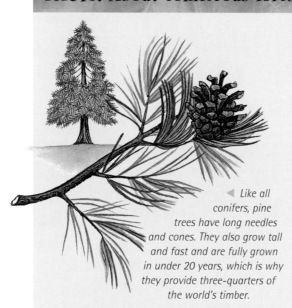

◀ Like all conifers, pine trees have long needles and cones. They also grow tall and fast and are fully grown in under 20 years, which is why they provide three-quarters of the world's timber.

• **Cold resistance**
Conifers are able to survive in cold areas with little water because instead of leaves they have thin, waxy needles that shed snow easily and lose very little water. (Water cannot be used by trees when it is frozen.) Their tall, narrow shape helps shed snow, too.

• **Evergreen**
Nearly all conifers are evergreen, which means that their leaves stay on all year round. Larches are an exception—their needles fall off in fall.

• **Plantations**
In various cold regions of the world, conifers are grown in narrowly planted rows on massive plantations to provide timber. They are fast growing and can also survive on soil that is too poor for other crops.

• **Life in a coniferous forest**
Coniferous forests are usually quite dense and dark, and so there is much less other plant life beneath the trees than there is in a deciduous forest—usually just fungi, ferns, and lichen.

• **Pine family**
Pines make up the largest family of conifers. This includes around 100 different species, such as the Scots pine, Corsican pine, and Loblolly pine.

• **Boreal forest**
The most extensive coniferous forests are found in the colder, northern parts of the world—mostly North America, Scandinavia, and Siberia.

• **Tree mix**
Most coniferous forests are made up of conifers like pines, spruces, and firs.

▲ *The giant redwood or sequoia trees of the Sierra Nevada in California are the world's largest living things, growing 330 feet or more tall. Some are among the oldest, too. There are redwoods here that date back to before the days of the Ancient Egyptians, 4,000 years ago.*

DATA: Big, old trees

- **THE TALLEST TREE**
  The tallest tree in the world is a coastal redwood in Redwood National Park, California,–365 feet.

- **THE OLDEST LIVING TREE**
  The oldest living tree is a 4,700-year-old bristlecone pine in California's White Mountains.

- **THE BIGGEST FOREST**
  The biggest forest is in Siberia–over 6.5 million square miles.

FACTS: Seeds and cones

- **Cone-bearers**
  Instead of flowers, conifers and cycads have male and female cones that produce and carry seeds.

- **Male cones**
  The smaller male cones grow in clusters and produce pollen grains that travel on the wind to fertilize the female cones.

- **Female cones**
  Once fertilized, female cones may take as long as three years to develop their seeds.

- **Female scales**
  Each scale of the female cone has one or more seeds attached to it. As they develop, they are protected within the hard cone. When they are ready, the scales open up and either release the seeds or fall away from the cone, taking the seeds with them.

▲ *Cones are very sensitive to changes in the dampness of the air. In dry weather, the scales shrivel and stand out stiffly. When it is damper, they absorb the moisture and close up neatly again.*

Mosses and ferns

NOT ALL PLANTS GROW FROM SEEDS. The very first plants to grow on land some 400 million years ago grew from tiny, dust-like cells called spores. These ancient plants, including mosses, liverworts, club mosses, horsetails, and ferns, still survive today, although none of them ever grow as big as they did in the time before seed-bearing plants appeared some 200 million years ago. They love damp, shady places and are often seen carpeting rocks along streams and growing all over trees in moist woodlands and steamy tropical rain forests–sometimes far above the ground.

FACTS: About ferns

- **Roots, leaves, and stems**
  Unlike mosses, ferns are "pteridophytes," or featherplants, and have roots and leaves, as well as veins to take food and water up and down inside the stem. Fern leaves are called fronds.

- **Tree ferns**
  Tree ferns are big ferns that can grow up to 82 feet tall, and they are abundant in moist tropical rain forests. They have no branches, and the fronds grow in a crown from the top of the trunk.

- **Passenger plants**
  Some ferns, such as bird's-nest fern and staghorn fern, grow on other plants without harming them. They get their moisture by collecting dripping rainwater.

- **Horsetails**
  Horsetails are similar to ferns, but they belong to a group called sphenophytes. Although today most are small, these plants grew more than 100 feet tall in the Carboniferous Period 300–355 million years ago.

  ▶ *Ferns grow from spores made on the underside of their leaves. The spores form a prothallus, which creates the embryo for a new fern to grow from.*

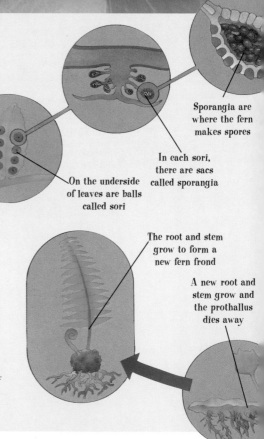

Sporangia are where the fern makes spores

In each sori, there are sacs called sporangia

On the underside of leaves are balls called sori

The root and stem grow to form a new fern frond

A new root and stem grow and the prothallus dies away

FACTS: About moss

- **Moss**
  Mosses and liverworts make up a group of their own called bryophytes. They form in thin cushions on walls, rocks, and old logs and have no true roots so they have to draw their moisture from the air through their stems and tiny threads called rhizoids. This is why they like damp places such as river banks.

- **Sponges**
  Sphagnum moss lives in bogs and can soak up to 25 times its own weight in water. It is the main constituent in peat bogs in Ireland and Scotland.

- **New moss**
  Moss spores make male and female cells, which swim together to create the embryo for a new moss.

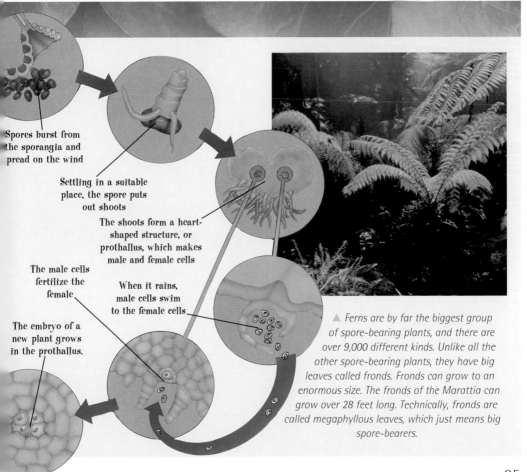

Spores burst from the sporangia and spread on the wind

Settling in a suitable place, the spore puts out shoots

The shoots form a heart-shaped structure, or prothallus, which makes male and female cells

The male cells fertilize the female

When it rains, male cells swim to the female cells

The embryo of a new plant grows in the prothallus.

▲ *Ferns are by far the biggest group of spore-bearing plants, and there are over 9,000 different kinds. Unlike all the other spore-bearing plants, they have big leaves called fronds. Fronds can grow to an enormous size. The fronds of the Marattia can grow over 28 feet long. Technically, fronds are called megaphyllous leaves, which just means big spore-bearers.*

Fungi and mushrooms

FUNGI AND MUSHROOMS grow in the ground like plants, but they are not plants at all. Fungi and mushrooms, along with toadstools, yeast, mildew and mold (like the mold on bread) all belong to a special group of organisms called Myceteae. Unlike plants, fungi have no green chlorophyll, so they cannot make their own food. So they have to get their food in other ways. Many fungi are parasites, which means they feed off living animals, plants, and other organisms. Others are "saprophytes" which means they live off the remains of dead plants and animals.

▶ *Fungi are both good and bad for us. Some kinds of fungi, such as mushrooms and cheese mold, are good to eat, but others are deadly poisonous. Some grow on plants and animals and make them ill, such as the aspergillus mold. Others provide antibiotic drugs. Yeast helps bread rise and beer ferment.*

FACTS: About parasites

▲ *Fungi live off other organisms. These fungi are growing on a tree, clinging on with hundreds of cotton-like threads called hyphae, which digest and absorb materials from the tree.*

- **Chemical rotters**
  Fungi rot the organism they are feeding on by sending out special chemicals called enzymes, which break down plant and animal cells.

- **Food source**
  Fungi absorb food from the rotting organism.

- **Blue cheese**
  The enzymes released by mold are what give blue cheese its flavor—and make bread mold toxic.

Destroying angel

Fly agaric

Honey fungus

Puffball

FACTS: What fungi are made of

- **Spreading threads**
  Fungi are made of cotton-like threads called hyphae, which spread out in a tangled mass through the soil—or into the tissues of the plant or animal the fungi are living on.

◀ *Sometimes, hyphae (pronounced hi-fee) bundle together to form what are called fruiting bodies—such as mushrooms and toadstools. But they can also make tiny pinheads, such as the mold on rotting fruit.*

Shaggy ink cap

Field mushroom

Oyster mushroom

Death cap

FACTS: Poisonous fungi

- **Fly agaric**
  Fly agaric makes the poison muscarine, which causes stomach pains and convulsions, and can occasionally kill. Fly agaric was once taken in small doses for its hallucinatory effect.

- **Death cap**
  The death cap and destroying angel toadstools look quite like harmless mushrooms—but they are deadly. Death-cap contains the poisons amanitine and phalloidine, which can kill a human within six hours of eating it, due to kidney and liver failure.

- **False morel**
  False morel makes the poison gyromitrin, which can create terrible stomach pains.

▶ *Fly agaric announces its deadly poison with its bright color. Eating even small amounts can completely knock you out.*

Algae

A KIND OF ALGAE was among the first living things to appear on Earth some three billion years ago. There are now many different kinds of algae, and although some are tiny, they are very important. They grow almost everywhere there is water, from the oceans to damp walls. Algae in the oceans not only provide food for creatures such as whales, but maintain the levels of oxygen in the air–and without this we could not breathe. Algae can draw energy from sunlight like most plants, but they have neither leaves, stems, roots, nor flowers. Indeed, many scientists don't put algae in the plant kingdom at all but in their own kingdom, called *Protoctista*.

FACTS: About lichens

◀ Lichens grow on bare rock, and can often be seen on stone walls and old stone buildings. But they are very sensitive to any pollution in the air–especially sulphur dioxide from coal-fired power stations–and will not grow where the air is dirty.

▼ Lichens grow in three kinds of shapes. Crusty, or "crustose," lichens grow in discs on stones and walls. Leafy, or "foliose," lichens grow on the ground or on trees, and their edges curl up like leaves. Shrubby, or "fruticose," lichens look like tiny bushes.

- **Algae and fungi**
  Lichens look like plants. But they are actually a remarkable partnership between algae and fungi. The algae are tiny green balls, and use sunlight to make food for the fungi. The fungi create a protective blanket above and below and act as a water store.

- **Reindeer food**
  The algae-fungi partnership enables lichens to live on bare rock faces and very harsh places such as Antarctica and on mountaintops. If things get too dry or cold, they simply go into suspended animation, ready for the good times to begin again. Some lichens provide the only food for reindeer in the Arctic.

Crustose lichen

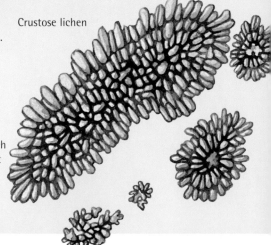

FACTS: About seaweed

- **Large algae**
  Seaweeds are very large algae that grow on seashores or get washed up on beaches. They are usually brown, red, or green in color. They tend to grow in the shallows because they need sunlight.

- **Brown and red**
  Brown algae such as kelp grow 50–65 feet down. Fern-like red algae grow at a depth of 100–200 feet.

- **Holding on**
  Seaweeds have a "holdfast," which looks like a mass of roots, but is just the seaweed's suckers for holding on to rocks despite crashing waves. They actually rely on the water to support them.

- **Natural floats**
  Some seaweeds have air-filled bladders to help them float near the surface.

- **Useful weeds**
  In many places, seaweed is gathered from the seashore to put on the land as fertilizer. It is also a valuable source of iodine and some antibiotics. "Alginates" from seaweeds help set ice cream.

Seaweed helps oxygenate the water and provides grazing for many sea creatures

- **Sea food**
  Seaweed may not look appetizing, but it is popular in Chinese and Japanese cooking. The red seaweed Porphyra is used in Wales to make a kind of pudding called 'laverbread'.

FACTS: About algae

- **Plankton**
  In the oceans, the most important plants are "phytoplankton"—tiny organisms that float in in the surface waters of the oceans and grow in huge numbers. These are food for a wide range of sea creatures.

- **Algal bloom**
  Sometimes algae grow in such huge numbers that they choke other life. These "algal blooms" can sometimes be caused in rivers by fertilizer pollution from farms.

▶ Most seaweeds stay submerged all the time, but many have to cope with the tides—and long periods when they are left high and dry out of water. Some can survive almost a day in baking sunshine, drying up, then returning to life when the tide comes in and refreshes them again. In fact, seaweeds are banded in the tide zone according to how long they can live out of water.

Plants for food

PLANTS PROVIDE the "staple" (basic or essential) food for most people around the world, and an area one and a half times the size of the United States is used for growing crops. Over 12,000 species of plant have been used for food at one time or other, but only about 150 or so are regularly grown as crops, including cereals such as wheat, rice, and corn, fruit such as oranges and bananas, root vegetables such as potatoes and yams, green vegetables such as cabbage and kale, and pulses such as soybeans and lentils. Some of these were first cultivated over 10,000 years ago.

FACTS: Fruit and vegetables

- **Citrus fruits**
  Oranges, lemons, grapefruits, tangerines, and limes are citrus fruits and are grown in huge quantities in places with Mediterranean climates. The fruits are picked in winter and often made into juice.

- **Fruit farms**
  Apples are grown in orchards, oranges are grown in groves, and bananas on plantations.

- **Potato blight**
  Potatoes come originally from the Americas, but they became the staple for poor Irish farmers in the 19th century. When the potato crop was ruined by a disease called "blight" in the 1840s, millions of Irish people starved.

▶ *Bananas are the major export of many countries in Central America, such as El Salvador and Honduras. They are picked while still green and semi-frozen for export by sea.*

Millet is grown in dry places such as Africa and is ground to make flour

Sunflower seeds are crushed to produce oil

▶ *These are just some of the plants grown for food. Many, including sunflowers, corn, and olives, are made into oil. The cereals can be ground to make flour, but rice is usually cooked as whole grains, while maize, millet, and sorghum (as well as oats) are typically made into a kind of oatmeal. Corn comes in two kinds. One gives the large head with lots of grains, known as sweetcorn or corn on the cob. Smaller-grained, smaller-headed corn is used for corn oil or cornstarch.*

Olives grow on trees in Mediterranean areas. They are eaten whole or pressed to make oil

Sorghum is a cereal grown in places such as Egypt and China

Wheat

Maize

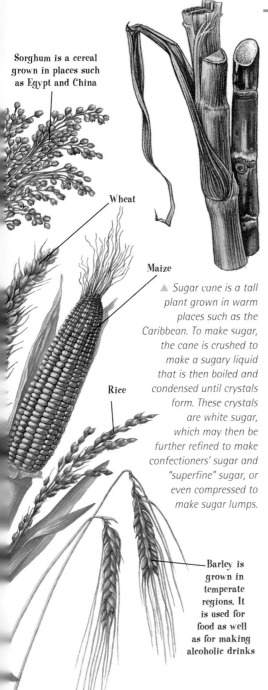

▲ *Sugar cane is a tall plant grown in warm places such as the Caribbean. To make sugar, the cane is crushed to make a sugary liquid that is then boiled and condensed until crystals form. These crystals are white sugar, which may then be further refined to make confectioners' sugar and "superfine" sugar, or even compressed to make sugar lumps.*

Rice

Barley is grown in temperate regions. It is used for food as well as for making alcoholic drinks

FACTS: About cereals

- **What are cereals?**
  Cereals are crops such as wheat, corn, rice, oats, rye, and barley. They are all grasses, and we eat the seeds or grain, leaving the stalks and leaves to rot into animal food called silage.

- **Wheat**
  Wheat provides the basic food for over one in three people in the world. Wheat grain is ground to make flour, which is then used to make things such as bread and pasta.

- **Rice**
  Widely grown in Asia, rice is the staple food for half the world's population. In China alone, 200 million tons are grown every year. There are over 40,000 types, including many long-grained rices such as Basmati rice used with Indian curries, medium-grained rices used for Italian risotto, and short-grained rice used for puddings. Brown rice is white rice with the husk on.

- **Paddy fields**
  Rice is the only cereal crop grown in water—in flooded fields called "paddies." Most of the work in producing it is done by hand. There are typically three crops a year.

▶ *Before processing, rice grains are enclosed in tough husks. Removing this outer layer makes brown rice; refining the grains even farther makes white rice.*

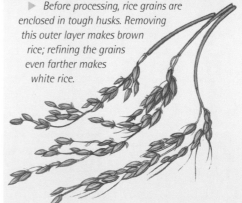

Herbs and spices

HERBS AND SPICES HAVE BEEN used to flavur food and to make medicines since prehistoric times. Herbs are small flowering plants, and there are hundreds of different kinds, each with its own special properties. Usually it is the leaves that are valued, but it can also be the flowers or the stem. Some, such as basil and oregano, are edible and are used in small quantities to flavor food. Others, like feverfew, are valued more for their medicinal qualities. Spices are strongly flavored seeds, roots, and bark that are usually ground into powder to add to food as it is cooked.

FACTS: About tea and coffee

- **Tea**
  Tea is the dried leaves of a small camellia bush that grows on hillsides in subtropical areas, especially in India and Sri Lanka, Japan, and China. The best tea grows slowly at high altitudes (up to 6,500 feet in places).

- **Black tea and green tea**
  There are two main kinds of tea: green tea and black tea. Green tea is picked and dried quickly, giving a mild flavor. Green tea is popular in China. Black tea is only partly dried before it is crushed in rolling machines, giving a much stronger flavor. Black tea is generally preferred in Europe.

- **Coffee**
  Coffee is made from the ground and roasted beans of the coffee bush. The beans are collected and soaked, then the husks are removed and the beans are dried, sorted, and roasted. The longer the roast, the stronger and darker the coffee.

- **Instant coffee**
  Coffee can be made into instant coffee powder by boiling coffee dry, or into instant coffee granules by plunging ground beans into liquid gas to freeze-dry them.

◀ For tea, tea pickers— mostly women— neatly pluck the young tips of the leaves by hand and put them in baskets slung over their shoulders.

◀ Coffee grows in the tropics in places such as Brazil, and the best coffee is grown on slopes 2,000–6,000 feet up. Coffee beans are not actually beans at all but a kind of berry, and are bright red when on the bush.

FACTS: About herbs

- **Herbal drugs**
  Many of today's medicines came originally from plants, including aspirin (from willow trees), morphine (from the seeds of the opium poppy), and quinine (from the bark of the cinchona tree of South America). An extract of the rosy periwinkle, called vincristine, is one of the drugs used against leukemia, a cancer of the blood.

- **Herb facts**
  Egyptian pyramid builders ate garlic because they thought it would give them strength; rosemary gets its name from the Latin *ros marinus* which means sea dew; bay leaves were used to crown poets and heroes in Ancient Rome; the Ancient Greeks called basil "King of Herbs;" the Latin name for sage is Salvia, which means "healthy," and sage is thought to have healing qualities; mint and the spice cinnamon keep moths away from clothes; oregano is used as a dye as well as a food flavor.

FACTS: About spices

- **Spice facts**
  It takes 400,000 hand-picked crocus flower heads to make 2 pounds of saffron; ginger is the root of a tall, grass-like plant that is harvested after flowering; even though it is a hot spice, chilis can cool you down because they make you sweat; cinnamon comes from the bark of a tree; nutmeg is the seed of a tree; star anise takes 15 years to grow.

- **Spice islands**
  Many spices come from the Moluccas in Indonesia, which were once known as the Spice Islands.

Opium poppy flower

Opium poppy seed head

Foxglove

White willow

Periwinkle

Feverfew

◄ Here are just a few of the many herbs and flowers valued for medicinal purposes. Foxglove in large doses is poisonous, but it yields the drug digitalis, used in small doses to treat heart problems. Feverfew was once thought of as an effective treatment for fever.

Tropical plants

The tropics are warm nearly all the time, and in the rain forests there is abundant moisture. The combination creates almost ideal conditions for plant growth, and tropical forests are not only lush but contain an astonishing variety of plants—including some of the world's most spectacular and strange. The rain forests are the world's richest plant habitats, containing over 40 percent of the world's plant species. No one knows exactly how many different plants there are. But botanists once counted over 180 species of tree alone in 2.5 acres of the Malaysian forest.

FACTS: Coping with drought

- **Deep roots**
  When there is no water on the surface, plants can often find moisture deep underground by growing long roots. Mesquite roots often grow as deep as 33 feet, and may be as long as 165 feet.

- **Tough leaves**
  In moist places, plants lose water by evaporation from their leaves. So desert plants usually have tough, waxy leaves that cut moisture loss to a minimum—and have as few leaves as possible.

▲ *The baobab of Africa and Australia survives in dry places by retaining moisture in its barrel-shaped trunk, which can be up to 30 feet thick.*

- **Cacti**
  Cacti live in American deserts. They have no leaves and a thick skin, so water loss is cut to a minimum. Their fat stems can hold huge amounts of water, which is why they are called succulents.

- **Prickly plants**
  Lush vegetation is so rare in deserts that animals eat anything. So cacti, prickly pears, and thorn bushes grow prickles to protect themselves.

◀ *Cacti have to pollinate, just like every other flowering plant, and so every few years they produce big colorful blooms in order to attract insects quickly.*

FACTS: About tropical water plants

- **Amazon lily**
  The world's biggest water plant is the Amazon water lily of South America. Its massive floating leaves grow up to 6.5 feet across and can sometimes support the weight of a child.

- **Water hyacinth**
  The water hyacinth is the world's fastest-growing water plant—so fast growing that it is thought of as a pest, especially since it chokes waterways and encourages mosquitoes.

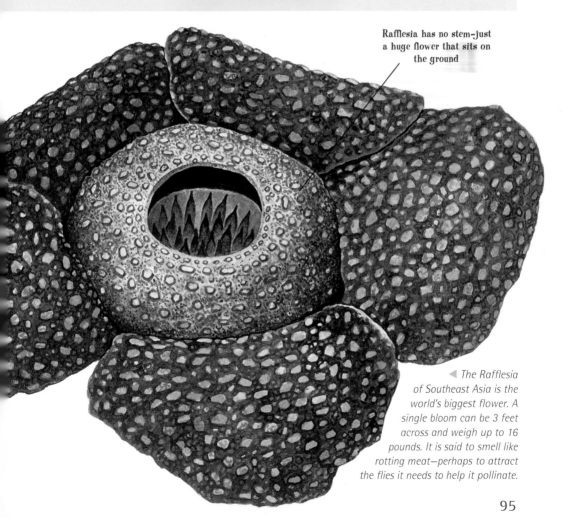

Rafflesia has no stem—just a huge flower that sits on the ground

◀ *The Rafflesia of Southeast Asia is the world's biggest flower. A single bloom can be 3 feet across and weigh up to 16 pounds. It is said to smell like rotting meat—perhaps to attract the flies it needs to help it pollinate.*

THE UNIVERSE

Planet Earth

THIRD PLANET OUT FROM THE SUN, our Earth looks from a distance like a great round blue jewel hanging in the darkness of space. It is blue because three-quarters of its rocky surface is under blue ocean waters, which shimmer in the light of the Sun. No other planet has this much water on its surface. Here and there, its rocky surface pokes up above the water to form half a dozen large continents and thousands of smaller islands. The very ends of the world are glistening white-the permanent polar ice caps.

FACTS: Earth measurements

- **The size of the Earth**
  Modern measurements show the distance around the Earth is 24,091 miles at the equator. The Earth's diameter at the equator is 24.9 miles—slightly larger than its diameter pole to pole, by 26.7 miles.

- **The weight of the Earth**
  The Earth weighs about 6,600 million billion tons.

- **The angle of the Earth**
  The Earth tilts over at an angle of 23.45°.

▼ Satellites have allowed the Earth to be measured more accurately then ever before. Satellites can detect movements of the continents of just a few fractions of an inch or small variations in the height of the sea's surface.

▲ The Earth looks round, but it is not a perfect sphere. Because it spins faster at the equator than the poles, it is actually shaped more like a tangerine, bulging slightly at the equator and flattened at the poles. So scientists used to describe its shape as an oblate spheroid (flattened ball). Now satellite measurements have detected other slight irregularities, so they call it geoid, which simply means Earth-shaped.

FACTS: Inside the Earth

- **Probing the Earth**
  Scientists have figured out what the Earth's interior is like from vibrations from earthquakes and underground explosions.

- **Crust**
  The Earth has a thin shell of solid rock called the crust, which varies from 3.5–7 miles thick under the oceans to 18.5–46.5 miles under the continents.

- **Mantle**
  Beneath the crust is a layer almost 3000 km deep, called the mantle. It is so hot here that the rock often flows like sticky molasses—only very, very slowly.

- **Core**
  Below the mantle is a core of metal, mostly iron and nickel.

- **Outer core**
  The outer portion of the core is so ferociously hot that the metal is always molten.

- **Inner core**
  The Earth's inner core is even hotter—estimated to be around 11,000°F—but the metal here is solid because pressures here are so great that metal simply cannot melt.

Inner core   Outer core   Mantle   Crust

▲ Earth has several different layers because the materials it is made of have separated out over billions of years. Dense metals such as iron sank to the center to form the core, while lighter rock-forming materials floated to the top to form the crust.

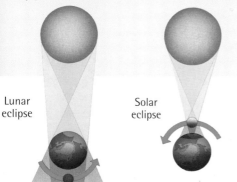

Lunar eclipse

Solar eclipse

◄ Every now and then, the Earth and the Moon move between each other and the Sun. This is called an eclipse because the planet in between "eclipses," or blocks out, the Sun. A lunar eclipse occurs when the Moon goes around behind the Earth into its shadow. A solar eclipse occurs when the Moon comes between the Sun and the Earth, casting a shadow a few miles wide on the Earth.

The Moon

Earthrise on the Moon

THE MOON IS THE BIGGEST, BRIGHTEST object in the night sky. It seems to shine almost like a pale sun. But it does not give out any light itself. It is just a big, cold ball of rock and shines only because it reflects sunlight. The Moon is the Earth's companion in space and circles around it continuously, just as the Earth circles the Sun. The Moon is about a quarter of the Earth's size and was probably formed shortly after the Earth, perhaps from hot splashes flung out as a small planet collided with the Earth.

FACTS: About the Moon

- **Pitted surface**
  The Moon's surface is pitted with craters—dents created by the impact of huge rocks early in its history.

- **Seas on the Moon**
  All over the Moon's surface are dark patches, which people once believed were seas. In fact, they are not seas at all, but vast plains formed by lava flowing from volcanoes that erupted early in the Moon's history.

- **"Moonths"**
  The word month comes from the Moon and the time it takes to go once around the Earth. It takes the Moon 27.3 days to circle the Earth, but it actually takes 29.53 days from one full moon to the next, because the Earth moves as well, and the Moon falls a little behind. This 29.53 days cycle is called a lunar month. However, the length of our calendar months was decided a few centuries ago by the Pope.

- **Watery Moon**
  In 1998, X-ray cameras on a U.S. space probe revealed that there are huge quantities of water on the Moon, in the form of ice under the Moon's surface.

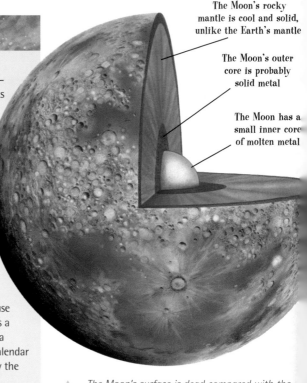

The Moon's rocky mantle is cool and solid, unlike the Earth's mantle

The Moon's outer core is probably solid metal

The Moon has a small inner core of molten metal

▲ The Moon's surface is dead compared with the Earth's. It has no atmosphere. The surface is just fine white dust, pitted with craters. Also, its rocky interior cool, not hot like the Earth's, and the volcanic activit' that constantly changes the Earth's surface has long since died out on the Moon.

▲ *The Moon is the only world beyond ours that people have visited. When Neil Armstrong set foot on it on July 20, 1969, he said famously, "That's one small step for a man, one giant leap for mankind."*

FACTS: On the Moon

- **Men on the Moon**
  The first men to land on the Moon were Neil Armstrong and Buzz Aldrin—in July 1969. Eugene Cernan is the last man to have walked on the Moon, in 1972.

- **High jumping**
  The Moon's gravity is only one-sixth of the Earth's, so everything is very light. Moon astronauts can jump easily—even in heavy space suits.

- **Footprints forever**
  Because there is no air, the sky on the Moon is inky black even in daytime, and there is no wind to disturb the dust. So the footprints left by the first men on the Moon will be there forever.

- **Day and night**
  Each day on the Moon lasts 655 hours (just over 27 days), and the temperature reaches 253°F — but the night is just as long and temperatures plunge to -387°F.

The phases of the Moon

Only the part of the Moon lit by the Sun is bright enough for us to see. But as it circles the Earth, the Sun shines on the Moon from changing angles, and we see more or less of the Moon at different times—and so the Moon appears to change shape over the course of a month as it circles the Earth. These changes are called phases.

▼ *During the first half of the month, the Moon grows from a crescent-shaped new moon, to a half-circle-shaped half moon, to a full moon. This is called waxing. In the second half, it gets smaller, or "wanes," through a half moon back to a crescent-shaped old moon—curving the opposite way from the new moon.*

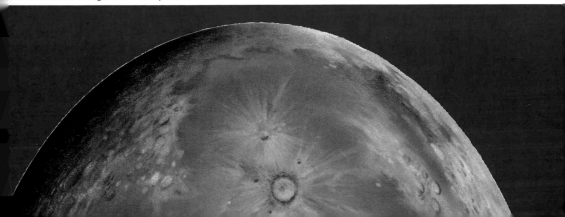

The Sun

THE SUN IS OUR LOCAL STAR, a vast, fiery spinning ball of hot gases–
three-quarters hydrogen and one-quarter helium. It is well over a million
times as big as the Earth. The gigantic mass of the Sun creates immense
pressures in its core. Such huge pressures fuse hydrogen atoms together in
a continual nuclear reaction that boosts temperatures to 27 billion°F. All this heat
turns the outer surface of the Sun into a raging inferno that burns so brightly that
it completely floodlights the Earth, over 93 million miles away.

FACTS: Inside the Sun

- **A bomb in the heart**
  Pressures in the Sun's core are many billions of
  times the pressure of the Earth's atmosphere.
  These pressures fuse so many hydrogen atoms
  together that it is as if billions of nuclear bombs
  were going off each second.

- **All down to Einstein**
  We owe our understanding of how the Sun
  produces heat and light to the famous scientist
  Albert Einstein (1879–1955), who showed how
  mass can be changed into energy.

- **Surface layers**
  The visible surface layer of the Sun is the
  photosphere. Above this lies the chromosphere
  and the corona.

- **Hot surface**
  Temperatures at the surface of the Sun are a
  phenomenal 11,000°F, enough to melt almost
  anything. Each square inch burns with the
  brightness of 300,000 candles.

- **The Sun's age**
  The Sun probably formed about five billion years
  ago, just a little before the Earth, which formed
  from the debris left over. It will burn out in about
  five billion years.

- **The solar wind**
  Streaming out from the Sun every second are
  more than a million tons of electrically
  charged particles. Earth is protected from
  this lethal stream, called the solar wind, by
  its magnetic field.

- **SOHO**
  The SOHO space observatory sits in space between
  the Earth and the Sun and monitors the Sun
  continually.

◀ *The Sun's energy is generated by nuclear reactions
in its core and makes its way to the surface over
millions of years.*

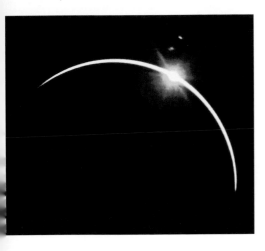

 DATA: The Sun

- DIAMETER
  The Sun is a medium-sized star 865,000 miles across–10 times the diameter of the Earth.

- MASS
  The Sun weighs 2,000 million trillion tons – over 300,000 times the weight of the Earth.

- ENERGY CONSUMPTION
  The Sun burns up more than four million tons of hydrogen fuel every second.

- ENERGY PRODUCTION
  The Sun's energy production each second could keep the Unied States supplied with electricity for 50 million years.

- CORONAL TEMPERATURE
  The temperature of the Sun's outer ring, or corona, is 2.7 million°F.

▲ *Every now and then, the Moon swings between the Sun and the Earth, blocking out the Sun and creating a shadow a few hundred miles wide on the Earth. This is called a solar eclipse. Sometimes, the Sun glints through a valley on the Moon's surface, as in this picture, creating an effect like a jewel on a ring.*

► *The heat from the Sun's core erupts on the surface in patches called granules. Here and there, giant flame-like tongues of hot hydrogen, called solar prominences, loop 62,000 miles out into space. Every now and then, too, huge five-minute eruptions of energy called solar flares burst from the surface. In places, there are dark blotches on the Sun's surface, called sunspots, over 50 times the size of Africa. They are dark because they are slightly less hot than the rest of the surface. The number of spots seems to peak every 11 years, and some scientists believe these peaks are linked to spells of stormier weather on Earth.*

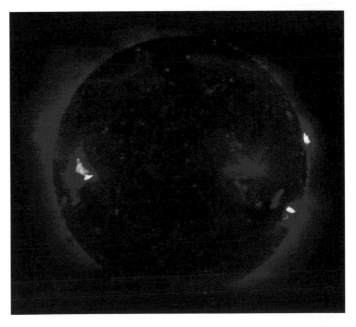

Inner planets

Mercury

THE INNER PLANETS are the four planets in the solar system that are nearest the Sun. Nearest the Sun is little Mercury, and then comes Mars, Earth, and Venus. All four are made of rock, unlike the big planets farther out, which are made mainly of gas. Because they are made of rock, they have a hard surface that a spaceship could land on, and they are sometimes called terrestrial (earth-like) planets. They all have an atmosphere of gas above the rocky surface–although Mercury's is very thin–but each is very different.

FACTS: About Mercury

◀ Mercury's atmosphere, also called its exoshere, is so thin that there is nothing to stop meteors from smashing into its surface—and nothing to smooth out any dents. So its surface is more deeply pitted with the scars of meteor impacts than the Moon's. All you'd see on a voyage across the surface would be vast empty basins, cliffs, and endless views of yellow dust.

- **Hot and cold**
  Temperatures on Mercury veer from one extreme to the other because its atmosphere is too thin to provide any insulation. In the day, temperatures soar up to 800°F, but at night they plunge to nearly -290°F.

- **Mercury's brief year**
  Mercury is so near the Sun that its orbit is very short. It gets around in just 88 days, compared with 365 days for Earth. On the other hand, it takes a long time to turn around—58.6 days. So its day lasts 58.6 Earth days.

- **Burning cold**
  Mercury has small ice caps at each pole—but the ice is made from acid, not water.

DATA: The inner planets

MERCURY
- Mercury is 28.5 million miles from the Sun at its closest and 43.3 million miles at its farthest.
- Mercury's diameter is 3,031 miles, and its mass is barely one-twentieth of Earth's.

VENUS
- Venus is 66.7 million miles from the Sun at its

closest and 67.7 million miles at its farthest.
- Venus's diameter is 7,520 miles, and its mass is about four-fifths that of Earth's.

MARS
- Mars is 141.6 million miles from the Sun.
- Mars's diameter is 4,217 miles, and its mass is just over one-tenth of Earth's.

FACTS: About Venus

▲ *Venus is the hottest planet in the solar system, and its surface is as barren as any desert on Earth. The build-up of carbon dioxide gas in its atmosphere has created a runaway "greenhouse effect," trapping so much of the Sun's heat that temperatures reach a scorching 878°F.*

- **Evening star**
  Venus reflects sunlight so well off its thick atmosphere that it shines like a star. But because it is quite close to the Sun, we can only see it in the evening just after the Sun has gone down, which is why it is sometimes called the evening star. We can also see it just before sunrise.

- **Thick air**
  Venus's atmosphere would be deadly to humans. It is very deep and thick, so pressure on the surface is enormous. It is also made mainly of poisonous carbon dioxide and filled with clouds of sulphuric acid gas belched out by the volcanoes on its surface.

FACTS: About Mars

- **High and deep**
  Mars has the biggest volcano in the solar system, called Olympus Mons, 15.5 miles high, three times higher than Mt. Everest. It also has a canyon called Valles Marineris that is 2,485 miles long and four times as deep as the Grand Canyon.

- **The red planet**
  None of the space missions to Mars so far have found even the remotest trace of life. But in 1996, NASA scientists found what they thought might be the fossil of a microscopic organism in a rock from Mars in the Arctic. So the search is on.

▶ *Mars is sometimes called the red planet because it is rusty red. The surface contains a high proportion of iron dust, and this has been oxidized (rusted) in its carbon dioxide-rich atmosphere. It has small ice caps.*

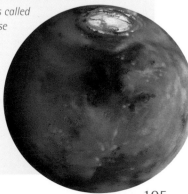

Giant planets

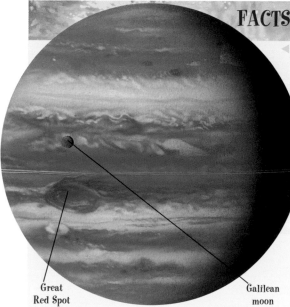

Saturn

OUT BEYOND MARS THERE are two planets far bigger than any others in the solar system. Jupiter and Saturn, the fifth and sixth planets from the Sun, are gigantic. Jupiter is twice as heavy as all the other planets put together and 1,300 times as big as Earth. Saturn is not that much smaller. Unlike the inner planets, though, they are both made mostly of gas, and only their core is rocky. This doesn't mean they are vast cloud balls. The huge pressure of gravity means the gas is squeezed until it becomes liquid or even solid.

FACTS: About Jupiter

Jupiter's surface is covered with a thin layer of swirling clouds of ammonia, indicating powerful storms. One storm called the Great Red Spot is 25,000 miles across and was first obseved in the 1660s..

• **Mighty magnet**
Jupiter's bulk and its fast spin churn up the metal insides of the planet so much that the planet becomes a giant dynamo, creating a magnetic field ten times as strong as Earth's.

• **Many moons**
Jupiter has 50 officially recognized moons, with 17 more awaiting confirmation. The four largest, Io, Europa, Ganymede, and Callisto, were discovered by Galileo as long ago as 1610, which is why they are called the Galilean moons.

Great Red Spot

Galilean moon

▼ *The power of Jupiter's gravity drags volcanoes of sulphur from the surface of its moon Io.*

• **Fast spinner**
Jupiter spins faster than any other planet. Despite its vast size, it turns around in just 9.8 hours, so the surface is moving at 28000 miles per hour!

• **Hydrogen deeps**
Jupiter is made mostly of hydrogen and helium gas, but this is squeezed so hard by the planet's gravity that it turns to liquid. Beneath Jupiter's thin atmosphere of ammonia, there is an ocean of liquid hydrogen 15,500 miles deep.

FACTS: About Saturn

▶ Saturn is the most beautiful of all the planets, with its pale butterscotch surface of ammonia gases and its huge halo of rings.

- **Saturn's rings**
  Saturn's rings are countless billions of tiny chips of ice and dust, few bigger than a refrigerator and most smaller than an ice cube. The rings are thin—no more than 164 feet deep—yet stretch over 46,000 miles out into space.

  ▼ Saturn's rings have definite bands, named with the letters A to G.

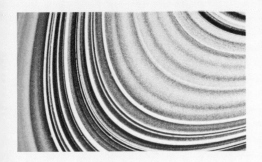

- **Light planet**
  Saturn may be big, but it is surprisingly light, weighing 600 billion brillion tons. If you had a large enough bath, it would float.

- **Most moons**
  Saturn has more moons than any other planet — 53 officially named so far, and more being discovered. Iapetus is black on one side and white on the other. Enceladus is covered with shimmering balls of ice. Tethys was once almost split in half by a giant meteor that left a giant crater. Titan is the only moon with an atmosphere.

- **Windy planet**
  The winds on the surface of Saturn are faster than those on Jupiter, roaring around at 1,100 mph.

 # DATA: About the giant planets

JUPITER
- Jupiter is 460.4 million miles from the Sun at its closest and 506.8 million miles at its farthest.
- Jupiter's diameter is 88,846 miles, and its mass is 318 times that of Earth's.
- It takes 11.86 years to orbit the Sun.
- Its surface temperature is -238°F.

SATURN
- Saturn is 837,000 million miles from the Sun at its closest and 936,000 million miles at its farthest.
- Saturn's diameter is 74,536 miles, and its mass is over 95 times that of Earth's.
- It takes 29.46 years to orbit the Sun.
- Its surface temperature is -292°F.

Outer planets

Neptune

OUT BEYOND SATURN are the seventh and eighth planets of the solar system: Uranus and Neptune. Unlike the other planets, these were unknown to ancient astronomers. They are so far away and so faint that Uranus was only discovered in 1781 and Neptune in 1846. Uranus and Neptune are giant gas planets like Saturn and Jupiter. Pluto can now neither be classified as a planet nor is it underdeveloped enough to be called an asteroid. In 2006, the International Astronomical Union finally declared Pluto to be a dwarf planet.

FACTS: About Uranus

- **Rollover planet**
  Unlike any of the other planets, Uranus does not spin at a slight angle. Instead it is tilted to its side and rolls around the Sun like a giant bowling ball. In summer, the Sun does not set for 20 years.

- **Blue planet**
  Uranus has an atmosphere of hydrogen and helium, but beneath that are oceans of liquid methane. It is this that gives the planet its beautiful blue-green color.

FACTS: About Neptune

Neptune has its own thin set of rings, similar to Saturn's.

- **Blue planet**
  Like Uranus, Neptune has a thin atmosphere of hydrogen and helium, but is mostly deep oceans of liquid methane. The methane makes Neptune a beautiful cobalt blue.

- **Long year**
  Neptune is so far from the Sun—over 2.5 billion miles—that its orbit takes 164.79 years.

- **Discovering Neptune**
  Neptune's moon Triton is the only moon to orbit backward. It is the coldest place in the solar system (-393°F) and looks like a green melon with pink ice cream on the ends—ice caps of frozen nitrogen. Its volcanoes erupt ice.

Uranus is so far from the Sun that temperatures drop to -346°F. Winds whistle through its atmosphere at 1,200 mph, whipping up huge waves in the icy oceans of methane below.

DATA: The outer planets

URANUS
- Uranus is 1.7 billion miles from the Sun at its closest and 1.9 billion miles at its farthest.
- Uranus's diameter is 31,763 miles, and its mass is over 14 times that of Earth's.

NEPTUNE
- Neptune is 2.76 billion miles from the Sun at its closest, and over 2.8 billion miles at its farthest.
- Neptune's diameter is 30,775 miles, and its mass is over 17 times that of Earth's.

- **Discovering Neptune**
  Neptune was discovered because in the 1840s two young mathematicians, John Couch Adams in England and Urbain le Verrier in France, predicted where it should be from the way its gravity made a slight difference to Uranus's orbit. The planet was actually spotted by John Galle from the Berlin Observatory on September 23, 1846.

  ▼ *This is a view of Neptune and its moon Triton taken by the Voyager space mission, which reached the planet in 1989.*

FACTS: About Pluto

 Pluto and Charon are so far away from the Sun that the Sun looks little bigger in their sky than a star, and shines as faintly as the Moon shines on Earth. So surface temperatures plunge to -364°F.

- **Pluto**
  Pluto is very, very small, which is why it took so long to spot. Initially, Pluto was called a planet, but it is now classified as a dwarf planet. It is five times smaller than the Earth and 500 times lighter.

- **Charon**
  Pluto is only twice as big as its companion moon Charon. So they circle around each other locked in space like a pair of weights on a barbell. If you stood on Pluto's surface, you would see Charon in the sky, appearing three times as big as our Moon, but never moving.

- **In and out**
  Pluto has an elliptical orbit that every now and then swings it closer to the Sun than Neptune.

Comets and meteorites

PLANETS AND MOONS are not the only things whirling round the Sun. Along with the Earth and its companions are thousands upon thousands of tiny bits and pieces of rock and ice of all shapes and sizes. Some are smaller than a car. Others are several hundred miles across. These lumps of space debris are called asteroids. Every now and then, a very large lump of debris swings in from the outer limits of the solar system, creating a comet in the night sky. And all the time, lumps of this debris streak through the Earth's atmosphere as meteors, some striking the ground as meteorites.

FACTS: About asteroids

- **The asteroid belt**
  Asteroids are little chunks of debris that never clumped together to make a planet when the solar system was young. There are probably a million or more lying in a belt circling the Sun between Mars and Jupiter.

- **Ceres**
  The first of the asteroids to be spotted—and the biggest—is Ceres, whih is as big as Ireland. The brightest is called Vesta, the only asteroid that can be seen with the naked eye.

- **The Trojan asteroids**
  The Trojans are two small groups of asteroids that circle the Sun on the same orbit as Jupiter.

▼ Asteroids were first discovered in 1801, after a group of astronomers, calling themselves the Celestial Police, began hunting for a missing planet they were certain lay somewhere between Mars and Jupiter. Nowadays, new asteroids are discovered frequently. Each is given an identification number and is named by the discoverer. Names vary from Greek goddesses to calculators.

▲ Every day, tons and tons of space debris rain down on the Earth, sometimes in such great concentrations that they make a golden rain in the night sky—called a meteor shower—as they hit the Earth's atmosphere and burn up. Meteors are space dust and rocks so small that they burn up long before they hit the ground. Meteorite are big enough to plunge right through the atmosphere and hit the ground. Most of these fall harmlessly into the ocean, and vary in size from lumps the size of shoe to the meteorite the size of a car that hit Namibia, Africa, in 1920, creating an enormous crater.

FACTS: About comets

▶ As a comet swings round the Sun, its tail changes direction. The tail contains so little solid matter that it is blown out easily by the solar wind, the stream of charged particles flowing away from the Sun—and so always points away from the Sun.

At the heart of a comet is a tiny nucleus of dust and ice

A tail of ionized atoms is blown out millions of miles behind the comet by the solar wind

- **Dirty snowballs**
  With their flaming tails, comets are the most spectacular sights in the night sky. But they are actually just dirty balls of ice, only a few miles across.

- **Visitors from afar**
  Many comets circle the Sun like the planets, but they have very long, stretched-out orbits and spend most of their time in the far reaches of the solar system. We see them only when their orbit brings them, for a few weeks, close to the Sun.

- **Glowing tails**
  The comet's tail is created as the comet hurtles toward the Sun and begins to melt. A vast plume of gas, millions of miles across, is blown out behind it by the solar wind, and this is what we see shining in the night as it catches the sunlight.

- **Periodics**
  Some comets, called Periodics, appear at regular intervals. Encke's comet comes every 1206 days. Halley's Comet comes every 76 years.

- **Speeding comets**
  Comets speed up as they near the Sun, sometimes reaching speeds of up to 1.2 million mph. But far away from the Sun they slow down to speeds of little more than 620 mph, which is why they stay away for so long.

▲ Halley's comet, discovered by Edmund Halley (1656–1742), appeared before the Battle of Hastings in 1066, and some say it was the star of Bethlehem.

111

Stars

A star in close-up: our Sun

THE FEW THOUSAND STARS you see twinkling in the night sky are just a tiny fraction of the trillions scattered through the Universe. Like our Sun, they are huge fiery balls of hot gas. They shine because they are burning. Deep inside, atoms of gas fuse together in nuclear reactions that boost temperatures to millions of degrees, making their surfaces glow. A star goes on glowing, sending out light, heat, radio waves, and radiation, until its nuclear fuel-mainly hydrogen gas-is used up.

FACTS: About giants and dwarfs

- **Giant stars**
  Most stars are much the same size as our Sun—about 0.9 million miles across. But some are giants 100 times as big, or supergiants over 300 times as big.

- **Dwarf stars**
  Dwarf stars are actually very small—smaller than the Earth. Very old stars can shrink under the power of their own gravity to even tinier neutron stars—no bigger than New York City, but so dense that they are as heavy as the Sun!

- **Starlight**
  The color of starlight tells us what the star is made of and how hot it is.

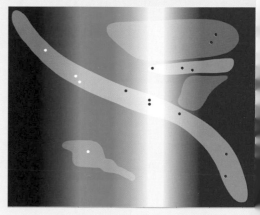

▲ The color of a star depends on how bright it is. The Herzsprung-Russell diagram shows how the hotter and whiter stars glow, the brighter they are; the redder and cooler they glow, the dimmer they are. All medium-sized stars behave like this and form a band, called the Main Sequence stars, across the middle of the graph. Giants, dwarfs ,and neutron stars fall outside this band.

◄ Stars vary in brightness or "magnitude," The Herzsprung-Russell diagram shows how we expect stars of a certain color to be a certain brightness, their Absolute Magnitude. But if a star is far away, it looks dimmer than expected. This is its Relative Magnitude.

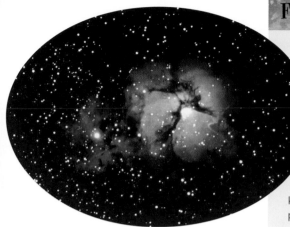

▲ *Stars are being born and dying all over the Universe. The bigger the star, the shorter its life. The biggest stars end their lives in gigantic explosions called "supernovas," which are, briefly, the brightest things in the night sky as incredibly hot gas billows away.*

DATA: Stars

- **THE BRIGHTEST-LOOKING STAR**
  Sirius, the Dog Star, is the brightest star in the night sky. But it is quite nearby (8.6 light-years) so its brightness is only because it is so close.

- **THE BRIGHTEST STAR**
  Eta Carina burns as brightly as 4.7 million Suns. A close contender is the Peony nebula star, with its light of about 3.2 million Suns.

- **THE BIGGEST STAR**
  No one knows what the biggest star is, but Antares is very big, 700 times bigger than our Sun.

- **OTHER STARS WITH PLANETS**
  At least nine other stars, including 51 Pegasi, are now known to have planets, as our Sun has.

FACTS: About constellations

- **Patterns in the stars**
  Ancient astronomers found their way around the heavens by looking for patterns of stars in the night sky. These patterns are called constellations. Astronomers now identify 88 of them, such as the Great Bear and Orion.

- **The Big Dipper**
  The Big Dipper, also known as the Great Bear or Ursa Major, is one of the best-known constellations in the northern sky. It points toward the North Star, indicating north.

- **Alpha and Beta**
  The stars in each constellation are named after letters in the Greek alphabet. The brightest star in each constellation is called Alpha, the next brightest Beta, and so on. So Alpha Pegasi is the brightest star in Pegasus, the Flying Horse.

▲ *Without constellations to help us, it would be hard to locate stars in the sky, but there is no real link between the stars in a constellation—the patterns they form are completely imaginary..*

Galaxies and nebulae

OUR SUN IS JUST ONE OF A MASSIVE collection of over 100 billion stars arranged in a shape like a spinning fried egg. This gigantic collection of stars is called the Galaxy, or Milky Way. It gets its name from the Greek for "milky," because we see it as a milky white band across the night sky. But the Milky Way is just one of many trillions of similar giant groups of stars, also called galaxies (with a small "g"), scattered throughout the Universe.

▲ On a clear night, fuzzy patches of light can be seen among the stars. Some of these patches are distant galaxies. But others are huge clouds of dust called nebulae, which are many times bigger than any star. Only a few, called glowing nebulae, actually glow themselves; most are bright because the dust reflects starlight, just as clouds on Earth reflect sunlight. This picture show the famous Horsehead Nebula in the constellation of Orion, so-called because it is shaped a little like a horse's head.

FACTS: About galaxies

▶ Spiral galaxies are spinning, pinwheel-shaped galaxies, like the Milky Way and Andromeda galaxies. They have a dense core of stars, surrounded by long whirling arms.

▶ Barred spiral galaxies are variations on spiral galaxies with a central bar from which arms of stars trail like water from a spinning garden sprinkler.

▶ Elliptical galaxies are huge egg-shaped galaxies sometimes containing over a trillion stars. They are the oldest galaxies of all, some over 12 billion years old.

▶ Irregular galaxies are different from the others in that they have no obvious shape at all, and may have formed from the debris of colliding galaxies.

▶ Stars start life in giant clouds of dust and gas called nebulae. Stars are born in these clouds as gravity pulls the dust into clumps—so ferociously that the pressure makes them glow.

- **Visible galaxies**
  Only three galaxies apart from the Milky Way can be seen with naked eye: the Large and Small Magellanic Clouds and the Andromeda galaxy.

- **Far lights**
  Galaxies contain many millions of stars, most as big as our Sun. But they are so far away that even with a reasonably good telescope, most look like blurs in the night sky. Andromeda, one of the nearest galaxies beyond the Milky Way, is over three million light-years away—over 17 trillion miles!

- **The size of galaxies**
  Galaxies are absolutely gigantic. Although they contain millions or even trillions of stars, they are mostly empty space, for the stars are far apart. If each star was a person, the nearest neighbour would be almost as far away as the Moon.

- **How many galaxies?**
  Astronomers estimate that there are something like 20 trillion galaxies in the Universe.

- **Spiral galaxies**
  Just as the planets spin around the Sun, so spiral galaxies seem to be spinning too, which is why they have trailing arms.

- **Groups**
  Galaxies are often clustered in Groups of 30 or more. The Milky Way is part of the Local Group.

The Milky Way is 100,000 light-years across and 1,000 light-years thick.

▶ The band of stars across the night sky called the Milky Way is an edge-on view of our own Galaxy, a vast cluster of stars 100,000 light-years across. It is a spiral galaxy, and our Sun is just one of millions of stars on one of the trailing arms. As it whirls around, it sweeps the Sun (and with it the Earth) in a huge circle 60 million miles every hour. The Sun travels over 100,000 light-years to go around once—and it will get around in 200 million years. So the dinosaurs had just appeared on Earth the last time it was where it is now.

Black holes

GRAVITY IS THE FORCE that holds the Universe together. It is the force that keeps the Earth in one piece, keeps us on the ground, and keeps planets circling the Sun and the stars together in galaxies. Yet it can also be so powerfully destructive that it can squeeze stars to nothing and suck galaxies into oblivion. When some giant stars burn out, there is nothing to hold them up and they start to collapse under the force of their own gravity. As they shrink, they get denser and denser, and their gravity becomes even stronger ... and so they get denser and denser, and their gravity becomes stronger still. Eventually, they become so small and dense that they may create a region in space called a black hole.

FACTS: About gravity and orbits

- **Orbits**
  Things stay in orbit when their forward momentum exactly balances the pull of gravity.

- **Earth's orbit**
  Earth stays on the same path around the Sun because it is bowling through space too fast to be drawn in by the pull of the Sun—yet not so fast that it can overcome the Sun's pull altogether and hurtle off into space.

- **Satellites**
  Satellites seem to hang in space because they are moving too fast to fall into the Earth.

Launched too slow, the satellite falls back to Earth

Launched too fast, the satellite hurtles off into space

Launched at the right speed, the satellite goes into orbit

◀ A satellite has to be launched at exactly the right speed and on exactly the right trajectory (path) to be placed successfully in orbit. The lower the orbit is to be, the faster it must go if it is to avoid being pulled down by gravity. For an orbit 22,245 miles above the ground, the satellite has to be going fast enough to complete an orbit in exactly 24 hours—the same time it takes the Earth to spin. So a satellite placed in this orbit stays in the same place above the Earth.

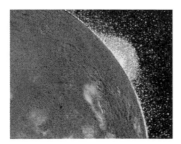

◀ The destructive power of gravity can be seen on Jupiter's moon Io. The giant planet Jupiter is so massive that its gravity alternately pulls and sucks so powerfully on Io as it revolves that the insides of the moon get incredibly hot— so hot that volcanoes burst onto the surface.

FACTS: About the search for black holes

- **Do black holes exist?**
  No one has ever seen a black hole. Indeed, we cannot be sure they actually exist. But the bright radiation from quasars (see below)—and from the center of our galaxy may be signs that black holes do exist.

- **Where are black holes found?**
  Some scientists think there is a giant black hole at the center of each spiral galaxy. Some believe there are tiny ones everywhere.

◀ *This bright galaxy may have a black core.*

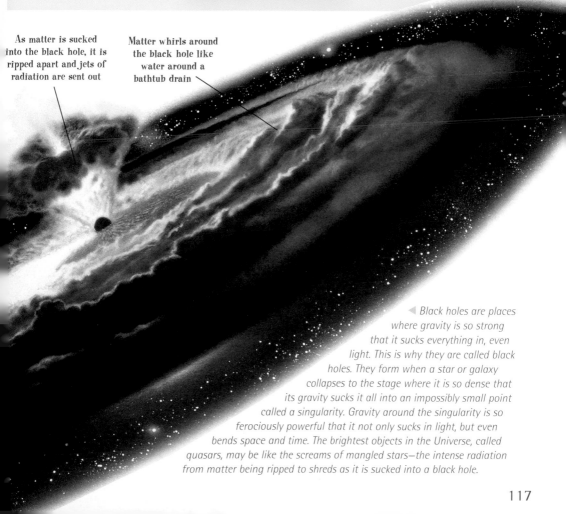

As matter is sucked into the black hole, it is ripped apart and jets of radiation are sent out

Matter whirls around the black hole like water around a bathtub drain

◀ *Black holes are places where gravity is so strong that it sucks everything in, even light. This is why they are called black holes. They form when a star or galaxy collapses to the stage where it is so dense that its gravity sucks it all into an impossibly small point called a singularity. Gravity around the singularity is so ferociously powerful that it not only sucks in light, but even bends space and time. The brightest objects in the Universe, called quasars, may be like the screams of mangled stars—the intense radiation from matter being ripped to shreds as it is sucked into a black hole.*

How far to the stars?

THE UNIVERSE IS VERY, VERY BIG. In fact, the distances between the stars are so huge that astronomers don't measure them in miles, but in light-years—which is how far light travels in a year. Light is the fastest thing in the Universe and travels at about 186,000 miles per second, so a light-year is about 5.9 trillion miles. The nearest star is 4.3 light-years away. The most distant objects so far discovered—very bright galaxies called quasars—are over 13 billion light-years away. That means their light takes over 13 billion years to reach us—so astronomers are looking at them as they were 13 billion years ago!

DATA: Distances in space

- **THE NEAREST PLANET**
  The nearest planet to Earth is Venus, which is over 24 million miles away.

- **THE FARTHEST PLANET**
  The farthest planet from Earth in the solar system is Neptune. It is also 30 times as far from the Sun as Earth.

- **THE NEAREST STAR**
  The nearest star is Proxima Centauri, in the constellation of the Centaur, which is 4.3 light-years away, or about 25 trillion miles away.

- **OUR NEIGHBORING GALAXY**
  One of the nearest galaxies outside our own is the Andromeda galaxy, 2.5 million light-years away.

- **THE FURTHEST GALAXY**
  The farthest galaxy yet seen is over 13 billion light-years away across the Universe.

- **DISTANCE TO THE MOON**
  At its nearest, the Moon is around 225,500 miles away; at its furthest nearly 252,000 miles.

- **DISTANCE TO THE SUN**
  At its nearest, the Sun is 91 million miles away; at its farthest, over 94 million miles.

- **PARSECS**
  Astronomers may measure large distances in parsecs. A parsec is 3.26 light-years. Parsec distances are calculated by using the geometry of "parallaxes"–the way a star seems to shift slightly in position in the night sky as the Earth moves around the Sun.

Distances in space are vast

◀ The distance to the Moon is measured to within a few feet by bouncing laser beams off mirrors left on the Moon by astronauts.

FACTS: Galactic distances

• **Standard candles**
To find the distance of a nearby galaxy, astronomers look for stars within it whose brightness they are sure of. These include stars called "cepheid variables," "supergiant stars," and giant exploding stars called 'supernovas'.

• **Very distant galaxies**
Astronomers cannot pick out individual stars in very distant galaxies, so they estimate the distance by tricks such as the Tully-Fisher technique, based on how a galaxy appears to be spinning. The faster it spins, the brighter it should be. So if it is dim, it must be far away.

• **Red shift**
The redder a distant galaxy looks, the faster it is moving away from us.

▶ The distance to the Sun and nearby planets is measured by bouncing radar beams off them. Space probes help with planets farther away.

▶ Distances to the nearer stars are generally worked out either by the parallax method (see parsecs) or by estimating their brightness. Astronomers can guess how bright a star should look compared to other stars from its color. If it actually looks brighter than it should, it must be nearby; if it looks dimmer, it must be farther away.

▼ Distances to the galaxies are figured out by looking for "standard candles," stars whose brightness we can be sure of. Really far off galaxies call for even more ingenious methods.

Figuring out distances

The method astronomers use to figure out the distance of an object in space depends on how far away it is. For nearby objects such as the Sun and the planets, they can use radar beams, and estimates can be accurate within a few thousand miles. They measure distances to nearby stars by gauging their brightness, and estimates are accurate only to within a few billion miles. Distances to far galaxies are accurate only to within a few billion light-years!

Space travel

THE AGE OF SPACE EXPLORATION began in 1957 when powerful rocket engines boosted the Russian satellite Sputnik 1 free of Earth's gravity. This was the start of an extraordinary series of adventures for mankind, which has seen scores of satellites put in space, man's first steps on the Moon, live broadcasts from Mars, and space probes venturing past the outer planets of the solar system. These probes have not only beamed back the first pictures of new, previously unknown, moons but have also provided remarkable insights into the nature of the Universe.

FACTS: About spacecraft

- **Rocket power**
  Very powerful rockets are needed to push a spacecraft clear of Earth's gravity—but once clear, such power is no longer needed. So rockets are made in separate stages, each of which falls away when its fuel is spent.

- **Space shuttles**
  In the early days, manned spacecraft could only be used once, with just a tiny capsule holding the astronauts falling back to Earth at the end of the mission. Launched in 1981, U.S. space shuttles were the first spacecraft that could be reused, landing back on Earth like an airplane.

- **Space probes**
  Unmanned space probes, guided by computer, have now visited all the planets, and probes have actually landed on Mars and Venus. In August 2012, the rover Curiosity landed on Mars to try and determine whether the planet could have supported life.

- **Slingshot effect**
  Space probes voyaging to the planets use gravity to help them travel huge distances on very little fuel. As they pass each planet, their gravity pulls them in and hurls them onward on a slightly different course, like a slingshot.

▲ The space shuttle was launched with solid fuel booster rockets that fell away but were then recovered. Typical shuttle missions included launching and repairing satellites and performing scientific experiments.

FACTS: About satellites and probes

- **Staying in orbit**
  Satellites stay in space because they are circling, or "orbiting," the Earth just too fast to be pulled down by Earth's gravity—but not so fast that they fly off into space.

- **Staying still**
  An orbit 22,245 miles above the ground takes exactly 24 hours—the same time it takes the Earth to spin once. So satellites on this orbit stay in exactly the same place above the Earth. This is called a geostationary orbit.

- **Hubble Space Telescope**
  Satellites not only give a clear view of the Earth from space, but a better view of space, too, because they are free from Earth's atmosphere. The Hubble Space Telescope, launched in 1990, gives extraordinary pictures of distant objects in space.

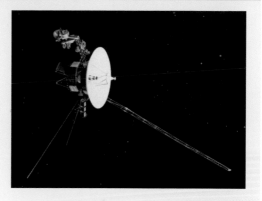

▲ *Spacecraft can be remarkably ungainly looking objects. Once they are free of the Earth's atmosphere, there is no need for streamlining and aerials and dishes stick out in all directions. This is the Galileo, launched in 1989 to explore Jupiter.*

DATA: Milestones in Space Exploration

- **THE FIRST LIVING CREATURE IN SPACE**
  Laika the dog was launched in a Russian satelite in November 1957. Sadly, she could not be brought back.

- **THE FIRST MAN IN SPACE**
  The first man in space was the Russian cosmonaut Yuri Gagarin, in April 1961.

- **THE FIRST SPACE WALK**
  In 1965, Russian cosmonaut Alexei Leonov was the first man to walk in space.

- **THE FIRST MEN ON THE MOON**
  U.S. astronauts Neil Armstrong and Buzz Aldrin stepped on the Moon on July 20, 1969.

- **REACHING VENUS**
  In 1970, a Russian probe landed on Venus.

- **PASSING SATURN**
  In 1979, the U.S. Pioneer 11 probe reached Saturn and discovered new moons.

- **REACHING NEPTUNE**
  In 1989, the U.S. Voyager 2 reached the planet Neptune.

- **MARS LANDING**
  In 1997, the Mars Pathfinder roved the surface of Mars, beaming back pictures.

121

History of the Universe

THE UNIVERSE PROBABLY BEGAN about 13 billion years ago. One moment there was nothing. The next there was a minute, unimaginably hot ball–and suddenly, the Universe burst into existence with the biggest explosion of all time, called the Big Bang, swelling at a totally astonishing rate. This explosion was so big that everything is still hurtling away from it, which is why the Universe is expanding. Even now, 13 billion years later, astronomers can still detect the faint afterglow, called the cosmic microwave background radiation, spread throughout the night sky.

FACTS: Expanding Universe

- **Receding galaxies**
  As astronomers observe space, they can see galaxies zooming away from us in all directions at astonishing speeds. The farther away they are, the faster they seem to be moving. This can only mean the Universe is expanding.

- **The Big Crunch?**
  Some scientists think the Universe will go on expanding forever. This is called the "Open Universe" idea. Others think gravity will put a break on its expansion. If there is a great deal of dark matter—matter we can't detect—it may be enough to make it all start to shrink again. Then it may end in a Big Crunch.

▶ We know how fast galaxies are receding because of the color of light from them. The faster they are receding, the more light waves from them get stretched out. When light waves are stretched they look redder. This is called red shift. The redder the light, the faster the galaxy is moving away.

FACTS: About how the solar system was born

- **Swirling cloud**
4.6 billion years ago, the solar system did not exist. There was just a hot, dark cloud of gases swirling round the Sun. The planets began to form as the cloud cooled and droplets began to clump together.

- **The birth of the Earth**
The Earth probably formed as gravity began to pull together clumps of star dust from around the Sun. But this early Earth was a molten ball.

▼ *No one knows where the material that formed the solar system came from. Some think it was the remnants of an exploded star, others the result of a collision between stars.*

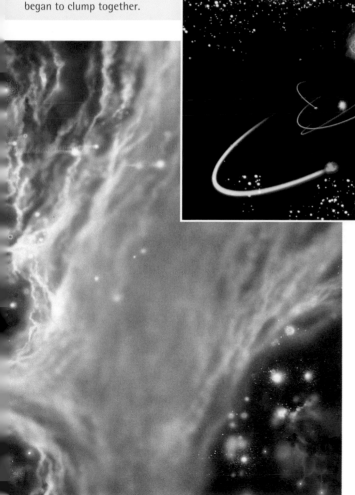

◀ *Scientists have figured out how the Universe began by mathematical calculations and experiments with huge machines called particle accelerators, which hurl atoms together. It started with a tiny hot ball that cooled by billions of degrees as it grew to the size of a football. In a split second, it swelled to create a space bigger than a galaxy in a period called inflation. Within this space, all the matter and energy and forces began to take the form we know in the Universe today. At first, it was a dense chaotic soup of particles and energy. But then atoms began to form, and the atoms formed clouds, and the clouds galaxies.*

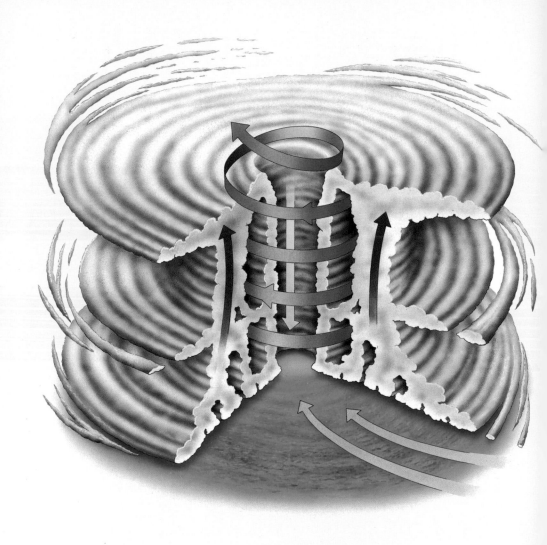

PLANET EARTH

Home planet

THE EARTH MAY SEEM QUITE STILL, but it is actually spinning around like a top at over 1,000 miles per hour – faster than any jet plane. It is also hurtling through the dark on its orbit around the Sun at over 66,000 miles per hour! Every year it covers 584,019,300 miles in its orbit around the Sun. The Earth's entire journey around the Sun takes exactly 365.242 days, which is why there are 365 days in our year. We make up the extra 0.242 days in our calendar with an extra day every fourth year, which is called a leap year– but then miss out a leap year every three centuries out of four.

FACTS: About latitude and longitude

▲ *Lines of latitude are called parallels because they form rings around the Earth parallel to the equator, which is latitude 0°. The North Pole is latitude 90°N.*

▲ *Lines of longitude, or meridians, run around the Earth from pole to pole, dividing the world up like the segments of an orange.*

- **Lines of latitude**
  Every place on the Earth's surface can be pinpointed by two figures: its latitude and longitude. Lines of equal latitude (called parallels) form rings around the Earth parallel to the equator. A place's latitude is given in degrees north or south of the equator.

- **Lines of longitude**
  Lines of longitude (called meridians) run around the Earth from north to south. A place's longitude is given as degrees west or east of the Prime Meridian which runs through Greenwich in London, England.

126

In spring, north and south get equal sun

When the north is tilted away from the Sun, it is winter here, but summer in the south

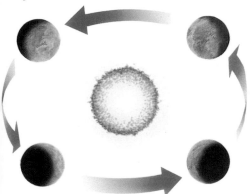

When the north is tilted toward the Sun, it is summer here, but winter in the south

In fall, north and south get equal sun

▲ *We get seasons because the Earth is always tilted over in the same direction. So when the Earth is on one side of the Sun, the northern hemisphere (the world north of the equator) is tilted towards the Sun, bringing summer here. At this time, the southern hemisphere is tilted away, and so gets winter. When the Earth is on the other side of the Sun, the northern hemisphere is tilted away, bringing winter, while the south gets summer.*

DATA: Our Home Planet

- **DISTANCE OF THE EARTH FROM THE SUN**
  At its nearest, called the perihelion, it is approximately 91.4 million miles away. At its furthest (the aphelion), it is around 94.5 million miles away. On average it is 93 million miles from the Sun.

- **SPIN TIME**
  The Earth spins around once every 23 hours 56 mins and 4.09 seconds. The Sun appears to come back to the same place in the sky once every 24 hours.

FACTS: About the time of day

- Time zones
  As the Earth spins, the Sun is always rising in one place and setting in another. So the time of day varies around the world. When it's dawn where you live, it's sunset on the other side of the world. To make it easier to set clocks, the world is split into 24 time zones, one for each hour of the day. As you go east around the world, you put clocks forward by one hour for each zone—until you reach a line called the International Date Line. If you cross the Date Line, you continue adding hours, but put the calendar a day back.

▲ *Half the world is facing the Sun and is brightly lit; the other half is facing away and in darkness. As the Earth spins around on its axis, each part moves into and out of sunlight, bringing day and night around the world. Because the Earth is turning eastward, the Sun appears to rise in the east and sink again in the west. The Earth turns once every 24 hours, which is why days are 24 hours long.*

Earth's atmosphere

WRAPPED AROUND the Earth is a thin blanket of gases called the atmosphere. This blanket is no thicker to the Earth than a peel is to an apple. Yet without it, the Earth would be as lifeless as the Moon. It gives us the air we need to breathe. It gives us clean water to drink. And it keeps us warm by trapping the Sun's heat-yet at the same time shielding us from the most harmful of its rays. It gives us weather, too, for everything we call weather is the churning of the atmosphere's lowest layer, next to the ground, as it is stirred by the Sun's warmth.

FACTS: About water in the air

- **Water cycle**
  All the water on Earth is forever being recycled in a process called the water cycle (see below).

- **Watery planet**
  Over 70 percent of the Earth's surface is covered by water. At any one time, though, just 1 percent is in the atmosphere. 97 percent is in the oceans. The rest is in lakes and rivers or frozen as ice.

- **Humidity**
  The air is full of invisible water vapor. The amount of water vapor in the air at any one time is known as its humidity.

- **Relative humidity**
  The total amount of moisture in the air is its "absolute" humidity. But the warmer air is, the more water it can hold, so meteorologists look at "relative" humidity, or rh, which is the percentage of moisture actually in the air relative to the maximum it could hold at that temperature.

- **Turning to water**
  As air cools, its rh must go up, because cool air can hold less moisture. Eventually, the rh reaches 100 percent and the vapor condenses into drops of water. This is called the dew point.

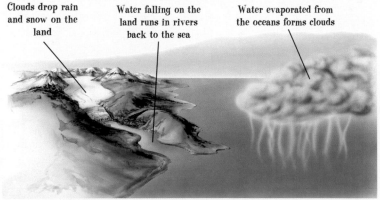

Clouds drop rain and snow on the land

Water falling on the land runs in rivers back to the sea

Water evaporated from the oceans forms clouds

The Sun's heat makes water evaporate from the oceans and rise into the air. As it rises, it cools and condenses into tiny drops of water, forming clouds. When the drops get big enough, they fall as rain or snow back into the oceans—or onto the land, where the water runs in rivers back to the sea again.

The atmosphere all looks like thin air, but scientists have shown that it has five or more layers, or "spheres," each with its own characteristics. We live in the lowest layer, called the troposphere. This layer is just 7.5 miles thick, but 75 percent of the atmosphere's gases sink into this layer. As you go higher and higher, the gases get more and more spread out, until by the time you are 500 miles or so up, the gases are so thin, or "rarefied," that the atmosphere fades off into space.

FACTS: About air pressure

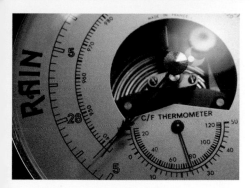

▲ Air pressure can be measured on a device called a barometer. Barometers help tell you if a storm is on its way, because storms are linked to low pressure. If the pressure drops sharply, you can be sure rain and wind are on their way.

- **Atmospheric pressure**
  At sea level, the atmosphere is so dense that there is a crush of air molecules. This crush creates enormous pressure in the air, called atmospheric or air pressure.

- **Wind and pressure**
  Air pressure varies from time to time and place to place. High pressure pushes air toward zones of high pressure, and this is what creates winds—air moving from high pressure to low pressure zones. The sharper the pressure difference, the stronger the wind.

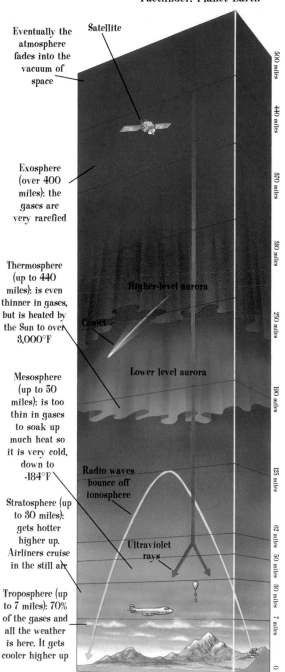

Eventually the atmosphere fades into the vacuum of space

Satellite

Exosphere (over 400 miles): the gases are very rarefied

Thermosphere (up to 440 miles): is even thinner in gases, but is heated by the Sun to over 3,000°F

Higher-level aurora

Comet

Lower level aurora

Mesosphere (up to 50 miles): is too thin in gases to soak up much heat so it is very cold, down to -184°F

Radio waves bounce off ionosphere

Stratosphere (up to 30 miles): gets hotter higher up. Airliners cruise in the still air

Ultraviolet rays

Troposphere (up to 7 miles): 70% of the gases and all the weather is here. It gets cooler higher up

500 miles
440 miles
370 miles
310 miles
250 miles
190 miles
125 miles
62 miles
50 miles
30 miles
7 miles
0

129

Weather

THERE ARE MANY DIFFERENT KINDS OF WEATHER–rain, snow, sun, wind, fog, mist, frost. But all of them are simply changes in the air caused by the varying effect of the Sun's warmth. Winds blow up, for instance, when the Sun heats some places more than others, setting the air moving. Rain falls when air warmed by the Sun lifts moisture high enough for it to form big drops of water when it condenses. Frost and snow occur when the power of the Sun is reduced. All weather comes down to three factors: the way the air moves (wind), its moisture content (humidity) and its temperature (warmth).

FACTS: About thunderstorms

- **Thunderclouds**
  Huge thunderclouds are built up by strong updrafts on a hot day or along a cold front. Eddies in the cloud hurl water drops and ice together so hard they become charged with static electricity. Positive particles clustering at the top of the cloud and negative particles at the bottom create a charge difference. Soon the charge difference builds up so much that lightning flashes from positive to negative.

▼ *Fork lightning flashes from cloud to ground. Sheet lightning flashes within the cloud. Lightning heats the air so much it bursts in a clap of thunder.*

Fronts

The stormiest weather in many places is linked to depressions (low pressure regions). A wedge of warm air intrudes into the heart of depressions, and the worst weather occurs along the edges of this wedge, called fronts where the warm air meets the cold. As the depression moves over, the fronts bring a distinct sequence of weather.

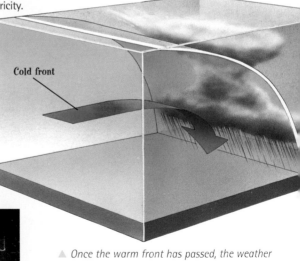

Cold front

▲ *Once the warm front has passed, the weather becomes milder and clearer for a while. But after a few hours, a build-up of thunderclouds and gusts of wind warn that the trailing edge of the wedge, called the cold front, is on its way. As the cold front passes over, the thunderclouds unleash short but heavy rain showers, and even thunderstorms, before calm returns.*

FACTS: About clouds and rain

- **Making clouds**
  Clouds form when water vapor rises with warm air, then condenses as the air cools in the upper air. It rains when the water drops in clouds get too heavy to float on the air.

- **Icy rain**
  Most rain comes from water droplets freezing into ice particles in a cloud. The particles grow into snowflakes, then melt into raindrops as they fall—or stay as snow if the air is cold.

- **Tropical rain**
  In the tropics, raindrops form inside tall clouds as small raindrops join up to make bigger drops heavy enough to fall as rain.

◀ *Rain clouds are gray because they are so thick with large drops of water that they block out the sunlight.*

▼ *Natural snowflakes are six-sided and consist of crystals that are mostly flat plates, but can be needles or columns. But under a magnifying glass, you can see their different intricate and beautiful shapes.*

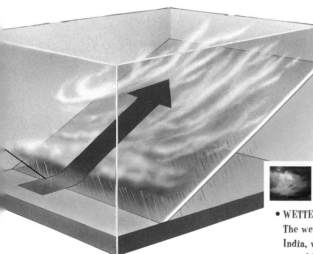

First to arrive is the leading edge of the wedge of warm air, or warm front, where warm air slides over old air. As it rises it forms banks of clouds along the front. So the coming of the warm front is heralded by feathery "cirrus" clouds high in the sky. Soon the clouds thicken until the sky is full of slate-gray "nimbostratus" clouds, which bring long periods of steady rain.

DATA: Weather

- **WETTEST**
  The wettest place on Earth is Mawsynram in India, which had 1,024 inches of rain in 1985– over 36 times the U.S. average.

- **THE COLDEST AND HOTTEST**
  The coldest recorded air temperature is -128.5°F in Vostok, Antarctica, and the hottest is Death Valley, which reached 134°F. Satellites have since recorded even more extreme ground temperatres.

131

Wind

ALL WIND IS SIMPLY AIR MOVING. Strong winds are air moving fast. Gentle breezes are air moving slowly. Air moves because the Sun warms some places more than others, creating differences in air pressure, which push the air arout. Warmth makes the air expand and rise, lowering air pressure. But where the air is cold and heavy, air pressure is high. Winds blow from areas where pressure is high, called anticyclones, to areas where pressure is low, called cyclones or depressions. The sharper the difference in pressure, the stronger the wind is.

FACTS: About hurricanes

◀ *Every summer, nine or so hurricanes develop in the eastern Atlantic and spiral westward to the Gulf of Mexico, tracked all the way by satellite. Here a hurricane's distinctive spiral of clouds is seen hitting the coast of Texas.*

▶ *Hurricanes are shaped like huge spiral layer cakes. Winds spiraling in toward the low pressure center, or eye, help line the thunderclouds into great walls of cloud towering into the sky.*

- **Hurricanes and typhoons**
  Hurricanes are the Atlantic version of the cyclone storms that batter eastern coasts in the tropics. In the Pacific they are known as typhoons.

- **What a hurricane does**
  When a hurricane strikes, trees can be ripped up and buildings flattened by winds gusting up to 225 mph. Vast areas can be battered and swamped by torrential rain, and coasts can be completely overwhelmed by the "storm surge"—the mound of sea water that builds up in the storm center.

- **Hurricane year**
  The hurricane season lasts from June to December in the northern hemishere, although occasionally some occur outside these months.

- **How hurricanes start**
  Hurricanes begin in the eastern Atlantic as thunderstorms set off by moist air rising over the warm ocean. If the water is warm enough, they pile up together, then begin to spiral westward across the ocean, growing bigger all the time.

- **Gaining power**
  By the time the hurricane has crossed the Atlantic, it is spiraling tighter and tighter around its center, or "eye." The eye shrinks to just 30 miles across, and winds howl around it at speeds of over 75 mph..

FACTS: About tornadoes

• **Twisters**
Tornadoes are tiny spirals of wind that sweep past in less than 15 minutes—but 185 mph winds and a low pressure center that sucks like a giant vacuum cleaner can toss people, cars, and buildings high in the air like toys. They are common from March to July in "Tornado Alley" in the Midwest.

• **Supercells**
Tornadoes are set off by giant thunderclouds called supercells. Winds whipping through the clouds set updrafts spinning. As they spin, they create a vortex that hangs from the cloud base down to the ground, like an elephant's trunk.

▲ Often it is the torrential rain and the storm surge of ocean water that do most of the damage in a hurricane, but the ferocious winds can also wreak havoc, blowing down trees and buildings.

• **The eye**
The air in the dead center or eye of the hurricane is at very low pressure, and is very calm. As the eye passes over, the winds may drop altogether and a small circle of blue sky may often be seen. But the lull is short-lived, for the rain and wind are at their strongest on either side of the eye.

• **Big wind**
A hurricane can be 500 miles across, and it can take 18 hours to pass over.

• **Hurricane warning**
Each hurricane is given a name and tracked by satellite to help give people plenty of warning that one is on its way.

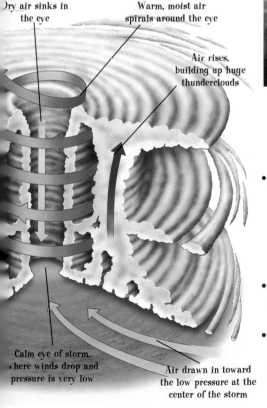

Dry air sinks in the eye

Warm, moist air spirals around the eye

Air rises, building up huge thunderclouds

Calm eye of storm, where winds drop and pressure is very low

Air drawn in toward the low pressure at the center of the storm

133

Structure of the Earth

THE EARTH IS NOT QUITE THE SOLID BALL it seems. Using sensitive equipment to detect the pattern of vibrations from earthquakes and big explosions, scientists have shown it has quite a complicated structure. Only a very thin shell, called the crust, is completely solid. Inside are a number of different layers, some solid, but some soft like thick molasses, while some of the core is molten metal. Atomic reactions in the core mean the Earth gets hotter and hotter as you go deeper toward the center, reaching nearly 11,000°F in the center–hotter than the surface of the Sun.

FACTS: Inside the Earth

- **Thin crust**
  The Earth's crust of rock is, on average, 25 miles thick under the continents and just 4.3 miles beneath the oceans.

- **Soft mantle**
  Beneath the crust is the mantle, nearly 1,900 miles thick and made of rock so warm it flows like molasses, only very, very slowly.

- **Metal core**
  In the center of the Earth is a core of metal (iron with a little nickel). The outer core is so hot it is molten. The inner core is even hotter, but pressures are so great the metal stays solid.

- **Crust edge**
  The boundary between the crust and mantle is called the Mohorovicic discontinuity.

- **Rigid top**
  The very top of the mantle is stiff and attached to the crust, so that they move as one—so scientists sometimes talk of the "lithosphere," which is the crust and the top of the mantle down to 60 miles.

- **Soft underneath**
  Beneath the lithosphere in the upper mantle is the softer "asthenosphere" down to 125 miles, where rock circulates very slowly.

▲ The world is a bit like a partly boiled egg, with a hard shell or crust, a white of semi-soft rock called the mantle, and a yolk or core of molten and solid metal.

- **Lower down**
  Below the asthenosphere is a third, stiffer layer within the upper mantle, called the mesosphere.

- **Mesophere**
  Heat makes the whole of the mantle churn very slowly, over millions of years. Sometimes big hot blobs rise right up from the core to the crust. These "superplumes" may create huge volcanoes.

▲ *The pulling apart of tectonic plates creates giant cracks in the Earth's surface. Usually, these cracks are hidden underwater on the ocean bed. But in Iceland, the crack that runs right down the middle of the Atlantic Ocean bed comes to the surface. Each side of this valley is a different plate, and they are slowly pulling apart.*

▼ *The giant plates that make up the Earth's hard shell or lithosphere are always moving, although very, very slowly. In some places, plates are crunching together, and one of the plates—typically a continent—rides over the other and forces it down into the Earth's interior. This process is called subduction. In other places— usually in mid-ocean on the seabed—plates are pulling apart. But even as they pull apart, so they gain new material as hot molten rock wells up through the gap and solidifies on the exposed edges. This is called mid-ocean spreading.*

FACTS: Moving plates

- **Tectonic plates**
  The Earth's rocky crust is broken into 20 or so huge fragments called tectonic plates. As these move slowly about, they set off earthquakes and volcanoes, and pile up mountain ranges.

- **Continental drift**
  As tectonic plates move, they carry the continents slowly around the world.

▼ *The Earth's crust is broken in 20 or so plates that carry continents as they move. Africa and South America were once joined. Europe is drifting slowly farther from North America.*

In the middle of the ocean, where plates are pulling apart, new molten rock wells up to create a series of ridges under the sea

Ocean

Deep trench in the ocean where a plate is subducted

Subducted plate pushed into the Earth's interior

In "subduction zones" plates are pushing together, pushing one plate beneath the other

Rock from the melting plate burns up to erupt through as volcanoes

Continent

Molten rock from the mantle

Plates pulling apart

Lithosphere

Asthenosphere

Plates pushing together

Subducted plate melting

History of the Earth

THE EARTH probably formed about 4.55 billion years ago from debris spinning around the Sun. At first, it was a molten ball, but it gradually cooled, and a thin crust formed around the outside. The first signs of life–probably bacteria–appeared nearly four billion years ago. But the first animals with shells and bones easily preserved as fossils did not appear until less than 600 million years ago. It is mainly with the help of such fossils that geologists have built up a picture of Earth's history since then. Very little is known about the four billion years before this, called Precambrian time.

Earth formed 4.55 billion years ago

Archean 4,600-2,500 million years ago (mya)

▲ *This spiral shows some events in Earth's history, starting with its origin at the center of the spiral and the coming of humans at the end. The scale is distorted because so little is known about what happened in the first 85 percent of Earth's history—so the last 15 percent is given much more space. If Earth's history were crammed into a day, humans would appear only at the end, just two seconds before midnight.*

FACTS: Geological time

- **Units of time**
  Just as the day is divided into hours, minutes, and seconds, so geologists divide the Earth's history into time periods. The longest are eons, billions of years long; the shortest are chrons, a few thousand years long. In between come eras, periods, epochs, and ages.

- **Fossil time**
  Because different plants and animals lived at different times in Earth's past, geologists can tell how long ago rocks formed from the fossils in them. Using fossils, they have divided the Earth's history since Precambrian times into 11 periods.

- **Geological column**
  Layers of rock form one on top of the other, so the oldest is usually at the bottom, unless they have been disturbed. The sequence of layers from top to bottom is called the geological column.

FACTS: About dating

- **Fossil dating**
  By looking for certain key fossils, geologists can tell whether one layer of rock is older than another so they can then place it within the geological column. This is called "biostratigraphy."

- **Absolute date**
  Fossils can only show if a rock is older or younger, not give a date in years—and many rocks don't contain fossils. To give an "absolute" date, geologists often use radioactivity.

- **Radioactive dating**
  After certain substances such as uranium and rubidium form, their atoms slowly break down into different atoms, sending out rays as they do so. The rays are called radioactivity. By assessing how many atoms in a rock have changed, geologists can tell how old it is.

Precambrian time:
The first lifeforms
(bacteria) appear, and
give the air oxygen

Cambrian Period:
No life on land, but
shellfish flourish in
the oceans

Ordovician Period:
Early fish-like
vertebrates appear.
The Sahara is
glaciated

Silurian Period:
First land plants.
Fish with jaws and
freshwater fish

Devonian Period:
First insects and
amphibians. Ferns and
mosses as big as trees

Proterozoic
2,500-590 mya

Carboniferous Period:
Vast warm swamps
of fern forests, which
form coal. First
reptiles

Permian Period:
Conifers replace ferns
as big trees. Deserts
widespread

Triassic Period:
First mammals. Seed-
bearing plants spread.
Europe in the tropics

Jurassic Period:
Dinosaurs widespread.
Archaeopertyx,
earliest known bird

Cretaceous Period:
First flowering
plants. The dinosaurs
die out

Tertiary Period:
First large
mammals. Birds
flourish. Widespread
grasslands

Quaternary Period:
Many mammals die
out in Ice Ages.
Humans evolve

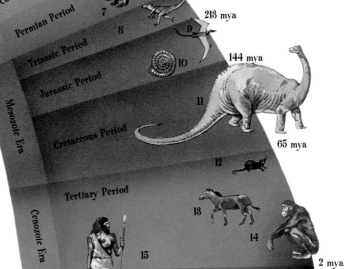

Precambrian

590 mya

Cambrian Period

505 mya
438 mya
408 mya

Ordovician Period

Silurian Period

Devonian Period

360 mya

Carboniferous Period

286 mya

Paleozoic Era

Permian Period

248 mya

213 mya

Triassic Period

144 mya

Jurassic Period

Mesozoic Era

Cretaceous Period

65 mya

Tertiary Period

Cenozoic Era

Quaternary Period

2 mya

Today

Key to lifeforms
1 Jellyfish
2 Trilobite
3 Acanthodian (jawed fish)
4 Cooksonia (early land plant)
5 Ichthyostega (early
 amphibian)
6 Dimetrodon (early
 mammal-like reptile)
7 Anteosaurus (early reptile)
8 Herrerasaurus (early
 dinosaur)
9 Pteranodon (early flying
 reptile)
10 Cephalopod (squid-like
 shellfish)
11 Brachiosaurus (dinosaur)
12 Crusafontia (small mammal)
13 Merychippus (early horse)
14 Proconsul (great ape)
15 Homo sapiens (early man)

Rocks

ROCKS ARE THE HARD MASS the ground is made of. You can only see bare rock exposed on the surface in a few places–cliffs, mountain crags, and quarries. But it is there everywhere, not far beneath the city streets or the thin covering of soil or vegetation. Some rocks are just a few million years old; some are almost as old as the Earth. But they all tend to be very tough solids made of tiny crystals or "grains" of naturally occurring chemicals called minerals. All these minerals came originally from the Earth's hot interior, but at the surface they form three kinds of rock: igneous, sedimentary, and metamorphic.

FACTS: About igneous, sedimentary, and metamorphic rock

▲ 90 percent of the Earth's crust is made from igneous rocks, like this granite, which is an intrusive rock and formed underground.

▲ Although most surface rock is igneous, 75% of the world's land surface is covered by thin layers of sedimentary rock like this limestone.

▲ Metamorphic rock such as this hornfels is rock made when other rock is altered by extreme heat or pressure.

- **Igneous rock**
  Igneous rock is formed from red-hot magma (molten rock) that wells up from the Earth's interior. Some erupts on the surface through volcanoes and cools to form "volcanic," or "extrusive," igneous rock. Some is pushed up under the surface, forming "intrusive" igneous rock.

- **Acid and basic igneous rock**
  There are many different kinds of rock. Some, like granite, are generally light in color and are made from quite acidic magma (rich in silica). Others, like basalt, are darker and made from basic magma.

- **Sedimentary rock**
  Sedimentary rock forms in thin layers from debris that settles mainly on the seabed and is then squeezed and cemented over millions of years into solid rocks. Some, like limestone, are made mainly from plant and animal remains. Most are made from fragments of rock worn away by the weather.

- **Metamorphic rock**
  Metamorphic rock is made when other rocks are crushed by movements of the Earth's crust or scorched by magma—and changed so much that they form a new kind of rock, such as marble or slate.

FACTS: About coal and oil

▼ *In the Carboniferous Period, there were huge tropical swamps filled with giant, tree-like ferns. It is these that most coal formed from, as the remains of the plants were buried and squeezed.*

1. Remains of swamp plants were first buried and squeezed to make peat

2. As they became buried deeper, heat and pressure changed the peat to brown coal

3. Further pressure changed brown coal to black bituminous coal and finally anthracite

- **Fossil fuels**
  Coal, oil, and natural gas are fossil fuels, which means they formed over millions of years from the remains of plants and small creatures.

- **Carboniferous swamps**
  Most coal formed from the remains of plants that grew in huge, warm swamps in the Carboniferous Period, 300 million years ago.

- **Oil bearing rocks**
  Oil formed from the remains of tiny plants and animals that lived in warm seas. As they died, they were buried and squeezed into oil, then collected in porous (sponge-like) layers of rock.

- **Crude oil**
  Oil usually comes up from the ground as thick, black "crude" oil and must be refined for use.

▼ *The materials rocks are made of are continually recycled to make new rocks in a process called the rock cycle. Magma from the interior cools to form igneous rock, which is gradually worn away by the weather. The fragments are washed down into the sea and settle on the seabed to form sedimentary rock. Both sedimentary and igneous rock may be altered into metamorphic rock—and all three are eventually broken down so that they too can be formed into new sedimentary rocks.*

1. Igneous rocks form from magma forced up from the Earth's interior

2. Weather wears away the rock, and fragments are washed into the sea, then settle on the seabed

3. Sediments buried under the seabed are cemented into layers of rock, then lifted up above the sea to be worn away again

139

Minerals

MINERALS ARE THE natural chemicals from which the Earth's crust is made. A few are powdery or resinous, but most are crystals. Usually, minerals occur as a mass of tiny crystals or grains. Occasionally, though, crystals grow as big as flagpoles. Geologists identify minerals by various factors including the color and shape of the crystal. There are 2,000 or so different minerals, but under a hundred are common. A handful of minerals are pure chemical elements that occur naturally, such as gold or silver. Most are compounds, of which by far the most common are silicates.

FACTS: Gems

- **Gems**
  Gems are especially rare and beautiful mineral crystals such as rubies and emeralds.

- **Veins and geodes**
  Many precious gems form either in veins, where hot volcanic fluid forces its way into a crack in the rock, or in gas pockets in cooling volcanic rock called geodes.

▲ Gems are rare because they only form naturally under very special conditions— usually deep within volcanic rocks. A few can now be made artificially, but these are not so precious.

- **Diamonds**
  Diamonds are very hard, very rare—and very old. They were probably made by the mighty collision of continents during subduction and taken deep into the Earth. They are only found because volcanoes bring them near the surface again after billions of years.

- **Colored gems**
  Many gems get their vivid colors from tiny traces of chemicals within them. Traces of iron turn common clear quartz into purple amethyst. Manganese turns quartz pink.

FACTS: About crystals

- **What are crystals?**
  Crystals are glassy-looking, brittle solids that form in regular shapes, with sharp corners and flat sides.

- **Crystal shapes**
  Crystals are regular, and there are only a certain number of possible basic regular shapes, called systems—cubic, pyramid, and so on. The crystals of each mineral fit into one of these systems.

▶ Minerals only rarely form in large, distinct crystals like these. Most of the time they form much smaller grains and are mixed in with other minerals in rocks. Granite, for instance, is made of the minerals feldspar, quartz, and mica, along with small amounts of other minerals. Quartz is a silicate mineral—the most common silicate mineral of all—but over 99 percent of it is actually mixed in with other minerals in granite and other rocks, such as sandstone.

Twists of silver

FACTS: Elements & silicates

- **Native elements**
  Native elements are minerals that occur naturally as pure chemical elements, including all those shown on this page.

- **Silicates**
  Silicates are minerals that form when the chemical elements silicon and oxygen—two of the most common elements on Earth—combine with a metal. There are over 500 of them, including quartz, olivine, and pyroxene.

▼ *Gold is rare but almost always found in pure form because it just won't mix with any other mineral.*

Bismuth rarely occurs in pure form in nature. It is usually mixed with sulphur

Silver rarely looks silvery in nature because exposure to air tarnishes the surface black

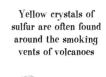

Copper only rarely occurs in pure form. Normally it is linked into minerals such as chalcopyrite

Yellow crystals of sulfur are often found around the smoking vents of volcanoes

Yellow fluorite is a rare mineral made of calcium and fluorine

The green crystals are uraninite, chemically uranium oxide, the main source of the metal uranium

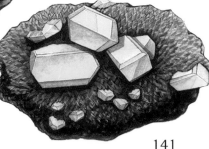

141

Volcanoes

VOLCANOES ARE PLACES where hot molten rock, or "magma," from the Earth's interior erupts on the surface. With some volcanoes, it oozes out gently and flows overground as lava—red-hot liquid rock. Others get clogged up with thick plugs of magma and then suddenly burst through in a mighty explosion that sends up jets of steam and hurls scorching fragments of debris from under the plugs thousands of feet in the air. Most volcanoes occur near the cracks between the giant tectonic plates that make up the Earth's surface, but a few occur at "hot spots" where plumes of hot magma rise under the crust.

FACTS: Types of volcanoes

- **Thick and thin magma**
  Volcanoes take many forms, but the most explosive volcanoes occur near subduction zones where the collision of tectonic plates creates a very thick, sticky "acid" magma that clogs up the volcano easily. Where plates are pulling apart, the magma is less acid and runs freely.

- **Cinder volcanoes**
  Most volcanoes are made of solidified lava, but some are mounds of ash.

◁ When the lava is quite runny, it floods out far and wide, creating a broad, gently sloping "shield" volcano.

◁ The thick lava from explosive volcanoes piles up steeply around the volcano, creating a cone.

◁ In "strato" volcanoes, alternate layers of ash and lava build up as ash falls on the lava flow from each eruption.

▷ The biggest eruptions are powered by a combination of steam and bubbles of carbon dioxide gas. Extreme pressure normally keeps them dissolved in the magma, but as the eruption begins the pressure drops and bubbles begin to form in the magma and swell rapidly. The eruption sends out three kinds of material apart from steam and gas—clouds of ash, solid fragments of the volcanic plug called tephra or volcanic bombs, and lava. Sometimes, lethal clouds of glowing ash hurtle down the slope.

▽ It is very hard to tell exactly when a volcano is going to erupt. But vulcanologists can get an idea by keeping a very careful watch on the slopes of the volcano, using laser rangefinders for accuracy. Any very slight change in slope might be the magma bulging up underneath, indicating an imminent eruption.

Eruptions begin with a build-up in pressure in the "magma chamber" beneath the volcano

Water heated under pressure underground by hot magma can burst onto the surface in a ferocious jet of steam and hot water called a geyser. The biggest geysers are hundreds of feet high.

Big eruptions can send so much ash into the upper air that they blot out the Sun and turn the world cool

Tephra vary in size from tiny "lapilli" to volcanic "bombs", which can measure over 3 feet across

Lava flows look spectacular, but it is the ash that is really deadly

FACTS: Famous eruptions

The eruption of Mount St. Helens in Washington state, in 1980 blew away the top and side of the mountain. The blast blanketed the forest far around with ash and flattened millions of trees in an area that covered over 230 square miles, as well as killing 57 people .

- **Big bang**
  The eruption of Krakatoa, east of Java, in 1883 was so loud that people heard it nearly 3000 miles away.

- **Gray skies**
  The eruption of Mt. Tambora in Java in 1815 sent up so much dust that the Sun was blocked out all around the globe, causing two years of poor summers.

- **Roman remains**
  When Mt. Vesuvius in Italy erupted in A.D. 79, the people of the Roman town of Pompeii were buried instantly. The remains of the city, almost perfectly preserved under the ash, were discovered in the 18th century.

- **Biggest in human history?**
  There was a giant eruption 20,000 years ago of Sumatra's Mt. Toba, which covered the entire island in ash 1,000 feet deep.

- **Biggest ever**
  One of the biggest-ever eruptions covered nearly all of India in lava 65 million years ago.

143

Earthquakes

EVEN A PASSING TRUCK can make the ground tremble, but most earthquakes are the ground shuddering as the huge tectonic plates that make up the Earth's surface grind past each other. Most of the time the plates slide past each other quietly. But they sometimes jam. Then pressure builds up until they suddenly lurch on again, sending shock waves radiating in all directions. The nearer a place is to where the earthquake began–called the epicenter on the surface–the more severe the earthquake is. The worst earthquakes can bring down mountains and destroy cities.

FACTS: Earthquake zones

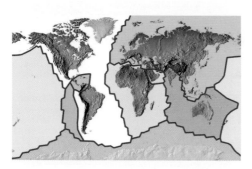

▲ *Earthquake zones—places that suffer earthquakes repeatedly—are near plate edges, such as southeastern Europe and the Pacific coast.*

- **San Andreas**
  The San Andreas fault in California is where two great plates slide past each other, often setting off earthquakes, such as that which destroyed San Francisco in 1906.

- **Predicting earthquakes**
  Earthquakes are hard to predict, but they are most likely to occur in earthquake zones—especially when there has not been one for some time. Seismologists use satellites and laser beams to detect slight movements and look for changes in the magnetism of rocks.

DATA: The worst earthquakes

- 856: 200,000 people killed; Damghan, Iran.
- 1138: 230,000 people killed; Aleppo, Syria.
- 1556: 830,000 people killed; Shaanxi, China.
- 1920: 200,000 people killed; Haiyhan, China.
- 1923: 144,000 people killed; Kwanto, Japan.
- 1948: 110,000 people killed; Ashgabat, Turkmenistan
- 1976: 255,000 people killed; Tangshan, China.
- 2004: 227,000 people killed; Sumatra, Southest Asia*
- 2010: 316,000 people killed; Haiti, Caribbean

The death toll of the Sumatran earthquake includes the highest number of casualties recorded as a result of a tsunami, which was triggered by the quake and hit coastlines in South Asia and East Africa on December 26.

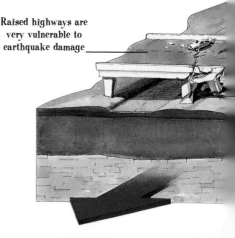

Raised highways are very vulnerable to earthquake damage

FACTS: About earthquake measurement

▲ *Seismometers detect tremors in the ground and display them on a seismograph. The strong vibrations of big earthquakes show as dramatic zig-zags.*

- Richter scale
  The severity of an earthquake, measured on a machine called a seismometer, is usually assessed on the Richter scale, which goes from 1 (slight tremor) to over 9 (severe earthquake).

- Mercalli scale
  The Richter scale gives the absolute magnitude (size) of an earthquake, but no idea of its effects. These are sometimes assessed on the Mercalli scale, which rates the damage done on a scale of 1 (barely noticeable) to 12 (total destruction).

Earthquakes usually last only a few minutes, but their effects can be devastating

Tall buildings are especially prone to earthquake damage

▽ *This picture shows the destruction that occurs when buildings lie directly over a fault in the Earth's crust. But the shock waves—called seismic waves—can be devastating even tens of miles from the epicenter. A great deal of damage is done by an earthquake itself, as the tremors shake buildings to pieces and snap roadways. But they can also fracture gas pipes and electricity cables and set off terrible fires.*

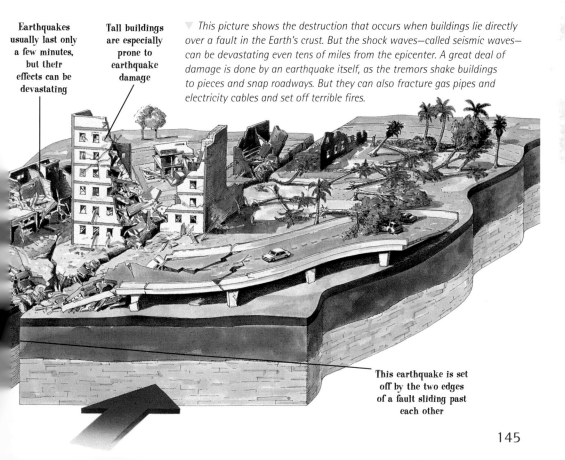

This earthquake is set off by the two edges of a fault sliding past each other

Mountains

MOUNTAINS LOOK FAIRLY PERMANENT, but they are continually being created and destroyed. Most of the biggest mountains are actually quite young in geological terms. The Himalayas of Asia, for instance, include the world's highest peaks, yet they were first raised less than 40 million years ago–and they are still growing today. Mountains are created in one of a number of ways. Most are created by the folding of rock layers as the huge tectonic plates that make up the Earth's surface crunch together. Others are created as crustal movements lift up huge blocks. Others are created by volcanic eruptions.

FACTS: About fold mountains

• **Fold ranges**
Most of the world's greatest mountain ranges—the Himalayas, the Andes, the Rockies, the Caucasus, and the Alps—are created by the crumpling edges of colliding tectonic plates. This is why they often form long narrow ranges along the edges of continents. The Himalayas were created by the collision of India with Asia.

• **Runny mountains**
The rock in mountains is not completely rigid. It flows a bit like very stiff molasses. So ranges such as the Himalayas are flowing out and getting flatter at the edges, at the same time as they are being pushed up.

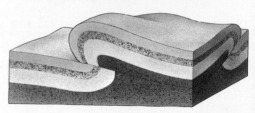

• **Dip and strike**
The angle at which folded rock layers are tilted is the "dip." This can be anything from a few degrees to over 90°. The direction of the fold is the "strike."

• **Upfold and downfold**
Downfolds (like a dish) are called synclines; upfolds (like an arch) are called anticlines.

• **Overturned folds**
Sometimes a fold may fold right over. This is called an "overturned" fold. If it folds so far that it rests on the next fold it is said to be "recumbent."

▲ *If tectonic plates continue pushing together, the folding may go well beyond a simple fold (top). First it overturns and the layers begin to snap (middle). Finally the layers snap altogether, creating a "nappe."*

146

The Alps were created by folding, but the dramatic shape of the Matterhorn, one of the highest Alpine peaks (over 13,000 feet high), was created by glaciers.

DATA: The highest mountains

- Everest in the Himalayas is the world's highest (29,029 feet).
- South America's highest is Aconcagua (22,835 feet).
- North America's highest is Mt. McKinley (20,322 feet).
- Africa's highest is Kilimanjaro (19,341 feet).
- Europe's highest is Elbrus in Russia (18,510 feet).
- Australasia's highest is Papua New Guinea's Mt. Wilhelm (14,793 feet).

FACTS: Faults & blocks

▶ As the tectonic plates of the Earth's crust jostle together, they may put rocks under such strain that they fracture, creating cracks, or "faults'," in the rock. Large blocks of rock may then be thrown up to create mountains.

A fault scarp is a cliff, exposed as a massive block of rock is thrown up or down

- **Where faults occur**
  Faults occur mainly in areas that are called "fault zones." These lie mostly along the edges of tectonic plates.

- **Normal fault**
  In most faults, the cracking of the Earth's crust as tectonic plates pull apart allows a block of rock to slip straight down. In a "wrench" fault, however, blocks slip sideways past each other. In a "reverse" fault, one block slides up over another as plates crunch together.

- **Horsts and rifts**
  If a block of rock is thrown down between two faults it may create a deep, steep-sided "rift" valley. If the block is thrown upward, it creates a high plateau called a horst.

▼ No mountain range lasts forever. Sooner or later they are worn down by the weather. Frost, for instance, may shatter rocks on mountain peaks, leaving the lower slopes littered with fragments known as scree.

Rivers

RIVERS RUN DOWN to the sea or lakes wherever there is enough rain or melting snow to keep them flowing. Even when it is not raining, most rivers in moist regions are kept flowing by water from underground. This is because a lot of rain does not flow directly over the land, but seeps into the ground—only to bubble up lower down, in places called springs. Most rivers are tiny when they start high up in the hills, tumbling over rocks and rapids. But they get bigger farther down as they are joined by tributaries (side rivers). As they near the sea, they run in broad, smooth-flowing curves called meanders.

Heavy rainfall and melting snow high up starts a river with plenty of water

High up, the river tumbles over rocks and rapids in steep, narrow valleys

FACTS: About river valleys

◁ *The Grand Canyon is one of the world's deepest river valleys, carved by the Colorado River over millions of years. The area is so dry that there is little rain to wear away the valley sides so these sides are often steep cliffs.*

• **River power**
Rivers continually batter their banks and beds with running water, sand, and pebbles. Over thousands of years, rivers can carve huge valleys out of solid rock.

• **Valley to plain**
To start with, river valleys are narrow, steep-sided and winding—and they are usually like this near their source in the hills. But, with time, they carve out broader, flatter valleys, and they meander over a wide "floodplain"—a flat area in danger of flooding when heavy rain or melting snow makes the river full.

Every river has a natural tendency to wind—especially in the lower reaches, where it is wide and deep and flows across a broad plain. Here, giant horseshoe-shaped meanders develop as the river wears away the outside bank of each curve and washes up sediment on the inside.

In the lower reaches, the river is broad and deep and flows through smooth channels of sediment, washed down from higher up

Where it meets the sea, the river may split into several branches, forming a "delta"

A river changes dramatically in character as it runs down toward the sea. High up, it is a small stream, tumbling over rocks because it is too small to wash them out of the way. Near the sea it flows through a smooth channel of silt and mud washed down by the river from higher up, over tens of thousands of years.

FACTS: About waterfalls

- **Where falls form**
  Waterfalls typically form where a river flows over a band of hard rock, as the water wears away the soft rock below.

- **'The smoke that thunders'**
  So much water flows over Victoria Falls in Zimbabwe—247,000 gallons every second—that the roar can be heard over 25 miles away.

The Angel Falls in Venezuela—named after a U.S. pilot, Jimmy Angel—is the highest waterfall in the world, plunging 3,212 feet.

DATA: The longest rivers

- The Nile in Africa is 4,146 miles long.
- The Amazon in S. America is 4,082 miles long.
- The Yangtze in Asia is 3,900 miles long.
- The Mississippi-Missouri in N. America is 3,740 miles long.
- The Danube in Europe is 1,775 miles long.

149

Oceans

ALMOST THREE-QUARTERS of the world is under water. There are five great oceans–the Pacific, the Atlantic, and the Indian–which all merge into the Southern Ocean around Antarctica–and the smaller Arctic Ocean. Then there are many smaller stretches of water called seas, including the Mediterranean, the Baltic and the Red seas. Yet until quite recently, the bottom of the oceans were as mysterious and unknown as the surface of Mars. Modern ocean surveys have now begun to reveal that the landscape of the ocean bed is as varied as that of the continents, with high mountains, vast plains, and deep valleys.

FACTS: About coasts

- **Eroded coasts**
  In some places, especially on headlands, coasts are worn away by waves crashing on bare rock. Hills are cut back to sheer cliffs, leaving behind platforms of rock washed over by the waves and, occasionally, isolated stacks of rock.

- **Sandy coasts**
  In other places, especially bays, material worn away is deposited as sandy and pebbly beaches and bars across river mouths.

- **Tides**
  In most places, the sea rises and then falls back again twice daily. These "tides" are created by the pull of the Moon's gravity, which creates a tidal bulge of raised water on opposite sides of the world. As the Earth turns beneath the Moon during the day, so the tidal bulge moves around the world.

▼ *Constant battering by waves and salty water gives coastlines their own unique range of landforms, including cliffs, headlands, and sandy bays.*

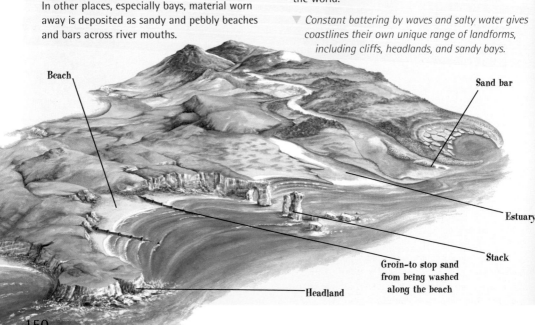

Beach

Sand bar

Estuary

Stack

Groin–to stop sand from being washed along the beach

Headland

FACTS: About the ocean bed

- **Ocean floor revealed**
  Since the 1970s, surveys using sound equipment and robot submarines have allowed oceanographers to lift away the ocean waters to create detailed maps of the ocean floor (right).

- **Shallow margin**
  Around the edge of each ocean is a shelf of shallow water called the continental shelf. At the edge of this shelf, the ocean floor plunges to the deep ocean floor, or "abyssal plain."

- **Seamounts**
  The abyssal plain is not completely flat but dotted, especially in the Pacific, with huge mountains known as seamounts, often thousands of feet high. In places, there are flat-topped seamounts called guyots, which may once have projected above the surface and been worn flat there.

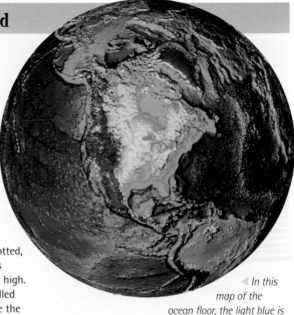

◀ In this map of the ocean floor, the light blue is the continental shelf and the dark blue is the abyssal plain.

▲ Sonar systems map the ocean floor by sending out high-frequency pulses of sound. The time it takes for the sound pulse to echo back from the ocean floor indicates how deep the ocean is.

DATA: The oceans

- **SEA AREA**
  The seas cover more than 139 million square miles of the Earth's surface. The biggest ocean is the Pacific, over 63 million square miles, more than a third of the Earth's surface.

- **WATER VOLUME**
  There is 324 million cubic miles of water in the oceans.

- **DEEP WATER**
  The average depth of the oceans is 12,238 feet—enough to cover most Alpine mountains.

- **DEEPEST WATER**
  The deepest point on the Earth's surface is the Challenger Deep in the Marianas trench in the western Pacific, which is 36,188 feet deep.

151

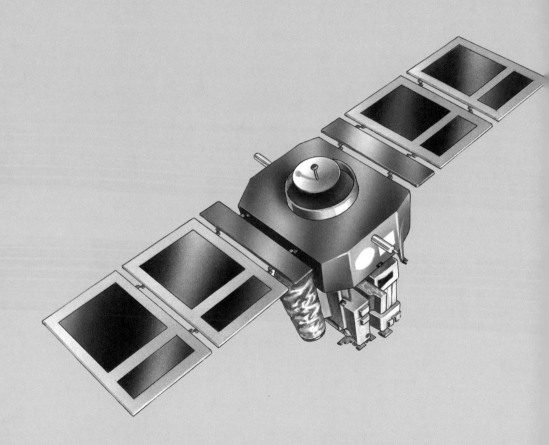

SCIENCE

Electricity

ELECTRICITY IS THE ENERGY that makes everything from toasters to tube trains work. It is also linked with magnetism. Together they form one of the basic forces that holds the Universe together–electromagnetism. Electricity starts with atoms and tiny parts of each atom called electrons. Just as magnets are drawn together, so electrons are drawn to the center of the atom. This attraction is called "electric charge." Electrons have a "negative" charge; atomic centers a "positive" one. It is the combined attraction of billions of tiny electrons to billions of tiny atom centers that creates electricity.

▶ Electricity is generated in power stations and sent across the country along big cables carried on towers called pylons, or along cables buried underground. The electricity is sent down these cables at very high voltage (high pressure) to make sure it reaches its destination.

▲ If a coil of wire is wrapped around a bar of iron, switching on the current turns the bar into a very powerful magnet, called an electromagnet, or solenoid. The gray curves show lines of magnetic force.

FACTS: Electromagnetism

- **Making electricity**
  When a coil of electric wire is moved near a magnet—or a magnet is moved near a coil—the magnetism draws electrons through the wire, creating an electric current.

- **Power stations and generators**
  Power stations make electricity using generators. In generators, turbines (like fan blades) are turned by running water or by steam heated by burning oil or coal, or by nuclear energy. The turning of the turbines turns banks of electric coils round magnets.

- **Electric motors**
  Just as moving magnets create electricity, so an electric current can make a magnet move. In electric motors, an electric current is sent through a coil wrapped round a magnet. The surge of electricity through the coil makes the magnet turn.

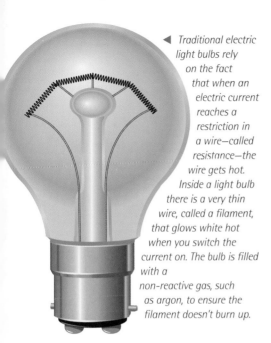

◀ Traditional electric light bulbs rely on the fact that when an electric current reaches a restriction in a wire—called resistance—the wire gets hot. Inside a light bulb there is a very thin wire, called a filament, that glows white hot when you switch the current on. The bulb is filled with a non-reactive gas, such as argon, to ensure the filament doesn't burn up.

FACTS: Static electricity

▶ Lightning is the release of the huge charge of static electricity made as raindrops collide in a thundercloud.

• **Static charge**
Static electricity is what makes dry hair get frizzy when you comb it and a sweater tingle if you pull it off too fast. It is called static because, unlike electricity in a circuit, it doesn't move. It is made when surfaces rub together. Electrons rub off one surface and onto to the other. The extra electrons give it a negative electric charge. This attracts surfaces that have lost electrons and so are positively charged.

FACTS: About electric currents

• **Currents and circuits**
Electric currents can move through certain materials in a continuous flow. But for the current to flow, there must be a complete loop, or circuit.

• **Free electrons**
Electric currents work like a row of marbles—flicking one jolts marbles down the row. The marbles are "free" electrons— electrons not attached to atoms.

• **Conductors**
Materials that have many free electrons, such as copper, make good conductors of electricity.

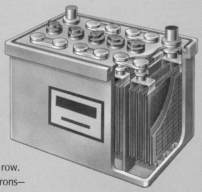

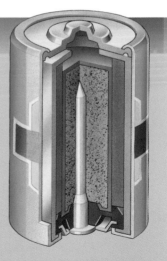

▲ Batteries use chemical reactions to create electricity. Each cell (part) has a positive and negative electrode. In a car battery, the electrodes are metal (usually lead) plates dipped in acid.

▲ Car batteries are called wet cell batteries. Flashlight and radio batteries are "dry cells." They often have electrodes of zinc and graphite (ground carbon).

Magnetism

MAGNETISM IS THE INVISIBLE FORCE between magnetic materials such as iron and nickel. It affects only a certain area around each magnet, called its "field." It is strongest at the two ends, or "poles," of the magnet and gets steadily weaker farther away. Magnetism sometimes attracts magnetic materials to each other; sometimes it repels them. Magnetism works in opposite ways at each of a magnet's poles, and whether two magnets snap together or spring apart depends on which poles meet. If the same poles of each magnet meet, they push each other away. If opposite poles meet, they pull together.

FACTS: About Earth's magnetic field

- **Magnet Earth**
  The Earth is a giant magnet—it behaves almost as if there was a giant iron bar magnet running through its middle from pole to pole.

- **Spinning core**
  The Earth gets its magnetism from its core of iron and nickel. Because the outer core is liquid and the inner core solid, they rotate at different rates. The circulating currents this sets up turns it into a giant solenoid.

- **Magnetosphere**
  Earth's magnetism not only affects magnets on the surface, but also electrically charged particles 37,000 miles out in space. The vast region of space affected is called the "magnetosphere." Without its protection, Earth would be exposed to the "solar wind," the lethal stream of charged particles whizzing from the Sun.

- **Why magnets point north**
  If you hold a magnet so that it can rotate freely, it always ends up pointing the same way, with one end pointing to the Earth's North Pole and the other to the South Pole. This is how compasses work.

- **Magnetic North**
  The Earth's magnetic field is slightly tilted, so compasses do not point to the Earth's true North Pole, but to a little way off northern Canada. This is called Magnetic North.

- **Magnetic dip**
  Magnets not only swivel to point north but also point down. This is called magnetic dip.

Lines of magnetic force created by Earth's magnetism

▲ There is not actually a giant bar magnet inside the Earth, but it is almost as if there was. The Earth's field, though, constantly varies from place to place and from time to time. Scientists can calculate changes that happened in the distant past from magnetic particles, frozen in rocks as they formed. This is called "paleomagnetism."

FACTS: Magnets

◀ *The effects of magnetic attraction are transmitted between objects affected by magnetism. So a magnet can pick up a string of paper clips.*

- **North and south poles**
  Every magnet has two ends: a north (north-seeking) pole and a south (south-seeking) pole.

- **Magnetic domains**
  Cut a magnet in half and you get two little magnets, each with north and south poles. You can go on dividing magnets into new magnets virtually down to atoms. This is because magnetic materials are made of tiny groups of atoms called domains, which are like mini-magnets.

- **Curie temperature**
  Iron loses its magnetic properties above 1,400°F, called the Curie temperature after Pierre Curie, the scientist who discovered this.

▼ Lines of magnetic force may be invisible, but they are real. Around a bar magnet, they form a hamburger shape. They crowd close together around the poles, where the field is strongest.

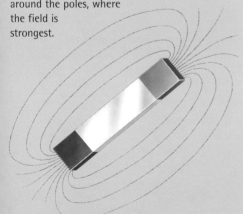

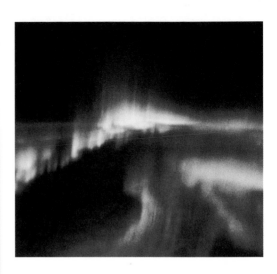

▲ *Auroras are spectacular curtains of light that ripple through the night sky above the poles. The aurora borealis (northern lights) is seen over the North Pole, and the aurora australis (southern lights) over the South Pole. Auroras occur because there is a gaping hole in Earth's magnetic field over the poles, where lines of magnetic force funnel in towards them. Every now and then, charged particles from the Sun stream in through the hole and cannon into air molecules at tremendous speed. The violent collisions make all the air molecules glow so brightly they light up the sky.*

▶ *The ancient Chinese were probably the first to make magnetic compasses, for telling fortunes as well as finding directions. But sailors everywhere have been using compasses to navigate for more than a thousand years.*

157

Electronics

ELECTRONICS ARE AT THE HEART of a huge range of modern technologies, from stereos to rocket control systems. All work by using electricity to send signals. Inside every electronic device there are lots of small electric circuits continually switching on and off, telling the device what to do. But electronic switches are not like electric light switches on the wall; they work automatically. The most basic switches are "transistors," which are made using special materials called semiconductors that change their ability to conduct electricity. Electronic systems work by linking lots of transistors together into "integrated circuits," "chips," and "microprocessors."

FACTS: About chips and microprocessors

• **Silicon chips**
In most integrated circuits, dozens or even thousands of tiny transistors are joined together in circuits that are packed inside a single tiny slice of silicon. This is called a silicon chip.

• **Mini-chips**
Chips are getting smaller and more sophisticated by the year. This is why even complex devices like powerful computers can be made pocket-sized.

• **Computer chips**
The most complicated silicon chips are "microprocessors" containing a million or more transistors. These are the brains in computers.

▲ *The biggest things in a silicon chip are not all its circuits and switches—the tiny patch in the center. The connectors that send its instructions to the rest of the machine—the teeth along the side of the chip—are much bigger.*

◀ *Liquid Crystal Display (LCD) screens are very thin and power-efficient, making them popular for all kinds of devices, such as televisions and computer displays.*
An LCD screen features millions of pixels, each containing a red, green, and blue liquid crystal. Electricity is passed through the crystals to control how much light, and which

colors, can escape from the screen. This results in high-resolution images and movies that look sharp and vibrant..

Look at an LCD screen close up and you may be able to see the individual pixels

FACTS: About computers

- **Binary code**
  Computers work electronically. Since electronic circuits can only be on or off, computers work by using a "binary" system. This codes all data as strings of 1's or 0's—ons or offs.

- **Bits and bytes**
  Each 1 or 0 in a computer is called a "bit," and bits are grouped together into bytes. This is why a computer's memory is measured in bytes. A kilobyte is 1,000 bytes. A megabyte is 1,000,000 bytes.

- **RAM and ROM**
  Some of a computer's memory, called the ROM (read-only memory), is built into its microchips. The RAM (random-access memory), takes new data and instructions whenever needed. Data can also be stored on flash drives that use electrical current to record and recall information at very high speeds.

▲ *Computers are often linked to the internet using WiFi technology, allowing them to send and receive data wirelessly using radio waves.*

▼ *Inside a computer are a number of microchips. At the heart is the Central Processing Unit (CPU). The CPU is what manages the computer's data, within guidelines set by the ROM, and processes and controls all the programs by sending data to the right place in the RAM.*

▶ *An optical mouse emits and then detects light, in order to know exactly how it is being moved. This information is used to control a cursor on the computer monitor.*

Fan
CPU
Graphics card
RAM chips
Disk drive
Power Supply Unit (PSU)

Solar panels provide electric power for both electronic devices and motorized tasks, such as adjusting stabilizers

Satellite and space technology depends on the sophisticated and compact control provided by electronic systems. Every spacecraft has its own onboard computers, and electronic circuits allow probes to be guided through elaborate tasks over millions of miles of space.

Radiation

RADIATION IS BASICALLY energy shot out by atoms at very high speeds. Some kinds of radiation are tiny particles splitting off from the atom. This is called radioactivity. But most radiation is tiny bursts of vibration, or "waves," such as X-rays, microwaves, radio waves, and light. Light is the only form of radiation you can see; all the rest are invisible. Radiation that comes in waves is called electromagnetic radiation because it is linked to electricity and magnetism. But the length of the waves varies. The waves in gamma rays are very short, but they pack in a lot of energy, which is why they can be dangerous. Radio waves are very long and low in energy, which is why they are used for radio broadcasts. The rest come in between.

FACTS: About radioactivity and nuclear energy

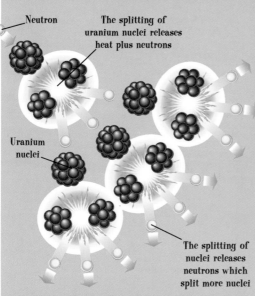

Neutron

The splitting of uranium nuclei releases heat plus neutrons

Uranium nuclei

The splitting of nuclei releases neutrons which split more nuclei

▲ Nuclear fission relies on a chain reaction between atomic nuclei. Tiny alpha particles called neutrons are fired at uranium nuclei, splitting them. This not only creates heat but sets free more neutrons which shoot away and split up more uranium nuclei, releasing more neutrons which split more uranium nuclei and so on. Control rods in the power plant absorb neutrons and prevent the chain reaction getting out of hand.

- **Radioactivity**
  Radioactivity is when an atom breaks down, or "decays," sending out radiation: lethal gamma rays (invisible electromagnetic waves) and two kinds of particle: "alpha" particles and "beta" particles.

- **Nuclear radiation**
  Nuclear bombs and energy both create radioactive material. Radioactivity from bombs is huge, controlled, and dangerous, causing death, radiation sickness, and birth defects.

- **Nuclear fission and fusion**
  In nuclear power stations, huge amounts of energy are released as heat from the nuclei of atoms by splitting them. This is called nuclear fission. Inside stars and in nuclear bombs, on the other hand, vast amounts of energy are unleashed when atomic nuclei are pushed together. This is called nuclear fusion.

▶ Nuclear bombs are the most devastatingly powerful bombs of all. They release so much energy so quickly that anything nearby is turned to dust, which billows up in a huge, mushroom-shaped cloud.

FACTS: Scans and X-rays

▼ *CT scans create a 3D picture of the inside of the body by making a complete circuit of the body along a particular "slice" with X-rays. A computer then constructs the X-ray slices into a 3D picture.*

The waves are scattered around the oven by a fan

Microwaves are created by a device called a magnetron

The patient is slid through the scanner as the X-ray gun rotates around her

▲ *Microwave ovens work by bombarding food with invisible microwaves. It is because they are electromagnetic that microwaves heat food so quickly. Molecules of water in the food are like magnets, and they are moved back and forth so quickly by the electromagnetic vibrations that they get very hot very quickly.*

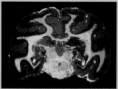

◄ *SQUID scans pick up the tiny radiation from firing nerve cells, and so show the brain working in detail.*

- X–rays

X-rays can be picked up on photos just like light, even though we can't see them. They have enough energy to pass clean through skin, but are stopped by muscle and bone. So muscle and bone show up in silhouette on an X-ray photo, giving doctors a vital view inside the body to help reveal problems.

- PET scans

PET (Positron Emission Tomography) scans detect particles called positrons to show blood moving.

 # DATA: Radiation

- **SPEED**

All electromagnetic radiation moves at the speed of light, 186,000 miles per second.

- **HALF LIFE**

Half the atoms in a bit of strontium decay radioactively in just nine mins. In uranium it takes 4.5 billion years.

- **BACKGROUND RADIATION**

Around 50 percent of the natural background radiation you are exposed to comes from radon gas seeping from rocks in the ground.

Light

LIGHT IS JUST ONE OF THE FORMS of electromagnetic radiation, but it is vital to us. It is the only form we can see–and without it we could see nothing. Plants grow by soaking up light, too, and changing it into food. And light from the Sun provides most of our warmth and energy. Yet although we are surrounded by light during the day, very few things give out light. The Sun, the stars, electric lights, and other things that glow are sources of light. But most things you see only because they reflect light from light sources. If they do not send out or reflect light, they are invisible, like air.

FACTS: About reflection and refraction

- **See-through**
  When light rays hit something, they bounce off, are absorbed, or pass through. Anything that lets light through, like glass, is "transparent." If it jumbles it on the way, like frosted glass, it is "translucent." If it stops light altogether, it is "opaque."

- **Reflection**
  When light strikes a surface, some or all is reflected. From most surfaces it scatters in all directions. But from mirrors and shiny surfaces, it bounces off in the same pattern it arrived, giving a mirror image.

- **Refraction**
  When light goes into something transparent, like glass or water, the rays are bent, or "refracted." This happens because light travels slightly slower through glass and water.

◀ The refraction (bending) of light by water makes a straw in water look as if it is bent up in the middle. Of course, it is completely straight.

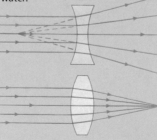

▲ When light is reflected off a mirror, it is reflected at just the same angle. The angle it hits, called the "angle of incidence," is the same as the "angle of reflection."

▲ Glass lenses are shaped so that light is refracted in certain ways. Concave lenses (above) spread them out. Convex lenses (below) focus them (bring them together).

▲ Combinations of lenses in binoculars and telescopes gather light rays together to make things look bigger and closer.

FACTS: About light waves

▲ *Most light contains a jumbled mixture of wavelengths. This is called "incoherent" light. But in laser light, all the waves are the same length and travel in step. This is called "coherent" light.*

- **Light waves**
  Light travels in waves, like ripples on a pond. The waves are tiny—2000 would fit across a pinhead.

- **Light packets**
  A light beam is made up of millions of tiny packets of energy called photons.

- **Wavelength**
  Every photon has its own distinctive wavelength. The color we see depends on the wavelengths of the photons.

- **Light from atoms**
  All light comes from atoms. When an atom is energized by, say, an electric spark or by heat, it becomes "excited" and its electrons are moved. As they settle back to their normal position, they let fire a photon.

FACTS: About color

- **Color**
  When we see different colors, we are seeing different wavelengths of light. Light that contains an equal mix of all colors, like sunlight, appears white.

- **Red buses**
  The colors of objects depend on what wavelengths they soak up and what they reflect. A red bus is red because it soaks up every color but red, and only bounces red back to your eyes.

- **Primary colors**
  You can make any color of light by mixing red, green, and blue light. You can make any color of paint by mixing cyan (a bluish color), magenta (a reddish color) and yellow paint.

▲ *Different colors are refracted different amounts. So white light splits into all the colors of the rainbow when it passes through a prism (a triangular block of glass).*

Levers & machines

IN EVERYDAY LIFE we take advantage of all kinds of machines, from toasters to TVs. But for a scientist, a machine is a device that makes life easier by reducing the effort needed to move something. There are always two forces involved in such a machine: a Load which is the force the machine is designed to overcome; and the Effort, which is the force used to move the load. The amount a machine cuts the effort you need to move a load is called the Mechanical Advantage. The mechanical advantage tells you how effective any machine is, whether it is a set of gears or a lever or a crane.

FACTS: About gears

- **How gears work**
  Gears can reduce work by spreading the effort over a greater distance. This can make it easier to cycle uphill or for a car to accelerate from a standstill. They are pairs of wheels of different sizes that turn one another. They often have interlocking teeth to avoid slipping.

- **Gear ratio**
  The number of times the wheel that is driving turns the wheel that is driven is called the gear ratio. With a ratio of 5:1, the driving wheel turns five times for every time the driven wheel turns.

▶ *Inside a gear box, there are four or five pairs of gear wheels. Changing gear means selecting the right pair to make sure the best combination of speed and force is transmitted from the engine to the wheels.*

▼ *The pedal wheel and cogs on a bicycle wheel don't actually touch, but they are gears too, for the chain connects them just like the teeth on gear wheels.*

- **Increasing force**
  With a big gear ratio, the driven wheel turns slower relative to the driving wheel. But though it turns slowly, it turns with more force. This is why you select a big gear ratio to ride a bicycle uphill. Although you have to pedal much faster, pedaling is less effort.

- **Increasing speed**
  With a small gear ratio, the driven wheel turns with less force, but turns faster. This is why you select a smaller gear ratio for riding along a level road.

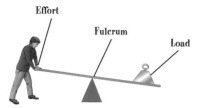

Effort · Fulcrum · Load

Some levers have the fulcrum between the load and the effort, like crowbars

Some levers have the load between the effort and the fulcrum, like wheelbarrows and screwdrivers

Some levers have the effort between the load and the fulcrum, like tweezers

A lever is a simple machine that makes it easier to move a load. If a rod is fixed at one point, but is free to swivel, it is a lever. The fixed point is called the fulcrum, and if you push on one end of the rod, your effort can be used to move a load on the other. This is called a turning effect. The further away from the fulcrum you apply your effort, and the nearer the load is, the more your efforts will be multiplied.

FACTS: About machines

- **Spreading the load**
  Machines do not give anything for nothing. The amount of effort to move a particular load is always the same. They make a load easier to move by spreading the effort over a greater distance.

- **Velocity ratio**
  The distance moved by the effort you apply divided by the distance moved by the load is called the velocity ratio. If the velocity ratio is greater than 1, the effort moves farther than the load. So you need less effort to move the load, but you have to apply it for longer.

- **Work**
  The sum of the effort you put in to move something is called the "work." Work is basically the force you apply multiplied by the distance the load moves. Moving a load of 1 pound over 10 feet always requires the same amount of work.

▼ *A mechanical digger uses powerful hydraulic (fluid-filled) systems to move its digging arms, but the same mechanical principles apply. The arms are levers and give the same mechanical advantage.*

Force & motion

A FORCE IS SIMPLY SOMETHING that pushes or pulls. Without forces, nothing in the Universe would happen. Every object in the universe has its own "inertia"–that is, it will not move unless it is forced to. So if something is moving, you can be sure it has been pushed or pulled. Similarly, once it is moving, it will go on moving forever, at the same rate and in the same direction, unless some force slows it down or speeds it up or pushes or pulls it off course. This is called "momentum." It is because heavy, fast-moving objects have a great deal of momentum that car crashes do so much damage.

FACTS: About gravity

• **Universal pull**
Gravity is the force of attraction that holds us all on the ground and holds the Universe together. In fact, every bit of matter in the Universe has its own gravitational pull and attracts every other bit of matter. The strength of the pull depends on how massive things are and how far they are apart. Massive objects nearby exert a strong gravitational pull. Light objects far away exert little pull.

▼ *When you kick a soccer ball, at first the power of your kick overcomes air resistance and gravity, and the ball climbs. But after a while, air resistance slows the ball and gravity pulls the ball down to the ground. So it loops through the air.*

▶ *A tightrope walker can balance on the high wire when gravity pulls down equally on each side. This happens when the exact middle of his weight, called the "center of gravity," is directly over the wire.*

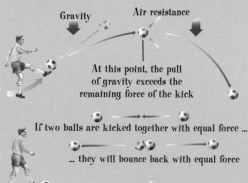

Gravity   Air resistance

At this point, the pull of gravity exceeds the remaining force of the kick

If two balls are kicked together with equal force ...

... they will bounce back with equal force

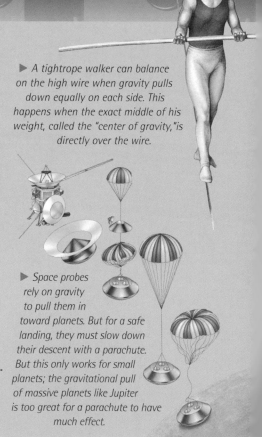

▶ *Space probes rely on gravity to pull them in toward planets. But for a safe landing, they must slow down their descent with a parachute. But this only works for small planets; the gravitational pull of massive planets like Jupiter is too great for a parachute to have much effect.*

When you measure the weight of an apple on a spring balance—or any other way—you are simply measuring the pull of gravity. The heavier the apple is—that is, the more mass it has — the more strongly it is pulled by the Earth's gravity, and so the farther it stretches the spring on the spring balance, which indicates its weight.

FACTS: Newton's Laws

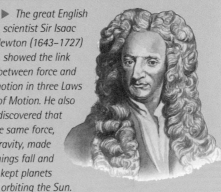

▶ The great English scientist Sir Isaac Newton (1643–1727) showed the link between force and motion in three Laws of Motion. He also discovered that the same force, gravity, made things fall and kept planets orbiting the Sun.

- **Mass and weight**
  When an object is heavy, we talk of its weight. But scientists use the word "mass." Mass is how much matter it contains. They use weight only for the force of gravity— that is, how strongly an object pulls or is pulled by gravity.

- **Acceleration by gravity**
  Like all forces, gravity makes things accelerate. So when things fall, they gain speed as they go down. On Earth they get faster at 9.8 m per sec.

- **Terminal velocity**
  As objects fall faster, the resistance of the air has more effect. Eventually, air resistance equals the pull of gravity and the object can fall no faster. It then falls at a steady speed. This speed is called the object's "terminal velocity."

- **Newton's First Law of Motion**
  Newton's First Law is about how an object accelerates (or decelerates) only when a force is applied.

- **Newton's Second Law of Motion**
  The Second Law is that the acceleration depends on the size of the force and the object's mass.

- **Newton's Third Law of Motion**
  The Third Law is that when a force pushes or acts one way, an equal force pushes in the opposite direction.

- **Dynamics and statics**
  The study of the way objects move when acted upon by forces is called dynamics. The study of things that do not move is called statics.

▼ Newton's laws work for every thing larger than an atom that moves in the Universe, from an opening bud to a speeding truck.

Energy

FOR ANYTHING TO HAPPEN, for things to move or even change–for chocolate to melt or a rocket to fly–you need energy. Scientists say energy is "the capacity to do work," and by this they simply mean energy makes things happen. It comes in many forms, from the chemical energy locked in sugar to the mechanical energy in a moving truck. But it always works in two ways: transfer or conversion. Energy transfer simply means it is moving from one place to another, like heat going up a chimney or a baseball being hit. Energy conversion occurs when it changes from one form to another–from steam-powered turbines to electric power in power stations, for instance.

FACTS: About solar energy

- **Solar power**
  Energy that arrives as light from the Sun gives us virtually all our energy, either directly by its warmth or indirectly by, for instance, providing the energy to grow plants that are eventually converted into coal for burning.

- **Solar panels and cells**
  Solar panels provide heat as water, sandwiched between sheets of glass, is heated by the Sun. Solar cells are light-sensitive chemicals that generate an electric current when hit by light.

▶ *Each solar cell generates only a tiny electric current, but connecting hundreds together can create a significant amount of electricity.*

▼ *Honda's record-breaking experimental solar-powered car showed just what could be done with a car run entirely on sunlight.*

▼ *Less than half the energy from the Sun that strikes the Earth reaches the ground, as 53% of it is absorbed or reflected on the way down through the atmosphere: 16% is soaked up by water vapor and dust in the air; 7% is scattered by the air; 3% is soaked up by clouds; 23% is reflected off clouds; and 4% is reflected by the land and oceans.*

Almost a quarter of the sunlight reaching Earth is reflected away off clouds.

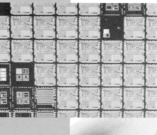

FACTS: Renewable energy

▲ To build up water pressure to turn the turbines and to even the flow, most hydroelectric power stations are built inside big dams.

- **Alternative energy**
Fossil fuels are irreplaccable and pollute the air, so there is a search for clean, renewable alternatives, including electricity generated by winds, the Sun (solar power), the tides, or waves.

- **Hydroelectric power (HEP)**
HEP is electricity generated by turbines turned by water. It is the only major alternative energy source.

FACTS: Energy sources

- **Fossil fuels**
90 percent of our energy comes from fossil fuels. About 40% comes from oil, 27% from coal, and 21% from natural gas. These sources are effectively non-renewable, since they took millions of years to make. So all the world's fossil fuels will eventually be used up.

- **Nuclear energy**
Nuclear energy is also non-renewable, but it uses fuel such as uranium so slowly that it will not run out in the near future. Unfortunately, it leaves a dangerous radioactive waste.

▲ When cars burn gasoline, they not only use up a non-renewable source of energy, they also fill the air with polluting exhaust fumes such as nitrous oxides.

Just 47% of sunlight is absorbed by the ground

◀ Flowers and other plants get their energy directly from sunlight in a process called photosynthesis. This allows them to use carbon dioxide in the air to create the energy-rich chemical sugars they need for growth. Humans, like animals, have to get their energy indirectly, by eating plants—or by eating animals that have themselves eaten plants.

Heat

HEAT IS NOT JUST THE WARMTH of the Sun or a fire; it is a form of energy, the energy of molecules moving. The faster molecules move, the hotter things are. When you feel the heat of a fire, you are simply being battered by millions of fast-moving air molecules–hurried up by millions of even faster-moving molecules in the fire. The fire heats the air because heat always spreads out, and something hot always makes its surroundings warm, too, as it itself loses heat and cools down. We measure how hot something is by its temperature. But temperature is just a measure of how fast the molecules are moving; heat is the total energy of all the moving molecules.

FACTS: About conduction, radiation and convection

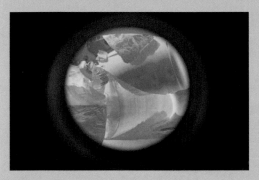

• **Convection**
Convection occurs when warm air rises through cool air, like a hot-air balloon. It rises because the warmth makes it expand, and so it becomes less dense and lighter than the cooler air around.

◄ *Infra-red radiation from the intense heat caused by silicon crystal meltdown.*

▼ *The heat of a candle flame heats up a nearby thermometer mainly by radiation, which travels in waves, just like light.*

• **Spreading heat**
Heat spreads in three ways: conduction, radiation and convection.

• **Conduction**
Conduction is the spread of heat through substances by direct contact—kind of like a relay race, as vibrating molecules cannon into their neighbors and set them moving, too. Good conducting materials like metals feel cool because they carry heat away quickly.

• **Radiation**
Radiation is the spread of heat as heat rays—invisible "infrared" electromagnetic radiation. Radiation moves through space spreading heat without direct contact.

FACTS: Pressure and heat

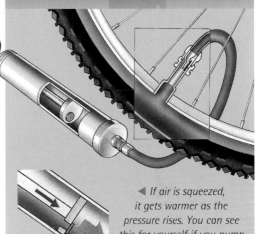

◀ Heat makes things expand. So thermometers can measure temperature by showing how much a liquid such as colored alcohol expands and rises up a tube. Everyday temperatures are measured in degrees— Fahrenheit (°F) or Centigrade (°C). Water freezes at 32°F which is also 0°C. Water boils at 212°F (100°C). The temperature of the surface of the Sun is about 10,000°F. Scientists use a scale called the Kelvin Scale, which starts at -459°F, so they would say that the Sun's surface temperature is around 5,800 K .

◀ If air is squeezed, it gets warmer as the pressure rises. You can see this for yourself if you pump up a bicycle tyre quickly. After a few pumps, it will feel quite warm. The pump works by squeezing air down through the tube with a plunger as you push down. On the upstroke, a one-way valve lets more air in.

- **What is pressure?**
  Pressure is the way water and air push against their surroundings. Molecules in air and water are always zooming about, and the pushing is actually all the molecules smashing into their surroundings.

- **Rising pressure**
  When air is squeezed, its pressure rises in proportion, because more molecules are squeezed into a smaller space. This is called Boyle's Law.

- **Heat and pressure**
  If air cannot expand, heating it up boosts its pressure in proportion, because heat makes the molecules zoom about faster and smash harder into their surroundings. But if it can expand, it swells in proportion instead. This is Charles's Law.

DATA: Temperatures

- **LOWEST TEMPERATURE**
  The lowest possible temperature is -468.67°F, when all molecules stop moving. This is called Absolute Zero. The lowest recorded on Earth was -128.56°F.

- **HIGHEST TEMPERATURE**
  The highest temperature may be 36 million°F in the heart of stars. The highest on Earth was 134°F.

Solids, liquids, & gases

NEARLY EVERY SUBSTANCE IN THE UNIVERSE is either a solid, a liquid, or a gas. These are said to be the three states of matter. They seem very different, but every substance can change from one to the other and back again, providing the temperature and pressure are right. Just as ice melts to water and water turns to steam when it gets hot, so every substance changes from solid to liquid to gas at certain temperatures. The temperature at which a substance melts from solid to liquid is called its melting point. The highest temperature a liquid can reach before turning to a gas is its boiling point.

FACTS: Three states of matter

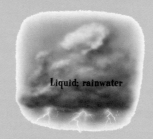

Gas: water vapor

Liquid: rainwater

Solid: ice

◀ A gas, like air, does not have any shape, strength, or fixed volume. This is because its molecules are moving fast enough to break the bonds that try to hold them together.

◀ A liquid flows and takes up the shape of any container it is poured into. This is because although bonds hold the molecules together, they are loose enough to fall over each other like dry sand.

◀ A solid has strength and a definite shape. This is because its molecules are bonded together firmly in a regular structure, and simply vibrate on the spot. The hotter it gets, the more they vibrate.

- **Melting**
  In a solid, molecules are held together tightly by bonds and simply vibrate on the spot. Heat makes them vibrate faster, until the bonds loosen. Eventually they become so loose that the neat structure breaks down, and the substance melts and flows all over the place.

- **Boiling**
  If the temperature goes on rising, the heat makes molecules zoom all over the place, until they move so fast that the molecules break away altogether. More and more molecules start shooting away from the surface as gas or steam. Eventually, all the liquid turns to gas.

172

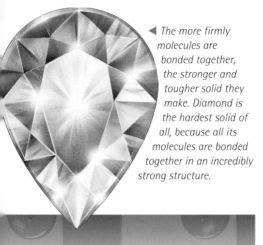

◄ The more firmly molecules are bonded together, the stronger and tougher solid they make. Diamond is the hardest solid of all, because all its molecules are bonded together in an incredibly strong structure.

FACTS: About solutions

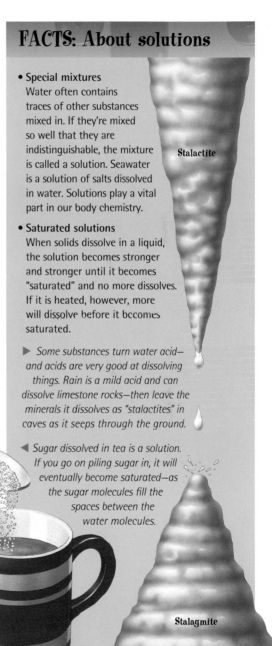

Stalactite

- **Evaporation**
  As a liquid heats up, more and more of its molecules break away from the surface, turning it to gas. This is called evaporation. When clothes dry, it is because water evaporates from them.

- **Condensation**
  When a gas cools, molecules slow down until bonds form between them, forming drops of liquid. This is called condensation. Water condensing from the air is called dew.

- **Ice, water, and water vapor**
  Water is the only substance commonly found in all three states: solid ice, liquid water, and gas. Water is called water vapor when it is a gas. Steam is actually lots of tiny drops of liquid water in air. Only when these drops evaporate does it turn to water vapor.

- **Space saving**
  Substances get smaller when they freeze as molecules pack tighter—except water. Water expands when it freezes, which is why ice bursts water pipes. It is also why ice floats, as it is less dense than water.

- **Special mixtures**
  Water often contains traces of other substances mixed in. If they're mixed so well that they are indistinguishable, the mixture is called a solution. Seawater is a solution of salts dissolved in water. Solutions play a vital part in our body chemistry.

- **Saturated solutions**
  When solids dissolve in a liquid, the solution becomes stronger and stronger until it becomes "saturated" and no more dissolves. If it is heated, however, more will dissolve before it becomes saturated.

▶ Some substances turn water acid— and acids are very good at dissolving things. Rain is a mild acid and can dissolve limestone rocks—then leave the minerals it dissolves as "stalactites" in caves as it seeps through the ground.

◄ Sugar dissolved in tea is a solution. If you go on piling sugar in, it will eventually become saturated—as the sugar molecules fill the spaces between the water molecules.

Stalagmite

Matter

MATTER IS EVERY SUBSTANCE in the Universe, from the tiniest speck of dust to the largest star–everything that is not simply empty space. Surprisingly, though, even the most solid-looking matter is mostly empty space too, for matter is made from tiny pieces called atoms. You cannot see them, or the space between them, because they are amazingly small. You could fit two billion atoms on the period at the end of this sentence. Scientists once thought they were the smallest things in the Universe–and that they were like tiny balls that could never be split or destroyed. But they are more like clouds of energy, and they too are mostly empty space, dotted with even tinier "subatomic particles."

FACTS: About atoms and subatomic particles

- **The atomic nucleus**
  The core of an atom is a cluster or "nucleus" of two kinds of particle: protons and neutrons. Protons have a positive electrical charge. Neutrons have none.

◀ *Protons are made from clusters of three quarks, held together by gluons. There are actually six different kinds of quark but only two–"up" quarks and "down" quarks–are long-lived, and this is what protons are made of.*

- **Electrons**
  Whizzing round the nucleus as fast as the speed of light are even lighter particles called electrons. Electrons are negatively charged.

▶ *Atoms are not really like this. All the particles are really just clusters of energy that probably only occur in certain places. But this is a good way to imagine them, with electrons whizzing round the nucleus.*

- **Atoms and ions**
  Most atoms have identical numbers of protons and electrons, so the electrical charges balance. An ion is an atom that has either lost or gained electrons, so it may be either positively or negatively charged.

- **Short-lived particles**
  By smashing atoms together at high speeds, scientists have found over 200 subatomic particles besides electrons, protons, and neutrons, but most of these last only a fraction of a second.

- **Quarks and leptons**
  Scientists believe that all particles are made from just two basic kinds: quarks and leptons. Electrons are leptons. Protons and neutrons are made from different 'flavors' of quark.

- **Atomic forces**
  Atoms can be split, but are usually held together by three forces—the electrical attraction between negative electrons and positive protons, and the "strong" and "weak" nuclear forces that bind together the particles of the nucleus. These forces, together with gravity, are the basic forces that hold the Universe together.

FACTS: About crystals

- **Crystal shapes**
  Crystals are hard, shiny solids formed in regular geometric shapes. Grains of salt, sugar, and sand are all crystals. So are diamonds. Each is made from a very regular structure of atoms, ions, or molecules.

- **Crystallization**
  When melted substances turn solid or dissolved substances leave solutions, they form crystals. This is called crystallization.

- **Crystallography**
  Crystallography is the study of crystals, usually using X-rays.

▲ *Most hard substances are crystals. A powerful microscope reveals the regular structure of crystals of sulphur. The colors are computerized.*

Water molecule

◀ *Atoms rarely exist alone. Usually they join up in small groups called molecules. Hydrogen atoms, for instance, exist in pairs or joined to other atoms. A molecule of hydrogen gas is a pair of hydrogen atoms. A water molecule is a pair of hydrogen atoms joined to an oxygen atom.*

Nucleus of protons and atoms

Around the nucleus whirl clouds of tiny negatively charged electrons

▶ *The study of matter is called chemistry. In the past most chemistry was done in laboratories— boiling and mixing chemicals in flasks and test tubes. Now a great deal of chemistry is done on computers, constructing molecules in cyberspace. In this way chemists have been able to create entirely new chemicals.*

The elements

ALL THE SUBSTANCES IN THE UNIVERSE are made up from 100 or so basic chemicals, or "elements," such as gold and oxygen.
Each element has its own unique character–and its own special atoms.
Each element has a different number of protons and electrons in its atoms, from hydrogen with one of each to lawrencium with 103. The number of protons and electrons in their atoms is really the only difference between the elements, but this difference has a huge effect on their nature. Nitrogen gas atoms, for instance, have seven protons and carbon have six, just one less, but they are totally different.

FACTS: Groups and Periods

- **Rows and columns**
  The Periodic Table of elements is laid out in rows called Periods and columns called Groups.

- **Electron shells**
  Electrons spin around atoms in up to 7 layers, or "shells." There is a limit to how many electrons can fit in each shell. Only 2 fit in the first shell, closest to the nucleus, 8 in the second, and 8 in the third. After that it gets complicated, but the outer shell never holds more than 8.

- **Shells and Periods**
  The number of electron shells an atom has increases down each Group. So every atom in each Period has the same number of electron shells. What varies is the number of electrons.

- **Electrons and Groups**
  Each Group is for elements with a certain number of electrons in their outer shells—and this is what determines an element's chemical properties. Every element in the same Group has similar properties.

- **Reactive to stable**
  Each Period starts on the left with a highly reactive "alkali metal" that has one electron in its outer shell. It ends on the right with a stable "noble gas," such as argon, which has eight electrons in its outer shell.

▼ All the elements can be displayed in order on a chart called the Periodic Table. The number of protons an element has in each of its atoms is called its Atomic Number, and the chart lists elements in Atomic Number order, starting with hydrogen at 1.

H
hydrogen
1

Above the name for each element is its abbreviation, or "formula": below is the Atomic Number

Li lithium 3	Be beryllium 4

The block of elements in the middle (yellow) is called the Transition metals

Na sodium 11	Mg magnesium 12

K potassium 19	Ca calcium 20	Sc scandium 21	Ti titanium 22	V vanadium 23	Cr chromium 24	Mn manganese 25	Fe iron 26	Co cobalt 27
Rb rubidium 37	Sr strontium 38	Y yttrium 39	Zr zirconium 40	Nb niobium 41	Mo molybdenum 42	Tc technetium 43	Ru ruthenium 44	Rh rhodium 45
Cs caesium 55	Ba barium 56	La lanthanum 57	Hf hafnium 72	Ta tantalum 73	W tungsten 74	Re rhenium 75	Os osmium 76	Ir iridium 77
Fr francium 87	Ra radium 88	Ac actinium 89						

This Group is called Alkali metals

This is the Alkaline-Earth Group

Ce cerium 58	Pr praseodymium 59	Nd neodymium 60	Pm promethium 61	Sm samarium 62
Th thorium 90	Pa protactinium 91	U uranium 92	Np neptunium 93	Pu plutonium 94

This row, called the lanthanides or rare earths, fits into Group 3

176

FACTS: About atomic mass and formulae

- **Atomic mass**
  Atomic mass is the "weight" of an atom of an element and corresponds to the average number of protons and neutrons in the nucleus.

- **Formula**
  Every element has a short name, or formula. Carbon is C, Hydrogen is H, Copper Cu, and so on.

▲ *Atoms of gold have 79 protons in their nuclei, and, on average, 118 neutrons. So its (relative) atomic mass is 197. The formula for gold is Au.*

These elements (purple) are called non-metals.

As the Atomic Numbers increase by one along each period, so the chemical properties change

These elements (blue) are called poor metals

The final Group on the right is the noble gases

He helium 2

B boron 5	C carbon 6	N nitrogen 7	O oxygen 8	F fluorine 9	Ne neon 10
Al aluminium 13	Si silicon 14	P phosphorus 15	S sulphur 16	Cl chlorine 17	Ar argon 18

Ni nickel 28	Cu copper 29	Zn zinc 30	Ga gallium 31	Ge germanium 32	As arsenic 33	Se selenium 34	Br bromine 35	Kr krypton 36
Pd palladium 46	Ag silver 47	Cd cadmium 48	In indium 49	Sn tin 50	Sb antimony 51	Te tellurium 52	I iodine 53	Xe xenon 54
Pt platinum 78	Au gold 79	Hg mercury 80	Ti thalium 81	Pb lead 82	Bi bismuth 83	Po polonium 84	At astatine 85	Rn radon 86

Eu europium 63	Gd gadolinium 64	Tb terbium 65	Dy dysprosium 66	Ho holmium 67	Er erbium 68	Tm thulium 69	Yb ytterbium 70	Lu lutetium 71
Am mericium 95	Cm curium 96	Bk berkelium 97	Cf californium 98	Es einsteinium 99	Fm fermium 100	Md mendelevium 101	No nobelium 102	Lr lawrencium 103

This row, called the actinides, fits into Group 3

FACTS: About metals

- **Metals**
  Metals are hard, dense, shiny solids. They conduct heat well. They are also good conductors of electricity because they are electropositive, which means electrons easily become "free."

- **Transition metals**
  Transition metals are metals in the middle of the Table like gold—shiny and tough, but easily shaped.

- **Lanthanides or rare earths**
  These silvery metals are called rare earths because they were once thought too reactive to stay in the ground unmixed with other elements for long.

FACTS: About noble gases

- **Nobly aloof**
  Group 0 is the far right group, called the noble gases. The outer shells of their atoms are filled up, so they do not react with other elements. They are sometimes called inert gases.

- **Bulb gases**
  Noble gases like argon and krypton are used in light bulbs because they are unreactive.

Chemicals & compounds

SOME SUBSTANCES, like gold, are made of just one element. Most are made of two or more elements joined together to make what is called a compound. Table salt, for instance, is a compound of the two elements, sodium and chlorine. A compound is usually very different in nature from the two elements that make it up. Sodium, for instance, is a metal that fizzes and gets hot when dropped in water; chlorine is a thick, green gas.

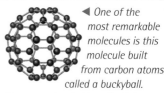

◀ One of the most remarkable molecules is this molecule built from carbon atoms called a buckyball. It was constructed by scientists as an experiment but may well have practical uses in the future.

FACTS: About chemical bonds

Atomic nucleus

Electrons in their shells

Sodium atom gives up an electron

Mutual electric attraction

Shared electrons

▲ Atoms are only stable when they have a full set of 8 electrons in their outer shells. Atoms that have too many or too few can get a full set by sharing electrons with other atoms. This makes a covalent bond.

Chlorine atom gains an electron

- Valency
Each atom joins only with a certain number of others—as if each only has so many hooks it can hang others on. This number is called its "valency."

- Chemical bonds
There are two main ways elements can combine: by sharing electrons in what are called "covalent bonds," or by losing or gaining them in "ionic bonds." "Metallic bonds" occur between huge numbers of atoms in a giant metallic lattice.

- Ionic bonds
Ionic bonds occur when atoms with just a few electrons in their outer shells donate them to atoms

▲ In ionic bonds, one atom donates an electron to another and so becomes negatively charged. The atoms are then bonded by mutual electrical attraction. This is what joins sodium atoms to chlorine atoms in salt.

with just a few missing from theirs. This makes the atom losing electrons positively charged and the other negatively charged (page 170)—so they stick together by electrical attraction.

- Covalent bonds
In covalent bonds, atoms share electrons. In water, two hydrogen atoms share electrons with one oxygen.

178

▲ Some substances make acids when they dissolve in water. Weak acids, like lemon juice or vinegar, taste tart. Strong ones, like sulfuric acids, are highly corrosive, burning, stinging, and even dissolving metals. The opposites of acids are bases, known as alkalis when dissolved in water. Weak bases like baking powder taste bitter and feel soapy. Strong ones, like caustic soda, are as corrosive as acids. Chemists use "indicators" such as litmus paper to test for acidity. Acids turn the paper red. Alkalis turn it blue.

▼ Strong acids are dangerous, but they can be useful in many ways. Sulfuric acid is used to make everything from fertilizers to paints. Crystals of salicylic acid (below), which occur naturally in willow trees, are used to make aspirin.

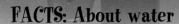

FACTS: About water

▶ Water molecules are made from two hydrogen atoms and an oxygen atom arranged in a V-shape. This is why the chemical formula is H_2O.

• **Water poles**
Water molecules are special. In sharing electrons with an oxygen atom, the electrons on each hydrogen atom are tugged to the side nearest the oxygen—leaving the far side "bare," and exposing the positively charged nucleus. This gives water molecules a + (positive) and a - (negative) end, and so they are called polar molecules.

• **Hydrogen bonds**
Pairs of water molecules bind together as + ends are drawn to - ends. These "hydrogen" bonds keep water liquid to 212°F, at which heat most similar substances are gases.

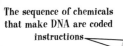

The sequence of chemicals that make DNA are coded instructions.

▲ The element carbon forms thousands of different compounds. Indeed, most of the "organic" compounds on which life depends are carbon compounds. The most remarkable of these is deoxyribonucleic acid, or DNA. DNA forms long molecules shaped like a twisted rope ladder. In the pattern of its rungs, DNA carries complete coded instructions for life—for everything from how a plant is to grow, to what color your eyes should be.

Amazing Questions

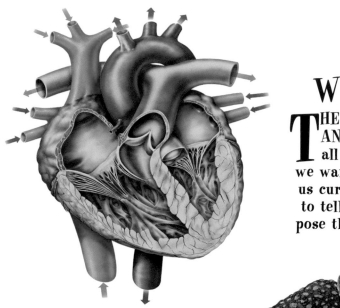

1. How many chambers has the heart?

Why questions?

THE WORLD IS A WONDERFUL AND FASCINATING PLACE, and yet all too often we are told not what we want to know about—what makes us curious—but what someone wants to tell us about. In this section, we pose the kinds of questions that you

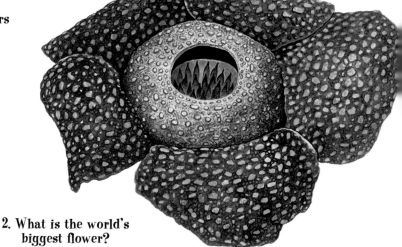

2. What is the world's biggest flower?

3. What's the smallest planet?

4. What's the Earth's core made of?

5. What's the smallest part of an element?

might ask if you had the chance–and answer these. On every spread too, there is a series of questions that we ask you–to give you a chance to test your general knowledge–or to challenge your friends and family. Here are some to get you going.

6. What is the world's biggest reptile?

How did scabious
get its name?

There are exploding
cucumbers in the
jungle: true or
false?

What tree is the
national symbol of
Canada?

Can plants cure
cancer?

What plant has t
different flowers

Where does chocolate
come from?

Which woodland
plant is good for a
kiss?

What plant amputates its own branches?

Plants

What plants have their own water tanks?

What is the strongest rope in the jungle?

Why don't all trees lose their leaves?

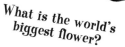

What is the world's biggest flower?

183

Plants of all kinds

What are plants?

THERE ARE OVER 400,000 KINDS of plants around the world, ranging from tiny single-celled organisms to giant trees, the largest living things. Most have green leaves and can make their own food from sunlight, which is why most don't need to move around like animals. But some microscopic plants can move like animals, even though they can make their own food, while others cannot move, but steal food from other plants.

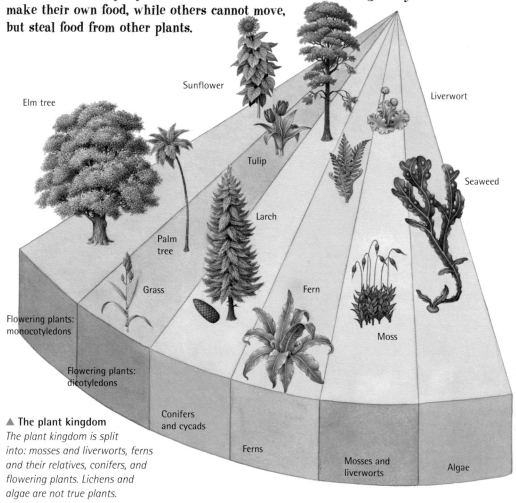

Sunflower

Elm tree

Liverwort

Tulip

Seaweed

Larch

Palm tree

Grass

Fern

Moss

Flowering plants: monocotyledons

Flowering plants: dicotyledons

Conifers and cycads

Ferns

Mosses and liverworts

Algae

▲ **The plant kingdom**
The plant kingdom is split into: mosses and liverworts, ferns and their relatives, conifers, and flowering plants. Lichens and algae are not true plants.

▶ Flowering tree
Deciduous trees like this bottlebrush are among over 400,000 species of flowering plants.

What is a flowering plant?

Flowering plants are plants that have flowers to make the seeds and fruits from which new plants will eventually grow. This doesn't only mean garden and wild flowers, but every herb, grass, fruit, shrub, and vegetable—all of which have tiny flowers. Another name for flowering plants is angiosperms.

Are any big plants not flowering plants?

Yes. Plants that make their seeds in cones, rather than in flowers. These cone-bearing plants, or conifers, are also known as gymnosperms. They include trees such as pines.

What are monocotyledons?

Flowering plants are either monocotyledons or dicotyledons. Monocotyledons begin from seeds with just a single leaf. They also tend to have longer, narrower leaves, like grasses, tulips, and daffodils. Dicotyledons start with two or more leaves from their seeds. Most flowering plants are dicotyledons.

Do all plants grow from seeds?

No, only flowering plants and conifers do. Ferns and mosses grow from tiny cells called spores, which can be seen only under a microscope.

Why are plants green?

Plants are green because they contain a green substance called chlorophyll. This plays a vital role in photosynthesis, the process by which plants make their food by absorbing sunlight. In photosynthesis, the plant changes carbon dioxide from the air, and hydrogen from water, into energy-giving sugars.

What is the stem?

A plant's stem not only supports the flowers and leaves; it is also a pipe to take water, minerals, and food up and down between the leaves and the roots. Water goes up through tubes called xylem. Food goes down to the roots through tubes called phloem. In herbaceous plants, the stem is soft and green. In woody plants like trees it is stiff and often covered with bark.

◀ Conifer
Conifers like pines are among the oldest of all plants, appearing 275 million years ago.

QUIZ

1 What are the biggest plants?

2 Seaweeds are a kind of algae: true or false?

3 How do plants get water?

4 Some plants eat meat: true or false?

5 Plants that take their food from other plants are called a) felons b) parasites c) clingers?

6 Some ferns can grow as big as trees, over 82 feet tall: true or false?

7 Plant spores can survive in outer space: true or false?

8 The oldest known plant is a creosote plant in California. It is thought to be: a) 250 years old, b) 1,260 years old c) 11,700 years old?

Answers
1. Trees; 2. True; 3. Through their roots; 4. True; 5. b)
6. True; 7. True; 8. c)

Flowering plants

What are flowering plants?

FLOWERING PLANTS are not just garden flowers and wild flowers with pretty blooms, but every herb, grass, shrub, tree, fruit, and vegetable, too. Indeed, nearly every plant except ferns, mosses, lichens and fungi is a flowering plant. The flowers may not be obvious, but all have flowers which create the seeds and fruits from which new plants will grow.

▲ **The largest seeds**
The largest seeds are double coconuts, weighing up to 40 pounds.

How do flowers make seeds?

Just as there are male and female animals, so a flower has male parts, known as stamens, and female parts, known as pistils. Seeds for new plants are made when pollen from the stamens meets eggs in the pistils.

Where are a flower's sex organs?

The female parts, or pistil, containing the ovaries where eggs are made, make up the thick, short stalk in the middle of the flower. The male parts, or stamens, which make pollen, are the spindly stalks around it.

Can flowers pollinate themselves?

Many flowers have both male and female parts. So some flowers can indeed pollinate themselves, and the pollen moves from the stamens to the pistil on the same plant. This is called self-pollination. Most flowers, however, are cross-pollinating. This means the pollen must be carried from the stamens of one plant to the pistil of another plant of the same kind.

Why are flowers such pretty colors?

Some flowers' pollen spreads on the wind. But others rely on insects such as bees and butterflies, or even birds and bats, to help them spread their pollen. Bright colors draw the bees to the flower to sip the flower's sweet juice or nectar. As they sip, they brush the flower's stamens and pick up pollen, which they carry to the next flower they sip.

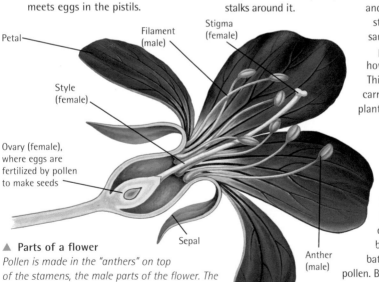

Petal

Filament (male)

Stigma (female)

Style (female)

Ovary (female), where eggs are fertilized by pollen to make seeds

Sepal

Anther (male)

▲ **Parts of a flower**
Pollen is made in the "anthers" on top of the stamens, the male parts of the flower. The female part, or pistil, is topped by a sticky "stigma," which traps the pollen. A long tube, or "style," takes it down to the ovary, where it meets the eggs to create the seeds.

186

Waxwing

Jay

◀ Seed spreaders
Some seeds are spread by the wind in feathery seed cases. But many are spread by insects, birds, and other animals. Birds like these eat fruits, and are drawn by their color. They digest the flesh, but the hard seed passes through the bird and emerges ready for germination.

Are fruits seeds?
No, they develop from the flower's ovary—and the hard pips inside are the seeds. Juicy fruits such as berries are called "true fruits" because they are made from the flower's ovaries alone. Apples and pears are "false" fruits because only the core is made from the ovary. Plums and cherries are "drupes" in which there are no pips, but the seed is held in a hard shell.

Are any vegetables fruits?
Potatoes and other root vegetables are plant roots, not seeds. But peas, beans, and other "legumes" are actually fruit, and the seeds are the peas and beans inside the pod.

How do seeds grow?
Each seed is the germ (start) of a new plant and contains the food it needs to help it germinate (grow into a plant). Growth starts with just a single root, or radicle, which grows down into the soil, and a single green shoot, or plumule, which grows up toward the Sun. Then the plant's seed leaves—its first leaves, like baby teeth—appear. Soon after, the main stem begins to grow, and true leaves sprout from this.

➤ Date palm
The sweet, sticky fruit of the date palm looks a little like a plum, but it is not a drupe. The stone of a date is actually the seed for a new tree, not the seed container like the plum stone.

QUIZ

1 How many pollen grains can a single American ragweed make in a day: a) 1,000 b) 100,000 c) 1 billion?

2 The flowers of the baobab tree are pollinated by bush babies: true or false?

3 How old are most oak trees before they start to produce acorns a) 4 months b) 4 years c) 40 years?

4 Are any seeds poisonous?

5 Do any flowers bloom just for a day?

6 What are the smallest seeds?

7 What are the world's oldest flowers?

6. Orchids; 7. Magnolias
glory and the day lily;
by birds; 5. Yes, like morning
save them from being eaten
1. c) 2. True; 3. c) 4. Yes, to
Answers

187

Trees and shrubs

What are trees?

ALTHOUGH SOME DWARF WILLOWS are just an inch or two high, most trees are much bigger; trees are the biggest of all plants. The biggest trees are the world's biggest living things, as tall as a skyscraper. They can grow big because they have huge numbers of leaves and hard, woody stems covered with a protective layer of bark.

What are conifers?

Conifers are among the oldest of all plants, first appearing over 275 million years ago. They get their name from the fact that they rely on cones rather than flowers to make the seeds for new trees. They usually grow tall and straight with hardly any big side-branches and, unlike "broad-leaved" trees, they tend to have narrow, needle-like leaves.

What is an evergreen?

An evergreen is a tree that keeps its leaves all year round. Each leaf lasts for years, and is usually a dark, waxy green. The leaves of trees that lose their leaves each year, called deciduous trees, are a lighter, yellow green.

▶ Going red

As days grow shorter and colder in autumn, the chlorophyll that makes leaves green breaks down in deciduous trees like the maple. This allows other colors—yellows, reds, browns, and golds—to shine through, giving the trees their beautiful fall hues.

Why do some trees lose their leaves every year?

Deciduous trees like oaks, ashes, and elms shed their leaves to cut down on moisture loss in seasons when water is harder to come by. In the tropics, they lose their leaves at the start of the dry season. In temperate regions, between the tropics and the poles, they lose them in autumn because water is much harder to come by in winter.

Why don't all trees lose their leaves?

In warm, moist places, like tropical rain forests, moisture is available all year round, so even broad-leaved trees can keep their leaves all year round. Conifers, too, can keep their leaves, because their narrow needles do not lose moisture nearly as quickly as the big leaves of broad-leaved trees, so they can survive through the winter, when water is short.

What are tree rings?

If a tree is cut across the trunk, you can see the trunk is marked by a series of rings called growth rings. These show how the tree has grown each year. The edge of the ring marks where growth ceased in winter. By counting the rings, you can tell how old a tree is. You can also tell whether a summer was good or bad for tree growth from just how wide each of the rings is.

What is heartwood?

Heartwood is the dark, dense dead wood found in the center of a tree trunk. It is surrounded by lighter, living "sapwood" which carries all the tubes that feed moisture and nourishment to the tree's leaves.

Life in a tree
An oak tree like this is home to countless animals and plants. Birds nest on branches and in holes, insects feed on the leaves and burrow in the bark, and fungi and ivy grow on the trunk.

Jay

Tawny owl

Woodpecker

Stag beetle

Ivy

Bracket fungi

QUIZ

1 The giant sequoia tree in California is the world's biggest living thing. Is it a) 138 feet b) 276 feet c) 505 feet tall?

2 Every tree can be identified by its leaves: true or false?

3 What tree is the national symbol of Canada?

4 What is the seed of the oak tree called?

5 Can trees warn other trees of caterpillar attacks?

6 Is the eucalyptus of Tasmania commonly known as a a) gum tree b) oil tree c) glue tree?

7 Are the pipes that carry a tree's sap called a) reeds b) xylem c) xylophones?

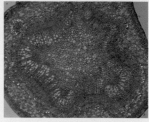

Answers
1. b) 2. True; 3. Maple;
4. Acorn; 5. Yes, willows
and alders send out airborne
chemicals; 6. a) 7. b)

189

Plants for food

What food do plants give?

PLANTS GIVE most of the world's people their "staple" food, the basic food they need for survival–whether it is bread, or oatmeal or soybeans. Fruit and vegetables provide us with most of the vitamins we need to keep us healthy. They also make some of the most delicious foods and drinks, from cherry pie to orange juice.

Why do we eat grass?
Cereals are the world's most important foods—including wheat, rice, corn, barley, oats, and rye—and they are all grasses. We usually eat their seeds, or "grain," leaving the stalks and leaves to rot to make silage to feed animals.

What is wheat?
Wheat is the most important of the cereals. It was first cultivated in the Middle East 12,000 years ago from the wild grass emmer. Now it provides the basic food for more than a third of the world's population. Wheat grain is usually ground into flour to make bread and pasta and many other things.

What was the Green Revolution?
From the 1940s, farmers in Europe and North America began growing special "high-yield" varieties of wheat, rice, and corn. These grow so fast and big they give bumper harvests—sometimes more than twice a year. Soon, the idea was adopted in India and elsewhere.

What's wrong with the Green Revolution?
High-yield crops only give big harvests if the land is well watered and the farmer uses a lot of fertilizer, pesticides, and machines—farmers now need to apply ten times as much nitrogen fertilizer to keep the soil fertile as they did in the 1950s. This not only poses much greater strains on the environment, but means small farmers may be put in debt to the suppliers of fertilizers, pesticides, and seeds.

What are root crops?
Root crops are plants cultivated mainly for their big, solid roots, such as potatoes, yams, cassava, and manioc. These roots are rich in carbohydrates, the food we need for energy.

▲ **Corn fed**
Corn comes in two main forms. One has a big head with big grains and gives us corn on the cob and sweetcorn (above). The other has a small head and small grains and gives corn oil and cornstarch.

▶ **Paddy fields**
In Asia, most people's basic food is rice, grown in flooded fields called paddies, where they can grow up to three crops a year. To keep the fields flooded on steep hillsides, farmers often have to build row upon row of terraces.

Where does chocolate come from?

Chocolate is made with cocoa powder, ground up from the roasted and fermented beans of cacao pods. The pods are the fruit of the cacao tree, which came originally from the Andes Mountains in South America, but is now grown mainly in West Africa and the Caribbean.

How many plants can be eaten?

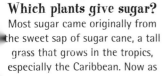

There are over 20,000 species of edible plant, but under 100 are usually grown as crops.

Which plants give sugar?

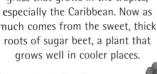

Most sugar came originally from the sweet sap of sugar cane, a tall grass that grows in the tropics, especially the Caribbean. Now as much comes from the sweet, thick roots of sugar beet, a plant that grows well in cooler places.

▲ **Prickly pear**
Different crops grow well in different places. In the hottest, driest parts of India, farmers often grow this cactus, called a prickly pear, which yields a sweet fruit.

Some rice terraces, like these in the Philippines, are thousands of years old

Most paddy rice is still planted and picked by hand

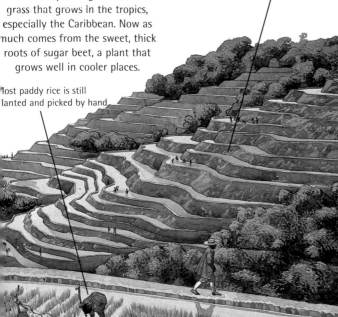

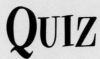

QUIZ

1 Is a fallow: a) a flower b) a kind of fruit c) a period in which soil is allowed to rest and recover?

2 Is a cash crop: a) an expensive haircut b) a banker's whip c) a crop a farmer grows to sell for money, not to eat?

3 What is a combine harvester?

4 Where did potatoes come from originally: a) Ireland b) North America c) India?

5 What plant gives most of our wine?

6 Japanese farmers use 45 times as much fertilizer per acre on their grains as farmers in Nigeria: true or false?

Answers
1. c) 2. c) 3. A machine that both cuts the wheat from the ground and separates the grain from the stalks; 4. b) 5. The grape vine; 6. True

Plants for health

Can plants heal?

YES. PLANTS HAVE BEEN USED as medicines since prehistoric times, and the effectiveness of some is beyond doubt. Many of today's most important drugs, such as aspirin, morphine, and quinine, came originally from plants. In some countries such as China, herbal remedies are still among the most widely used of all medicines, although not all are equally effective.

▲ Poppy power

The opium poppy is the source of opium, which oozes from the unripe seed head when cut with a knife. Opium is the source of the powerful drug morphine, used to help ease extreme pain. It is also the basis for the milder painkiller codeine, used in cough medicines. Opium can also be turned into the dangerously addictive drug heroin, which is why it is sometimes grown in secret. Afghanistan is the leading producer of opium poppies.

▶ Plants for health: key
1. Periwinkle
2. Feverfew
3. White willow
4. Opium poppy
5. Foxglove

How can a willow cure a headache?

People used to chew willow bark to ease pain. In the last century, scientists discovered this worked because willow contains a certain chemical, also found in meadowsweet. This chemical was later used to make aspirin.

Why might foxglove stop your heart?

Foxglove in large doses is highly poisonous. But it also yields the drug digitalis, used in small doses to treat heart problems.

Can plants cure cancer?

No drug yet known can cure cancer. But an extract of the rosy periwinkle, vincristine, is very effective against leukemia, a cancer of the blood.

1

2

Why might a gin and tonic help cure malaria?

The tropical disease malaria once killed millions of people. Then it was discovered that it could be treated with quinine, extracted from the bark of South America's cinchona tree. Quinine also gives the bitter flavor in tonic water.

How did feverfew get its name?

"Feverfew" comes from the plant's Latin name *febrifuga*, which means "driving away fever," and it was once thought an effective treatment of fever. It is still used to alleviate headaches today.

What is ginseng?

Ginseng is a plant related to ivy, prized in China for 5,000 years. Its powdered root helps relieve tiredness and is said to relieve kidney disease and headaches.

Why did women put deadly nightshade in their eyes?

Deadly nightshade has poisonous, red berries. The juice of these berries is used to make the drug atropine, which makes the pupil bigger for eye examinations. In the Middle Ages, women put this juice in their eyes to make their pupils wider and more attractive, which is why the plant is also called "belladonna," from the Italian for "beautiful woman."

5

4

◄ Medicinal plants
In the past many herbs were grown for their medicinal properties, and scholars wrote huge books listing the healing qualities of thousands of plants. One of the most famous was "The Complete Herbal" of Nicholas Culpeper (1616–1654). Today, doctors are more skeptical about the value of all these herbs. But many important drugs are based on plants, and scientists are discovering more and more all the time.

QUIZ

1 Oranges are good for preventing colds: true or false?

2 The coca in Coca-Cola is the same coca plant that the dangerous drug cocaine comes from: true or false?

3 Coffee beans contain the stimulating drug caffeine: true or false?

4 Is someone who studies plant medicine: a) a vegetarian b) a herbalist c) a plantain?

5 The wild yam–a bit like a turnip–helps with birth control: true or false?

6 Dock leaves are good for nettle stings: true or false?

7 Rubbing beets on the skin cures spots: true or false?

8 Lungwort gets its name because it is good for lung problems: true or false?

Answers
1.True; 2. True; Coca-cola originally contained coca and cola, a nut that contains the pick-me-up caffeine; 3. True; 4. b) 5. True; 6. True; 7. False – but it makes all of your face equally red! 8. True

Plants for materials

What kinds of materials can plants be used for?

PLANTS PROVIDE A HUGE range of materials, used for all kinds of purposes. The most important is wood for building and paper, perhaps, but there is also cotton for clothes, cork for wine bottles, oils, rubber dyes, rope and string, and much more besides.

▲ **Cotton head**

Many of our clothes are made from cotton—or cotton mixed with man-made fibers. Cotton is a natural fiber that comes from the cotton flower, a plant that grows in warm regions. Its seed pods, or "bolls," hold a dense mass of fluffy fibers, which can be separated into strands of cotton "lint." It is the lint from which cotton cloth is woven.

What plants make paper?

Most paper is made from wood pulped into a soft white mush. Many conifers are planted especially for paper. But natural forests are also a source. The main trees are spruce and pine, but aspen, poplar, and eucalyptus are used, too. In Asia, paper may be made from bamboo. Paper can also be made from grasses, straw, and sugar cane.

What trees make wood?

All trees are woody, but we use the work "timber" to describe wood that is used to make things Timber is either softwood or hardwood. Softwood comes from fast-growing conifers like pine, larch, fir, and spruce, which grow in colder places. Hardwood is from slow-growing broad-leaved trees such as oak. It also comes from tropical trees like mahogany.

▲ **Reed hut**

In the past, people made the most of plants that were available locally. Some of the first boats and houses were made from reeds pulled from marshes. The Ancient Egyptians and South Americans made boats of weed. The Marsh Arabs of southern Iraq still do.

▶ **Wooden houses**

When most people still lived in the countryside, before the Industrial Revolution of 200 years ago, only the houses of the very rich were built mainly of brick or stone. Most ordinary houses were built with timber frames and even walls, and were often roofed by thatches made from reeds and straw.

Plant carrier

When tankers carry oil, the fuel we use to run cars and fire power stations, they are in fact carrying the ancient remains of plants and animals.

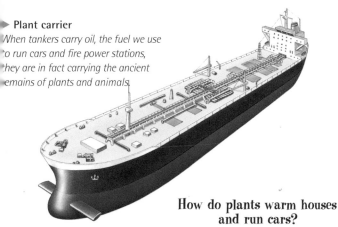

What are fossil fuels?

Fossil fuels are fuels like coal, oil, and natural gas, made mainly from the remains of plants that died long ago. The remains were buried underground and gradually squeezed and concentrated into fuels over millions of years. Coal was made from giant ferns that grew in huge swamps 300 million years ago; oil from tiny plants and animals that lived in warm seas.

How do plants warm houses and run cars?

Plants provide 80 percent of all our fuels—for running cars, keeping houses warm, and generating power. In developing countries, most people cook and keep warm by burning wood they gather from forests and shrubs. In Brazil, they run cars not on gasoline but on a fuel like diesel, tapped from the copaiba tree. In Europe, North America, and many other places in the world, the main fuels are fossil fuel—that is, coal, oil, and natural gas.

QUIZ

1 How do plants give plastics?

2 Where does mahogany come from?

3 What plant is sunflower oil made from?

4 Cork comes from the sea: true or false?

5 Does ivory come from a plant or an animal?

6 What connects bicycle wheels with tropical plants?

7 What color dye did ancient Britons make from the leaves of the yellow flower woad?

8 Why does a madder plant make you redder?

Answers
1. Most plastics are made from either oil or coal; 2. Tropical rain forests; 3. The seeds of the sunflower; 4. False; cork comes from the bark of the cork-oak tree; 5. Animal; the elephant; 6. The tires are made of rubber, which comes originally from the sap of the rubber tree; 7. Blue; 8. Madder is a flower that gives a red dye

Woodland plants

What are woodland plants?

WOODLANDS are the home for plants that prefer the shady conditions under the trees to full sunlight. There are spring flowers like bluebells and primroses, summer flowers like foxgloves and rosebay willow herb, shrubs like brambles and hawthorn, as well as ferns, mosses, and fungi.

Why do primroses bloom in spring?

Like many flowers of deciduous woodlands, primroses bloom in spring before the leaves have grown thick on the trees, so that they get plenty of sunshine. Many other woodland flowers bloom in spring for the same reason, including wood anemones, oxlips, daffodils, lesser celandines, bluebells, early purple orchids, and dog's mercury. It is flowers like these that give the woodland floor a colorful carpet every spring.

▼ **Woodland plants**
This picture shows just some of the many wildflowers and other plants that grow on the woodland floor. Although all the flowers are shown in bloom here, they do not all bloom at the same time. Each has its season, keeping the floor alive with color for many months of the year.

Why are dead trees good news?

When big trees die and come crashing down through the branches, they create a clearing in the wood called a glade. Here sunlight can reach the woodland floor again, allowing all kinds of plants to sprout anew, including flowers such as foxgloves and rosebay willow herb and all kinds of fungi, such as fly agaric, which thrive on the rotting wood.

What plant has two different flowers?

Wood sorrel has a big spring flower to attract the bees that spread its pollen, and another smaller flower in summer to make seeds.

Which woodland plant is good for a kiss?

At Christmas, many people still hang up a sprig of mistletoe and kiss beneath it. Mistletoe is a parasitic plant with white berries that clings to trees such as apple, hawthorn, poplar, and willow and puts its roots into them. The custom goes back to the druids, the white-robed priests of ancient Britain over 2,000 years ago, who used to cut down mistletoe with a golden sickle to use in their sacred rites.

What is a coppice?

Since early times, people living in woodland areas have cut down trees to allow new, straight shoots to grow through. This is called coppicing, and ensured a good supply of straight poles for fencing and making tools.

Are fruits seeds?

No, they develop from the flower's ovary—and the hard pips inside are the seeds. Juicy fruits such as berries are called "true fruits" because they are made from the flower's ovaries alone. Apples and pears are "false" fruits because only the core is made from the ovary. Plums and cherries are "drupes" in which there are no pips, but the seed is held in a hard shell.

Woodland plants: key

1. Lords-and-ladies
2. Wood anemones
3. Honeysuckle
4. Fly agaric
5. Wood Blewit
6. Bluebells
7. Orchid
8. Primrose
9. Rhododendron

QUIZ

1 What poison do foxgloves contain a) arsenic b) cyanide c) digitalis?
2 What trees are used to make most baseball bats?
3 King Alfred's cake fungus gets its name because it looks like burned buns: true or false?
4 What is a bloody cranesbill?
5 Fungus sharpens knives: true or false?
6 In spring, the faint ringing of bluebells can be heard in woods: true or false?
7 Elizabethan lords used lords-and-ladies for a) cooking b) stiffening their collars c) smoking?
8 Ferns are the world's oldest trees: true or false?

Answers
1. c) 2. Ash
3. True; 4. A crimson flower;
5. True, the razor strop fungus was used to sharpen razors
6. False; 7. b) 8. True, there were forests of ferns 300 million years ago

Tropical plants

What makes tropical plants different?

▲ The Rafflesia has no leaves, and the only part of the plant above ground is the huge, blotchy red and white bloom. It is a parasite, and beneath the ground is a tangle of thread-like roots growing inside the roots of lianas and gaining nourishment from them.

THE TROPICS ARE WARM nearly all the time, and in the rain forests there is abundant moisture. The combination creates almost ideal conditions for plant growth, and the forests are not only lush but contain an astonishing variety of plants–including some of the world's most spectacular and strange.

What is the world's biggest flower?

A single bloom of the Rafflesia of Southeast Asia can be over 3 feet across and weigh 15 pounds or more. The titan arum is even bigger, at 10 feet tall, but is made of many small flowers, not a single bloom like Rafflesia.

What is the world's worst-smelling flower?

The Rafflesia may not only be the world's biggest flower; it may also be the foulest smelling. Some people call it the stinking corpse lily and say it smells like rotting meat. The stench is said to draw the flies it needs to pollinate.

How many plants are there in the rain forest?

The rain forests are the world's richest habitats, containing over 40 percent of the world's plant species. No one knows exactly how many different plants there are. But botanists counted over 180 species of tree alone in 2.5 acres of the Malaysian forest.

Do plants grow on trees?

The forest is so dense that to get nearer sunlight, small plants called epiphytes wrap their roots around high branches and grow there. The commonest epiphytes are bromeliads.

What is the strongest rope in the jungle?

The liana is a vine or creeper that dangles down from trees in the rain forest. It is so strong that monkeys and other forest animals can use lianas to swing through the trees. The vine is actually a very long stem. The liana's roots are in the ground, and its leaves are in the sun above the trees.

What are the world's largest leaves?

Palm tree leaves can be very big. The leaves of raffia palms and the Amazonian bamboo palm can grow up to 65 feet long.

▶ What makes the rain forest so rich in plant life is that plants don't just grow in the soil. Trees are adorned not only with dangling creepers and vines, but many plants that actually grow in the tree including bromeliads, orchids, ferns, and mosses—and plants called air plants which get enough moisture from the air alone.

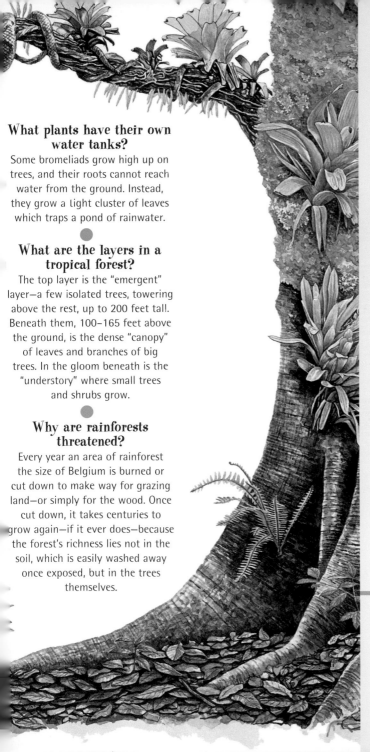

What plants have their own water tanks?

Some bromeliads grow high up on trees, and their roots cannot reach water from the ground. Instead, they grow a light cluster of leaves which traps a pond of rainwater.

What are the layers in a tropical forest?

The top layer is the "emergent" layer—a few isolated trees, towering above the rest, up to 200 feet tall. Beneath them, 100–165 feet above the ground, is the dense "canopy" of leaves and branches of big trees. In the gloom beneath is the "understory" where small trees and shrubs grow.

Why are rainforests threatened?

Every year an area of rainforest the size of Belgium is burned or cut down to make way for grazing land—or simply for the wood. Once cut down, it takes centuries to grow again—if it ever does—because the forest's richness lies not in the soil, which is easily washed away once exposed, but in the trees themselves.

QUIZ

1 Is the world's biggest rain forest in a) Brazil b) India c) Australia?

2 The world's fastest-growing plant is Myanmar's giant bamboo. In a day, it can grow a) 2 inches b) 4 inches c) 18 inches?

3 Flowers grow on tree trunks in the jungle: true or false?

4 There is a plant in the jungle that eats frogs: true or false?

5 There is a plant in the jungle that strangles trees: true or false?

6 There are exploding cucumbers in the jungle: true or false?

7 Lianas can strangle monkeys: true or false?

False, except by accident
shoots seeds up to 26 feet; 7.
squirting cucumber bursts and
strangler fig does; 6. True, the
Venus flytrap does 5. True; the
1. a) 2. c) 3. True; 4. True, the

Answers

199

Water plants

What plants grow in water?

The very first plants developed in water, then gradually colonized the land as they evolved. Since then many new plants–called aquatic plants–have learned to live in water, including flowers like water lilies, water hyacinths, and grass-like plants such as reeds, rushes, and papyrus.

Do plants float?

Yes, the leaves of flowers like the water lily and hyacinth float on the surface. But the leaves are on long, flexible stalks that reach down to the lake or river bed, and the roots are firmly anchored in the mud. Even so, they cannot survive in fast-moving water.

Why don't floating plants sink?

Because some plants have air sacks in their stems and leaves. Others, like the water lily, have leaves that turn up at the edges so that they float like boats.

What is the world's biggest water plant?

The floating leaves of the giant lily of the Amazon in South America grow 6 feet across and are strong enough to bear the weight of a child.

What water plant did the Pharaohs write on?

The papyrus is a giant reed that grows 10 feet tall along the Nile River. The Ancient Egyptians discovered 5,000 years ago that the pith of papyrus stems could be used to make paper. Although paper is now made from wood pulp, we owe the word to the papyrus reed.

Why are water hyacinths a nuisance?

The purple flowers of the floating water hyacinth are attractive, but the plants can spread rapidly, choking waterways and blocking the path of boats.

How do river plants cope with the current?

To survive in anything but the very slowest-flowing rivers, water plants have to anchor themselves with firm roots to save themselves from being washed away, and their leaves must be feathery, like those of the fanwort, to avoid offering resistance to the water. The river water crowfoot can survive in quite fast-flowing streams because its leaves are streamlined.

What water plant eats bugs?

The bladderwort is a plant of swamps that develops underwater bladders on its stem. When an insect such as a water flea touches a trigger on one of these bladders, the bladder springs open and sucks in the bug with the inrushing water.

Why don't all lakes have plants?

Because the chemical composition of the water varies. Lakes filled by water draining from lime-rich soils tend to to be rich in plant life. Those near acid soil are more sterile.

▼ **Water life**

Slow-flowing rivers and shallows in lakes are often densely packed with all kinds of water plants. Most plants are rooted to the bed, but a few get all the nutrients they need directly from the water. Some plants are hidden underwater. Some float on the surface. Plants such as rushes and reeds are called emergents because they grow up out of the water.
Key: *1. Bulrushes 2. Frogbit 3. Water crowfoot 4. Water lily 5. Yellow flag iris 6. Water plantain*

QUIZ

1 What water flower was adopted as a symbol by French and English kings?

2 What important food crop is grown in water in China?

3 Do lakes last forever?

4 How do water plants keep out the rain in parts of England?

5 Amazonian Indians make cartwheels out of water-lily leaves: true or false?

6 What water plants did the Egyptians make boats from?

7 What water plants was Moses found among?

8 The pollen of most water plants spreads by floating on the water: true or false?

Grassland plants

Are grasslands all grass?

AT FIRST GLANCE grasslands look as uniform and unvaried as a lawn-just mile upon mile of green grass. But a closer look reveals that there are, for a start, many types of grass, including tussock grass, marram grass, meadow grass, blue grass, and many more-and mixed in with the grasses are a rich variety of herbs and flowers.

▲ **Rokerboom**
There is too little water for most ordinary trees in tropical grasslands like the veld of South Africa. So, like the baobab of the savanna, the rokerboom tree has developed a huge swollen trunk that acts as a water store to help it survive through dry periods.

▼ **South American pampas**
The pampas stretches across Argentina, Uruguay, and southeastern Brazil, forming the largest area of temperate grassland in the southern hemisphere. Many parts of the pampas are dominated by tussock grasses like those seen in the foreground.

Do grasslands have any other name?

They have special names in every continent. In North America they are called prairies. In South America, they are called pampas. In northern Asia, they are the steppes. In South Africa, they are the veld. In Australia, the bush. In Britain, grasslands occur mostly on chalk hills and are called downs.

Where do grasslands occur?

Grasslands occur all over the world where there is only moderate rainfall—mostly in the heart of continents, far from the sea—or where the ground is so dry and well-drained that only grass will grow.

Why don't trees grow in grasslands?

Because trees need a lot of water. Grasslands are too dry. The few trees that do grow in grasslands, such as the baobab and the rokerboom, have immensely thick trunks that are very good at retaining moisture.

What is meadow grass?

Meadow grass is the most common of all grasses, found in grasslands all over the world. This is the grass that people use in lawns. It is almost always green because although each plant lasts only a few years, they continually produce fresh seeds, so new grass is springing up all the time.

▶ Acacias

Acacia trees, sometimes known as thorn trees because of their prickly thorns, are the most widespread trees of the African savanna, and their flat tops are a distinctive part of the savanna landscape. They have formed a remarkable partnership with ants that helps them survive. The acacia's leaf stalks secrete a nectar that attracts ants. In return, the ants attack any animal that tries to browse on the leaves. They also help spread the acacia's seeds.

QUIZ

1 What animals are raised on the pampas?

2 What large animal used to roam the prairies?

3 What animals are raised on Australian grasslands?

4 Which state in the U.S. is famous for its bluegrass a) California b) South Carolina c) Kentucky?

5 What is a billabong?

6 What color is prairie soil a) brown b) black c) yellow?

7 On which continent would you find a gaucho?

8 What is a big cattle farm on the prairies called?

9 What was a prairie schooner?

10 What grass would you find on sand dunes a) sedge grass b) rye grass c) marram grass?

Why do farmers like rye grass?

Rye grass is the grass that many farmers grow for cows to graze on, and to make hay for feeding livestock from. Typically, new pastures are sown with either pure rye grass or mixed rye and clover.

What wild flowers grow on grasslands?

Vetches, trefoils, worts, orchids, and various herbs are among the many flowers native to grasslands.

Which garden flowers come from grasslands?

From the grasslands of Europe and Asia come flowers such as adonis, anemones, delphiniums, and scabious. Flowers from the prairies of North America include the coneflower, the sunflower, and the blazing star.

How did scabious get its name?

The juice was said to cure scabies and other skin diseases.

Answers
1. Cattle; 2. Bison; 3. Sheep; 4. c) 5. A lake in Australia; 6. b) 7. On the pampas in South America: a gaucho is a cowboy; 8. A ranch; 9. A settler's covered wagon; 10. c)

203

Desert plants

Do any plants grow in the desert?

A DESERT IS A PLACE where very little rain falls–but only rarely is there no rain at all, and wherever there is a little moisture, some especially adapted hardy plants, such as cacti, will survive.

How do plants find water in the desert?

When there is no water on the surface, plants can often find moisture deep underground by growing long roots. Mesquite roots often grow as deep as 33 feet, and may be as deep as 165 feet.

How do plants save water?

Wherever water is short, plants have developed ways of saving water. Other plants lose a great deal of water by evaporation from their leaves. So desert plants usually have tough, waxy leaves—and plants that live in extreme conditions cut down their leaves to a minimum.

▶ Saguaro
The saguaro of Mexico and the American Southwest is the biggest cactus of all. It can grow up to 65 feet tall and 2 feet thick.

What plant amputates its own branches?

The branches and trunk of the quiver tree are filled with a soft fiber that can store water. But in severe drought, it seals off branches to save moisture loss through the leaves. The branch end looks like an amputated limb.

▲ Oasis

In places in the Sahara Desert in Africa, water-bearing rocks are exposed at the surface, creating an oasis where moisture-loving plants such as palm trees can flourish.

QUIZ

1 Is a half-man a) a mythical camel b) a desert monkey c) a prickly desert plant?

2 How quickly does the Joshua tree of the Mojave Desert grow a) 1 inch a year b) 4 inches a year c) 4 feet a year?

3 What happens to the shriveled brown leaves of a resurrection tree after it rains?

4 Where do some owls live in the deserts?

▼ Cactus in flower

Cacti have to pollinate just like every other flowering plant, and so every few years they produce big, colorful blooms in order to attract insects quickly.

What is a window plant?

Some plants, such as pebble plants, escape the drying heat of the desert by growing partly underground. But the window plant grows almost entirely underground. It is like a cigar poked down into the ground. All that is visible on the surface is the end, a little green button—the plant's window to the Sun.

How do cacti survive in Death Valley?

Cacti are the most impressive of all desert survivors. They are remarkable plants that live in American deserts. They have no leaves and a very thick skin, so water loss is cut to a minimum. Their fat stems are able to hold huge quantities of water, which is why they are called succulents.

Why is cactus prickly?

Lush vegetation is so rare in the desert that animals eat anything available. So plants like cacti, as well as prickly pears and thorn bushes, grow prickles to protect themselves from being eaten.

◄ Blooms in the desert

When it rains in the desert, seeds that have lain dormant during the long drought suddenly burst into brief bloom.
Key: *1. Saguaro 2. Evening primrose 3. Prickly pear*

5 What is the hottest desert?

6 How often does it rain in Chile's Atacama desert— every a) 5 years b) 20 years c) 400 years?

Answers
1. c) 2. b) 3. The leaves turn green; 4. In holes in cacti; 5. The Sahara, where it often gets to 104°F; 6. c)

205

Mountain plants

What plants live on mountains?

THE WEATHER GETS COLDER, windier, and wetter the higher you go up a mountain. Some mountain tops are even permanently covered with snow. So the plants that grow on mountains have to be hardy, and they usually get smaller the higher you go, varying from big trees such as conifers on the lower slopes to tiny flowers, low grasses, and mosses higher up.

▼ Alpine flowers: key
1. Alpine bluebell 2. Alpine gentian
3. Mountain avens 4. Edelweiss
5. Purple saxifrage

What is the tree line?

Above a certain height, it gets too cold for trees to grow well. This is the tree line. It varies according to local conditions, but gets lower toward the poles. It is about 7,200 feet in the Swiss Alps.

Can plants survive on rock faces?

The purple saxifrage and starry saxifrage have tough, penetrating roots that exploit cracks and crevices, enabling them to colonize the narrowest rocky ledges. Their roots anchor so firmly that they were once thought to be able to actually crack the rock. The word saxifrage means "stone-breaker."

Why do some alpine flowers have big blooms?

There are few insects to pollinate flowers high up on the mountainside, so flowers like purple saxifrage and the snow gentian produce big colorful blooms to ensure that insects don't waste time searching for them.

QUIZ

► Edelweiss
The edelweiss can grow at very high altitudes in the Alps, sprouting out from cracks in the rocks, because its blooms and leaves are covered with a coat of woolly hairs that protect it from the cold.

How do alpine flowers cope with a short summer?

High up near the snow line, the time available for growing after the snow melts in spring is very short. So the alpine snowbell makes the most of each summer by developing its flower buds the previous summer. They lie dormant through the winter under a protective blanket of snow, ready to burst through at the first thaw.

How do plants survive in the cold ?

Plants have evolved various different ways of coping with the cold. Some cover themselves with a coat of woolly hairs, like edelweiss, or have thick, waxy leaves. The Himalayan saussurea is almost all wool. Others, like the daisies of Tasmania, pack their stems into a tight, padded cushion.

Can plants freeze?

Few plants can survive being frozen, but many can thrive under the snow. Snow acts like a blanket, keeping ice and wind at bay, and saves the plant from being frozen to death. Alpine grasses stay alive and green under the snow, ready to grow again as soon as it melts.

Where are there dandelions as big as trees?

On Mount Kenya in Africa, baking daytime sun and icy mountain nights have created giant groundsels. Elsewhere, groundsel is a small plant similar to dandelions— but on Mt. Kenya it grows over 33 feet tall! The European lobelia is a tiny plant, too—but on Mt. Kenya, lobelias grow huge.

◄ Alpine flowers
Above the tree-line, many small flowers thrive, including cinquefoil, stonecrop, and campion, besides those shown.

1 What is the snow line?

2 How much colder does it get for every 1000 feet you climb a) 5.4°F b) 7.2°F c) 9.6°f?

3 Do fir trees lose their leaves in winter?

4 In the Alps, which side of the mountain is warmest: the north or the south?

5 Where might you find alpine flowers in an ordinary garden?

6 Is gentian violet a) an antiseptic b) an artist's color c) a uniform?

7 In Switzerland, is edelweiss a symbol of a) good luck b) spring c) purity?

8 Edelweiss means in German a) lazy good-for-nothing b) snow bell c) noble white?

9 Is Mt. Kenya in the tropics?

10 Which berries grow on mountains a) gooseberries b) blueberries c) bilberries d) strawberries e) crowberries?

Answers
1. The lower limit of permanent snow; 2. a) 3. No; 4. The south, because it faces the Sun; 5. A rockery; 6. a) 7. c) 8. c) 9. Yes; 10. b), c), and e)

Arctic plants

Do plants grow in the Arctic?

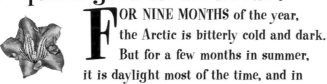

FOR NINE MONTHS of the year, the Arctic is bitterly cold and dark. But for a few months in summer, it is daylight most of the time, and in this brief respite from the worst of Arctic weather, a surprising variety of plants–over 900 species–spring up.

Why does it never get dark in the Arctic summer?

In summer, the Sun sets for only a few hours in the middle of the night. This happens because the Earth is tilted over. As the Earth makes its year-long journey around the Sun, the part of the Earth tilted toward the Sun gradually shifts north, then south. In the Arctic summer, the Earth has reached the point in its journey where the North Pole is tilting most toward the Sun.

▶ **Arctic flowers: key**
1. Saxifrage
2. Snowbell
3. Avens
4. Willow herb
5. Saxifrage
6. Stonecrop
7. Arctic poppy

Why are trees shorter than daisies?

Willow trees grow in the Arctic, but because of the fierce Arctic wind, they never grow more than 4 inches tall. Instead, they spread out along the ground.

Why do Arctic plants like skulls?

Nutriment is so scarce in the Arctic that plants take what there is. So when an animal such as a musk ox dies, seeds make the most of its corpse, and Arctic flowers often spring up inside the skull.

How do some plants melt snow?

Some plants have dark leaves and stems. When the Sun shines, their dark color soaks up the Sun's warmth and melts the snow.

How do plants cope without bees to pollinate them?

There are so few bees and butterflies in the Arctic that many Arctic flowers find other ways of spreading their pollen. Some flowers, like mustard, rely on the wind. Others rely on flies, and so only put out yellow or white flowers, since flies are color blind.

What is the tundra?

Tundra is a region so cold that no large trees grow—only dwarf trees, shrubs such as heathers, grasses, and other small plants. There is a vast area of tundra stretching through the north of Canada, Siberia, and Scandinavia, and into Greenland. There is tundra on high mountains, too.

6

7

Why are many Arctic plants evergreen?

Leaves grown the previous summer are ready to make the most of the brief summer. Over the winter, they are protected by dead leaves.

Do plants grow in Antarctica?

Most of Antarctica is covered with snow and ice all year round, so very few plants can survive here, unlike the Arctic. Yet there are fungi and lichen growing within 300 miles of the South Pole, and two species of flowering plant are native to Antarctica.

Why is snow pink in Antarctica?

Some algae live in the snow, just below the surface, but the UV rays from the Sun are so bright in snow that the algae must protect itself with red pigment. The red algae turns the snow pink.

◄ Arctic bloom
Full-size trees will not grow in the Arctic tundra, but the brief summer sees it bursting into life. Grasses and sedges, mosses, and lichens thrive, along with various small flowers such as saxifrages, ovens, and Arctic poppies, especially adopted to survive the cold.

QUIZ

1 Gentian is used to make a bitter tonic for stomach complaints—true or false?
2 Which flower blooms nearest the North Pole a) snowdrop b) bluebell c) Arctic poppy?
3 Lichen growing in Antarctica may be the world's oldest living things. Are they a) 1,000 years old b) 10,000 years old c) 100,000 years old?
4 In Antarctica, the temperature can drop to a) -5°F b) -128°F c) -482°F?
5 Is the North Pole in Antarctica or the Arctic?

Answers
1. True; 2. c) 3. b) 4. b) 5. The Arctic

What creature turns
green with rage?

Why do elephants
have trunks?

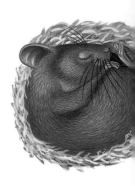

How do seals keep
warm?

Why does a
woodpecker peck
wood?

Which bird never
sees the sunset?

Why does a beaver
slap its tail on the
water?

What's the noisiest
creature in the
Amazon jungle?

What frog make
Indian arrows
deadly?

Why is a flamingo pink?

What bird has a beak as big as its body?

Animals

Do bears hug?

How does a giraffe drink?

What is a female deer called?

Rain forest animals

What animals live in rain forests?

THE LUSH, WARM RAIN FORESTS of the tropics are home to more species of animal than any other habitat in the world. Huge numbers of small, tree-dwelling creatures especially live here–scores of different reptiles such as snakes and lizards, hundreds of different kinds of birds, and perhaps more than a million different insects.

What creature turns green with rage?

The chameleon is a strange tree lizard with swivelling eyes, a long tail that coils up, and an amazingly long, sticky tongue, which darts out to catch flies. But what is strangest of all is that the chameleon can change its skin color, either when it is in a certain mood—in a rage, for instance—or to camouflage itself by blending in perfectly with its background.

What frog makes Indian arrows deadly?

The sweat of the poison-arrow tree frogs of Central and South America is deadly to humans. Local Indians collect the poison by holding the frogs over a fire to make them sweat, then scraping the sweat off into a jar. If they want their arrows to kill, they dip the tips in the poison jar.

▲ Toucan
The toucan uses its big beak to fight rival males and to eat fruit and birds' eggs. But no one knows just why it is so colorful.

◀ Poisonous frog
Some tree frogs like the kokoi and the poison-arrow have a poison much more deadly than any snake. Their bright colors act as a warning.

▲ Three-toed sloth
Sloths live in the jungles of South America. They live in trees, climbing and hanging upside down, using their long claws as hooks.

What bird has a beak as big as its body?

The toco toucan has a huge, brightly colored beak 9 inches long—longer than its body. It doesn't overbalance because the beak is full of holes inside and so is very lightweight.

What snakes squeeze victims to death?

"Constrictor" snakes like pythons wrap their coils around a victim and squeeze until they suffocate.

What is the slowest creature in the jungle?

Hanging upside down in the trees, the three-toed tree sloth takes a minute to lope just 10 feet. On the ground, it can manage only 6.5 feet.

What's the noisiest creature in the Amazon jungle?

Howler monkeys have a sound-box in their throats, which resonates very loudly. When a small group howls together, the din can be heard over 1.8 miles away.

What's a prehensile tail?

Monkeys in North, Central and South America often have prehensile tails. Monkeys in Asia and Africa don't. They are muscular tails that can curl to grip things like a hand, which is very useful for swinging through trees.

What's a jaguar?

A jaguar is the biggest cat in the Americas. It looks like a leopard, but it is larger and has a shorter tail. Its spot pattern is also slightly different.

▼ The reticulated python
This python, which lives in the forests of Asia, grows up to 33 feet long and can swallow a goat whole—and then not eat for a month.

QUIZ

1 The sloth moves so slowly that plants grow on it: true or false?

2 What is the world's smallest bird?

3 What is the world's loudest bird: a) the great bittern b) the golden eagle c) the Indian peacock?

4 How much poison from the kokoi frog's sweat does it take to kill a man: a) 1 ounce b) 1 quart c) 0.00001 ounce?

5 Cockatoos have been heard talking to each other in English: true or false?

6 In the 1800s, please in Britain used blue morpho butterflies as brooches: true or false?

Answers
1. True, algae grows in its fur, making it look green; 2. The bee hummingbird is just 2.25 inches long; 3. c) 4. c) 5. False, they can mimic a few words but not converse; 6. True

Woodland animals

What creatures live in the woods?

MANY DIFFERENT ANIMALS live in woodlands in the temperate zone, in between the tropics and the poles. The leaf litter beneath the trees teems with tiny creatures-worms, millipedes, ants, and other insects-all of which draw predators such as spiders, shrews, and mice. The trees themselves provide a haven for many insects, birds, and small mammals.

Why does a woodpecker peck wood ?

A woodpecker clings to tree trunks, propped up by its stiff tail, and rapidly hammers its long, powerful beak against the trunk. The idea is to bore a hole for nesting or to get at insects and larvae, which the woodpecker licks out with its long, worm-like tongue. The tip of the tongue is barbed so that the bird can harpoon tiny insects deep inside narrow tunnels.

Where do badgers live?

Badgers live in families in extensive burrows called setts, which they dig out with their broad, powerful forepaws. Typically, setts are in woodlands, but they may also be in fields or even garbage dumps. Each sett has a sleeping chamber, and the bedding inside this chamber is changed frequently.

What do foxes eat?

Foxes eat all kinds of food. They often hunt at night for small animals such as voles and rabbits. But they also eat beetles, worms, and berries. They are scavengers too, and in recent years, foxes have been seen in towns going through garbage cans for scraps. Occasionally, when food is scarce, they take farmers' chickens.

Why are foxes cunning?

Foxes are intelligent hunters with a very keen sense of smell, sight, and hearing. But it was the people who hunted them—on horseback with hounds—and farmers whose chickens had been stolen who have labeled them cunning as they cleverly elude capture.

◀ Red fox
The fox is like a small dog, but the red fox, with its russe coat, large ears, bright ambe eyes, and big, bushy tail i unmistakable

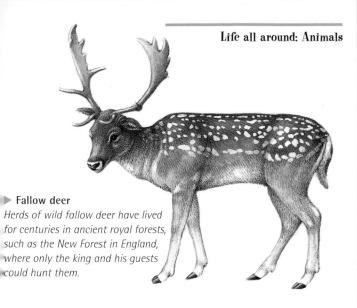

Fallow deer
Herds of wild fallow deer have lived for centuries in ancient royal forests, such as the New Forest in England, where only the king and his guests could hunt them.

QUIZ

What are antlers?

Antlers are the hard, spiky branchesd bones on a deer's head. They are used as weapons, like horns, but antlers are different from horns and only male deer have them. Horns are permanent bony growths covered with horn, but antlers are covered with a hairy skin, called velvet, and grow then drop off once a year.

What happens in the woods at night?

Many small mammals, such as shrews, moles, squirrels, mice, weasels, stoats, ferrets, and foxes, go hunting. So, too, do night-flying birds such as the nightjar, which sleeps camouflaged on the ground by day. And so does the tawny owl, which preys on the small mammals.

What are the smallest woodland carnivores?

Weasels, stoats, and polecats are very fierce, despite their small size, and are able to kill animals that are much larger such as rabbits.

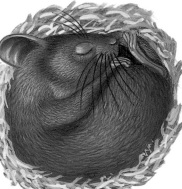

Wood mouse
ike many woodland mammals, vood mice go into a sleepy stage, lmost like hibernation, in winter. his helps them save energy when ood is scarce.

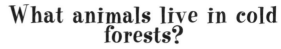

Cold forest animals

What animals live in cold forests?

THE FOREST TREES OF THE COLD NORTH are mainly conifers, like pine trees. Many woodland creatures feed on the pine leaves and cones, including chipmunks, crossbills, and various insects such as pine-shoot moths. There are also animals that prey on these creatures, such as pine martens, owls, wolves, and bears.

What do bears eat?

Brown bears eat almost anything. Fruits and berries, honey straight from bees' nests, fish, and carrion (corpses left by other animals). They also hunt small mammals. They can even catch fish by scooping them out of the river with their paw. The technical name for such wide-ranging eaters is "omnivore."

Do bears hug?

The idea that bears hug their victims to death is a superstition. They usually kill any animals they hunt with a swift blow or "cuff" from their huge, strong forepaws— or with a bite from their sharp teeth.

▲ **Raccoon**
Raccoons live near water because they often feed on frogs, crabs, water snails, and small fish.

What is the woodland bandit?

The raccoon of the forests of North America looks like a bandit because of the distinctive black eye mask across its white face. Equally distinctive is its big, bushy black and white striped tail.

Do pine martens live in pines?

Pine martens are small creatures that are similar to weasels. They don't actually live in pine trees, but they are incredibly agile climbers—one of the few predator that can catch a squirrel in a tree

◄ **Big and brown**
Bears usually move around on all fours, but they can often stand up to reach berries in trees. A standing male brown bear is over two metres tall – quite a bit taller than a man.

What's a moose yard?

In deep snow, a moose can easily be overcome by a marauding puma, or cougar. So when herds of moose get together in winter, they trample out big flat areas of snow called "yards." Here they can get a good enough footing to give them a fighting chance of using their antlers and hooves on an attacker.

Why does a beaver slap its tail on the water?

To warn other beavers of approaching danger.

Do reindeer pull sleighs?

Reindeer, or caribou, are among the longest-domesticated creatures on Earth. The people of Siberia were using them to pull sleighs and for riding over 7,000 years ago.

◀ **The winter trek**
In winter, when the weather in the cold north gets bitter and foraging for food can be difficult, reindeer begin a long trek to the south. In the past, they used to migrate in herds a quarter of a million strong.

▶ **Big feller**
Beavers can bring down literally scores of small trees to build dams and their homes in the river, gnawing through them with their two razor-sharp front teeth.

QUIZ

1 What do they call a pine marten in Russia?

2 What's the difference between a reindeer and a caribou?

3 What's a beaver's home called?

4 Which animal has the biggest horns?

5 Why's a grizzly bear grizzly?

6 What's the difference between a moose and an elk?

7 What is a lynx?

8 Do wolves really howl at the Moon?

Answers
1. A sable; 2. None, a caribou is the North American name for a reindeer; 3. A lodge; 4. A moose; 5. It has gray hairs among the black; 6. None, moose is the North American name for an elk; 7. A small wild cat; 8. No, but they do howl at night to communicate with the rest of the pack

Animals of cold seas

What animals live in the Arctic?

THE WEATHER GETS SO BITTERLY COLD in the Arctic that it is hard to imagine how any creatures can live there, yet a surprising number do–in the sea, including seals and whales; in the air, such as the Arctic tern; and on land, such as the polar bear, the Arctic fox, and the Arctic hare.

▶ **Big bird**
The albatross is the world's largest seabird, over 10 feet from wingtip to wingtip.

Which bird never sees the sunset?

The Arctic tern lives in the Arctic only during the summer, when the Sun never completely sets. At the end of the summer, it makes an incredible 12,500-mile flight to the other end of the world to catch the summer in Antarctica, where it remains daylight for months on end, too.

Are seals fish or mammals?

Despite their streamlined, fish-like shape, seals are warm-blooded mammals. Just like other mammals, they have babies that feed on their mother's milk.

How does the snowshoe hare get its name?

The snowshoe hare, which turns white as snow in winter, gets its name from its huge feet, which act like snowshoes when it bounds easily across the softest snow. Long hair grows between the toes, both to stop the toes from sinking into the snow and to keep the hare's feet warm.

How do seals keep warm?

On land, mammals rely on the air trapped in thick fur to keep them warm, but this is no good in the water. Seals have only a thin layer of fur, but they instead have a layer of fatty blubber under their skins up to 4 inches thick.

Harp seal

◀ **Ice birds**
Penguins are Antarctica's most distinctive inhabitants. Penguins can't fly and they waddle ungainly on land, but they are agile swimmers, using their wings as flippers.

QUIZ

1 What is the biggest penguin?

2 What bird makes the longest migration?

3 What sea mammals have two long tusks?

4 What color do Arctic foxes become in winter?

5 What do seals eat?

6 How many kinds of animals breed in Antarctica: a) 1 b) 8 c) 49?

7 What ox lives in the Arctic?

8 How do whales breathe out?

9 Which is the largest meateater in the Arctic?

How do Emperor penguins keep their eggs warm?

Emperor penguins are the only birds to lay their eggs in the bitter Antarctic winter. They keep them warm by resting them on their feet, tucked under their belly.

Do all penguins live in Antarctica?

All species of penguin live in the southern hemisphere, and most live in or near Antarctica.

What is the biggest creature of cold seas?

The blue whale, the biggest creature in the world, which grows over 100 feet long and weighs from 100 to 200 tons.

How do whales communicate?

By clicks, whistles, and low-pitch rumbles that echo hundreds of miles through the water. The humpback whale sings like this.

▼ **Seals and sea lions**
Seals and sea lions are different. Only sea lions have external ears and also back flippers that they can use to move about on land.

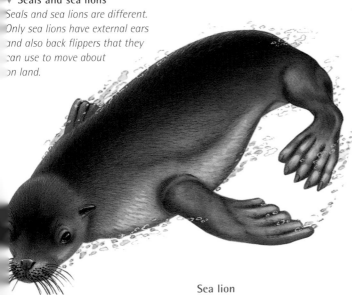

Sea lion

Answers
1. Emperor penguin; 2. Arctic tern; 3. Walrus; 4. White; 5. Mainly fish; 6. b), four kinds of seal, two kinds of penguin, the southern skua, and the snow petrel; 7. Musk ox; 8. Through the blowhole on top of their heads; 9. Polar bear

219

African animals

What animals live in Africa?

AFRICA IS HOME TO SOME of the world's most spectacular animals. The tropical forest in the center is home to many different kinds of monkeys and the gorilla. In the bush country or savanna beyond live such magnificent creatures as elephants, lions, giraffes, rhinos, hippos, zebras, and many more.

▲ Amboseli, Kenya
Many of Africa's most spectacular animals have been reduced almost to extinction by hunters who call them "Big Game." Now many animals are protected inside safari parks such as the Amboseli in the shadow of Mount Kilimanjaro.

How do lions hunt?

Although they sometimes attack young giraffes or weak buffaloes, lions' main prey is antelopes. Lions hunt silently, usually in small groups—lying in wait for the antelopes at waterholes or creeping stealthily through the grass. When they near their prey, they make a sudden sprint, then pounce, sinking their sharp fangs into their victim's neck. Meat is so nutritious that one kill is usually enough to last a lion for days.

Why do elephants have trunks?

An elephant uses its trunk for all kinds of different tasks. The trunk is used mainly for feeding, and the elephant pulls off grasses and leaves with it and stuffs them in its mouth. But the elephant also uses the trunk to suck up water, which it then drinks or uses to spray itself clean. The trunk is the elephant's nose, too, and an elephant may often put its trunk in the air to sniff the wind. The trunk is even used for caressing baby elephants.

▶ Big bird
Africa is home not only to the largest land mammal, the elephant, but the largest bird, too—the ostrich. Ostriches can reach 8 feet tall. They can't fly, but they can run fast, and their long legs can inflict a hefty kick.

◀ Deadly huntress
Male lions with their big manes may look impressive, but it is the females, called lionesses, that do most of the hunting.

How can you tell an African elephant from an Asian elephant?

African elephants are generally bigger than Asian elephants. African elephants have much bigger ears and much longer tusks. The Asian elephant also has a slightly humped back and just one finger-like lip on the end of its trunk, while the African has two. The African elephant lives on hot, dry plains, while the Asian lives in shady forests.

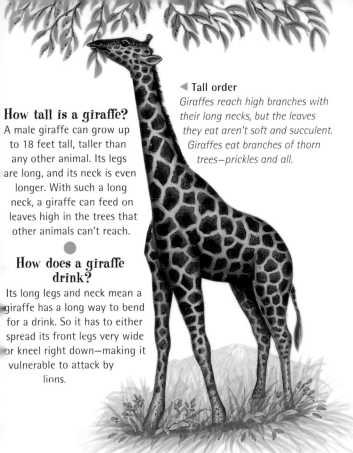

How tall is a giraffe?

A male giraffe can grow up to 18 feet tall, taller than any other animal. Its legs are long, and its neck is even longer. With such a long neck, a giraffe can feed on leaves high in the trees that other animals can't reach.

◀ **Tall order**

Giraffes reach high branches with their long necks, but the leaves they eat aren't soft and succulent. Giraffes eat branches of thorn trees—prickles and all.

How does a giraffe drink?

Its long legs and neck mean a giraffe has a long way to bend for a drink. So it has to either spread its front legs very wide or kneel right down—making it vulnerable to attack by lions.

Can hippos swim?

A hippo spends most of its day in or near water, only coming out at night to feed on plants. Yet it cannot really swim. Instead, it walks or runs along the river bed, often at amazing speeds, only coming up for air occasionally.

What is a gnu?

A gnu or wildebeest is a large African antelope that migrates across the plains between waterholes in huge herds.

Why do zebras have stripes?

Zebras' stripes seem hard to miss. But in the shimmering heat of Africa, they act as camouflage, blurring the zebra's outline, like shadows of grass, especially when the zebra is moving slowly.

How many kinds of zebra are there?

Three: the common, the mountain, and Grevy's zebra. The Grevy is the biggest and brays like a donkey.

QUIZ

1 What's the world's fastest runner?

2 How fast can an ostrich fly?

3 What's a group of lions called?

4 What's the world's biggest mammal?

5 What animal has a horn on the end of its snout?

6 How can you tell a male lion from a female?

7 What's an okapi?

8 What are elephant's tusks made of?

9 Do zebras neigh like horses?

Answers
1. The cheetah, reaching speeds of up to 68 mph; 2. An ostrich can't fly at all; 3. A pride; 4. The blue whale; 5. A rhinoceros; 6. An adult male has a big mane, but a lioness has not; 7. A relative of the giraffe; 8. Ivory; 9. No, they bark or bray.

221

Wetland animals

▲ Cool crocodile
Crocodiles adjust their lives to the weather, basking on the bank to warm up, but slipping into the water when it gets too hot.

What animals live in wetlands?

WETLANDS ARE AMONG THE WORLD'S most precious animal habitats, havens for many wild creatures. They are home not only to big animals like crocodiles and alligators, but to smaller creatures like nutrias (or coypus) and voles, and numerous birds, insects and, of course, fish.

What's the difference between a crocodile and an alligator?

Alligators are generally rounder and fatter, with short, blunt snouts. Crocodiles are slightly thinner, and their snouts are longer and narrower. Crocodiles also have a fourth tooth on the lower jaw that can be seen when their mouths are shut.

Are crocodiles like dinosaurs?

Crocodiles may be the nearest thing to dinosaurs alive today. Many dinosaurs may have had the same scaly skin and creatures very like crocodiles lived in the early Triassic Period, 200 million years ago, when the dinosaurs first appeared. But dinosaur's legs were underneath, not sticking out to the side like a crocodile's. Some people believe that dinosaurs' nearest living relatives are birds.

A crocodile's teeth do not overlap when the jaw is closed, unlike an alligator's

Are there any other creatures like crocodiles?

Crocodiles belong to a group of animals called the crocodilians. Besides various species of crocodiles and alligators, the group includes smaller crocodile-like animals called caimans and gharials. Caimans have bony plates on their bellies. The gharial has a distinctive long, thin snout.

▼ Wetland hunter
Crocodiles live in the rivers and swamps of the tropics. They are fearsome hunters, with massive, snapping jaws—yet it is their tail that is most lethal. Crocodiles lie in wait in the shallows, looking for all the world like a log, until animals come to drink at the water. Then they make a sudden lunge at their victim, drag it into the water and stun it with a blow from their tail, and drown it.

The eyes and nostrils stick out of the water even when the crocodile is submerged

Why is a flamingo pink?

For a long while, flamingos in zoos kept losing their delicate pink color and fading to white. Then keepers realized the problem was due to their diet. Flamingos feed on a certain kind of algae, and these algae contain chemicals called cartenoids that are responsible for the pink. If a flamingo does not get these algae, it does not get the cartenoids, and its color fades.

◀ A spoon bill

A spoonbill is a large wading bird that paddles through swamps in the tropics, dragging its long spoon-shaped bill through the water from side to side. It is searching for shrimp and other small water creatures, and when it finds a meal, it snaps the bill shut on its victim like a pair of spring-loaded sugar tongs.

QUIZ

What's special about Okavango?

The Okavango Delta in Botswana is one of the world's largest wetlands, swelling to 8,500 square miles in the wet season. A continual outflow and inflow of water keeps the water fresh and turns it into an astonishingly rich habitat—home to hippos, crocodiles, and elephants, as well as antelopes and countless birds and fish. But the Delta is coming under increasing threat from human activities.

The crocodile's tail is immensely powerful

1 **What's so remarkable about the mudskipper?**

2 **What gives the proboscis monkey of Borneo its name?**

3 **Where would you find a terrapin?**

4 **What is the Everglade kite?**

5 **Is it true that a mother crocodile carries her babies between her teeth?**

6 **Can crocodiles climb trees?**

7 **Can leeches be good for you?**

Many crocodiles have been killed for their shiny, scaly skin

Answers
1. It can survive out of water;
2. Its big red nose; 3. In a swamp; 4. A rare bird of prey that lives in the swamps of Florida; 5. Yes; 6. Yes; 7. Yes, their saliva contains a substance that can reduce blood clotting after surgery.

Mountain animals

What animals live on mountains?

COLD AND WINDY mountaintops are among the harshest environments in the world, but surprisingly many animals can survive there, including hunting animals such as pumas, or cougars, and snow leopards, as well as sure-footed grazers, such as mountain goats, chamois, ibex, and yaks.

▲ Lammergeier
The huge lammergeier is one of the few birds that can survive in high mountain peaks. They are superb gliders, floating over the slopes looking for carcasses for hours, seemingly without effort.

▼ Himalayan Snowcock
The Himalayan Snowcock is one of the highest-living of all birds, nesting at over 13,000 feet up in the Himalayan Mountains. Its gray and white plumage blends perfectly with the landscape of gray rock and snow.

Why does the lammergeier drop its dinner?
The lammergeier is a kind of vulture found in Africa and southern Europe. Food is scarce in the mountains, so the lammergeier has learned to feed on the toughest hide and bones in a carcass, too tough for other animals. But some bones are too tough even for the lammergeier. So it drops the bones again and again from a great height onto its own chosen rock (called an ossuary)—until the bone smashes and the bird can get at the soft marrow inside.

What is the world's biggest bird of prey?
The condors of California and the South American Andes are the world's biggest birds of prey with huge wings over 10 feet across, and weighing up to 26.5 pounds. They are actually vultures that feed on carcasses, and can soar for hours on the buffeting winds that howl through the peaks while they wait for an animal to die.

▲ Yak pack
In Tibet, the docile yak has been domesticated and is used as a pack animal, as well as for milk and meat, and for its woolly coat.

What is highest living mammal?
The yak is a remarkable ox with huge curved horns and a very shaggy coat that lives in the Himalayan mountains of Tibet, the world's highest mountains. Protected from the cold by its coat and able to eat the toughest grass it can survive over 19,000 feet up among the peaks.

▶ **Snow cat**
The snow leopard is a big cat that lives in the Himalayan mountains. It has a beautiful pale coat with dark markings, which has sadly made it a target for fur poachers.

QUIZ

1 What big cat lives in the steamy Amazon jungle and the icy peaks of the Rocky Mountains?

2 Which of these animals is in the camel family: a) llama b) alpaca c) guanaco d) vicuna?

3 What is the biggest British bird of prey?

4 How do you say ptarmigan?

5 The lynx is a big cat that lives on mountains. Is it bigger than a dog?

6 What are an eagle's claws called?

7 What is an ibex?

How do mountain goats climb?

Mountain goats are incredibly nimble climbers, able to get up the steepest slopes and leap from crag to crag with amazing agility. Their secret lies not only in their sense of balance but in their hooves. A mountain goat's hooves have sharp edges that dig into rock crevices. They also have slightly hollow soles that act almost like suction pads.

What is a chamois?

A chamois is a tiny animal that leaps around the highest peaks in Europe. It is a kind of goat-antelope, with the face and horns of an antelope and the mountaineering abilities (and smell) of a goat.

What dogs live in mountains?

The timber wolf looks somewhat like a German Shepherd. It has been driven from lowland forests in North America, but many still survive high in the mountains, hunting their prey in packs.

What animal can jump highest?

The puma, also known as the cougar or mountain lion, can jump an astonishing 18 feet into the air to get into a tree or jump up on a ledge. This is the equivalent of jumping up to an upstairs bedroom window—and much higher than any kangaroo, which can only jump 10 feet or so.

What was the highest climbing cat?

In September 1950, a four-month- old kitten belonging to a little Swiss girl named Josephine Aufdenblatten began following a group of climbers. Remarkably, it followed them all the way to the top of the highest Alpine peak, the 14,692-foot-high Matterhorn.

What happens in winter to a mountain hare's coat?

Like the coat of many animals in snowy places, the mountain hare's coat, or "pelage," turns white so that it is much harder for predators to spot against the white of the snow.

Answers
1. Puma (cougar); 2. All four; 3. Golden eagle; 4. TAR-mig-un; 5. It is bigger than a dog but smaller than a wolf; 6. Talons; 7. A kind of mountain goat

225

Desert animals

Do animals live in the desert?

Deserts are hard places for animals to live. They are very dry and often very hot, too. Many insects, spiders, and scorpions, as well as lizards and snakes, have adapted to life under these harsh conditions, but mammals such as the camel survive here, too.

▲ **Sand cat**
The desert even has its own predatory cat—the sand cat. It is quite small, and by hunting only at night, it can survive in hot deserts.

How do kangaroo rats save water?
The kangaroo rat gets its name from its big hind legs. It can survive even in California's Death Valley because it gets its water from fats in its food and saves water by eating its own droppings.

What antelope lives in the desert?
The Sahara Desert has its own large antelope, the addax. It never needs a waterhole, because it gets all its water from its food.

How do camels cope with the desert sand?
Camels' feet have just two joined toes to stop their feet from sinking into soft sand or snow, in the case of the Bactrian camel of Central Asia. They also have nostrils that close up completely to block out the sand, and double rows of eyelashes to protect their eyes from both sand and the Sun's glare.

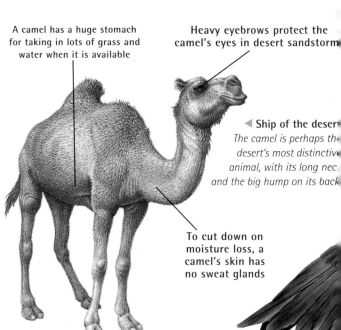

A camel has a huge stomach for taking in lots of grass and water when it is available

Heavy eyebrows protect the camel's eyes in desert sandstorms

◀ **Ship of the desert**
The camel is perhaps the desert's most distinctive animal, with its long neck and the big hump on its back

To cut down on moisture loss, a camel's skin has no sweat glands

What does a camel have a hump for?
The camel's hump is made of fat, not water as some people insist. But the fat can be broken down within the body and converted to both energy and water, whenever food and water are scarce.

▶ **Bearded vultures**
Vultures gather to feed around the carcasses of dead animals. Here the vultures are bearded vultures, which get their name from the clump of black bristles under their beaks; the carcass is of an antelope.

226

Desert hedgehog

Fennec fox

Jerboa

▲ The burrowers

A number of small animals cope with the desert heat by resting in burrows or sheltering under stones in the day, and only coming out to feed in the cool of the night. The fennec fox also has big ears to help it keep cool by radiating heat.

Do birds live in the desert?

Although many birds, like vultures, live in fairly dry parts of the world, only a few live in true deserts. Among these is the sand grouse. They rest under bushes during the day, then fly hundreds of miles at night to watering places. They soak up water in their breast feathers to help protect their young from the Sun.

Do vultures hunt?

No. Vultures are mainly scavengers, which means they feed on animals that have died already, or been killed by other animals such as lions. Their strong claws and beaks are for tearing carcasses apart. Each species feeds on a different bit of the carcass. So small Egyptian vultures wait until big lappet-faced vultures have finished before diving in.

QUIZ

1 What is a gila monster?

2 How many humps does a camel have?

3 What is a dromedary?

4 Where is a scorpion's sting?

5 How do lizards survive the desert heat?

6 What is the biggest desert in the world?

7 What continent does the kangaroo rat live on?

8 What is the biggest animal in the desert?

Answers
1. A Mexican desert lizard with a poisonous bite; 2. The Asian or Bactrian has two and the Arabian has one; 3. An Arabian camel for racing; 4. The tip of its tail; 5. By sheltering under rocks during the hottest part of the day; 6. The Sahara; 7. North America; 8. The camel

227

Seashore life

What makes the seashore special?

WATER IS CONTINUALLY moving up and down the seashore as waves roll up and down, and as the tide rises and falls. So creatures that live on the seashore have to be well adapted to surviving long periods out of water–or long periods in salt water. The seashore, then, has its own special creatures, including crabs, anemones, and a range of shellfish such as barnacles and limpets.

Common gull

▼ Rock pool
Rock pools are seashore aquariums full of all kinds of sea life.
Key:
1. Mussels
2. Starfish
3. *Cladophora* (algae)
4. Gem anemone
5. Common prawn (shrimp)
6. Bladder wrack (seaweed)
7. Common goby
8. Dog whelk (sea snail)
9. Barnacles
10. Sugar kelp
11. Cockle
12. Limpet

▶ Crab
Crabs have a hard shell, eight legs, and two powerful pincers for grabbing prey. They scuttle along the beach or the seabed sideways.

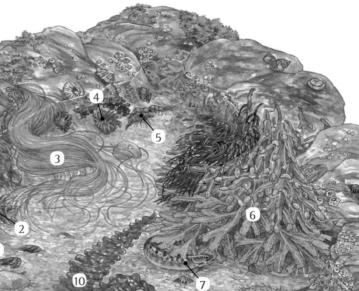

▶ Puffin and guillemot

A huge number of birds live by the sea, feeding on the seashore or diving for fish in the sea. Most have webbed feet for swimming, waterproof plumage, and sharp bills for gripping fish. The puffin's big colorful beak can hold up to 11 fish at once. Puffins live in burrows on clifftops. Guillemots nest in big, closelypacked colonies on narrow cliff ledges.

Guillemot

Puffin

What lives in rock pools?

Rock pools are pools of seawater left behind on seashore rocks as the tide goes out. They can get so warm and salty in the sunshine that they have their own special range of creatures, including shrimps, hermit crabs, fish-like blennies and gobies, anemones, and sea slugs.

What creature looks like a blob of jelly?

The beadlet anemone looks just like a blob of purple jelly stuck on the rocks when half uncovered by the tide. But when they are completely submerged, they open to reveal a ring of tentacles that they use to trap the small creatures they feed on. They look a little like flowers, which is how they get their name, but even though they never move, they are in fact carnivorous animals.

What is a mollusc?

Molluscs are a huge group of creatures including slugs and snails, clams and oysters, and octopuses and squids that live mostly in water or damp places. They are mostly soft, squishy creatures, but octopuses and squids are protected by stinging tentacles and shellfish and snails by shells.

What creatures live on beaches?

Sandy shores often look completely lifeless, but just below the surface are often all kinds of creatures burrowing in the sand to escape from the drying wind and sun, and also from hungry predators. They include razor clams, lugworms, sea cucumbers, small crabs, and burrowing sea anemones. Some filter food from seawater; others eat tiny particles from the sand. Along the hightide line you might see sandhoppers, which look like tiny yellow woodlice, feeding on rotting seaweed.

QUIZ

1. Puffins talk to each other by growling: true or false?

2. What does a sea urchin use its spikes for?

3. How many legs do barnacles have?

4. Why do fiddler crabs waggle their pincers a) to attract a mate b) to swim c) to frighten prey?

5. What color are lobsters?

6. The sooty tern can fly nonstop for 10 years: true or false?

7. Kittiwakes get their name because they dive toward sleeping cats: true or false?

8. The common gull feeds on garbage dumps in big cities: true or false?

Answers
1. True; 2. Walking; 3. 10; 4. a) 5. Blue. They only turn red when cooked; 6. True; 7. False; 8. True

12

Australian animals

▲ **Dingo**
The dingo is Australia's own wild dog, the only large carnivore. But it is a scavenger, not a hunter.

▲ **Wombat**
Wombats look a little like bears, but they behave more like rabbits, living in burrows and feeding on bark, roots and grass.

▶ **Kangaroo**
The kangaroo is the biggest of the marsupials. But a newborn kangaroo is smaller than a thumb—and blind and deaf—when it makes its amazing way up through its mother's fur from the birth opening, up through her belly fur, and into the pouch.

What's strange about Australian animals?

AUSTRALIA HAS ANIMALS LIKE NOWHERE else in the world. Its land links to Asia were cut off millions of years ago, and a unique set of pouched animals called marsupials developed, along with many other unusual creatures.

What are marsupials?
Babies of ordinary mammals grow fully inside their mother before they're born. Marsupial babies grow only partially, and are born so tiny they can't survive in the open. After they're born, they crawl into a pouch on their mother's belly and stay there until they're big enough to climb out.

Can marsupials fly?
No, but squirrel-like creatures called gliders come close. They have big flaps of skin stretched between their legs, so when they leap from tree to tree, they can glide long distances. The best flier is the great gliding possum.

Is the koala a bear?
No. It looks just like a big teddy bear, but the koala is not related to any bear. It is a marsupial belonging to a group of animals called phalangers, which includes the possum. When born, a baby koala crawls into its mother's pouch. After six months, it climbs around onto her back and rides piggyback.

What bird sounds like a chainsaw?
The male lyre bird is one of the world's weirdest-sounding birds. To attract a female, it imitates any sound it hears—including machines. It mimics a chainsaw starting up and hacking through wood, for instance, so well that people are fooled into thinking they're hearing the real thing.

What's a Tasmanian devil?
A fierce little marsupial that lives in Tasmania and looks like a cross between a black rat and a dog. It eats rats, wallabies, and birds—not to mention sheep, chickens, and poisonous snakes.

▲ Koala and baby
Koalas eat only the leaves and bark of certain eucalyptus, or "gum," trees. So they live only in a small area where these trees grow in eastern Australia.

▼ Marsupial mole
Many creatures in the rest of the world have their marsupial equivalent in Australia—even the humble mole.

How far can a 'roo jump?
Kangaroos' huge back legs help them jump huge distances. They can bound along at nearly 30 miles per hour, covering 33 feet or so at every single leap.

What's a duck-billed platypus?
The duck-billed platypus is a mammal with four legs and fur—but with webbed feet and a beak like a duck's. What's more, it is a "monotreme" which means it is one of the few mammals that lays eggs.

QUIZ

1 What is a baby kangaroo called?

2 What is a wallaby?

3 Is a wallaby bigger than a kangaroo?

4 What do bandicoots eat?

5 Is a cuscus: a) a Middle-Eastern meal b) a possum c) a very awkward man?

6 What does "playing possum" mean?

7 Is a quoll or dasyure a kind of: a) rat b) bat c) cat?

8 How does the kookaburra get its name?

9 What is a thorny devil, and is it dangerous?

Answers
1. A joey; 2. A small kangaroo-like animal; 3. No; 4. Insect larvae; 5. b) 6. Playing dead, as a possum does to escape predators; 7. c) 8. From its rippling call; 9. A harmless thorny lizard

Freshwater animals

What animals live close to rivers and lakes?

THE RIVERS AND LAKES of the world teem with all kinds of small creatures–small mammals such as voles, water rats, and otters, birds such as kingfishers and herons, insects such as dragonflies and water boatmen, and, of course, various kinds of freshwater fish, such as trout.

Why do some birds have long thin legs?

Birds that have long thin legs are generally wading birds, such redshanks, avocets, and curlews. They need their long legs for wading through the water to look for insects and worms. The biggest wading birds are herons, storks, and flamingos.

Why do ducks have bills?

Ducks have broad, flat bills because they feed on insects that live in the water. The broad bill enables them to scoop up a big gulp of water and filter out the insects. "Dabbling" ducks like mallards and widgeons simply upend in shallow water. "Diving ducks" like scoters dive to the bottom.

How does a kingfisher catch fish?

By sitting on a perch above the water silently watching for fish. When it sees a minnow or a trout, the kingfisher dives into the water in a flash, then flies back to its perch, tosses the fish in the air, and swallows it.

Why do frogs have long legs?

To help them jump huge distances to escape predators. A small frog can jump several feet – the equivalent of a human jumping the length of a football field. Frogs also have strong front legs to withstand the shock of landing.

What's a tadpole?

A tadpole is a young frog, soon after it emerges from its egg. A tadpole looks like a little black fish, but after seven weeks or so it will grow two back legs and get a frog face. After 10 weeks, its legs are quite long and it has front legs as well. By 12–14 weeks, the tail is gone and it emerges from the water as a frog.

▲ **Otter**
Otters live close to rivers and lakes all over Europe, North America and northern Asia. Their lithe, powerful bodies make them strong swimmers, and they can dive for five minutes at a time.

▲ **Barheaded goose**
Geese, ducks, and swans are all water fowl, with webbed feet and long, supple necks for reaching down into the water.

◀ **Common frog**
Frogs have two big swiveling eyes to help them judge distances when jumping and catching flies.

How do young otters spend their day?

Otters are mainly nocturnal animals, coming out of their dens in the river banks at night to hunt for fish in the river. But young otters are among the most playful of all animals, and they can often be seen during the day tumbling and rolling happily around on the bank, sliding down mud chutes, and leaping in and out of the water.

What's a coypu?

A coypu, or nutria, is a large water rodent, over 40 inches long and related to the guinea pig. It comes originally from South America, but was brought to Europe by fur farmers and has escaped to thrive in rivers and marshes.

Is a water vole a rat?

No, though people sometimes call them water rats. The vole prefers clean water, unlike the rat. The water vole is now becoming very rare, partly due to mink predation.

Why don't fish sink?

Because they have a special air bag inside their bodies called a swim bladder. This acts like the air in a lifejacket, keeping the fish afloat. Without it, the fish would have to swim continuously.

Why don't fish drown?

Fish breathe through gills, not lungs. Gills are rows of feathery brushes under flaps on the fish's head. The fish gulps in water through its mouth and lets it out through the gill covers. As the water passes over the feathery surfaces of the gill, they absorb oxygen from the water just as our lungs do from the air.

What is the main predator in European rivers?

The pike can grow to over 65 pounds. Long and sleek, with a large mouth full of sharp teeth, it is a deadly hunter that lurks among the weeds waiting for unwary fish, or even rats and birds, waiting to pounce. This is why it prefers deep ponds and slow rivers.

◀ Fish
Bream is a common freshwater fish that was once the staple diet of poor people in Europe. Rainbow trout has been introduced to European rivers from North America, with only partial success.

Bream

Rainbow trout

QUIZ

1 Do water voles eat any meat?

2 What bird is famous for its boom?

3 What is a water boatman?

4 What is an amphibian?

5 What is a young eel called?

6 What is the real name for an otter's den ?

7 What fish leaps up waterfalls?

8 What is a young dragonfly called?

9 How many legs does a crayfish have?

10 What is the jelly called frog spawn?

Grassland animals

What animals live on grasslands?

SOME GRASSLANDS ARE HOT. Some are quite cool. But they are all home to large herds of grazing animals such as antelope, buffalo, and horses, and the animals that prey upon them, such as lions, cheetahs and other big cats.

Wildebeest

Why do antelopes have long legs?

There is nowhere for a large animal to hide in open grasslands, so nearly all grassland animals are fast runners with long legs.

How fast can an antelope run?

Cheetahs can reach nearly 70 mph when chasing antelopes, but only over a short distance. The pronghorn antelope has been timed at 41 mph for over 10 miles and at 60 mph over nearly 650 feet. A race horse sustains over 40 mph over a 1.2 mile race.

Are all antelope horns the same?

There are over 60 species of antelope living in Africa and South Asia—and each has differently shaped horns.

▲ **Grazing herds**
Grasslands in the tropics are the home of vast herds of antelope of various kinds. In the last century, herds of 10 million springboks, hundreds of miles long, were sometimes seen in South Africa.

▲ **Cheetah**
The fastest runner in the world, the cheetah shows an astonishing turn of speed over a short distance to catch gazelles—a kind of antelope.

Which is the biggest antelope?

The biggest antelope is the giant eland of Africa, which has now become very rare. It stands over 6 feet tall at the shoulder, and weighs almost 2,200 pounds. The smallest is the royal antelope, which is very tiny indeed—no bigger than a hare.

What's odd about cheetahs?

Cheetahs are not like other big cats. In fact, some scientists think they are not that closely related. They have a much longer, flatter head than other cats. They also have permanently extended claws on the end of very long legs.

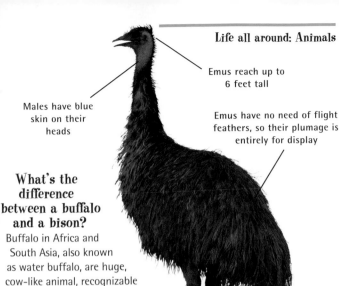

Emus reach up to
6 feet tall

Males have blue
skin on their
heads

Emus have no need of flight
feathers, so their plumage is
entirely for display

What's the difference between a buffalo and a bison?

Buffalo in Africa and
South Asia, also known
as water buffalo, are huge,
cow-like animal, recognizable
by their gigantic curved horns.
North American buffalo, also
called bison, are very different
creatures with huge, low-slung
heads, a big hump, and a shaggy
coat. They were once common in
both Europe and North America.

Do horses have toes?

Yes. All the big grazing animals
have toes, even hooved animals.
They are divided in two big
groups. Ungulates, including
horses, rhinos, and tapirs, have an
even number of toes on each
foot. Artiodactyls, such as pigs,
cows, and camels, have an odd
number of toes.

What are the world's biggest birds?

The world's biggest birds are all
flightless birds, including the
ostrich and the cassowary, with
very long legs for running and
long necks. The biggest of all is
the North African ostrich, which
lives on the fringes of the Sahara
Desert and grows up to 9 feet tall.

◄ Emu
*The emu is a
giant bird that lives
in Australia. It has
virtually no wings and can't fly,
but like ostriches and cassowaries,
it can run very fast on its long,
powerful legs. Emus are somewhat
inquisitive birds. They feed on fruit
and insects but may often steal
coins and keys.*

What was the biggest bird ever?

Bones found in New Zealand show
that until 1,000 years ago, there
was a bird called the moa that
was as tall as an elephant. When
the first bone was found in 1839,
some people thought that it did
indeed belong to an elephant. It
was the prominent 19th-century
British naturalist Richard Owen
who figured out what the bone
really belonged to.

QUIZ

1 How do cows 'chew the cud'?

2 What is an animal that eats plants called?

3 What animal has the longest horns of all?

4 How fast can an ostrich run: a) 12 mph b) 25 mph c) 37 mph?

5 What is an oryx?

6 What are prairie dogs?

7. Is it true that prairie dogs kiss each other when they meet?

8. How does a springbok get its name?

9. Were horses' ancestors bigger or smaller?

Answers
1. By rechewing partially digested food; 2. A herbivore; 3. Water buffalo; 4. c) 5. A kind of antelope; 6. Large, hamster-like creatures that live in big burrows beneath the prairies; 7. Yes; 8. By springing up to 10 feet straight up; 9. Smaller

Deep-sea animals

What creatures live in the sea?

LIFE BEGAN IN THE OCEANS, and now a huge range of creatures live there. There are thousands of kinds of fish, from tiny gobies to giant whale sharks. There are also many shellfish, including molluscs like clams and squids, and crustaceans like shrimp and lobsters–not to mention echinoderms like sea urchins and sea cucumbers. Then there are various reptiles like sea snakes, amphibians like turtles, and even a few mammals like seals and whales.

▼ **The great white shark**
Sharks have powerful jaws and double rows of razor-sharp teeth. When the outer row wears out or breaks, the inner row moves forward to replace it.

How big are whales?
Most full-grown whales are quite big, but the biggest of all—the blue whale—is absolutely gigantic. It is the largest creature that has ever lived. An average Blue whale is over 98 feet long and weighs over 100 tons. Some can grow twice as heavy. The biggest ever caught weighed 210 tons.

Are dolphins and whales related?
Yes. Dolphins are a kind of whale. In fact, the biggest of the 42 kinds of dolphin is called the killer whale. Together, whales, dolphins, and porpoises are known as cetaceans.

▲ **Giant turtle**
The leatherback is the world's biggest turtle. It can grow up to 10 feet long and weigh more than 4,400 pounds.

What is the fiercest shark?
The great white shark is one of the biggest and most fearsome of the sharks. Attacks by sharks on humans are quite rare, but most of the time it is great whites that are the culprits. They live all around the world in warm waters, and can grow up to 23 feet long. Their double rows of razor-sharp teeth can rip through sheet steel.

▶ Different levels in the sea

Different creatures live at different levels in the sea.

1. Dolphin
2. Jellyfish
3. Plant plankton
4. Zoo (animal) plankton
5. Tuna
6. Turtle
7. Whale
8. Squid
9. Deep sea fish, including angler fish and gulper eel

How do fish stay afloat?

Fish stay afloat because they have a special air bag inside their bodies called a swim bladder. Without this, they would have to swim all the time. As a fish swims deeper, the extra pressure of water squeezes more gas made in the blood into the bladder. As the fish swims up again, this extra gas is let out, so the fish floats easily.

Are any fish poisonous?

Quite a few, such as the pufferfish. The most poisonous is the stonefish, whose fins have spines containing a deadly neurotoxin that can kill in minutes.

How do fish breath underwater?

Fish get oxygen from the water just as we get oxygen from the air. But they absorb the oxygen through gills, which are feathery brushes under flaps on the side of the fish's head. To take oxygen in, the fish gulps water through its mouth, swashes it over the gills, and lets it out through the gill flaps.

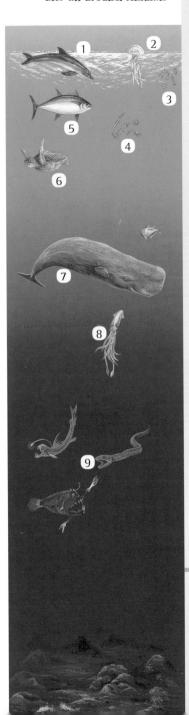

QUIZ

1. What shark has a head shaped like a mallet?

2. Some fish can fly up to 650 feet over the water; true or false?

3. What fish has a long lancelike nose?

4. Some fish can survive many days out of water: true of false?

5. The catfish makes a noise like a bagpipe with its swim bladder: true or false?

6. Parrot fish get their name because they eat nuts like parrots: true or false?

7. What whale is famous for its singing?

8. What fish can blow itself up to three times its normal size?

Answers
1. The hammerhead shark; 2. True, flying fish can; 3. Swordfish; 4. True; 5. True; 6. False; 7. The humpback whale; 8. The pufferfish

What was the
Stone Age?

Who were the
first farmers?

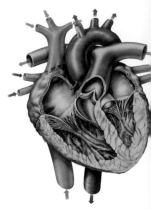

Who built the first
roof gardens?

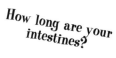

Who first wore
trousers?

Why does vomit
taste sour?

What food makes
you grow?

How long are your
intestines?

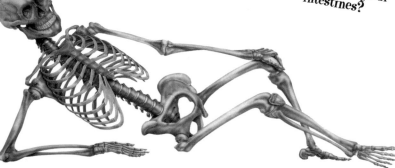

Why is blood red

What's a brain?

How do you smell?

People

Why do ears pop?

How many muscles does a football player have?

Why do we have two eyes?

Human origins

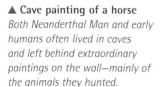

▲ Cave painting of a horse
Both Neanderthal Man and early humans often lived in caves and left behind extraordinary paintings on the wall—mainly of the animals they hunted.

Who were the first hominids?

Some of the oldest remains of hominids date from around four million years ago and belong to a group of creatures called *Australopithecus*, meaning "southern ape," who lived in Africa. Most walked upright like humans but were little more than 3 feet tall. They had a smallish brain, jutting ape-like jaws, and hairy bodies, and lived on fruit and vegetables.

When did the first humans live?

THE FIRST TRUE HUMANS lived about 30,000 years ago, but there were human-like creatures millions of years earlier. Scientists call these human-like creatures hominids, and there were many different kinds. The earliest hominids were much like apes, with long arms and a big jaw, but over time they evolved (changed) to become more and more like humans. Hominids and apes probably had the same ancestor–an orangutan-like creature that lived in Africa six million years ago.

Who first used tools?

Humans are not the only creatures to use tools. So do many animals such as sea otters. All early hominids probably did. But the first hominid to use tools with skill was *Homo habilis,* or "Handy Man," who appeared in Africa about two million years ago. *Homo habilis* was the first really human-like creature. He had a large brain and used tools to cut hides to make clothes and food for eating.

●

Where did hominids live?

All early hominids lived in Africa, and only began to spread out farther two million years ago. The first humans may have come from Africa, too.

◄ Making fire
Learning to make fire was one of Homo erectus's *greatest achievements. It not only kept him warm in winter, allowing him to live in cold places. It also meant he could cook food, and so eat meat.*

▲ Ancient home
Early humans were usually nomadic and lived in tents made of hide, bones, and sticks rather than permanent houses.

Homo habilis
(Handy Man)

Australopithecus
(Southern Ape)

Who were the first hunters?

The earliest hominids were vegetarians, like apes. But about 1.5–2 million years ago, a kind of hominid called *Homo erectus*, or "Upright Man," began to hunt and eat meat. *Homo erectus* could light fires, cook food, and hunt with wooden spears. He was also the first hominid to spread out of Africa, and remains have been found as far away as Russia and Indonesia.

Who was Neanderthal Man?

We humans belong to a group of creatures called *Homo sapiens*, or "Wise Man," and Neanderthal Man was the first of these, appearing about 100,000 years ago. He had a bigger brain than ours and a rugged body, but no one knows why he died out.

Life all around: People

Prehistoric flint spearhead

What was the Stone Age?

Until humans discovered how to make tools from bronze about 6,000 years ago, humans made their tools from stone. So all of human history from the time *Homo erectus* appeared two million years ago until the beginning of the Bronze Age 6,000 years ago is called the Stone Age. The Stone Age is divided into three periods: the Paleolithic, or Old Stone Age, from two million to 12,000 years ago; the Mesolithic from 12,000 to 9,000 years ago; and the Neolithic, or New Stone Age, from 9,000 to 6,000 years ago.

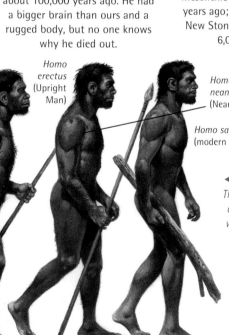

Homo erectus (Upright Man)

Homo sapiens neanderthalensis (Neanderthal Man)

Homo sapiens sapiens (modern human)

◀ **Evolution of humans**
This series shows some of our ancestors, beginning with Australopithecus *on the far left and ending with us humans, called by scientists* Homo sapiens sapiens, *on the right. The first human was called Cro-Magnon Man and lived about 30,000 years ago.*

QUIZ

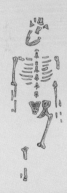

1 Early hominids made clothes from wool: true or false?

2 Early humans hunted dinosaurs: true or false?

3 Place the following ages of prehistory in the right order: the Iron Age, the Stone Age, the Bronze Age.

4 The first hominids lived in northern Canada: true or false?

5 Which of these is the most ancient: a) Java Man b) Neanderthal Man c) Cro-Magnon Man?

6 The oldest almost complete skeleton of a hominid is a) Bill b) Methusalah c) Lucy?

241

Peoples of the world

What are ethnic groups?

ETHNIC GROUPS ARE GROUPS of people who belong to the same race, nationality, religion, or culture. Irish people, for instance, come from the nation of Ireland or have ancestors who do. Jews are people descended from the ancient Hebrews of the Middle East and follow the Jewish religion. Many African Americans are descended from the West African peoples who were taken to the Americas as slaves in the 17th, 18th, and 19th centuries.

▲ Easter Island
Huge, stone statues on Easter Island in the Pacific were made by Polynesian peoples thousands of years ago.

Who are Afro-Caribbeans?

Afro-Caribbeans are descended from African slaves taken to work in the Caribbean. Since the 1950s, many have moved to Britain, other parts of Europe and the Americas.

Who are Caucasians?

The word Caucasian is used to describe white people whose ancestors came from Europe. The word comes from the Caucasus mountains in southern Russia.

◄ Masai warrior
The Masai are nomadic people of East Africa. Many have given up the nomadic life and now live in towns.

Who lives in Africa?

In North Africa, in countries like Egypt, most people are Arabs. But south of the Sahara are over 800 native African groups, each with its own lifestyle and culture. Descendants of European colonists live here, too.

Who are nomads?

Nomads are people like the Bedouins of North Africa and the Middle East, the Mongols of Asia and the Masai of Africa who move around the country taking their shelters with them.

► Maoris
Maoris are the people who first settled in New Zealand 1,000 years ago, coming over the Pacific from the Polynesian islands in large sailing canoes.

▲▶ Ethnic clothes
In the past, people from different ethnic groups could be recognized by their traditional way of dressing, like the Polish woman in traditional costume on the right. But now most people wear modern western-style clothing, like the children above.

Who lives in South America?

In the country, groups of Native American peoples still survive. But in cities there is a mix, including people descended from: Spanish settlers who came in the 1500s; marriages between Spanish settlers and Native Americans; African slaves brought here in the 18th century; and more recent European immigrants.

▶ Oaxaca woman weaving
The Oaxaca of Mexico are among several Native American peoples who survived after the Spanish arrived in the 1500s. They are famous for their woven cloth.

Who lives in North America?

North America was originally inhabited by Native Americans. Today, most people are descended from Europeans who have come here over the centuries, from immigrants from South and Central America, and African Americans.

● Do peoples move about?

In history, whole peoples have migrated or moved huge distances. The Polynesians spread across the Pacific from South America, thousands of years ago. Asian peoples crossed into Alaska from Siberia 11,000 years ago and spread south to become Native Americans. The Anglo-Saxons of England came originally from northern Europe.

QUIZ

1 In 2012, what did the world population reach: a) 700 million b) 7 billion c) 70 billion?

2 How many babies are born every minute in the world a) 2 b) 167 c) 15,000?

3 Are mestizos a) sausages b) shoes c) offspring of marriages between Native Americans and Spanish settlers?

4 Which country has the most people: a) Russia b) India c) China?

5 What is the world's most crowded large country a) Australia b) Bangladesh c) Italy?

6 Is a kimono a) a Japanese silk gown b) a Chinese fruit c) a large lizard?

Answers
1. b) 2. b) 3. c) 4. c), China has around 1.4 billion people; 5. b) 6. a)

243

The first farms

Who were the first farmers?

EARLY PEOPLES mostly lived in small bands and moved around hunting animals and gathering food from wild plants. Then, about 12,000 years ago, some people learned to herd animals such as sheep and goats to provide a ready supply of food. Others learned to sow the seeds of wild plants to grow crops. This happened at different times in different parts of the world. The earliest farms were created by the people of the Middle East around 11,000 years ago. But there were farms long ago in China, India, and Central America, too.

▼ Ancient Egyptian farmers

The development of farms led to the creation of the world's first great civilizations—including that of Ancient Egypt, where the pyramids were built. Egypt's farms were alongside the Nile River, which not only provided water, but brought rich silt soil in its floods to an area that would otherwise be desert.

What were the first crops?

The first crops were grown from the seeds of wild grasses that gave wheat and barley. One of the oldest known kinds of wheat is one called emmer. Vegetables such as peas were also grown on early farms.

How did farming change people's lives forever?

For the first time, people had no need to move around looking for food. They could settle in one place and build first villages and then towns. At Jarmo in Iraq, there are the remains of 24 mud huts where 150 people lived around 11,000 years ago.

What new skills did people learn?

To begin with, farming was mixed with hunting, but the extra food meant people were free to do other tasks. Soon some people became skilled in things such as building houses and food stores, weaving cloth, and making pots. They also learned how to use metals—first bronze in the Bronze Age and then iron in the Iron Age.

What were the first inventions?

Once they were settled in farms, people began to invent all kinds of things to make life easier. They learned how to make pots from clay around 9,000 years ago. At about the same time, they learned how to grind grain into flour in shallow bowls called mortars using club-like stone pestles.

How did they plant seeds?

At first, farmers planted seeds simply by dropping them in holes made with a stick. Then someone learned that you could get better results if you turned over the soil a bit and carved out long furrows to put the seeds in with a blade called a plow.

When was the wheel invented?

Sometime before the wheel was invented, people may have moved heavy loads using tree trunks as rollers. The first wheels were probably slices of tree trunk with a rod or axle pushed through. A platform could rest on the axle to make a cart. By about 5,200 years ago, solid wheels made of short planks of wood bolted together were being used in Mesopotamia in the Middle East.

QUIZ

1 Is a sickle a a) bout of feigned illness b) small black fruit c) curved blade for cutting the ears off grain?

2 What did early farmers make from wheat and barley?

3 Why did early farmers drive cattle over their grain harvest?

4 Was the farming area by the Middle East's Tigris and Euphrates rivers called the a) Grain Belt b) Fertile Crescent c) Golden Triangle?

5 5,000 years ago is about a) A.D 3,000 b) 7,000 B.C. c) 3,000 B.C.?

6 Is crop rotation a) spinning a horsewhip b) turning grains to face the Sun c) using fields for different crops each year to preserve the soil?

The first cities

What were the first cities?

ONCE EARLY PEOPLE BEGAN to settle in one place in the Middle East around 11,000 years ago, families soon grew, and villages grew into cities. They were places where those who governed the land lived, craftsmen made things, and people came to buy and sell things—not only food grown in the countryside around them, but metal goods, cloth, jewels, spices, and much more besides.

What's the world's oldest city?

No one knows for certain, but one of the oldest is Jericho in the Middle East. The ruins of some of the city walls date back over 11,000 years. They were massive stone structures perhaps 23 feet tall. There were also many other cities in the Middle East at least 7,000 years ago.

Were there any early cities in China?

Chinese civilization began over 7,000 years ago when the Yang-Shao people built the first villages on the land between the Hwang-Ho and Wei-Ho rivers.

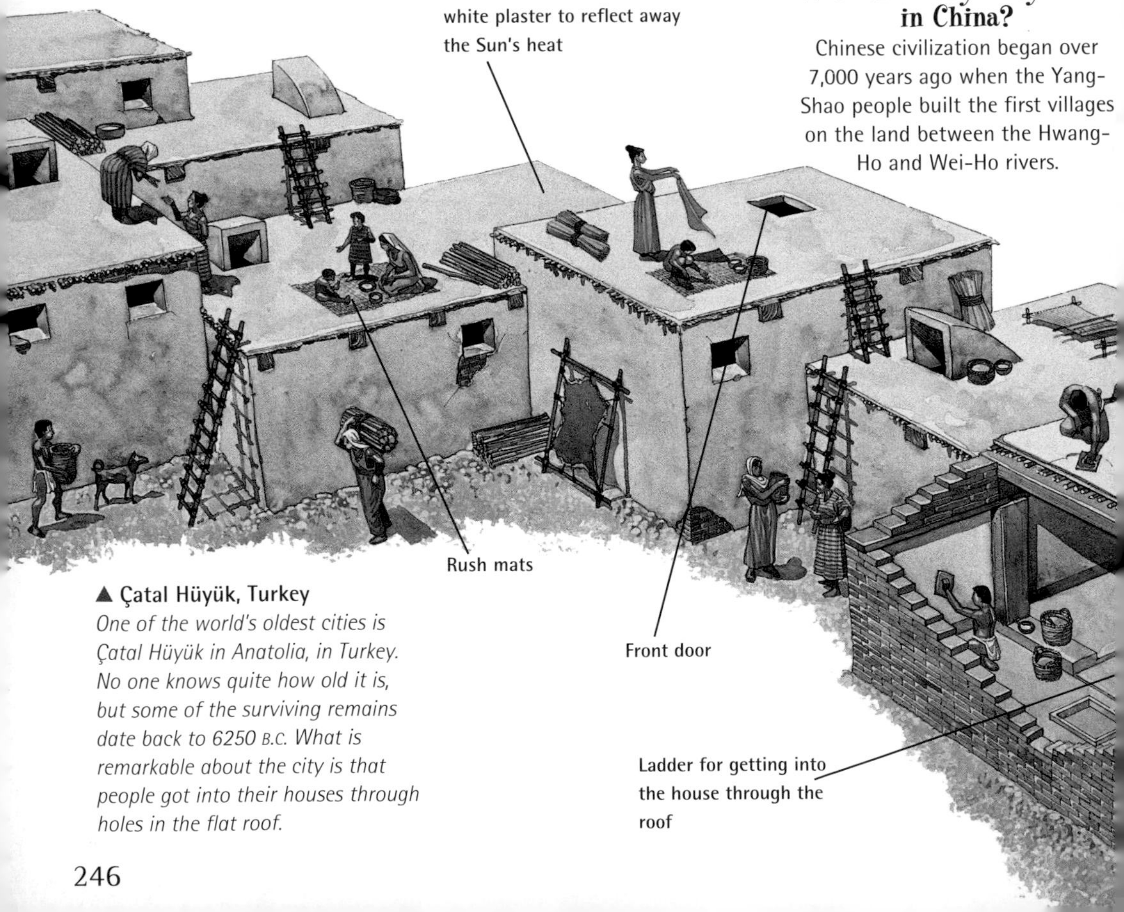

Walls and roof covered with white plaster to reflect away the Sun's heat

Rush mats

▲ **Çatal Hüyük, Turkey**
One of the world's oldest cities is Çatal Hüyük in Anatolia, in Turkey. No one knows quite how old it is, but some of the surviving remains date back to 6250 B.C. What is remarkable about the city is that people got into their houses through holes in the flat roof.

Front door

Ladder for getting into the house through the roof

Who built the first roof gardens?

6,000 years ago, the civilization of Sumer began to flourish on the fertile land between the Tigris and Euphrates rivers in modern Iraq. Here people built the great cities of Ur and Eridu. One of the centerpieces of Ur was the ziggurat, a temple built like a step-sided pyramid—with trees and lush gardens on top.

Where did writing begin?

Writing did not begin in any one place, but in the Middle East in Sumeria, in China, and in Central America independently. The first written symbols were probably used by rulers to show their power and by city officials to record and label food and other things. One of the earliest systems of writing is "cuneiform," used in Sumer and Babylon, which used wedge-shaped marks on clay tablets.

Holes filled with daub (mud and straw)

Walls built with mud bricks

Framework built from wooden posts and beams

What were the hanging gardens of Babylon?

Babylon was first built 3,800 years ago. But it reached its height under King Nebuchadnezzar II in the 6th century B.C. Its beautiful hanging gardens were one of the wonders of the world. They were planted high on a ziggurat (see left) to remind Nebuchadnezzar's queen of her mountain home.

Who were the pharaohs?

The pharaohs were the kings of the civilization of Ancient Egypt on the banks of the Nile River. The pharaohs ruled for nearly 3,000 years, from 2920 B.C., and left behind astonishing monuments to their power and wealth—not only the great pyramids and statues in the desert, but fabulous treasures in their tombs, including mummies, writing, and beautiful gold and jeweled objects.

What is civilization?

The word "civilization" comes from the Latin word for city dweller. It is the highly organized, settled way of life—complete with rules and laws, as well as writing—that came with the creation of the first cities.

QUIZ

1 What ancient city was carved from desert stone a) Stonehenge b) Ur c) Petra in Jordan?

2 Pyramids were built in Mexico 2,800 years ago: true or false?

3 What ancient civilization was based in Crete: a) Aztec b) Minoan c) Persian?

4 What was a chariot?

5 What would you ask a scribe to do?

6 What did the Ancient Egyptians write on?

7 Are the ruins of the ancient city of Mohenjo-Daro in a) Pakistan b) Arizona c) Turkey?

Clothes and costumes

When did people first wear clothes?

NO ONE CAN BE SURE WHEN people stopped going naked. But the first clothes were probably animal skins people wrapped around themselves to keep off the cold. It was when people began to farm and settle in villages that the earliest actual clothing was worn. At first, clothes were just skirts and shawls built up from twisted tufts of wool and flax. But by about 6,000 years ago, people had learned to spin and weave cloth, and sew it to make nice clothes.

Who were the first fashion victims?

Over 5,000 years ago, the women of ancient Sumeria wore beautiful colored clothes, along with fancy headdresses, and gold and silver earrings and necklaces studded with jewels, such as lapis lazuli and carnelian.

Who first wore cosmetics?

It may have been the women of Ancient Egypt, who had elaborate make-up, including eyeliner, skin powder, and lipstick. They mixed ground malachite (copper ore) and galena (lead ore) with oil to make kohl to line their eyes. They made lipstick and rouge from red ocher, and also painted their nails with henna.

▼ All kinds of clothes?
Today, fewer and fewer people wear distinctive traditional clothes. Instead, people everywhere wear the shirt, trousers, skirt and jacket made popular in Europe and North America.

Muslim girls often wear a veil called an aba or chador covering their whole body and head

Sari, a traditional Indian dress made of silk or artificial material

Traditional turban from central Asia

Jellaba, a traditional smock worn in North Africa.

Smocks are common in China

Baseball cap

▲ Warm skins
Animal skins have provided clothes for many tens of thousands of years, especially in very cold places where wool and cotton are too thin. The Inuits and Saami people of the far north traditionally dress in skins.

Who invented silk?
The Chinese discovered how to make silk thread from the cocoon of the silkworm caterpillar almost 5,000 years ago. According to legend, it was the Princess Si-ling-chi who found that the cocoon could be separated into threads in hot water. She was known thereafter as the Silk Goddess.

●

Who first wore platform shoes?
Chopines were worn by women in Italy in the Renaissance in the 1400s. The biggest belonged to prostitutes in Venice, whose soles were built up to a height of 80 cm or more — as a high as a chair.

Who wore togas?
Togas were wraps of beautiful light cloth often worn by men in Ancient Rome over their tunics. The early togas were simple and worn with both ends thrown over the shoulder. But in later years, they became more elaborate. Officials had togas edged in a special purple dye.

●

Who first wore trousers?
The ancient Celts of Britain wore pants over 2,000 years ago, and so did the Chinese. Dutch and English sailors revived them in Europe in the 16th century. But it took French Revolutionaries of the 1790s to make them popular.

●

What is a crinoline?
The underskirt of steel hoops Victorian women wore to make their dresses fuller.

QUIZ

1 Is a jerkin a) a pickled cucumber b) a violent throwing action c) a medieval waistcoat?

2 Tudor men wore codpieces on their tights: true or false?

3 What kind of cloth came from De Nîmes in France?

4 Where were parkas invented?

5 What kind of boots are named after a British general?

6 Georgian boys wore dresses: true or false?

7 Some crinolines were so large, women had to go through double doors sideways: true or false?

8 Who wears the most armor today?

7. True; 8. Ice hockey players
Inuits; 5. Wellingtons; 6. True;
jeans; 4. In the Arctic by
blue material used to make
1. c) 2. True; 3. Denim, the
Answers

249

Eating

Why do we eat?

MOST OF THE FOOD YOU EAT is fuel, burned by your body for energy to keep you going. It gets this mainly from substances in food called carbohydrates and fats. But you also need to eat small amounts of food such as proteins to help repair and build body cells, and tiny traces of chemicals called vitamins and minerals the body cannot make itself.

Where does food go when you eat it?

Your food goes down through your body in a long tube called the alimentary canal. When you swallow, food slides down your gullet or esphagus into the stomach, where it churns around for a few hours. Then it is squeezed into a long, coiled tube called the small intestine, where nourishing parts of the food are absorbed into the blood. The rest then passes on into a larger tube called the large intestine, and the waste, or feces is pushed out through the anus.

How long are your intestines?

Your intestines are coiled up so much that if you unwound them, they would be over three times as long as your body—20 feet.

◄ **Digestive system**
If you could see your digestive system through your body, this is what you would see. Most of the system is the alimentary canal, the long tube that takes food through your body.

How is food broken down?

Food is broken into the small molecules the body needs by a process called digestion in two ways. First, food is broken up mechanically by chewing and by the squeezing muscles of your digestive system. Second, it is attacked chemically by acids, such as the bile and hydrochloric acid in your stomach, and by biological chemicals called enzymes, mixed in with your saliva and stomach juices.

What are carbohydrates?

Carbohydrates are foods made of kinds of sugar like glucose and starch. Foods such as bread, rice, potatoes, and pasta, as well as sweet things, are rich in carbohydrates.

What is fat?

Fats are greasy foods that won't dissolve in water. Some are solid, like cheese and meat fat. Others are oils. Fats are usually stored by the body as energy reserves, rather than burned up at once like carbohydrates.

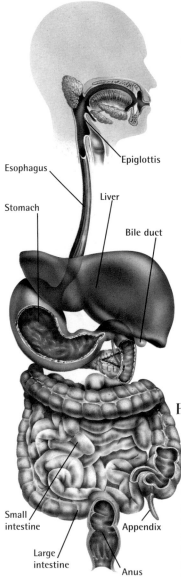

Esophagus

Epiglottis

Liver

Stomach

Bile duct

Small intestine

Appendix

Large intestine

Anus

◄ A healthy diet

A healthy diet contains just the right amount of each kind of food your body needs, and no more. The bulk of your diet must be solid food like carbohydrates, but it must also contain enough fat, plenty of protein, and the right vitamins and minerals.

What food makes you grow?

To grow, your body needs proteins, the natural substances from which cells are built. Proteins are made from 20 basic chemicals called "amino acids." The body can make 12 of these. The other eight you must get by eating protein-rich food such as milk, fish, meat, eggs, and beans.

Why are teeth different?

Different teeth do different jobs. The flat "incisors" at the front have sharp edges for slicing through food. The pointed "canine" teeth just behind are good for ripping chewy food. The big flat-topped "premolars" and "molars" toward the back of your mouth are good for grinding food into a small, mushy ball ready to be swallowed.

QUIZ

1 How many teeth do most grown-ups have: a) 12 b) 32 c) 64?

2 Why does vomit taste sour? Is it because a) you've eaten sour food b) your stomach is full of acid c) vomit gets rid of body poisons?

3 Vitamin C helps your body fight infection. What foods do you get it in?

4 What are the teeth you had as a baby called?

5 How long can you survive without eating: a) 2 days b) 20 days c) 300 days?

6 How long can you survive without drinking: a) 2 days b) 20 days c) 300 days?

7 What kind of food is meat mostly: a) carbohydrate b) fat c) protein and fat?

► Inside a tooth

To chew food every day, your teeth must be incredibly hard-wearing. The outside of a tooth is made from enamel, the hardest substance in your body. Inside that is dentine, a material as hard as bone. In the center is a pulpy mass of blood and bones.

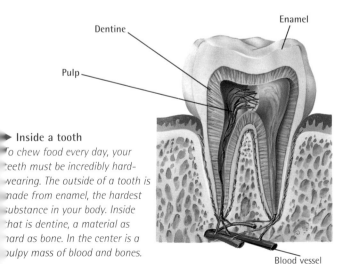

Dentine

Pulp

Enamel

Blood vessel

Breathing & circulation

Why do we breathe?

JUST AS A FIRE NEEDS air to burn, so every cell in your body needs a continuous supply of oxygen to burn up the food it gets in the blood. The cells get their oxygen from the air you breathe in. Without oxygen your body cells quickly die–and brain cells die quickest of all. If you stopped breathing for very long, you would soon lose consciousness, your brain would be damaged, and eventually you would die.

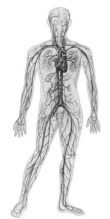

▲ Blood vessels
Arteries rich in oxygen carry bright red blood. Veins, which return carbon dioxide to the lungs, are bluer.

How does your body get oxygen?

Every time you breathe in air through your nose or mouth, the air rushes down your windpipe into your lungs. Your lungs are spongy bags inside your chest, filled with millions of minute branching airways. At the end of each airway is an airsac, or alveolus, with walls so thin that oxygen can seep through into the tiny blood vessels wrapped around it.

What do you breathe out?

Most of what you breathe out is the air you breathed in, minus a little less oxygen. But it also contains a little waste carbon dioxide brought to the lungs from your body cells in the blood.

How does oxygen get to each body cell?

This is what your blood circulation is for. Driven by the pumping of the heart, blood circulates through an intricate network of blood vessels all the way around the body again and again, every 90 seconds or so. As it passes through the lungs, it picks up oxygen as it washes around the airsacs. The heart then pumps this oxygen-rich blood throughout the body. As the blood returns to the lungs, it carries with it the waste carbon dioxide from the cells.

Why dos the heart have two sides?

Your heart has two sides because your body has two blood circulations. The left side of the heart pumps blood through the lungs to pick up oxygen, and take it to the right of the heart. This is called pulmonary circulation. The right side pumps oxygen-rich blood around the body and back to the left of the heart. This is called the systemic circulation.

Artery taking oxygen-poor blood to the lungs

Veins bringing oxygen-rich blood back from the lungs

Right atrium, where blood is held ready to be pumped

Right ventricle, the heart's pumping chamber

How does your heart pump?

Your heart has walls of muscle that contract automatically once a second or more. As they contract, they squeeze blood into the blood vessels. The entrances of each of the heart's two pumping chambers, or ventricles, have little flaps, or valves, to ensure that blood can only enter and leave one way.

Why is blood red?

Oxygen is carried through the blood inside red blood cells. Red blood cells can carry oxygen because they contain a remarkable substance called hemoglobin. Hemoglobin glows bright red when it is carrying oxygen but fades to dull purple when it loses oxygen.

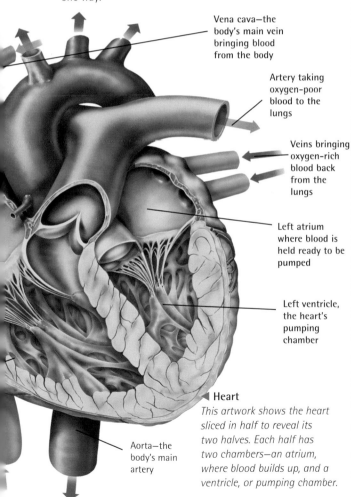

Vena cava—the body's main vein bringing blood from the body

Artery taking oxygen-poor blood to the lungs

Veins bringing oxygen-rich blood back from the lungs

Left atrium where blood is held ready to be pumped

Left ventricle, the heart's pumping chamber

Aorta—the body's main artery

◀ **Heart**

This artwork shows the heart sliced in half to reveal its two halves. Each half has two chambers—an atrium, where blood builds up, and a ventricle, or pumping chamber.

QUIZ

1 How many miles of airways are there in your lung:
a) 4 miles b) 429 miles
c) 1,490 miles?

2 Your heart is in the middle of your chest, slightly to the right: true or false?

3 Blood carries food as well as oxygen to the body cells: true or false?

4 Your pulse-the rate your heart beats-is normally 300 beats a minute: true or false?

5 What are the major blood vessels that carry blood away from the heart called?

6 Are the tiniest blood vessels called: a) filigrees b) venioles c) capillaries?

7 Smoking damages which body tissue?

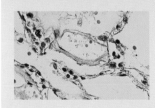

Moving

Why do you have bones in your body?

WITHOUT BONES, YOU WOULD FLOP on the floor like a spoonful of jelly. Your bones make the strong, rigid framework called the skeleton that supports your body. It not only provides an anchor for your muscles, but supports your skin and and other tissues. It also provides a protective casing for your heart, brain, and other organs.

How many bones do you have?
A baby's skeleton has over 300 bones, but some fuse together as it grows. You probably now have 206 bones—although some people have extra bones in their back.

What's inside a bone?
The very center of many bones is a core of soft, jelly-like material called bone marrow. This where your blood cells are made.

Why are bones strong?
Their tough outer casing combines two materials—one that makes them flexible and another that makes them stiff. The flexible material is strong, stretchy strands called collagen. The stiff material is hard deposits of the minerals calcium and phosphate.

Why don't bones weight you down?
Bones are incredibly light despite their strength because they are full of holes. Inside the casing is a criss-cross honeycomb structure of struts called trabeculae.

What are joints?
Joints are places where two bones meet. A few joints, such as those in the skull, are completely rigid. But most joints allow the bones to move, and the end of each bone is shaped to allow it to move in a particular way. The knee is a hinge joint that lets the lower leg swing back and forward. The hip is a ball-and-socket joint that lets you rotate your leg all around.

What do muscles do?
Muscles make parts of your body move. They work by making themselves shorter, so that they pull things together. When the muscle on the front of your upper arm gets shorter, it pulls up your forearm.

Are there different kinds of muscle?
The outside of your skeleton is covered with muscles called skeletal muscles, which you use to make your body move. But there are also muscles inside your body called involuntary muscles, which move food through your digestive system and control your blood flow without you being aware of it. A third kind of muscle works your heart.

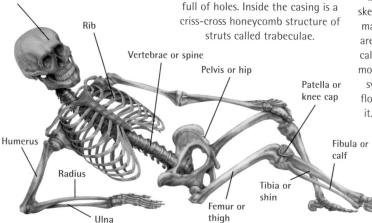

Skull

Rib

Vertebrae or spine

Pelvis or hip

Patella or knee cap

Humerus

Radius

Ulna

Femur or thigh

Tibia or shin

Fibula or calf

◀ Skeleton
Your skeleton is tough, light framework of over 200 bones.

▼ Inside a muscle

A muscle is made of bundles of fibers, each made of strands called fibrils, which are in turn made up of myofibrils.

Muscle fiber

Fibril

Myofibril

Myosin filament

Actin filament

Why do muscles work in pairs?

Muscles work in pairs because they can only pull themselves shorter. They need a partner working the opposite way to pull them out again. On your upper arm, you have biceps muscles at the front, which shorten to lift your forearm. You have triceps muscles at the back to pull it lower again.

How do muscles work?

Muscles are made of bundles of tiny fibers that get thicker and shorter when the muscle is working. Each of the fibers is made of interlocking strands of two materials, actin and myosin. The myosin has little chemical hooks that twist and tug on the actin to make the muscle shorter.

●

How are bones and muscles attached?

Muscles are attached to bones by tough cords called tendons. Bones are bound together by tough cords called ligaments.

Different kinds of joints

Ball-and-socket joints like the shoulder and hip allow free movement in many directions.

The swivel joint between your skull and spine lets you turn your head to the left and right.

In your thumbs, two saddle-shaped bone ends fit snugly to combine strength and free movement.

Hinge joints like those in the knee and elbow swing only two ways, like a door, but are strong.

QUIZ

1 Your biggest muscle is in your buttocks: true or false?

2 How many muscles do you have a) 650 b) 860 c) 1,170?

3 What fuel do muscles run on a) glucose sugar b) hydrocarbons c) gas?

4 What are the muscles in the top of your chest called a) petrels b) pectorals c) dorsals?

5 Which is the longest bone in your body?

6 What mineral is good for your bones?

7 How many muscles does the average football player have?

Seeing

How do you see things?

YOUR EYES ARE A LITTLE like tiny TV cameras. At the front is a lens called the cornea–the disc in the center of your eye. This projects a picture onto an array of light-sensitive cells called the retina lining the back of your eye. The retina then sends signals to your brain.

How do you see when it's dark?

In order to see well in dim light, your pupils open wider to let in more light. In the dark, it gets up to 16 times bigger. The sensitivity of the retina increases too, by up to 100,000 times. But the retina becomes less sensitive and the pupil narrows in very bright light. Even so, very bright light can damage the eyes, which is why you should never look directly at the Sun.

Why do we have two eyes?

Each eye gives a slightly different view of the same thing. The nearer a thing is, the greater the difference between the view. These slight differences combine in the brain to give us an impression of 3D depth and solidity, and allow you to judge easily just how far away things are.

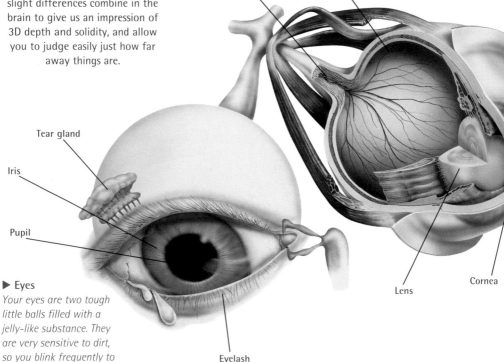

Optic nerve to the brain

Retina (light-sensitive layer)

Tear gland

Iris

Pupil

Lens

Cornea

Eyelash

▶ Eyes
Your eyes are two tough little balls filled with a jelly-like substance. They are very sensitive to dirt, so you blink frequently to wipe away dust, and they are washed by tears.

► Color mix

All the colors you see are contained in white daylight. If you spin this wheel of color, the colors would mix to look white.

What are rods and cones?

Rods and cones are the two kinds of light-sensitive cell in your retina. Rods tell you how bright light is. Cones tell you what color it is. Rods are much more sensitive than cones and work even in dim light. Cones don't work well in dim light, which is why colors look gray at night.

How do you see in color?

It was once thought that there are three kinds of cones in the eye—some sensitive to red light, some to green, and others to blue. So some scientists think you see colors simply as different mixtures of these three "primary" colors. Others think there are pairs of cones sensitive to blue and yellow, red and green, and the color you see depends on which half of the pair is stimulated most by the light.

What's in your eyeball?

Eyes are filled with a jelly-like substance called vitreous humor which is very clear to let you see well.

What are primary colors?

Primary colors are three basic colors that can be mixed in different proportions to make every other color. The primary colors of light are blue, green, and red. But when mixing paint you use three different primary colors—yellow, magenta (a kind of purplish red), and cyan (a greenish blue).

What is nearsightedness?

Not everyone sees equally well. Nearsightedness occurs when your eyeball is slightly stretched out, so you can only see things nearby clearly without glasses or contact lenses. Farsightendness means you only see distant things clearly.

What is your iris?

The iris is the ring around the dark center, or pupil, of your eye. It contracts or expands to open the pupil wider, or to close it.

◄ **Flipped flower**
As rays of light focus through the cornea, they cross over. So the picture in your eye is flipped upside down, although your brain sees it as normal.

QUIZ

1 Which has the sharpest sight, in order: a) human b) fly c) eagle?

2 Astigmatism means: a) your eyes are different sizes b) you tend to blink frequently c) you see things magnified more in one direction than the other?

3 Everybody has a blind spot right in the middle of their eye: true or false?

4 Everyone has one strong eye and one weak: true or false?

5 Pupils get their name because the picture they give is small, like schoolchildren: true or false?

Answers
1. c), a), b) 2. c) 3. True;
4. True; 5. True

Hearing

How do you hear?

SOUND REACHES YOUR EAR AS VIBRATIONS in the air. Your outer ear funnels sound into a tube into your head called the ear canal. Inside, the sound hits a taut wall of thin skin called the eardrum and makes it vibrate like a drum. As the eardrum vibrates, it rattles three little bones, called ossicles, which knock against the "cochlea," deep inside the ear. The cochlea is filled with fluid, and as it is knocked waves run through the fluid, and the waves move hairs attached to nerves. The moving of the hairs tells your brain about the sound.

▼ Inside the ear
The flap of skin on the side of your head is only the entrance to the real ear. Inside are all the complex mechanisms of the middle ear, designed to pick up the faintest vibrations in the air and amplify them enough for the hearing nerve to respond to.

Why do you have two ears?
So that you can tell which direction a sound is coming from. You can pinpoint sound because a sound to the left of you is slightly louder in your left ear than in the right ear, and vice versa.

What is earwax?
Earwax is a yellow-brown waxy substance made in the glands lining the ear canal. Its purpose is to trap dirt and germs and prevent them from getting into the inner ear. It is slowly eased out of the ear.

Why do ears pop?
When you fly up or down in a plane, the air pressure may change before the air inside your ears can adjust. The popping occurs when pressure evens out again.

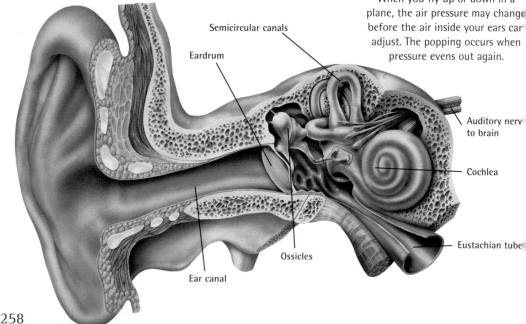

Semicircular canals

Eardrum

Auditory nerve to brain

Cochlea

Eustachian tube

Ossicles

Ear canal

▶ Inside the cochlea

The vibrations of a sound are amplified (made much bigger) by the time they reach the cochlea of the inner ear, but they are still very tiny. So inside the cochlea is a remarkably sensitive mechanism that picks up every slight movement of the fluid.

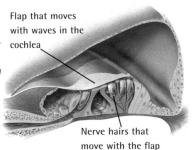

Flap that moves with waves in the cochlea

Nerve hairs that move with the flap

How is sound measured?

Sound is measured in decibels. Decibels go up geometrically—that is, three decibels is twice as loud as two, and four twice as loud as three, and so on.

How loud is a pin dropping?

About 10 decibels—just about the quietest sound you can hear. A whisper is about 20 decibels. Some animals hear even quieter sounds.

How loud is a jet?

Close up, a jet engine is about 140 decibels. This kind of noise is genuinely painful to the ears, and can do lasting damage. Indeed, any continuous sound over 90 decibels can be damaging.

How do your ears help you balance?

Next to the cochlea is a cluster of three fluid-filled rings called semicircular canals. These canals act like tiny levels, telling you when you are tilting one way or the other, as the fluid moves inside the canal.

What are the ossicles?

The ossicles are three linked bones in the middle ear. They all have Latin names and a simple English equivalent: hammer or malleus, anvil or incus, stirrup or stapes.

Hammer

Anvil

Stirrup

▲ Ossicles

Sounds are transmitted through the middle ear by the tiny ossicle bones. The hammer bangs against the anvil like a blacksmith's hammer on an anvil. The stirrup gets its name because it is shaped like a rider's stirrup.

QUIZ

1. The cochlea is named after the snail: true or false?

2. The nerve hairs inside the cochlea are called a) the ear trumpet of Obi b) Copper's flute c) the organ of Corti?

3. Is the scientific name for your outer ear: a) pinna b) sinna c) dinna?

4. Humans can hear much higher-pitched sounds than dogs: true or false?

5. Sound travels through the air in a) waves b) straight lines c) little lumps?

6. What is the loudest sound in space?

7. The pitch of a sound is measured in a) Hertz b) Akes c) Paynes?

8. Sound travels faster through water than air: true or false?

9. The ear is connected to the top of your throat: true or false?

Taste, smell, and touch

How do you taste things?

YOU TASTE THINGS BOTH WITH taste buds on your tongue and also by using other senses. Your taste buds can primarily detect the difference between sweet, salty, sour, and bitter flavors, and a savory flavor known as "umami." But when you eat, other sensations–heat and cold, texture, and especially smell–also come into play. It is these extra sensations that help you tell the difference between a huge range of foods.

▲ Taste bud
The taste buds contain clusters of cells with hairs on the end. When these hairs are washed over by saliva, they react if the saliva contains the right taste.

▼ Cheese tastes
Taste buds can detect little real difference between all these cheeses. But other senses such as smell combine with taste to reveal the range of flavors.

What are taste buds?

Taste buds are clusters of special cells set in tiny wells in your tongue—so tiny that there are 10,000 of them altogether. As you chew, tiny particles of food dissolve in saliva and trickle down into the taste buds. Each taste bud reacts to a particular kind of taste—sweet, salty, sour, bitter, or umami. If the food contains the right flavor, the taste bud is triggered and it immediately sends off a message down nerves to your brain.

Where do you taste sweet and sour things?

Your taste buds are hidden away inside tiny bumps on your tongue called papillae. Taste buds that respond most to sweet tastes are on the tip of the tongue. Salty flavors are detected most strongly just behind on the sides of the tongue. Sour things set off taste buds on the sides of your tongue farther back. Bitter tastes hit the back of your tongue. Umami flavors are detected mainly at the center of your tongue.

How do you smell?

Smells are tiny particles in the air. As you breathe in, some of these particles travel up your nose and dissolve in the mucus. They then drift toward a small patch at the top inside called the olfactory epithelium. This tiny patch is packed with 10 million smell receptors. These smell receptors react to chemicals dissolved in the mucus and send messages to your brain.

How do you feel things?
You feel things touch your skin because your skin is packed with different kinds of receptors that can tell you whether things are hard or soft, hot or cold, rough or smooth to the touch.

Where can you feel things?
There are sense receptors in almost every part of your skin. But some places, like your hands and face, have lots of receptors and so are very sensitive. Other places on the body—the small of your back, for instance—have very few and so are not so sensitive.

How do you know how hard someone's pushing?
When someone touches you, the receptors in the skin send off signals to your brain. The harder the touch, the faster the nerves send signals.

Which parts of the body are most sensitive to heat?
Your elbows and feet are more sensitive to heat than many other parts of the body. This is why mothers sometimes test the bathwater for babies to make sure it isn't too hot by putting their elbow in the water.

QUIZ

1 Sometimes you can't taste things if your nose is blocked with a cold: true or false?

2 By the age of 20, you will have lost 20 percent of your sense of smell: true or false?

3 Dog's noses are a) 100 times more sensitive than humans b) 10,000 times c) 1 million times?

4 Babies have a better sense of smell: true or false?

5 How far can you smell underwater a) 3 feet b) 60 feet c) 800 feet?

6 Sense receptors connect to which part of the brain: a) the midbrain b) the brain stem c) the cortex?

7 Taste buds last only a day: true or false?

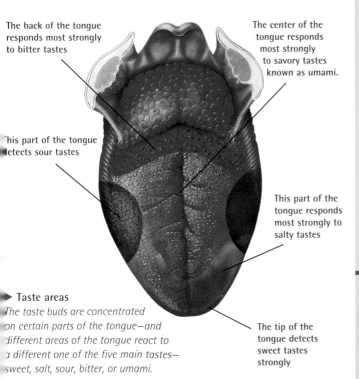

The back of the tongue responds most strongly to bitter tastes

The center of the tongue responds most strongly to savory tastes known as umami.

This part of the tongue detects sour tastes

This part of the tongue responds most strongly to salty tastes

The tip of the tongue detects sweet tastes strongly

► Taste areas
The taste buds are concentrated on certain parts of the tongue—and different areas of the tongue react to a different one of the five main tastes—sweet, salt, sour, bitter, or umami.

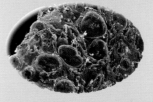

Answers
1. True; 2. True; 3. b)
4. True; 5. None; you can't smell underwater; 6. c)
7. False: taste buds last a week before the body replaces them

Thinking

What is a brain?

YOUR BRAIN IS an amazing package of 100 billion tiny nerve cells, each connected with up to 25,000 others. This huge number of interconnecting nerve cells is what makes your brain so smart-enabling it to do everything from analyzing all the signals coming from your senses to controlling your body-and thinking.

What goes on in the brain?
Different things happen in different parts of the brain. The center of the brain is right at the top of the neck where nerves from the spine join it. This is where body functions you don't have to think about—like breathing and heart rate—are controlled. Just behind this is the "cerebellum" which controls balance and coordination. Wrapped around the outside is the cerebrum, where you think and complex tasks like speaking and actions you decide on are controlled.

What is the nervous system?
The nervous system is your body's hot line carrying messages from the brain to every organ and muscle in your body—and sending back a constant stream of information to your brain about the world both inside and outside your body. It is made from long strings of special nerve cells or neurons.

What is the central nervous system?
The brain and the spinal cord (the bundle of nerves that runs through the middle of your backbone) together make what is called the Central Nervous System, or CNS. All the body's nerves radiate out from the CNS in branches. This is why severe damage to the spine can make someone paralyzed.

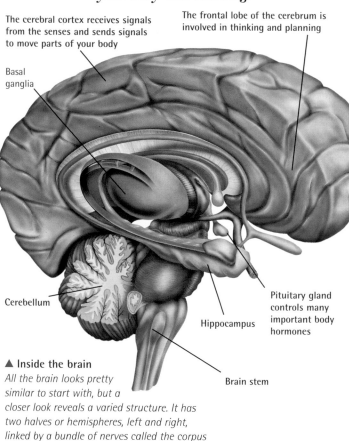

The cerebral cortex receives signals from the senses and sends signals to move parts of your body

The frontal lobe of the cerebrum is involved in thinking and planning

Basal ganglia

Cerebellum

Hippocampus

Pituitary gland controls many important body hormones

Brain stem

▲ Inside the brain
All the brain looks pretty similar to start with, but a closer look reveals a varied structure. It has two halves or hemispheres, left and right, linked by a bundle of nerves called the corpus callosum. In the center are a collection of different structures, each with its own task.

Where in your brain do you see things?

All your senses are received in a part of the brain called the cortex, which is like the brain's rind, the outer layer of the brain at the top. The part of your brain that registers what you see is called the "visual cortex." This is right at the back of the brain.

What does a brain look like?

It looks like a large, soggy, pinkish gray walnut on the outside. This is because the outer part of the brain is made of masses of nerves called gray matter, which are wrinkled up to get as much inside your head as possible.

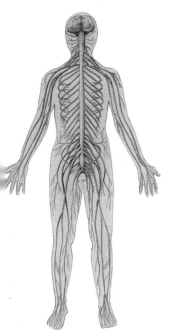

▲ Juggling
Skills like juggling, which require tremendous coordination, are gradually programmed into the cerebellum at the back of the brain.

What's the difference between the brain's two halves?

The left side of your brain controls the right side of your body; the right side controls the left. Most people are right-handed because the left side of the brain is dominant. In left-handed people, the right side of the brain is dominant. Since the part of the brain that controls speech is in the left of the brain, and the part of the brain that controls awareness of space is in the right, some people believe left-handed people are likely to be good at art and design.

◀ Nerves in the body
Nerves link your brain to every part of the body. Like branches on a tree, the nerves spread out from the central nervous system (the brain and spinal cord). Motor nerves control movement. Sensory nerves send signals back to the brain. Sensory and motor nerves are usually paired.

QUIZ

1 The small club-shaped part of the brain center that controls moods, willpower, and learning is called the a) hippo-potamus b) hippocampus c) cortex?

2 The brain is the only part of the body that can survive without oxygen: true or false?

3 Boys' brains are bigger in relation to their bodies than girls': true or false?

4 The tiny gaps between the ends of nerves are called a) gates b) prolapses c) synapses?

5 The brain goes to sleep when you do: true or false?

Answers
1. b) 2. False: even a few minutes without damages the brain; 3. False: the reverse is true; 4. c) 5. False

263

Growing

How do you grow bigger?

YOUR BODY IS MADE UP OF MILLIONS of tiny packets called cells, nearly all of them so tiny they can be seen only under a powerful microscope. You grow as these cells divide in two again and again to make new cells. This is called cell multiplication and happens most when you're young. You look young because most of your body is made from new cells.

What makes you grow?
You grow bigger mainly because the pituitary gland in your brain sends out a chemical in the blood called "growth hormone." When this hormone is released into the blood from time to time, it tells body cells to divide and multiply.

▼ **Body changes**
Most people in the richer parts of the world live until they are 70 or more, and some live until they are 100. During their lives, their body will have gone through many changes, gradually growing during childhood, then slowly deteriorating once they are adults.

You stop growing when you are an adult, and may have children of your own

At puberty, the body changes shape and sexual organs begin to mature

As people get older, they begin to slow down and become less fit and active

During childhood, legs and arms grow longer and adult teeth grow

Older people may become quite frail, and their senses usually weaken

A two-year-old is about half the height it will be when an adult

Babies often learn to crawl before they take their first tottering steps

What is puberty?

You are born with sexual or reproductive organs—the organs that enable you to have children when you are an adult. Puberty is the time of your life when they develop in the right way for you to have children. Puberty comes at different ages in different people. Girls typically reach puberty at 11 or 12. Boys reach it at 13 or so.

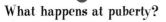

What happens at puberty?

Puberty is the time when your body begins to change from a child's into an adult's. A girl begins to grow breasts, and her hips become wider, and she grows hair around her genitals. Eventually she starts her monthly periods of menstruation. A boy's testicles begin to grow and produce sperm. He begins to grow hair on his chin, and his voice deepens.

What happens when you grow old?

By the time you are 20 or so, you are fully grown. From then on, your body starts to slowly deteriorate. People age at different rates, but by the time you are 65 or so, you will be less fit, and less able to run and jump. Your hair will probably be gray or white. You may be bald if you are a man. Your skin will become wrinkled. You may stoop. You will find all your senses less sharp. All the same, all body cells except for nerve cells are continually being renewed, even when you old.

1. Before cell division begins, each chromosome is copied, and the two copies coil up into dark rods that join to make an X-shaped pair

2. The pairs of chromosomes line up across the center of the cell. They stick to tiny threads that grow across the cell

3. The threads begin tugging in opposite directions. The pairs split in half, and each half is pulled to the opposite end of the cell

4. A new nucleus starts to form around the cluster of chromosomes at each end of the thread. Each cluster of chromosomes is identical

5. A membrane grows around the two new nuclei, and eventually the old cell divides down the middle to create two brand new cells

▲ How cells grow

New human cells are made when old cells split in half. This is how your body grows when you are young, and how body cells that are worn out are replaced by new ones. The process of cell division is called mitosis, and ensures that each new cell is identical and gets a copy of the cell's instructions or chromosomes.

QUIZ

1 The part of your body that grows quickest until you are five is a) the brain b) the legs c) the tongue?

2 A doctor who specializes in treating children is called a) a neurologist b) a pediatrician c) a pedologist?

3 Your brain goes on growing all your life: true or false?

4 The rate at which you grow is controlled by a chemical released by the pituitary gland in your brain: true or false?

5 The tallest man who ever lived was a) 6 feet 2 inches, b) 8 feet 11 inches c) 16.5 feet?

6 What part of your body is almost as big when you are a baby as it will be when you are an adult?

Answers
1. a) 2. b) 3. False;
4. True; 5. b)
6. Your head

265

What's the biggest creature that
ever lived on land?

Where does sand
come from?

Was Australia ever
joined to Africa?

What is a wadi?

Do glaciers ever
melt?

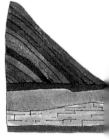

How do we know
dinosaurs existed?

Could we ever visit the center of the Earth?

Was New York ever in the tropics?

Earth

How does frost break rock?

How long do earthquakes last?

When did the first humans appear?

How hot is it in the Earth?

Earth's history

How old is the Earth?

Earth formed 4.55 billion years ago

Archean Period

Precambrian Period

Proterozoic Period

THE EARTH IS ABOUT 4.55 BILLION YEARS OLD. Scientists know this from analyzing meteorites—lumps of rocky debris that have fallen to Earth from space and probably formed at the same time as the Earth. They can tell the age of a meteorite by studying atoms in it. When the meteorite formed, certain atoms in it began to break up at a constant rate. By analyzing just how far they have broken up, scientists can tell exactly how old the meteorite is. This is called radioactive dating.

How is Earth's history divided up?

Just as the day is divided into hours, minutes, and seconds, geologists divide the Earth's history into different time periods. The longest are eons, which are hundreds of millions of years long. The shortest are chrons, which are just a few thousand years long. In between come eras, periods, epochs, and ages.

What do we know about Earth's early history?

We know only a little about the first four billion years of Earth's history, called the Precambrian, because fossils from that time are rare. But we know a great deal about the last 590 million years, since the beginning of the Cambrian Period, and this is split into 11 periods.

How can you tell how old a rock is?

Many rocks form from mud and other sediments on sea and river beds. When living things die, their remains are sometimes preserved in sediments like these. Because different plants and animals lived at different periods in Earth's history, geologists can tell how long ago the rocks formed from the fossils they contain.

When did the dinosaurs live?

The dinosaurs first appeared during the Triassic Period, about 220 million years ago. They became widespread over the next 150 million years, during the Jurassic and Cretaceous periods. Then, about 65 million years ago, they suddenly died out—perhaps because a huge asteroid struck the Earth and turned it cold.

Key:
1. Jellyfish
2. Trilobite
3. Acanthodian (jawed fish)
4. Cooksonia (early land plant)
5. Ichthyostega (early amphibian)
6. Dimetrodon (early mammal-like reptile)
7. Anteosaurus (early reptile)
8. Herrerasaurus (early dinosaur)
9. Pteranodon (early flying reptile)
10. Cephalopod (squid-like shellfish)
11. Brachiosaurus (dinosaur)
12. Crusafontia (small mammal)
13. Merychippus (early horse)
14. Proconsul (great ape)
15. Homo sapiens (early man)

QUIZ

Earth's history

This illustration shows the major time periods of Earth's history and some of the characteristic fossil creatures and plants that help geologists identify rocks from each of these different periods.

Key to periods:
Archean: 4,600–2,500 million years ago (mya)
Proterozoic 2500-590 mya
Cambrian 590 mya
Ordovician 505 mya
Silurian 438 mya
Devonian 408 mya
Carboniferous 360 mya
Permian 286 mya
Triassic 284 mya
Jurassic 213 mya
Cretaceous 144 mya
Tertiary 65 mya
Quaternary 2 mya

1 Is a meteorite a a) ball of rock from space b) kind of ancient rock c) kind of dinosaur?

2 The Earth formed from the remains of an old star: true or false?

3 What was the first living thing on Earth?

4 What period in Earth's history did the swamps that gave us coal form in:
a) Precambrian
b) Carboniferous
c) Quaternary?

5 How old is the oldest rock ever found a) 38,000 years b) 380 million years c) 3.8 billion years?

6 When did the first modern humans appear?

Cambrian Period
Ordovician Period
Silurian Period
Devonian Period
Carboniferous Period
Permian Period
Triassic Period
Jurassic Period
Cretaceous Period
Tertiary Period
Quaternary Period

Paleozoic Era
Mesozoic Era
Cenozoic Era

Answers
1. a) 2. True; 3. Bacteria
4. b) 5. c)
6. Cro-Magnon Man lived around 30,000 years ago

269

Fossils

What are fossils?

FOSSILS ARE THE RELICS of plants and animals that have been preserved for many thousands or millions of years, usually in stone. They may be the remains of living things–bones, shells, eggs, seeds, and so on. Or they may just be signs, such as footprints or scratchmarks, left behind.

▼ **Fossils**

There are many different ways in which once living things can be fossilized.

Key:

1. Spider in amber, the hardened resin of ancient trees
2. Leaves turned to carbon
3. Trace fossil: footprint preserved in hardened mud
4. Fossilized shark's teeth
5. Trilobite: ancient shellfish
6. Petrified (turned to stone) logs

What is the oldest fossil?

The oldest fossils, not counting microscopic traces of bacteria, are "stromatolites." These are fossils of giant pizza-like mats, made by colonies of billions of microscopic cyanobacteria. Some of these date back over 3 billion years!

How do fossils form?

When an animal dies, its soft parts rot away quickly, but if its bones or shell are buried quickly in mud, they may eventually turn to stone.

When a shellfish dies and sinks to the seafloor, its old shell gets buried in mud. Over millions of years, water trickling through the mud dissolves away the shell, but minerals in the water fill its place, making a perfect cast.

How do scientists tell a fossil's age?

From the rock it is found in. They know how old rocks are relative to each other because layers of rock form on top of each other, so the lowest layers are oldest. Measuring the fossil's radioactivity gives a more precise date.

▼ Big lizard
Iguanadon was one of the first dinosaurs identified, by the fossil hunter Gideon Mantell in the 1820s. Mantell found a fossilized claw of the iguanodon, and realized that it was very similar to that of a modern iguana (a kind of lizard)—only 20 times as big! Mantell thought it had four legs like an iguana. We now know it only had two.

Q<small>UIZ</small>

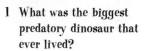

1 What was the biggest predatory dinosaur that ever lived?

2 There once were flying dinosaurs as big as airplanes: true or false?

3 There were creatures on land long before there were any in the sea: true or false?

4 Coal is the fossilized remains of swamp plants: true or false?

5 Woolly mammoths (large, hairy, elephant-like creatures) were found preserved in a) sugar b) ice c) sand?

6 Which of these shelled creatures was related to squids: a) ammonite b) cockle c) brachiopod?

Why do geologists study fossils?

The simplest way to tell the age of a rock is from the fossils it contains. Many species only lived at certain times during Earth's history. So if a rock contains a species that dates from a certain time, the rock must have formed at that time, too. Useful fossil species for dating are called index fossils. These index fossils include certain ancient kinds of shellfish called trilobites, graptolites, brachiopods, crinoids, ammonites, and belemnites.

What do fossils tell us?

It is from the study of fossils that fossil scientists have learned how plants and animals evolved on Earth. They have found that most species only lived for a short time, before being superseded by another better adapted to the conditions of the time.

How do we know dinosaurs existed?

Because they left behind a huge number of their fossilized remains. No one knew what they were for a long time. In China, people thought they belonged to dragons. Then, in the 1820s, an English naturalist named William Buckland recognized them for what they were. Now hundreds of species of dinosaur have been identified from fossils, and recently, a clutch of dinosaur eggs was discovered with the babies inside.

What's the biggest creature that ever lived on land?

Many dinosaurs were huge, but the largest were the plant-eating sauropods, which had long necks for browsing on trees. The biggest may have been the brachiosaurus which was at least 46 feet tall and 82 feet long—four times as tall as an elephant and six times as long.

Continental drift

Have the continents always been the same?

NO. THEY MAY LOOK VERY FIXED, but the continents are moving slowly all the time. Sometimes they crunch together. Sometimes they break apart in the middle. But they are always drifting about the world, like ice floes on a pond. This is called continental drift.

How fast are the continents moving?

The speed continents move varies from place to place. North America is drifting away from Europe at about three-fourths of an inch a year—the same rate a fingernail grows. This might seem slow, but over millions of years, it can move continents thousands of miles.

Why could South America and Africa fit together like a jigsaw?

Because they were once joined together—along with all the other continents—in a giant supercontinent that geologists call Pangea. About 200 million years ago, Pangea began to break up, and the fragments have drifted apart to form today's continents.

What happens when continents crunch together?

The edge of one continent may well be crumpled up. These crumples, or folds, form high mountain ranges. The Himalayan mountains were thrown up where India crashed into Asia. Indeed, the Himalayas are getting higher, because India is still pushing into Asia.

Is it just the continents that move?

No. The whole of the Earth's surface is broken into 20 or so giant fragments called tectonic plates, and all of these move around. The continents are simply carried on top of these moving plates, like cargo on a raft.

220 mya The continents were joined together as Pangea

▶ **Pangea**

The map of the world has been changing over time. 220 million years ago (mya), there was just one supercontinent, Pangea, and one giant ocean, Panthalassa. By analyzing the alignment of magnetic particles in rocks (which set pointing north like compasses), geologists have traced how the continents have drifted since.

200 mya Pangea split into two landmasses, Gondwanaland in the south and Laurasia in the north

135 mya The South Atlantic opened between South America and Africa. India broke off and drifted towards Asia

QUIZ
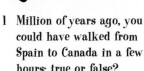

1 Million of years ago, you could have walked from Spain to Canada in a few hours: true or false?

2 What continent was once attached to the south coast of Australia?

3 Which two continents crashed together to form the Alps?

4 The San Andreas fault in California is the gap between two tectonic plates: true or false?

5 Tides in the sea occur because the continents are moving: true or false?

6 There were once dinosaurs in Antarctica: true or false?

7 Was the Sahara always a desert?

▶ **Ice cover in the Ice Age**
At times during Earth's history, in cold periods called Ice Ages, many parts of the world have been covered with thick ice. Because continents have drifted, even the Sahara was once glaciated!

Was New York ever in the tropics?

Yes. 250 million years ago, the place where New York is now was on the equator, and it was a boiling-hot desert. It was in this hot desert that the sandstone formed that gave New York its famous brownstone houses. 300 million years ago, New York was a steamy swamp.

Why do the continents move?

Probably because they are carried along by moving currents of molten rock in the Earth's interior. Just as bubbles rise to the surface in boiling soup, so giant streams of molten rock rise up through the Earth's hot interior. When they come up beneath the surface, these "convection currents" spread out sideways, carrying the continents with them.

Was Australia ever joined to Africa?

Yes, about 200 million years ago the north coast of Australia was joined to the southeast coast of Africa.

40 mya Europe split from North America, and the continents began to drift to their current positions

The future The Pacific will shrink and the Atlantic will get wider. Africa will split along the Great Rift Valley in the east

Answers
1. True; 2. Antarctica; 3. Europe and Africa; 4. True; 5. False; 6. True; 7. No

273

Structure of the Earth

What's inside the Earth?

THE HARDY, ROCKY SURFACE OF THE EARTH, called the crust, is just a thin shell. Inside, the Earth gets hotter and hotter until at the very center the temperature reaches 11,000°F—hotter than the surface of the Sun. So just beneath the crust, there is an ocean of half-molten rock thousands of miles deep called the mantle. Beneath this, in the Earth's center is an outer core of molten iron and nickel. In the inner core, pressure is so intense that the metal cannot melt despite the heat.

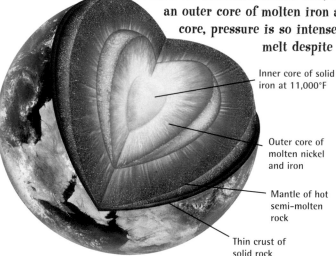

Inner core of solid iron at 11,000°F

Outer core of molten nickel and iron

Mantle of hot semi-molten rock

Thin crust of solid rock

▲ Inside the Earth
Beneath the thin shell called the crust, the Earth churns and bubbles like soup, and at the boundary of the Earth's core there may be continents and oceans like those on the surface.

How big is the Earth's crust?

The Earth's crust is surprisingly thin. Proportionally it is not much thicker than the skin on an apple. It is thickest beneath the continents. But even here it is no more than 44 miles thick at most. It is thinnest beneath the oceans, often less than 5 miles thick.

How do we know what the Earth is like inside?

From the vibrations of earthquakes. Long after the ground stops shaking, the reverberations from earthquakes shudder through the Earth. Sensitive detectors can sense them on the far side of the world. Just as you can hear the difference between metal and wood if you tap them with a spoon, so scientists can "hear" the Earth's interior from the pattern of earthquake waves.

Could we ever visit the center of the Earth?

No one has ever managed to drill more than 7.5 miles down. Even at this depth, pressures are so great and rock so hot and soft that drill bores close up as fast as they are drilled. It seems unlikely then that anyone will ever get through the thin crust to the mantle, let alone down to the core.

What's the mantle made of?

The mantle is made of rock, like the crust. But the most common substances are minerals that are rare on the surface, like perivskovite and olivine.

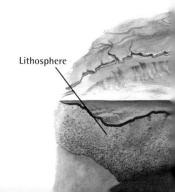

Lithosphere

Where does the crust end?

The crust meets the mantle along a boundary called the Mohorovicic discontinuity. Chemically, this is a distinct break. But the top of the mantle is just as rigid as the crust. So scientists often group the top of the mantle together with the crust and call it the lithosphere. "Litho" means "stone." Beneath the lithosphere is a layer that flows like very, very, sticky molasses called the asthenosphere.

▼ **Crack in the Earth**
The Earth's surface is cracked in many places. One of the biggest cracks is under the middle of the oceans. Here the tectonic plates that form the Earth's rigid shell, or lithosphere, are pulling apart. As they do, molten rock from the mantle oozes up, cools, and solidifies, forming a long ridge of rock.

Are there any gaps in the crust?

Yes, the crust—or rather, the lithosphere (see left) — is actually broken into 20 or so giant sections called tectonic plates. Molten material from the mantle oozes up along the cracks, creating volcanoes—especially where they are pulling apart.

How hot is it in the Earth?

In the lithosphere, the temperature climbs 95°F every 3,300 feet you go down. In the mantle, temperatures climb to 5,400°F. The core reaches 11,000°F.

QUIZ

1 How thick is the Earth's mantle a) 190 miles b) 1,900 miles c) 19,000 miles?

2 In 1864, the famous book *Journey to the Center of the Earth* was written by a) Nathaniel Hawthorne b) Charles Dickens c) Jules Verne?

3 There may be continents on the Earth's core: true or false?

4 There are oceans hundreds of miles below the Earth's surface, in the mantle: true or false?

5 What do the Earth beneath the crust and an old fireplace in common?

6 Some caves reach right down into the mantle: true or false?

7 Which one is lightest (least dense): a) the Earth's crust b) its mantle c) its core?

8 The world's deepest borehole in the Kola Peninsular in Russia goes down: a) 0.6 miles b) 7.5 miles c) 217 miles?

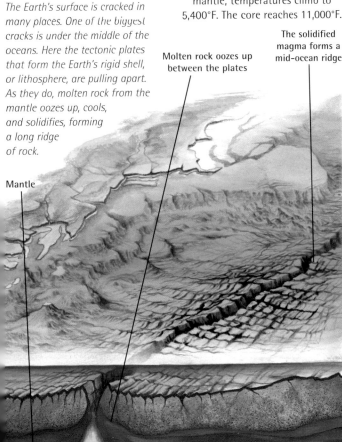

Molten rock oozes up between the plates

The solidified magma forms a mid-ocean ridge

Mantle

Answers
1. b) 2. c) 3. True! 4. Probably true: scientists have found evidence in minerals from the mantle; 5. Both are called mantles; 6. False; 7. a) 8. b)

Mountain building

▲ The Himalayas
The Himalayas are the world's highest mountains, including such soaring peaks as K2 (28,251 feet), Kanchenjunga (28,169 feet) and Lhotse (27,940 feet) as well as Everest.

What are the world's highest mountains?

THE WORLD'S HIGHEST MOUNTAINS are the Himalayan mountains in Asia to the north of India. Here are all the world's 10 tallest mountains, including Mount Everest, the very highest mountain of all, 29,029 feet high. But each continent has its high mountain range. There are the Andes in South America where there are many peaks over 20,000 feet, the Rocky Mountains in North America, and the Alps in Europe.

Have mountains always been there?

New mountains are being created all the time—although it takes many millions of years. Most of the world's highest mountains were formed quite recently in Earth's history. The Himalayan mountains, for instance, have been built up within the last 40 million years—and they are still growing even today.

How are mountains made?

Some mountains are created by volcanic eruptions, but most mountains are thrown up by the tremendous power of the Earth's crust moving. Some mountains are huge slabs called fault blocks, or "horst" that are thrown up by powerful earthquakes. The biggest ranges, though, are created by the crumpling of rocks as the great plates that make up the Earth's crust squash together. Mountains that form like this are called fold mountains. The Alps, Himalayas, and Andes are all fold mountains.

▼ Folding mountains
Whether they are made from sediments settling on the seabed or from volcanic plateaus, most rocks form in flat layers. But as the plates of the Earth's crust move together, folds form as the layers are squeezed horizontally.

As plates of the Earth's crust push together, layers of rocks get pushed up in folds

If the plates continue pushing, the layers may overturn and snap

Eventually the layers may begin to snap altogether, creating a "nappe"

Where do mountains form?

Fold mountains are usually thrown up where the edge of a continent is crumpled as it collides with another tectonic plate. The Andes, for example, were crumpled up right along the edge of South America, as the plate beneath the Pacific ocean crunched into it. When two continents collide, the mountains may be huge. The Himalayas are being thrown up where the Indian plate is driving into Asia.

▼ Block mountains

The movement of tectonic plates can put rocks under such strain that they fracture, creating cracks called faults in the rock. Large faulted blocks of rock may then be thrown up to create mountains.

When did mountains form?

Fold mountains are usually created in fairly short mountain-building phases. By short, geologists mean a few tens of millions of years, rather than hundreds. In different parts of the world, geologists identify different phases from the past. In North America, there are phases called the Huronian, Nevadian, and Pasadenian. In Europe, there were the Caledonian, Hercynian, and Alpine. Most of today's major mountain ranges were formed in the last 50 million years.

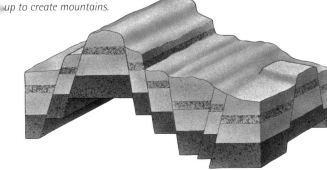

Will mountains always be there?

No, each mountain range is slowly worn down by the weather, and by rivers and moving ice, over millions of years. Scotland's Caledonian mountains and North America's Appalachians were once among the world's highest, but are gradually being worn flat. Other parts of the world that are now completely flat were once mountainous.

Why are some mountains snow-capped?

Air gets colder as you get higher. Above a certain level, called the snow line, it is always too cold for snow to melt, so it stays on the mountaintop all year round. The snow line is 16,400 feet up in the tropics, 8,858 feet in the Alps, and at sea level at the Poles.

QUIZ

1 What is the highest mountain in North America?

2 How high is the Vinson Massif in Antarctica: a) 12,512 feet b) 14,725 feet c) 16,066 feet?

3 Mt Everest is gaining height: true or false?

4 The Black Forest in Germany is a) fold mountains b) fault block mountains c) volcanoes?

5 Which continent has no mountains over 16,400 feet?

6 A syncline is a) a steep slope b) a downfold in rock c) a bad habit?

7 What is Japan's highest mountain–and how did it form?

Volcanic eruptions

What are volcanoes?

VOLCANOES ARE PLACES where molten rock from the Earth's hot interior comes up through the ground. The molten rock is called magma, and sometimes it just oozes slowly onto the surface as a red hot stream called lava. Sometimes, though, the magma builds up underground and then bursts through in a huge explosion called an eruption. When this happens, steam and ash are thrown high into the air, ash and hot cinders rain down far around the volcano, and streams of lava gush from the neck of the volcano.

▲ **Crater**
Around the top of a volcano's vent, there is usually a wide mouth called a crater. Occasionally, the entire top of the volcano collapses into the magma chamber to form a huge crater called a caldera.

▼ **Types of volcano**
No volcano is quite the same. Each has its own shape and way of erupting—and each eruption is slightly different. But there are three main kinds of volcano: shield volcanoes, cone volcanoes, and composite volcanoes.

How does the magma get out through the ground?
Before it emerges, magma builds up in a space underground called the magma chamber. The pressure of magma bubbling up underneath builds until it pushes magma up to the surface—either through a pipe called a vent, or a crack called a fissure.

Are all volcanoes made of lava?
No, some are made of ash, and some are made of alternate layers of lava and ash.

Are all volcanoes the same?
No. There are many different kinds. The kind of volcano depends mainly on the nature of the magma. When magma is low in silica, it is very runny. It gushes out from cracks in the ground and flows out over wide areas and hardens to form what are called shield volcanoes, because they are shaped like shields. When magma is high in silica, it piles up around the vent. A tall cone is built up in successive eruptions. It is these cones that make the most distinctive volcanoes, like Mount Fuji in Japan, and Kilimanjaro in Kenya.

Shield volcanoes are formed by gentle eruptions of runny lava

Cone volcanoes are built up by successive eruptions of sticky, acidic lava

QUIZ

Lava stream
The red hot stream of molten rock called lava looks frightening, but it is rarely lava that kills people in a volcano eruption. The real killers are usually the clouds of choking ash that bury the landscape far around—or worse still, high speed flows of mud or glowing ash called nuée ardenté.

Where are volcanoes found?

Volcanos are found mainly along the boundaries between the great tectonic plates that make up the Earth's surface—and in particular, a ring around the Pacific Ocean called the Ring of Fire. They are also found on "hot spots"—places where columns of hot rock bubble up under the crust and burn through.

What is a dormant volcano?

Some active volcanoes erupt almost continuously, but others go quiet for periods and so are said to be dormant. If they never erupt, they are extinct.

Why do some volcanoes erupt explosively?

When the magma is very thick and sticky, it can clog up a volcano's vent. When it finally bursts through, it is like popping the cork of a champagne bottle. Steam and carbon dioxide gas dissolved under pressure in the magma boil and bubble violently as the pressure is released, and these bubbles drive the magma in an explosive froth up through the vent. The old clog is shattered to smithereens by the explosion, forming ash and cinder that are hurled for miles around the volcano.

1 Which is the tallest volcano in Japan?

2 What volcano erupted and buried the Ancient Roman town of Pompeii in Italy a) Etna b) Stromboli c) Vesuvius?

3 Edinburgh Castle is built on an extinct volcano: true or false?

4 Most of the world's active volcanoes are on land: true or false?

5 Can volcanoes change the world's weather?

6 Vulcanologists try to predict eruptions by looking for a slight swelling in a volcano: true or false?

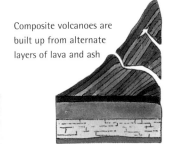

Composite volcanoes are built up from alternate layers of lava and ash

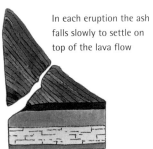

In each eruption the ash falls slowly to settle on top of the lava flow

Earthquakes

What are earthquakes?

EARTHQUAKES ARE A SHAKING of the ground. Some are so slight they can barely rock a cradle. But some are so violent they can shake down mountains and destroy cities. All kinds of things can set off small earthquakes, from the rumbling of heavy traffic to the eruption of a volcano. But the biggest earthquakes are set off by the shuddering of the vast tectonic plates that make up the Earth's surface as they grind slowly together underground.

What sets off an earthquake?

Tectonic plates are sliding past each other all the time, but sometimes they jam. Then the rock bends and stretches for a while until the strain gets so much that it snaps and the plates lurch on again. The snapping of the rock and sudden jolting of the plates sends shock waves out in all directions. When these waves reach the surface, they create earthquakes.

Where do earthquakes start?

The starting point of an earthquake underground is called the hypocenter or focus. The epicenter is the point on the surface above the hypocenter. Earthquakes are strongest at the epicenter, and get gradually weaker farther away.

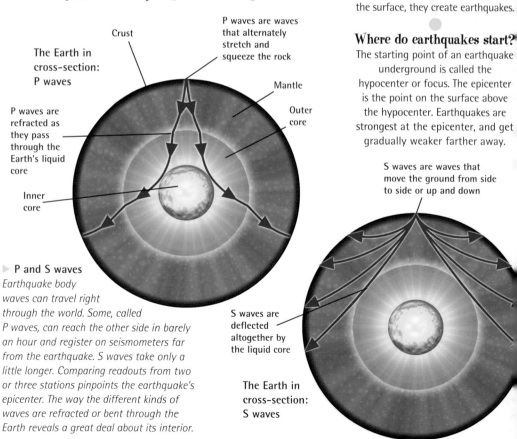

Crust

The Earth in cross-section: P waves

P waves are waves that alternately stretch and squeeze the rock

Mantle

Outer core

P waves are refracted as they pass through the Earth's liquid core

Inner core

S waves are waves that move the ground from side to side or up and down

▶ P and S waves
Earthquake body waves can travel right through the world. Some, called P waves, can reach the other side in barely an hour and register on seismometers far from the earthquake. S waves take only a little longer. Comparing readouts from two or three stations pinpoints the earthquake's epicenter. The way the different kinds of waves are refracted or bent through the Earth reveals a great deal about its interior.

S waves are deflected altogether by the liquid core

The Earth in cross-section: S waves

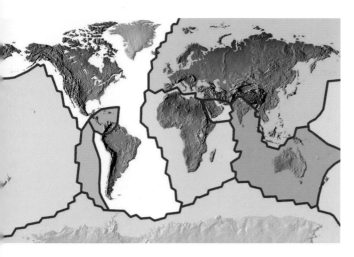

Earthquake zones
Earthquakes tend to occur mostly along the boundaries of tectonic plates. Places like Japan and Mexico are particularly prone to quakes.

What are earthquake zones?

Earthquake zones are places particularly prone to earthquakes. Most of these lie on or near the edges of tectonic plates. Many major cities, such as Los Angeles, Tokyo, and Mexico City, lie in earthquake zones.

How long do earthquakes last?

Most earthquakes are over quickly, lasting less than a minute. The longest, which hit Alaska in March 1964, lasted just four minutes.

How are quakes measured?

With a device called a seismometer, which responds to vibrations and records them on a computer display.

What are earthquake waves?

Earthquake, or "seismic," waves are the vibrations from earthquakes. There are two main kinds. Body waves travel underground at huge speeds, and can vibrate all around the world. Surface waves travel out along the surface from the epicenter and are much slower, but it is these that do the real damage in an earthquake. Surface waves called Q waves shake the ground from side to side, bringing down tall buildings. Surface waves called Rayleigh waves shake the ground up and down, and seem to roll through sandy or muddy ground like waves in the sea.

What is the Richter scale?

The Richter scale shows an earthquake's magnitude—that is, how strong the waves are on a seismometer. Each point indicates a tenfold increase in size. A really big earthquake is at least 6 on the Richter scale.

QUIZ

1 Which Japanese city was devastated by an earthquake in 1995: a) Kobe b) Nagasaki c) Tokyo?

2 What is the name of the fault that sets off earthquakes in California?

3 Which year was San Francisco burned to the ground after an earthquake: a) 1854 b) 1906 c) 1937?

4 Giant waves called tsunami are set off by a) tidal movements b) volcanoes c) undersea earthquakes?

5 The ancient Chinese detected earthquakes with brass frogs: true or false?

6 Earthquakes can make rock rise and fall like tides in the sea: true or false?

Answers
1. a) 2. San Andreas; 3. b)
4. b) and c) 5. True
6. False

281

Weathering

How do hills wear down?

HILLS AND MOUNTAINS are all worn flat eventually. It takes many thousands or even millions of years, but the combined attack of the weather, chemicals in rainwater, running water, wind, glaciers, and various other "agents of erosion" will wear them flatter and flatter. Valleys will get broader, hilltops will get lower, ridges will get narrower until at last an entire mountain range is turned into a lowland plain.

▲ Grand Canyon.

The Grand Canyon was carved by the Colorado River as it cut down through the Colorado Plateau, which was lifted up thousands of feet in a massive movement of the Earth's crust.

What is weathering?

Although rock is hard, the assault of the weather will turn even the hardest granite into soft clay over time. The weather breaks down rocks through the attack of moisture, heat and cold, and chemicals in rainwater. Usually only rocks near the surface are affected, but water trickling down through the ground can weather rocks far underground. The more extreme the climate, the faster rock weathers.

How does frost break rock?

When water freezes, it expands by almost a tenth. So when it freezes inside cracks in rocks, it can push them apart. This expansion can exert a pressure of 6,600 pounds on an area of rock the size of a postage stamp. As water freezes and thaws again and again inside cracks, this pressure can shatter rocks entirely.

What is scree?

Scree is the huge piles of angular rock you often see littering mountain slopes.

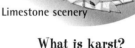

Limestone scenery

What is karst?

Streams and rainwater absorb carbon dioxide gas from the soil and air, and so become a weak acid called carbonic acid. Most things are unaffected by this acidity, but limestone is very easily corroded by this acid. So when limestone is near the surface, water trickling down through the rock can dissolve huge holes in it. This can create a spectacular landscape of gorges, caves, and jagged rock called karst, after the Karst region of Bosnia.

◄ Uluru

Uluru, or Ayers Rock, is a dome of sandstone in the middle of the Australian bush. Deep furrows down its side testify to the erosive power o running water even in this dry place.

Wave rock
This fantastically curved rock was carved by floods of water in much wetter times. A dry climate has preserved its shape since.

What is exfoliation?

In dry areas, rocks often flake off in leaves at the surface. This is called exfoliation. It was once thought this was due to extremes of heat and cold. Now scientists think it is caused by the growth of salt crystals in water that seeps into the rock.

What are tors?

Tors are outcrops of rock often seen on the tops of hills on granite moors, such as Dartmoor in England. The tor began as bedrock beneath a hilltop, but as water trickled into cracks, it rotted away below the ground—except where there were massive blocks with few cracks. These massive blocks were left standing out above the ground as the rotted rock around was worn away.

What happens to weathered rock?

Fragments of weathered rock roll downslope to be washed away by rivers, creep down slowly, or get gradually worn finer and form the basis for soil.

◁ **Shattered peak**
Thousands of years of frost have shattered the peaks of high mountains like the Matterhorn, creating sharp, craggy, broken ridges and a jagged rock summit.

QUIZ

1 In China there is a spectacular range of pointed limestone hills made of eroded limestone. What are they called?

2 The corroded grooves in limestone are a) tongue and groove b) brett and pull c) clint and gryke?

3 The flaking of rock on the Yosemite dome in California is caused by the removal of the weight of rock above: true or false?

4 Rabbits make rock vulnerable to erosion by their burrowing: true or false?

5 What's the main erosive force on mountain tops?

Answers
1. Guilin Hills;
2. c) 3. True; 4. True;
5. Frost shattering

283

Rivers

What makes rivers run?

RIVERS ARE KEPT RUNNING BY RAINFALL. The rain does not always run off the land directly into rivers. Sometimes it sinks into the ground on hilltops and emerges lower down through holes called springs. Sometimes it is frozen into ice and snow for a while and does not reach the river until it melts. But without rain every river will stop running eventually. The more it rains, the fuller the river will be. Floods usually occur a little while after heavy rainstorms, or after winter snows melt in spring.

High in the hills, a small stream tumbles over rocks in a narrow V-shaped valley

Farther downstream, rivers flow in smooth channels made of their own deposited material.

Oxbow lake formed by a cut-off meander

Toward the sea, the river may flow across the broad plains of silt it has washed down

As tributaries join, the river grows bigger

▶ Changing river

Near its start, high in the hills, streams simply tumble this way and that over rocks in steep valleys. But as they become broad rivers farther down, they begin to flow in smooth channels made entirely of fine material worn away higher up and washed down by the river.

Lower down, the river may wind across the valley floor in broad meanders

Why do rivers wind?

All rivers tend to wind, especially as they near the sea, where they often wind in horseshoe shape bends called meanders. The biggest meanders occur where the river flows wide and smooth through soft muddy banks. They form partly because of the way water in the river spirals, and partly because of the way the river wears away its bed and banks in some places, and deposits grains of mud and sand in others.

Where do rivers start and end?

Rivers start off as small streams high in the hills. As they flow downhill, they are joined by other streams, called tributaries. They grow bigger and bigger, and at last flow into a sea or lake.

How do rivers shape the land?

Over many thousands of years, rivers can wear away the land. First, they carve downward to create deep V-shaped valleys. Then they swing sideways to widen the valleys, eventually, into broad plains. They may also bury the valley floor or plain in fine silt.

As it nears the sea and slows down, the river may drop its sediment load and split into branches

What is a waterfall?

A waterfall is a place where a river flows straight over a ledge of rock and plunges vertically. Typically, waterfalls occur where the river flows across a band of hard rock. The river wears away the soft material, leaving the hard rock barely touched. The world's highest waterfall is Angel Falls in Venezuela, which plunges 3,212 feet.

What is a delta?

Deltas are areas of sediment—sand, silt, and mud—piled up in a river's mouth, as the river hits the sea, or a lake, and slows down. Often the river splits up into many smaller branches called distributaries.

How do rivers move silt and sand?

Rivers carry their "load" of sediment in three ways. Big stones are rolled along the river bed. Smaller grains are bounced along the bed. The finest grains float in the water.

What is an oxbow lake?

An oxbow lake is a small lake formed where a river meander has been cut off. The river wears away the outside bend of the meander, making its neck narrower and narrower, until the river cuts through, cutting off the meander.

QUIZ

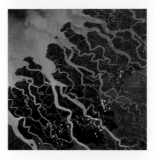

1 The Mississippi River forms a delta as it enters the sea: true or false?

2 River flow reaches its peak a) just before a rain storm b) during a rain storm c) just after a rainstorm?

3 What is the world's longest river?

4 Is river braiding a) where rivers branch b) where rivers wear their banks away c) raised river banks?

5 The Orinoco River, a tributary of the Amazon, flows uphill: true or false?

Glaciers

What are glaciers?

GLACIERS ARE RIVERS OF SLOWLY moving ice that form when it is too cold for snow to melt. Nowadays, they form only in high mountains and toward the North and South Poles. But in the past, during cold periods called Ice Ages, glaciers were far more widespread. Huge areas of North America and Europe were under ice, and the ice left dramatic marks on the landscape.

How do glaciers form?

Glaciers form when new snow, which scientists call névé, falls on top of old snow. The weight of the new snow compacts the old snow into denser snow, which the scientists call firn. In firn, all the air is squeezed out, so it looks less like fluffy snow and more like white ice. Over time, the ice is compacted more and more until it turns into thick white glacier ice and begins to flow, very slowly, downhill.

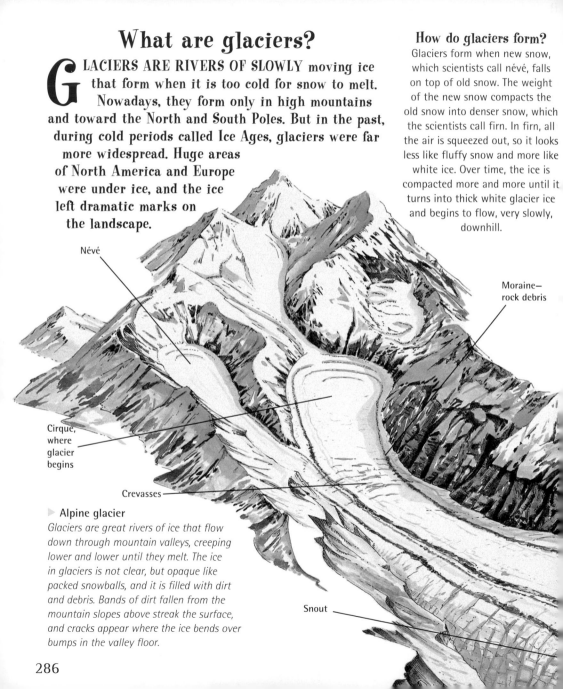

Névé

Moraine—rock debris

Cirque, where glacier begins

Crevasses

Snout

▶ **Alpine glacier**
Glaciers are great rivers of ice that flow down through mountain valleys, creeping lower and lower until they melt. The ice in glaciers is not clear, but opaque like packed snowballs, and it is filled with dirt and debris. Bands of dirt fallen from the mountain slopes above streak the surface, and cracks appear where the ice bends over bumps in the valley floor.

How do glaciers shape the land?

Glaciers move very slowly, but their sheer weight and size give them enormous power to carve out the landscape. They carve out huge U-shaped valleys, gouge out great bowls in hills called cirques, and truncate (slice away) entire hills and valleys. They can also move huge amounts of rock debris and then drop it in large, distinctive piles called moraines.

Do glaciers ever melt?

Yes, they are melting all the time. As they flow downhill into warmer air, the end, or "snout" of the glacier melts. But snow falling up in the mountains replenishes the top of the glacier and keeps it from shrinking—unless the climate begins to warm.

What are fjords?

Fjords are very deep inlets in the coasts of Norway, New Zealand and Canada. They were carved out by glaciers in the last Ice Age, then flooded by the sea.

▲ Icebergs

Icebergs are large floating chunks of ice that break off the end of ice sheets, ice caps, and glaciers and float out to sea.

When was the Ice Age?

There is not just one Ice Age. There have been four in the last billion years, and each of these has many colder periods called glacials and warmer ones called interglacials. There have been 17 glacials in the last 1.6 million years, and the last ended just 10,000 years ago.

Why do Ice Ages happen?

They are probably caused by regular wobbles of the Earth's axis, called Milankovitch cycles.

QUIZ

1 Where is the world's longest glacier?

2 Glaciers flow an average of 6.5 feet a) a year b) a day c) a second?

3 What did the ship *Titanic* hit before it sank?

4 The largest iceberg ever was almost as big as Denmark: true or false?

5 In 1913 an iceberg was seen floating past the Statue of Liberty: true or false?

6 The landscape of Norfolk in England was shaped by ice: true or false?

7 What continent has the biggest area of ice?

8 What are the cracks in glaciers called?

Answers
1. Antarctica; 2. b) 3. An iceberg; 4. True; 5. False; 6. True; 7. Antarctica; 8. Crevasses

287

Deserts

What are deserts?

DESERTS ARE VERY DRY PLACES where it hardly ever rains. Some deserts are very hot, like the Sahara Desert in Africa. Some are very cold, like Antarctica. In hot deserts, what little rain there is quickly evaporates, so there is little water available for plants. So plants are very scarce in the desert. Indeed, most deserts are bare rock, rubble, or sand, with no soil.

▼ **Desert landforms**
The bare, dry landscape of the desert has its own distinctive range of landforms. With no water to round hills, the landscape is jagged, and filled with odd-shaped rocks sculpted by the wind, as well as seas of sand dunes.

Key:
1. Mushroom rock
2. Sand dunes
3. Sand ripples
4. Deflation hollow (blown out by wind)
5. Oasis

Where do deserts occur?

Many deserts occur in the subtropics—that is, just outside the tropics. Due to the natural circulation of air around the world, the air in this area of the world is very calm, clear, and dry. The Sahara and the Great Australian Desert are subtropical deserts. Some deserts, like Chile's Atacama, occur in the lee of mountain ranges that act as a barrier to rain-bearing winds. A few deserts are near sea coasts and are dry because cool ocean currents dry the air.

How hot are deserts?

Hot deserts can be the hottest places in the world, because there is no moisture in the air to block the Sun's rays. Summer temperatures in the Sudan desert in Africa can soar to 56°C, hotter than anywhere else in the world. But even here it can get cold at night, because the heat escapes through the clear skies.

Are all deserts sandy?

No. Deserts that are vast seas of sand are actually quite rare. Just as many deserts are pebbly or rocky.

Are there any rivers in the desert?

Some rivers, like Egypt's Nile River, start in wet regions outside the desert and flow right through it and out the other side. Others flow only when it rains, leaving a dry river bed most of the year round. Rivers like these are called ephemeral.

Mushroom rock

Barchan

Wind

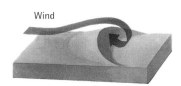

▲ **Wind action**
*Wind plays an important part in
shaping the desert landscape. Wind
bouncing sand along the ground
can undercut rocks to create
distinctive mushroom-shaped rocks.*

What is a sand dune?

A dune is sand blown into a
mound by the wind. Dunes come
in many different shapes and sizes,
including stars, long ridges (called
seifs), and crescents (barchans).
It all depends on how sandy it
is, and where the wind blows
from. Barchans are moved along
gradually as sand is blown up one
side and rolls down the other.

What is a wadi?

A wadi is a gorge cut by rivers in
the desert when it rains. Most of the
time it is completely dry, but after a
rain storm it can fill suddenly with
water in a flash flood.

How is a sandy desert landscape shaped?

Since desert sand is very dry, it
is easily blown up by the wind,
and the desert has its own range
of landforms sculpted from sand
hurled by the wind. The high
temperatures mean that rocks can
easily be corroded by salts as well—
or even baked to breaking point.

QUIZ

1 How much of the world's
land surface is covered
by desert: a) a tenth b) a
fifth c) one-half?

2 What is the world's
biggest desert?

3 Vast areas of Central Asia
and China are covered by
a thick layer of yellow
dust: true or false?

4 What is an oasis?

5 Buttes are a) sheer-sided
rocks b) deep dry gorges
c) the end of a valley?

6 The technical name for
wind action is a) alluvial
b) aeolian c) ventilation?

7 Where is Uluru, or Ayers
Rock?

8 There used to be snow in
the Sahara Desert: true or
false?

Coasts

How do waves shape coasts?

ON EXPOSED COASTS, the pounding of waves can wear away solid rock, undercutting hills to create sheer cliffs. As the cliffs are worn back farther, they leave behind a wide ledge of rock at sea level called a wavecut platform, or upstanding remnants of the cliff called stacks. On sheltered coasts, however, waves can build up the coast, washing in sand to create beaches.

▼ Coastal landforms

Constant battering by waves and seawater gives coasts their own range of landforms. In exposed places such as headlands, the coast is rocky, with steep cliffs, wavecut rock platforms, stacks, and even natural rock arches. In sheltered places, sand worn away from the headlands piles up as beaches.

Sand piles up as beaches in bays

Where does sand come from?

Sand is what is left after material broken off cliffs and rocky coasts has been battered this way and that in the sea for many years.

What is shingle?

Shingle is like sand, but with much bigger grains, the size of small peas, rather than sugar. Water sorts different grades of grain out, so that some beaches are pebbly, some are shingly, and some are sandy.

Waves wear expos headlands into clif and stacks

▲ **Blowhole**
Sometimes, the sheer pressure of water from a breaking wave may force water up through a crack to burst through the top of a cliff like a fountain. This is called a blowhole.

▲ **Rock arch**
As waves wear away the base of a cliff over the years, they may eventually wear right through a headland, creating a natural rock arch, if the rock higher up stays intact.

▲ **Stack**
As the waves continue to wear away at the base of the cliff, the rock arch gets wider and eventually is so weak that it collapses, leaving just a column called a stack.

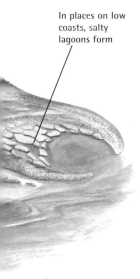

In places on low coasts, salty lagoons form

How are waves made?

Waves begin as wind blowing across the open sea whips the surface into ripples. If the wind is strong enough and blows far enough over the water, the ripples build into waves. The stronger the wind and the greater the distance (called the fetch) it blows, the bigger the waves. In big oceans like the Atlantic and Pacific, the fetch is so big that huge "swells" build up.

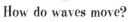

How do waves move?

Waves move like a relay race. The water in them barely moves, but simply goes around in a circle, like the roller on a conveyor belt.

What are tides?

Tides are the slight rising and falling of the sea—usually twice a day—as the Earth turns round. They are caused by the pull of the Moon's gravity on the waters of the oceans.

Why do waves break?

Waves break when the water becomes so shallow that the water cannot complete a circle. Instead, water rolling round the top of the wave spills forward onto the beach, then falls back.

QUIZ

1 Groynes on a beach are a) barriers of rock b) sand bars c) fences put up to to stop sand from being washed along the beach?

2 What is a bight?

3 Sand moves along a beach when waves hit the beach at an angle: true or false?

4 A coast with lots of islands is called a) an archipelago b) an insular coast c) an escarpment?

5 What is an ebb tide?

6 Spring tides are a) tides that happen only in spring b) tides that race up and down c) the most extreme tides each month?

7 What is a long, narrow continental-size inlet?

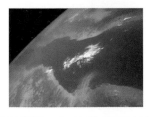

Answers
1. c) 2. A very large bay;
3. True: this is called longshore
drift; 4. a) 5. A falling tide;
6. c) 7. A gulf

291

Caves

What are caves?

CAVES ARE LARGE NATURAL HOLES UNDERGROUND. Some are little bigger than a kitchen cabinet. Others are bigger than a cathedral. The biggest caves are called caverns. Some are single caves. Others are huge networks of chambers linked by long passageways through the rock.

How do caves form?

Caves form in many ways. Some are the old pipes that lava flowed through in volcanoes. Some are created when earthquakes crack the rock. Some are opened up by the sea. But the biggest and most extensive caves are usually in limestone. Streams and rainwater absorb carbon dioxide gas from the soil and air, turning it into a weak acid. Limestone has plenty of cracks called joints. As the acid water trickles down through these joints into limestone, it gradually dissolves away the rock underground. As more and more of the rock around a joint is dissolved away, it forms a cavern.

▲ **Stalactites and stalagmites**
Hanging needles and pillars formed by dripping water can turn limestone caverns into natural cathedrals.

What is a pothole?

Because limestone rock has so many cracks or joints, most streams quickly disappear into the ground. The hole down which a stream runs into the ground is called a swallowhole. Over time, mild acids dissolved in the water may corrode the crack in the rock into a deep vertical shaft. This is a pothole. Sometimes streams plunge into them as spectacular waterfalls.

▶ **Limestone underground**
Slightly acidic water trickling down through cracks in limestone gradually eats away the rock underground, opening up caverns and potholes. Below a certain level, called the water table, the rock is completely saturated with water, and the caverns are flooded.

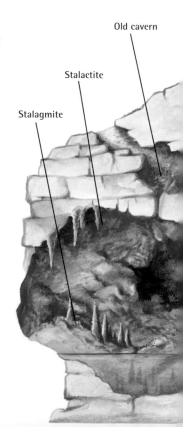

Old cavern

Stalactite

Stalagmite

What are stalactites and stalagmites?

Stalactites and stalagmites are formations made by water dripping through the ceiling of a limestone cavern. Calcium carbonate dissolved in the water forms long, icicle-shaped deposits that hang from the ceiling. These are called stalactites. As water drips from a stalactite onto the cavern floor, calcium carbonate is also deposited on the floor, piling up in a narrow pinnacle called a stalagmite. Eventually, the stalagmite and stalactite may actually meet to form a pillar from floor to ceiling.

Do caves last forever?

No. Although some are very old, most are gradually corroded away. As more and more of the roof rots away, it gets weaker and may eventually collapse, leaving just a large hole in the ground, called a polje. If an entire interlinked string of caverns collapses, it may create a long, cliff-walled valley called a gorge, though gorges may also form in other ways.

What are gallery caves?

Gallery caves are long, dry, tunnel-like caves originally formed by an underground stream, but left dry when the water table (the level of water) in the rock dropped.

QUIZ

1 The world's longest cave network is Mammoth Cave in Kentucky. It is a) 13 miles long b) 125 miles long c) 348 miles long?

2 The world's biggest single cave is the Sarawak Chamber in Sarawak. It is big enough to hold a) a house b) a football stadium c) New York City?

3 What is the technical name for an expert on caves?

4 There are huge caves under the ocean, created by waves: true or false?

5 Stalagmites and stalactites are covered with material that makes them shine in the dark: true or false?

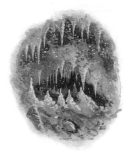

Swallowhole   Pothole or   Cavern   Joint
                ponor

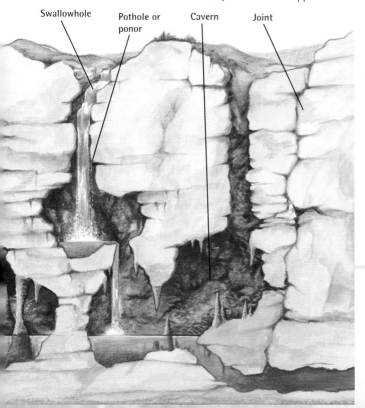

Why does the
Moon shine?

How hot is the
Sun?

Who were the first
men on the Moon?

How many stars
are there in the
sky?

How do rockets
work in space?

How do satellites
stay up?

Is there life on
Mars?

Why do stars twinkle?

How did the Universe begin?

Space

Why is Venus pink?

The Earth

What is the Earth?

THE EARTH IS ONE OF THE EIGHT PLANETS that continually circle the Sun, making up the solar system. It is the third planet out from the Sun, between Venus and Mars, and like them and Mercury, the planet nearest the Sun, it is a ball made largely of rock. What makes it special is the fact that its surface is two-thirds covered by water. It is also the only planet with oxygen in its atmosphere. Without water and oxygen, there would be no life.

How was the Earth formed?

No one is absolutely sure how the Earth began. But most astronomers think that about five billion years ago there was just a vast cloud of hot gas and dust circling around the newly formed Sun. Then gradually, parts of this cloud began to clump together, pulled together by gravity. These clumps grew to form the planets.

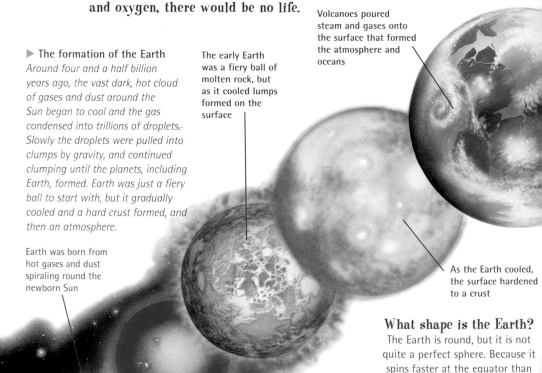

▶ **The formation of the Earth**
Around four and a half billion years ago, the vast dark, hot cloud of gases and dust around the Sun began to cool and the gas condensed into trillions of droplets. Slowly the droplets were pulled into clumps by gravity, and continued clumping until the planets, including Earth, formed. Earth was just a fiery ball to start with, but it gradually cooled and a hard crust formed, and then an atmosphere.

The early Earth was a fiery ball of molten rock, but as it cooled lumps formed on the surface

Volcanoes poured steam and gases onto the surface that formed the atmosphere and oceans

Earth was born from hot gases and dust spiraling round the newborn Sun

As the Earth cooled, the surface hardened to a crust

As more and more droplets and grains of dust clumped together, the newborn Earth congealed into a red-hot ball

What shape is the Earth?

The Earth is round, but it is not quite a perfect sphere. Because it spins faster at the equator than at the poles, the Earth is flung out a little at the equator and so bulges here. Scientists describe the Earth's shape as "geoid," which simply means Earth-shaped.

QUIZ

How far is Earth from the Sun?

About 93 million miles on average, but it varies according to the time of year. At its closest, in January, it is 91 million miles. This is called the perihelion. At the furthest point, or aphelion, on July 4, it is over 94 million miles away.

The crust cooled to form continents

How long does the Earth take to turn?

The Earth turns around in 24 hours, which is why days are 24 hours long. Actually, it takes 23 hours, 56 minutes and 4.09 seconds to turn around, but because the Earth moves round the Sun as well as turning, it takes exactly 24 hours for the Sun to return to the same place in the sky.

Why do we have leap years?

It takes the Earth just over 365 days to go around, which is why a year is 365 days. The journey actually takes 365.242 days, not 365. To make up for the 0.242 days and keep the calendar in step with the Earth, we add an extra day to February every fourth year, the leap year. Even this doesn't make it quite right, so a leap year is left out at the end of three centuries out of four.

Does the Earth tilt over?

Yes. It spins around on a line between the poles called its axis. The axis is tilted over at 23.5° in relation to the Sun.

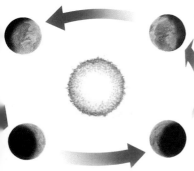

◀ Seasons
We get seasons because the Earth is always tilted over in the same direction. So when the Earth is on one side of the Sun, the northern hemisphere (the world north of the equator) is tilted toward the Sun, bringing summer here. When the Earth is on the other side of the Sun, the northern hemisphere is tilted away, bringing winter. The seasons are reversed in the south.

1 How old is the Earth:
   a) 46,000 years b) 4.6
   million years c) 4.6
   billion years?

2 How far is it around the
   Earth at the equator,
   about a) 15,000 miles
   b) 25,000 miles
   c) 55,000 miles?

3 The astronomer who
   first realized Earth goes
   around the Sun was a)
   Ptolemy b) Copernicus c)
   Hubble?

4 The Earth is moving
   around the Sun at
   50,000 miles per hour:
   true or false?

5 The Earth is spinning at
   over 25,000 miles per
   hour: true or false?

Answers
1. c) 2. b) 3. b) Nicolaus
Copernicus (1473–1543);
4. True; 5. False; it takes 24
hours to spin 25,000 miles

The Moon

What is the Moon?

THE MOON IS A BALL OF ROCK, about a quarter of the size of the Earth. The Moon is held close to the Earth, like a ball on a string, by the mutual pull of the Moon and Earth's gravity. It circles continually around the Earth, taking about a month to go around, and as it goes around it also turns slowly on its axis, taking exactly the same time to go around–nearly 30 times slower than the Earth, which spins round in 24 hours.

◀ **Inside the Moon**

The Moon has a very thick crust of solid rock (about 93 miles thick), a very cool mantle of softer rock beneath, and a tiny metal core.

▼ **Changing Moon**

As the Moon circles the Earth over the course of a month, we see different amounts of its bright, sunlit side, so it appears to change shape. The changes are called the phases of the Moon. The phases are, from left to right: New Moon, Half Moon, Gibbous Moon, Full Moon, Gibbous Moon, Half Moon, Old Moon. When it is growing bigger it is said to be waxing; when it is growing smaller it is said to be waning.

Why does the Moon shine?

The Moon is by far the brightest thing in the night sky. Indeed, it is so bright that you can often see it in the sky during the day, too. But it does not have any light of its own. Moonlight is simply the Sun's light reflected off the white dust on the Moon's surface.

What are the Moon's seas?

The large dark patches on the Moon that look like seas are, in fact, ancient lava flows from volcanoes.

QUIZ

▶ **Solar circle**

When the Moon swings in between the Sun and the Earth, it blocks off the Sun from a small region on Earth for a few minutes. This is a solar eclipse.

Why does the Moon change shape?

It doesn't, but looks as if it does because as it circles the Earth we see its bright, sunny side from different angles. At New Moon, it is between the Sun and the Earth, and we catch just a crescent-shaped glimpse of its bright side. Over the first two weeks, we see more and more of its bright side until at Full Moon, we see all of it. Over the next two weeks, we see less and less until we get back to a sliver, the Old Moon.

How long is a month?

It takes the Moon 27.3 days to circle the Earth, but 29.53 days from one Full Moon to the next, because the Earth moves as well. This 29.53-day cycle is a lunar month. Calendar months are entirely artificial.

What is an eclipse?

As the Moon goes round the Earth, it sometimes passes right into Earth's shadow, where the Sun's light is blocked off. This is called a lunar eclipse. Sometimes, the Moon passes between the Sun and the Earth and blocks off the Sun's light from a bit of the Earth. This is called a solar eclipse.

Who were the first men on the Moon?

The first men on the Moon were U.S. *Apollo 11* astronauts Neil Armstrong and Buzz Aldrin. The *Apollo*'s lunar module landed Armstrong and Aldrin on the Moon on July 20 1969.

1 Why does the Moon look the same size as the Sun?

2 Why does the Moon look like cheese?

3 There is water on the Moon: true or false?

4 A Harvest Moon is a) a golden moon b) a kind of cheese c) the bright full moon of harvest time?

5 The footprints left by the astronauts on the Moon in the 1960s are still there: true or false?

6 The terminator is a) Arnold Schwarzenegger b) the boundary between the Moon's dark and bright sides c) The dark side of the Moon?

Answers
1. Because the Moon is much, much closer; 2. Because its surface is pitted with craters; 3. True; 4. c) 5. True; 6. a) and b)!

The Sun

What is the Sun?

THE SUN IS A STAR, just like all the others you see in the night sky. The only difference is that it is just 93 million miles away, not many billions. It formed about 5 billion years ago after an earlier, much bigger star blew up, and now, in middle age, burns yellow and fairly steadily, giving the Earth daylight at remarkably constant temperatures. It will probably burn for another five billion years before burning out.

Above the chromosphere is the Sun's halo-like crowning ring, called the corona

The chromosphere is a thin layer through which dart tongues called spicules, making it look like a flaming forest

Core where the Sun fuses hydrogen nuclei to create enormous heat

Convection currents in the Sun's mantle

The photosphere is a sea of boiling gas, and gives us the heat and light we get on Earth

▶ Inside the Sun
The Sun is not just a flaming ball. Although it is made almost entirely of hydrogen and helium, its structure is complicated. Like the Earth, it has a core, and this is where most of the heat is produced, taking 10 million years to reach the surface. Above that are a number of different layers, including (in order outward): the photosphere, the Sun's visible surface; the chromosphere; and the corona, its glowing, white-hot atmosphere.

Sunspot

QUIZ

▲ Solar prominences

Solar prominences are giant flame-like tongues of hot hydrogen that loop well over 62,000 miles out into space—as far as the Moon from the Earth.

High above the chromosphere are prominences

How hot is the Sun?

The surface of the Sun is a phenomenal 11,000°F, and would melt pretty nearly anything. But its core is much, much hotter, at over 28 million°F!

Why is the Sun hot?

The Sun gets its heat because pressures deep in its core are enormous. Pressures are so great that the nuclei (centers) of hydrogen atoms are fused together as helium atoms. This nuclear fusion reaction—the same reaction that makes atomic bombs explode—releases a huge amount of heat.

How big is the Sun?

The Sun is medium-sized for a star, but it is over 170 times as big as the Earth. It is about 365,000 miles across and weighs just under 2,000 million trillion tons.

What is the solar wind?

The solar wind is the stream of radioactive particles that is blowing out from the Sun all the time at hundreds of miles a second. These particles are so dangerous that life on Earth would be destroyed if the Earth were not protected from the wind by its magnetic field. A little of the wind creeps in through the clefts above the poles, creating the light displays in the sky known as aurorae.

What are sunspots?

Sunspots are dark blotches that can be seen on the Sun's surface with special instruments. They are dark because they are about 3,600°F cooler than the rest of the surface. They usually appear in groups and move across the Sun's face as it rotates—in about 37 days at the equator and 26 days nearer the poles. The average number varies, reaching a maximum every 11 years, and may be linked to storm spells on Earth.

What are solar flares?

Flares are eruptions from the Sun's surface that spout into space every now and then. They last about five minutes, but they have the energy of one million atom bombs.

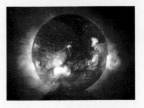

The night sky

How many stars are there in the sky?

WITHOUT A TELESCOPE, you can probably see almost two thousand stars in the sky at night if your eyesight is reasonably good. With the most powerful telescopes of all, it is possible to see many millions. But even this is just a tiny fraction of all the stars in the Universe. Astronomers guess that there are perhaps 200 billion billion altogether, most of them as big as or bigger than our Sun.

▼ Observatory

Because the world is turning, observatory telescopes have to turn too in order to follow the pattern of stars. So the telescope here is mounted on a turntable, and the roof turns with it. The dish to the right is a radio telescope.

What is an observatory?

An observatory is a place where astronomers study the night sky. Although some are located near cities for convenience, the air near cities is dirty and the light from cities makes night viewing hard. So most observatories are situated high on mountaintops, far away from cities, to give as clear a view as possible.

What can you see in the night sky?

The biggest and brightest thing is the Moon. Everything else is just pinpoints of light to the naked eye. Most are stars. But you can also see five of the planets—Mercury, Venus, Mars, Jupiter, and Saturn—if you look at the right time. Occasionally, you may see comets and meteors shooting through the sky. The pale band across the middle of the sky called the Milky Way is actually a concentration of the stars of our own local Galaxy.

How powerful are astronomers' telescopes?

In the last century, the most distant objects astronomers could see were about 15,000 light-years away. Now powerful telescopes enable them to see galaxies 13 billion light-years away. If it could focus on nearby things, a telescope this powerful would enable you to read this book from well over 328 feet away.

How do astronomers study the night sky?

In the past, they would stare at it for hours on end through a telescope, recording where every pinpoint of light was. Nowadays, the view through the telescope is usually recorded electronically, and astronomers study the electronic image on a computer screen.

January

July

◄ **Night sky**
The pattern of stars in the night sky is fixed, and has hardly changed since prehistoric times. But as the Earth moves, so we see a changing view of the pattern. So the pattern of stars gradually arcs through the sky during every night as the Earth turns. Each night, the pattern begins slightly farther on. Only after a year, when the Earth has completed its journey, does the pattern start in the same place again.

QUIZ

1 What is light pollution?

2 The SOHO space telescope is targeted on a) the Moon b) Uranus c) the Sun?

3 Which famous scientist was the first to look at the night sky through a telescope?

4 With a powerful telescope, you can see the equipment left behind on the Moon by the Apollo missions: true or false?

5 A light-year is the distance light travels in a year: true or false?

6 Where is the largest telescope in the world?

What are radio telescopes?

The stars are beaming a range of radiation at us. Some, called visible light, is the light we can see. Most is invisible, with wavelengths too long or too short for our eyes. But though we can't see them, special telescopes can pick them up and so see much more of the stars than we could by visible light alone. Radio telescopes are telescopes that respond to radio waves. They use dishes to focus the rays rather than lenses, and the dishes are often hundreds of feet across. Other telescopes respond to radiation bands such as microwaves, X-rays, and submillimeter wavelengths.

What are space telescopes?

Looking at the night sky through our atmosphere is like looking through frosted glass. So astronomers send up electronic telescopes on satellites to get a clear view into space. The most famous is the Hubble Space Telescope, launched in 1990.

Can you see other planets?

Until recently the only planets known were those around our Sun, but astronomers have now observed a few very big planets circling around other stars, too.

▼ **Gazing at the sky**
A small telescope enables amateur astronomers to see much dimmer stars.

Answers
1. The light from cities that makes it hard to see the night sky; 2. c) 3. Galileo; 4. False; 5. True; 6. In Spain, the Gran Telescopio Canarias

303

Space travel

Why do you need a rocket to go into space?

TO ESCAPE FROM THE PULL OF EARTH'S GRAVITY demands the power that only a rocket can provide. But traveling through the emptiness of space doesn't. So spacecraft are usually boosted into space by powerful launch vehicles–rockets designed to fall away in stages when the spacecraft is on its way.

How do rockets work in space?

There is nothing to push on in space, but rockets move forward because the burning gas swells inside the rocket burners. As it swells, the gas pushes the rocket forward.

▼ **Lunar module**
The lunar module was the small part of the Apollo 11 *spacecraft that detached to carry astronauts Armstrong and Aldrin down to the Moon's surface for the first Moon landing in 1969.*

When was the first space flight?

The first space flight was made in October 1957 by Russia's *Sputnik 1.* The second, a month later, launched a dog named Laika into space in *Sputnik 2.* Sadly, Laika never came back.

What is the Space Shuttle?

Early spacecraft were used for one flight only, but the US Space Shuttles were the first reusable spacecraft. They were launched on the back of rockets like all spacecraft, but could glide back to Earth and land just like an airplane, and so could be used again and again.

▶ **Rocket power**
Some rockets such as boosters burn a solid rubbery fuel, but most are powered by liquid fuel. Since this only burns with oxygen, the rocket also carries a tank of liquid oxygen. The fuel and the oxygen mix in a combustion chamber, and then they are ignited.

The payload— the satellite or crew—are in just a tiny section on top of the rocket

The liquid fuel and the liquid oxygen are stored in separate tanks

Fuel and liquid oxygen mix in the combustion chamber and swell ferociously as they burn, giving the rocket thrust

The second stage of the rocket w come int action when th first falls away

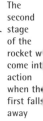

▶ Men on the Moon
Astronaut Neil Armstrong salutes the U.S flag during the Moon landing of July 21, 1969—the first manned landing on another world.

▼ Space shuttles in action
Space Shuttles were used for anything from ferrying scientists to space labs, to repairing satellites.

How many planets have spacecraft been to?
The first successful planetary spacecraft was *Mariner 2*, which flew past Venus in 1962. *Mariner 10* reached Mercury in 1974. The *Vikings 1* and *2* landed on Mars in 1976. The *Voyager* spacecraft flew past Jupiter (1979), Saturn (1980–81), Uranus (1986), and Neptune (1989) before heading out of the solar system.

Why are things weightless in space?
Astronauts orbiting the Earth float around as if they are weightless. In fact, they are not, but the spacecraft is hurtling around the Earth so fast it counteracts the effect of gravity. It is as if the astronauts were in a lift falling so fast they float off the ground.

What are space stations?
Space stations are bases in space where astronauts can live and work. The Russian *Mir* orbited Earth from 1986 to 2001. The first crew docked at the giant International Space Station (ISS) in 2000. Hundreds of astronauts from different countries have now visited the ISS on missions.

Where can astronauts go?
Except for the manned missions to the Moon, all the spacecraft that have been sent off to explore the planets are robot craft, guided automatically by computer, and by radio signals from Earth. They have to be automatic, because it is very hard to bring them back to Earth. The furthest humans are likely to go is Mars.

How do satellites stay up?
By circling the Earth so fast that they never come down—like a ball thrown very hard. The closer they are to Earth, the faster they have to go.

QUIZ

1 Who was the first man in space?
2 What did Neil Armstrong say when he stepped onto the Moon?
3 You can see TV pictures from Mars live over the internet: true or false?
4 To escape Earth's gravity, spacecraft need to travel at least: a) 248.5 mph b) 2,485 mph c) 24,855 mph?
5 There is a Russian space station orbiting Venus: true or false?
6 How many manned missions to the Moon were there a) 1 b) 6 c) 22?
7 Who was the first man to walk in space?

Answers
1. Yuri Gagarin in 1961;
2. "One small step for a man; one giant leap for mankind";
3. True; 4. c) 5. False; 6. b)
7. Alexei Leonov in 1965

305

Satellites

What are satellites?

SATELLITES ARE OBJECTS that orbit (circle) around planets. There are natural satellites, like our Moon, and the moons that orbit planets such as Jupiter and Saturn. But in the past few decades, we have launched more and more man-made satellites. These tiny spacecraft are designed to stay in space orbiting the Earth to perform all kinds of tasks, from land use surveys to speeding up worldwide telephone communications.

▶ Satellite
Most satellites get their power from panels of solar cells that turn sunlight into electricity. The panels are hinged to ensure that they always face the Sun. Many satellites also have little gas jets to turn the satellite around and ensure that it is positioned exactly right.

Are all satellite orbits the same?

No. The orbit chosen for a satellite depends on its purpose. Many satellites are launched into what is called a low orbit, about 186 miles above the Earth. A low-orbit satellite circles the Earth in about 90 minutes. Low-orbit satellites are the cheapest to launch, since it requires a low-power rocket to get them up. To get a satellite into a high orbit—above 18,640 miles—the satellite has to be launched first into a high orbit with one set of rockets. A second set then fires to steer it into the correct orbit.

When were the first satellites launched?

The first artificial satellite was *Sputnik 1*, launched by the Soviet Union in 1957. Three years later, *Tiros 1*, the first weather satellite was launched. Then, in 1962, the *Telstar* satellite beamed the first live television pictures across the Atlantic.

How do satellites stay up?

The Earth's gravity stops satellites from flying off into space, but they stay up because they are moving too fast through space to fall back to Earth. To stay in orbit, the satellite must fly fast enough not to fall but not so fast that it whizzes off into space. Gravity gets weaker farther from the Earth, so the higher the orbit, the slower the satellite needs to fly to stay up.

Why do they bother with high orbits?

It costs a lot to launch a satellite into a high orbit. But an orbit 22,236 miles above the Earth takes 24 hours, the same time as it takes the Earth to spin around. If a satellite in this orbit is above the equator, it always stays above the same place on the ground. This "geostationary" orbit is used for many weather and communications satellites.

QUIZ

◀ **Orbiting satellite**
There are now hundreds of observation satellites in space designed to look back down on Earth, for anything from science to spying. Cameras on board spy satellites can now give such high resolution that they can pick out individual buildings and even people.

▶ **Land and sea**
Most satellite photos are in artificial colors to penetrate the atmosphere better.

What is a polar orbit?

Polar orbiting satellites circle the Earth from Pole to Pole about 350 miles above the ground, covering a different strip of the surface each time around. So eventually, the satellite scans the entire surface in detail.

How are satellites launched?

Satellites are launched into space either by rockets, or carried up by space shuttles. Shuttles can only reach heights of a few hundred miles, so can only place satellites in low orbit. But some satellites have little rockets to move them up to a higher orbit.

What is a communications satellite?

Communications satellites transmit around the world anything from TV pictures to telephone calls. Each word of a telephone call from, say, London to Australia is bounced around the world off the satellite on a beam of microwaves.

What's GPS?

GPS is the Global Positioning System. This is a network of satellites in space that allows people with a GPS device on land, on sea, or in the air to fix their position accurately to within a few feet.

1 **About how many satellites are launched every year: a) 10 b) 30 c) 100?**

2 **Satellite measurements have shown that there are hills and valleys on the ocean surface: true or false?**

3 **You can see some satellites in space with the naked eye: true or false?**

4 **How many satellites are there in space: a) 170 b) 550 c) over 1,500?**

5 **The U.S. Department of Defense (the Pentagon) knows exactly where every single satellite is all the time: true or false?**

6 **What is the launch path of a satellite called?**

7 **What kind of orbit do TV satellites have?**

Answers
1. c) 2. True; 3. True;
4. c) 5. True;
6. Trajectory;
7. Geostationary

307

Inner planets

What is the solar system?

THE SOLAR SYSTEM is the Sun and all the planets and other bits and pieces that circle round it. There are eight planets altogether–four rocky inner planets near the Sun including the Earth, and four farther out away from the Sun. The bits and pieces include comets, tiny lumps called asteroids, and meteors.

◀ Mercury
Mercury hurtles around the Sun in just 88 days (compared to 365 for the Earth). But it takes 59 days to turn once on its axis. This means the Sun comes up only once a year. But once it's up it stays up for 176 days!

What are the inner planets?

The inner planets are, in order away from the Sun: Mercury, Venus, Earth, and Mars. All four are quite small compared with some of the outer planets like Jupiter, and all four are made mostly of rock. Because they are made of rock, they have a hard surface on which a spacecraft could land, and are sometimes called the "terrestrial" (earth-like) planets. Space probes have landed on both Venus and Mars.

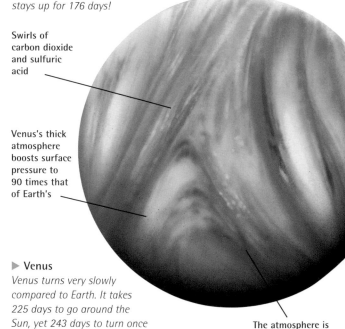

Swirls of carbon dioxide and sulfuric acid

Venus's thick atmosphere boosts surface pressure to 90 times that of Earth's

The atmosphere is made from fumes of gases from volcanoes

How hot is Mercury?

Mercury is so near the Sun that daytime temperatures soar to 806°F, more than enough to melt lead. But its atmosphere is so thin that it loses all this heat at night, when temperatures plunge to -292°F!

▶ Venus
Venus turns very slowly compared to Earth. It takes 225 days to go around the Sun, yet 243 days to turn once around. So a day on Venus is longer than its year.

Why is Venus pink?

Venus is pink because it has an atmosphere so thick we can never see the surface of the planet. The atmosphere is made of white fumes of carbon dioxide and pink clouds of sulfuric acid, so it would be deadly for humans. The atmosphere is so deep that the pressure on the ground would be enough to crush a car to foil.

Why is Venus so hot?

Venus is the hottest planet in the solar system, with surface temperatures of 878°F. The build-up of carbon dioxide gas in its atmosphere has created a runaway "greenhouse effect," trapping the heat from the Sun like the panes of glass in a greenhouse.

Why is Venus called the evening star?

Venus's thick atmosphere reflects light so well it shines like a star. But because it is quite close to the Sun, we can only see it in the evening, just after the Sun sets. By midnight, it has disappeared. But it may become visible again just before sunrise.

What volcano is three times as high as Mt. Everest?

The surface of Mars is much more stable than Earth's, and there is no rain or running water to wear down the landscape. So mountains can be very high. One volcano, called Olympus Mons, is 15 miles high—three times as high as Mount Everest!

Is there life on Mars?

When the *Viking* space probes landed on Mars in the 1970s, they found it completely lifeless. But in 1996, microscopic fossils of what might be mini-viruses were found in a meteor from Mars. Future space probes may reveal microscopic life beneath the surface.

▼ Mars

Mars is sometimes called the red planet because it is rusty. The surface has a lot of iron dust, which has been oxidized (rusted) by the carbon dioxide in its atmosphere.

Mars has small polar ice caps

Markings on Mars's surface were once thought to be signs of civilization—but they are purely geological

QUIZ

1 Venus turns backward (in a direction opposite to that of its orbit): true or false?

2 There are ancient pyramids on Mars: true or false?

3 For a few hours during Mercury's day the Sun goes backward through the sky: true or false?

4 What is the name of the space probe that landed on Mars in 1997?

5 Which of the inner planets has moons?

6 Mercury has ice caps of yellow acid: true or false?

7 Which planet is closest to Earth?

8 Which planet has the shortest year?

9 Are there volcanoes on Venus?

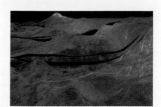

Answers
1. True; 2. False; 3. True; 4. *Mars Pathfinder*; 5. Mars and Earth; 6. True; 7. Venus; 8. Mercury (88 days); 9. Yes

Outer planets

What are the outer planets?

THE OUTER PLANETS BEYOND MARS are, in order away from the Sun: Jupiter, Saturn, Uranus, and Neptune. These are all very, very big—much bigger than the inner planets like Earth and Mars. They are also made mostly of liquid gas rather than rock. So spacecraft could never land on them.

▶ **Uranus**
Uranus is the seventh planet out from the Sun, and rolls around it almost on its side.

Which is the biggest planet?

Jupiter is 82,846 miles across, 272,946 miles around and twice as heavy as all the planets put together. Although it is 1,300 times as big as the Earth, it is only 318 times as heavy, because it is made largely of liquid hydrogen and helium.

▼ **Saturn**
Saturn is the most beautiful of all the planets, with its shimmering pale butterscotch atmosphere and its halo of rings.

Like Saturn, Uranus has rings, but much smaller

Great Red Spot

Saturn's rings occur in broad bands, labelled with the letters A to G outward

What are Saturn's rings?

◀ **Jupiter**
High speed winds—six times faster than hurricanes on Earth— whir through Jupiter's atmosphere, creating bands of curling clouds on the surface—including a whirlpool called the Great Red Spot, or GRS, which has been there at least 300 years.

Saturn's rings are the planet's shining halo, first noticed in 1659 by Dutch scientist Christiaan Huygens (1629–95). They are made of countless billions of tiny chips of ice and dust—few bigger than a refrigerator and most the size of ice cubes. The rings are incredibly thin—no more than 164 feet deep – yet they stretch over 46,000 miles out into space.

QUIZ

Neptune receives so little heat from the Sun that the surface is -346°F

Winds of hydrogen and helium roar round at over 1,243 miles per hour

▼ Neptune

Neptune is the eighth planet out from the Sun—up to 2.5 billion miles. It is so far away from the Sun that it takes 164.79 years to go around just once. So its year is 164.79 Earth years.

1 Which planet is farthest from the Sun?

2 Comets are made mostly of ice: true or false?

3 Saturn would float if you could find a bathtub big enough: true or false?

4 Which planet is named after the Roman god of the sea?

5 The surface of Jupiter is spinning at over 28,000 mph: true or false?

6 Saturn's moon Enceladus is made mainly of sugar: true or false?

7 On Uranus in spring, the Sun rises and sets backward: true or false?

8 Which planet has the most moons?

9 Jupiter glows like a big light bulb: true or false?

How many moons have the outer planets?

All the outer planets have lots of moons. Jupiter has over 50, Saturn at least 53, Uranus 27 and Neptune 13. Some of them are almost as big as the planet Mercury. Saturn's moon Titan is exciting astronomers because it has an atmosphere—the only moon in the solar system with one—so it may be able to support some form of life.

When were Uranus and Neptune discovered?

Unlike the planets closer to the Sun, Uranus and Neptune were completely unknown to ancient astronomers. They are so far away from us and so faint that they can only be seen through powerful telescopes. Uranus was discovered only in 1781, and Neptune in 1846. They were both visited by the *Voyager* space probe between 1986 and 1989.

▶ Pluto and Charon

Pluto was discovered in 1930 and was considered the ninth planet until 2006, when it was reclassified as a dwarf planet. Pluto is five times smaller than Earth, and its largest moon, Charon, is almost half Pluto's size.

Why is Neptune turquoise?

Neptune and Uranus are both bluey turquoise in color because their surfaces are completely covered by deep oceans of liquid methane (the same gas often used for heating and cooking).

How cold is it on Pluto?

Pluto is so far from the Sun, the Sun looks just like a star in the sky, and temperatures plunge to -364°F. Each day on Pluto lasts 6.39 Earth days—but a year lasts 248.54 Earth years, during which time Pluto travels well over 900,000 miles.

Stars

What are stars?

STARS ARE HUGE FIERY BALLS OF GAS. They shine because they are burning. Deep inside, hydrogen atoms fuse together to form helium as they are squeezed by the star's gravity. This nuclear reaction unleashes so much energy that the core of the star reaches millions of degrees and makes the surface glow-sending out light, heat, radio waves, and many other kinds of radiation.

How big are stars?

Our Sun is an average-sized star. There are "red giant" stars 20 to 100 times as big. There are also supergiants like Betelgeuse 500 times as big and 435 million miles across. There are also smaller stars too, such as white dwarfs that are smaller than the Earth and neutron stars just 9.5 miles across. These are remnants of old stars that have collapsed under their own gravity.

Stars begin life when clumps of gas and dust in nebulae are pulled together by gravity

As gravity squeezes the clumps, they begin to get hot

Only big enough clumps get hot enough to start the fusion reaction

Nuclear fusion begins as hydrogen atoms fuse together to make helium. The heat makes the star glow

▶ Star life

Stars are born when clumps of gas in space are drawn together by their own gravity, and the middle of the clump is squeezed so hard that temperatures reach 18 million°F—enough to start the nuclear fusion reaction that makes stars glow. All this happens inside vast clouds of dust and gas called nebulae.

QUIZ

What is a constellation?

Constellations are patterns made by stars that astronomers use to find their way around the night sky. There is no link at all between the stars in a constellation; it simply looks that way. They were given names like the Great Bear and Orion by astronomers long ago. There are now 88 recognized.

Why do stars twinkle?

They twinkle because the Earth's atmosphere is never still, and starlight twinkles as the air wavers. Light from the nearby planets is not distorted as much, so they don't twinkle.

How hot are stars?

The surface temperature of the coolest is 6,300°F. The brightest, hottest stars are over 72,000°F.

What is the brightest star?

The nearer a star is, the brighter it appears. So some of the biggest brightest stars in the Universe appear quite dim simply because they are far away. The star that seems the brightest from Earth is Sirius the Dog Star, which is 26 times brighter than the Sun. But the hypergiant Cygnus OB2 No. 12 is 810,000 times brighter than our Sun but is almost 6 billion light-years away, so it seems quite dim.

What is the nearest star?

Apart from our Sun, the nearest star is the faint Proxima Centauri, just over 4 light-years away (25 trillion miles). The nearest visible to the naked eye is Alpha Centauri, 4.35 light-years away.

If the heat made in the core pushes out as hard as gravity pulls in, the star stabilizes and burns steadily for billions of years

1 What constellation is named after a fish?

2 What star shines at the dead center of the northern sky?

3 The constellation Pleiades is named after a) three sisters b) seven sisters c) twelve sisters?

4 The group of stars called the Plough in Europe is called in North America a) the Big Dipper b) the Panhandle c) the Scythe?

5 The constellation Cygnus is named after a god who became a swan to seduce a girl: true or false?

6 The Dog Star has a companion star called the Pup Star: true or false?

7 Betelgeuse gets its name because it is the color of beetle blood: true or false?

Answers
1. Pisces; 2. Polaris, the North Star; 3. b) 4. a) 5. True; 6. True; 7. False

313

The life of a star

How long do stars live?

THE BIGGEST, BRIGHTEST STARS are the shortest-lived, many surviving less than ten million years. Medium-sized stars like our Sun last much longer–ten billion years or more. Small stars may last much, much longer.

▼ The end of a star
Toward the end of a star's life, its hydrogen is burned up and it shrinks to burn helium. When the helium runs out, the outer layers cool and it swells to become a red giant. The biggest stars continue swelling to become supergiants with cores so pressurized that carbon and silicon fuse to make iron.

Why do stars die?

Stars die when they have exhausted their vast supplies of nuclear fuel. When the hydrogen runs out, they switch to helium. When helium runs out, they quickly exhaust any remaining nuclear fuel then either blow up, shrink, or become cold.

What is a supernova?

A supernova is a gigantic explosion that finishes off a supergiant star. For just a brief moment, the supernova flashes out with the brilliance of billions of Suns. They are rare and short-lived, but there is always one somewhere in the Universe.

What are the oldest stars?

The oldest stars are not stars at all but look like them because they are so far away. Some of these "quasi-stellar radio objects," or quasars, are so far away, the light we see left them 13 billion years ago.

Once iron forms in its core, the star does not release energy but absorbs it

What are nebulae?

Nebulae are giant clouds of gas and dust spread throughout the galaxies. Some of them can be seen through telescopes because they shine faintly as they reflect starlight. Others, called dark nebulae, can only be seen because they hide the stars behind with an inky black patch. It is in these dark nebulae that stars are born.

The collapse of a supergiant star triggers an explosion like a gigantic nuclear bomb called a supernova

As it absorbs energy, the star suddenly and catastrophically collapses in a few seconds to little bigger than a planet

QUIZ

1 Supernovas can send out more energy in a few seconds than our Sun in 200 million years: true or false?

2 Stars called pulsars, which beam out regular radio signals, are called LGMs. LGM stands for: a) Little Green Man b) Low Gas Matter c) Light Generating Masses?

3 A sugar cube of neutron star weighs a) 10 tons b) 10 million tons c) 100 million tons?

4 Red dwarf stars glow red because they are made of coal: true or false?

5 Astronomers have discovered alcohol in the clouds called nebulae: true or false?

What is a white dwarf?

White dwarfs are the small white stars formed as stars smaller than our Sun lose their surface gas altogether and shrink. Yet they are much bigger than neutron stars, which are all that is left of a supergiant star after a supernova explosion. Neutron stars are unimaginably dense.

Answers
1. True; 2. a), because the signals are so regular, it was once thought they might be aliens; 3. c) 4. False; 5. True

Galaxies

What are galaxies?

OUR SUN IS JUST ONE of a vast concentration of over 100 billion stars, arranged in a shape like a spinning fried egg, over 100,000 light-years across. This huge star city is called the Milky Way, or simply the Galaxy, because we see it as a pale band across the night sky—the word "galaxy" comes from the Greek for "milky". But earlier this century, astronomers realized that the Milky Way is not the only star city in the Universe. In fact, there are billions of similar star groups scattered throughout space. These are also called galaxies (with a small "g").

Why is the Milky Way just a band across the sky?

Because we are seeing it edge-on. We are out on one edge, looking in toward the center, and the Milky Way as viewed in our sky is the narrow layer of stars stretching away from us. If we could travel millions of light-years out at right angles to the Milky Way, we would see that it is indeed spiral.

Where is the Earth?

The Earth and the solar system are on one of the Milky Way's spiral arms, about 30,000 light-years out from the center.

▼ **The Milky Way**

Our view of the Milky Way is of a pale, blotchy white band that stretches right across the night sky. A powerful telescope reveals that is made of countless stars. It is actually an edge-on view of our Galaxy.

The trailing arms of stars are embedded in a ball of dark matter

Our Galaxy is whirling rapidly, sweeping the Sun and other stars around at 62 million mph

There is a concentration of stars at the heart of the Galaxy

Irregular
galaxy

Spiral
galaxy

Barred spiral
galaxy

▶ Galactic shapes
There are four main kinds of galaxy, but the distinction between them is not always completely clear.

Is our Galaxy turning?

Yes, it is whirling around so fast it sweeps us along at 62 million miles per hour! We go once around the Galaxy, a journey of almost 100,000 light-years, in just 200 million years. But we are so much a part of the Galaxy we only know we are moving by watching distant galaxies.

The Sun is just one of the stars in the Galaxy, located on an arm 30,000 light-years out

What is a spiral galaxy?

A spiral galaxy is one of the four kinds of galaxy. It has spiralling arms of stars like a giant Catherine wheel. They trail because the galaxy is rotating rapidly. Our Galaxy is a spiral galaxy.

Where is the next galaxy?

The Milky Way's nearest neighbor is the only other galaxy you can see with the naked eye, the Andromeda galaxy, which is about 2.5 million light-years away. But there are 30 or so galaxies in our own neighborhood, called the Local Group, which is itself part of a cluster of 3,000 galaxies.

Is there anything else but stars in a galaxy?

The Milky Way and other spiral galaxies look flat like a fried egg. In fact, they may be shaped more like burgers—and all we are seeing is the meat in the burger. The "bread" is mysterious stuff called dark matter, because it can't be seen or detected in any way. We only know it is there because of the way its gravity affects the stars. It may be that more than 90 percent of the mass of the Universe is dark matter.

QUIZ

1 Every now and then galaxies crash into one another: true or false?

2 The Large Magellanic Cloud is a) a nebula b) a kind of thundercloud c) a galaxy?

3 What creatures dominated the Earth the last time our spiral arm of the Galaxy was in the same place ?

4 The biggest structure in the Universe is the Great Wall of galaxies. It is a) 4,000 b) 4 million c) 500 million light-years thick?

5 Which astronomer first showed there were galaxies beyond our own a) Copernicus b) Herschel c) Hubble?

Distant objects

How big is the Universe?

BIGGER THAN YOU CAN possibly imagine. Venus, the nearest planet, is 24 million miles away at its nearest. The dwarf planet Pluto is 3.7 billion miles away. The nearest star, Proxima Centauri, is 25 trillion miles away. The nearest galaxy beyond our own is 25,000 light-years away. The farthest object astronomers can see is over 7.4 billion trillion miles away–and the Universe must stretch way beyond that, and is getting bigger by the second.

▲ Candle power
The farther away a candle is, the dimmer it looks. The same is true of stars—and this is how astronomers measure how far away the stars are.

How are distances given in space?
Distances are so great in space that they can't be measured in feet or miles. Instead, they are measured in light-years and parsecs. A parsec is 3.26 light-years.

A black hole is a place where gravity is so strong it sucks everything in, even light

What is a light-year?
Light is the fastest thing in the Universe, traveling at almost 186,000 miles a second. It gets to the Earth from the Moon in the blink of an eye. It takes eight minutes for light to reach us from the Sun and four YEARS to reach us from the nearest star. A light-year is the distance light travels in a year, which is 5,878,000,000,000 miles—just under six trillion miles!

Black holes form when a star or galaxy gets so dense that it collapses under the pull of its own gravity

▶ Quasar
Quasars are so bright we can see them billions of light-years away. Their energy may come from gas being sucked into a black hole in their center

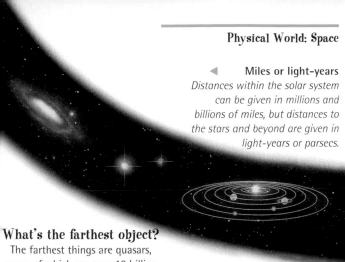

◄ **Miles or light-years**
Distances within the solar system can be given in millions and billions of miles, but distances to the stars and beyond are given in light-years or parsecs.

QUIZ

1 At its nearest, the Moon is a) 12,836 miles b) 225,623 miles c) 700,541 miles away?

2 The distance to the Moon is measured with laser beams bounced off mirrors left on the surface by space probes: true or false?

3 About how far from Earth is the Sun: a) 31 million b) 93 million c) 176 million miles?

4 Andromeda is 15 billion billion miles away. How many light-years is this?

5 The star Deneb is 3,200 light-years away. Who was ruling in Egypt at the same time as we see it?

6 How soon could you get to the Sun and back at the speed of light?

What's the farthest object?

The farthest things are quasars, many of which are over 10 billion light-years away. This means we are seeing them as they were over 10 billion years ago—over five billion years before the Earth was formed, and shortly after the dawn of the Universe.

How do they measure how far a star is?

Distances to nearby stars can be measured by the parallax method. As the Earth circles the Sun, a nearby star seems to shift a little compared to stars farther away, as our viewpoint changes slightly. By measuring how much it shifts, we can figure out how far off it is.

How do they measure how far to more distant stars?

The farther away a star is, the dimmer it looks. But some stars burn brightly while others glimmer. So it's hard to tell if a dim star is far away or just feeble. But the color of a star shows how bright it really is. If you know how bright a star really is from its color, you can figure out how far away it is by comparing this with how bright it looks.

How far away are galaxies?

Beyond about 30,000 light-years, stars are too indistinct to detect their color accurately. So for objects at this distance, we look for "standard candles"—that is, a star whose brightness we know. The dimmer it looks compared to how bright it should look, the farther away it must be. Standard candles include supernovas and fluctuating stars called cepheid variables.

What is red shift?

When a galaxy is moving rapidly away from us, the waves of light from it become stretched out— that is, they become redder. The greater this red shift, the faster the galaxy must be moving away from us.

Are the galaxies moving?

Studying red shifts has shown that every galaxy is moving away from us. The farther away it is, the faster it is receding. The most distant galaxies are receding at almost the speed of light.

The Big Bang

How did the Universe begin?

THE UNIVERSE began with the biggest explosion of all time, called the Big Bang. One moment there was just an unimaginably small, incredibly hot little ball. A moment later, the Universe burst into existence with a gigantic explosion. Within a split second, all the forces that shape the Universe were created, and so, too, was all the matter. The explosion was so big that material is still hurtling away from it in all directions at astonishing speeds.

What was the early Universe like?

The early Universe was very small, but it contained all the matter and energy in the Universe today. It was a dense and chaotic soup of tiny particles and forces— and instead of the four forces scientists know today, there was just one superforce. But this original Universe lasted only a moment. After just three trillionths of a trillionth of a trillionth of a second, the superforce split to create the separate forces we know today.

QUIZ

Can you see the Big Bang?

Astronomers can see the galaxies hurtling away from us in all directions. They can also see the afterglow of the Big Bang—as low level microwave radiation coming toward us from all over space. This is called microwave background radiation. In 1992, the Cosmic Background Explorer (COBE) made a complete map of the background.

When did the galaxies and stars form?

Galaxies and stars probably began to form about 300 million years after the Big Bang, from curdled lumps of hydrogen and helium gas. Some astronomers think they formed as large clumps and broke into smaller clumps. Others think they formed as clumps packed tighter and tighter.

What will happen in the future?

No one knows if the Universe will go on growing. It all depends on how much matter it contains. If there is more than the "critical density," gravity will put a brake in its expansion, and it may soon begin to contract again to end in a Big Crunch. If there is about the same, it may already be in a "steady state," neither expanding nor contracting. If there is much less than the critical density, it will go on expanding forever. This is called the Open Universe.

How old is the Universe?

We know that the Universe is getting bigger at a certain rate by observing how fast distant galaxies are moving. By calculating how long it took everything to expand to where it is now, we can wind back the clock to the time when the Universe was very small. This suggests the Universe began somewhere between 13 and 15 billion years ago. However, studies of globular clusters of stars suggest some stars in our galaxy may be 18 billion years old.

What was there before the Universe began?

No one has the remotest idea. Some people think there was a weird ocean, beyond space and time, full of potential universes continually bursting into life. Ours was one of the successful ones. There may be others.

How do scientists know what the early Universe was like?

They don't for certain, but they can get a good idea from mathematical calculations based on laws of physics today, and from experiments with huge machines called colliders and particle accelerators. These recreate conditions in the early Universe by using magnets to accelerate particles to astonishing speeds in a special tunnel, then smashing them all together.

1 What was the first chemical element to form?

2 Which scientist wrote a book called *A Brief History of Time*?

3 How old is the Earth?

4 The Universe is getting bigger, but only the space between the galaxies is stretching: true or false?

5 Which formed first: the Milky Way or the Sun?

6 Two of the four basic forces in the Universe hold the nuclei of atoms together. What are the other two?

7 Is the Andromeda galaxy getting nearer to us or farther away?

8 Astronomers can detect sounds from the far side of the Universe: true or false?

Answers
1. Hydrogen; 2. Stephen Hawking; 3. 4.6 billion years; 4. True; 5. The Milky Way; 6. Gravity and electromagnetism; 7. Farther, like all galaxies; 8. False, there are no sounds in space

What substance has the highest melting point?

What did Newton learn from an apple?

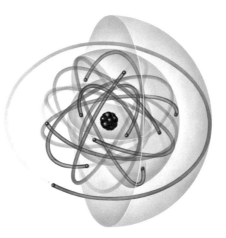

How big are atoms?

Why are racing bicycles made of light materials?

Why don't the bottoms of lakes freeze?

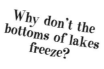

Which frog makes arrows deadly?

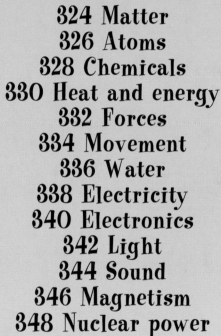

Why is laser light special?

Science

Can sound travel in a vacuum?

Why does hair get frizzy?

What is virtual reality?

Matter

What is matter?

MATTER IS EVERY SUBSTANCE in the Universe—everything that is not simply empty space. There are three different forms, or "states," of matter—solid like a brick, liquid like water, and gas like air. Every substance can change from one state to another and back again, providing the temperature and pressure are right.

▲ Freezing

When a liquid cools, the molecules slow down enough for regular bonds to grow between them. When water freezes to snowflakes, beautiful crystals form.

▼ Water cycle

Water is the only substance to exist naturally on Earth in all three states—solid ice, liquid water, and the gas water vapor. Water is called water vapor when it is a gas; steam is actually lots of tiny drops of water.

What is a solid?

When a substance is solid, it has strength and a definite shape. Every substance is made from minute bits called molecules, which are much, much too small to see. In a solid, the molecules are bonded together firmly in a regular structure. Like all molecules, they are moving all the time, but in a solid, molecules simply vibrate on the spot. The hotter it gets, the more they vibrate.

What is a liquid?

A liquid is substance in a state like water, which flows and takes the shape of any container it is poured into. It does this because although bonds hold its molecules together, the bonds are loose enough for molecules to roll over each other like dry sand.

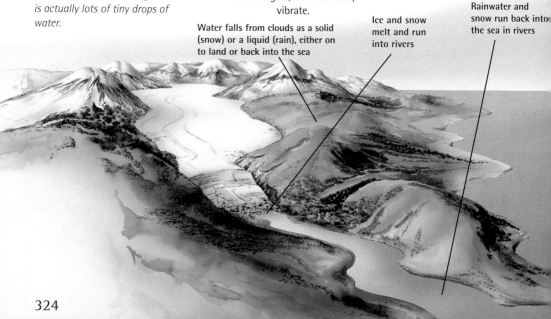

Water falls from clouds as a solid (snow) or a liquid (rain), either on to land or back into the sea

Ice and snow melt and run into rivers

Rainwater and snow run back into the sea in rivers

Solid

▲ **Loosening bonds**
It is the bonds between the molecules it is made from that make a substance solid, liquid or gas. As the temperature rises, the molecules move more and the bonds get looser.

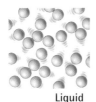
Liquid

Gas

What is a gas?

A gas is when a substance is in a state like air. It does not have any strength, shape or volume. The molecules move so fast that they break any bonds that might hold them together.

What happens when things melt or boil?

When a solid melts, it turns to liquid because heat makes the molecules vibrate so much that they break the bonds that hold them together. If it gets even hotter, the molecules zoom all over the place, and some move so fast they break away from the surface of the liquid altogether, turning to gas.

As seawater is warmed by the Sun, some of it evaporates (turns to vapor) and begins to rise up through the air on warm air currents

As it rises through the air and cools, water vapor condenses (turns to liquid) and forms clouds

QUIZ

1 **What is the boiling point of water a) 122°F b) 212°F c) 1,832°F?**

2 **Helium has the lowest freezing point of any substance. Is it a) -456.96°F b) -53.5°F c) -12.2°F?**

3 **Tungsten has the highest melting point of any metal. It is a) 608°F b) 6,188°F c) 14,234°F?**

4 **What substance has the highest melting point?**

5 **What is condensation?**

6 **What is melting point?**

7 **Which metal is liquid at normal temperatures?**

8 **Clouds contain water in which states of matter?**

Answers
1. b) 2. a) 3. b) 4. Carbon;
5. The change from gas to liquid;
6. The temperature at which a substance changes from a solid to a liquid; 7. Mercury; 8. All three

Atoms

What is an atom?

ATOMS ARE THE TINY BITS, OR "PARTICLES," of which every substance is made. They are far too small to see. Two billion of them would fit on the dot on the top of this "i." Scientists once thought they were the smallest things in the Universe–and that they were tiny hard balls that could never be split or destroyed. Now they know atoms are more like clouds of energy, and are mostly empty space, dotted with even tinier "sub-atomic" particles.

▲ Helium nucleus
The nucleus of an atom of helium is one of the smallest—though not as small as hydrogen. It combines two protons with two neutrons.

What's inside an atom?

Right in the center of every atom, like a pea in a basketball, is a dense core, or "nucleus," containing two kinds of tiny particles—protons and neutrons. Around the nucleus are even tinier particles called electrons, whizzing around at the speed of light.

How big are atoms?

They are about a ten-millionth of a millimeter across and weigh 100 trillionths of a trillionth of a gram. The smallest atoms of all are hydrogen atoms.

Electrons behave as if they were stacked around the nucleus in different levels, like layers of an onion. The levels are called shells

The particles of the nucleus are held together by a force called the strong nuclear force

Electrons are held to the nucleus by electrical charge—because they have an opposite electrical charge than the protons in the nucleus

The nucleus is made from particles called protons and neutrons, which are made, in turn, of even smaller particles called quarks

▶ Inside an atom
Atoms don't really look like this, but it is a good way to think of them. Most of an atom is empty space, but right in the center is a nucleus of protons and neutrons, held together by special nuclear forces. Around the outside whizz electrons, held in place by the opposite electrical charge on the protons.

There is only room for a certain number of electrons in each shell

Sodium atom gives up an electron

Mutual electric attraction

Chlorine atom gains an electron

◀ **Ionic bond**

Atoms are only stable if they have a full set of electrons in their outer shells. They can get this by bonding with other atoms to make molecules. In "ionic" bonds one atom donates an electron to the other and becomes negatively charged. The atoms are then bonded by mutual electrical attraction. This is how sodium atoms bond with chlorine atoms to make salt molecules.

QUIZ

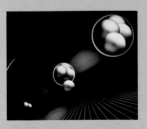

1 The smallest atom is hydrogen, which has one proton in its nucleus. Meitnerium is the biggest. It has a) 30 protons b) 40 protons c) over 100 protons?

2 Who first split an atomic nucleus in 1919 a) Newton b) Dalton c) Rutherford?

3 Scientists think quarks are stuck together by gluons: true or false?

4 All particles are either quarks or leptons: true or false?

5 An atom with a full outer shell of electrons, like argon, does not react with others: true or false?

6 A new chemical element is made when an atom gains a proton: true or false?

What is an electrical charge?

Protons have a "positive" electrical charge, which just means they attract electrons. Electrons have a "negative" electrical charge, which means they attract protons. Neutrons have no charge. Most atoms have the same number of protons and electrons, so their charges balance out. The charge on electrons drives them apart. If they were not attracted to the protons, the electrons on an atom would fly off.

What is an ion?

An ion is an atom that has either lost one or more electrons, making it positively charged (cation) or gained a few, making it negatively charged (anion).

What are molecules?

Some atoms cannot exist by themselves, and so join up with others—either of the same kind, or with others to form chemical compounds. A molecule is the smallest particle of a substance that can exist on its own.

How many kinds of sub-atomic particle are there?

At least 200, besides electrons, protons, and neutrons. But most are created in special conditions and last only a split second.

What are the smallest particles?

Protons are made of tiny particles called quarks. Electrons are also tiny. But the smallest of all are neutrinos.

▶ **Covalent bond**

Atoms are only stable when they have a full set of electrons in their outer shell. Atoms that have too many or too few can get a full set by sharing electrons with other atoms. This makes a "covalent" bond.

Shared electrons

Electrons in their shells

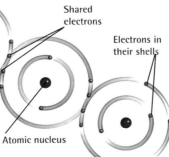

Atomic nucleus

Chemicals

What are chemical elements?

CHEMICAL ELEMENTS ARE substances that cannot be split up into other substances. Gold is an element because it cannot be split. Water is not, because it can be split into the elements hydrogen and oxygen. What makes each element different are the atoms it is made from. Each element is made from atoms with a certain number of protons in their nucleus. Atoms of gold have 79 protons in their nucleus; atoms of hydrogen have 1.

How many elements?

The number of known elements is constantly increasing, as scientists discover ways to create new ones in addition to the 90 or so that occur naturally on Earth.

What is the Periodic Table?

Devised by the chemist John Dalton (1766-1844) the Periodic Table is a chart on which all the elements can be arranged according to the number of protons in the nucleus. Columns are called Groups, rows are called Periods. Each Period contains elements with atoms that have the same number of electron shells. In each Period, the number of protons (and so the number of electrons) in the atom goes up one by one. Elements in the same Group have the same number of electrons in the outer shell of their atoms, and so have similar properties.

▶ **The Periodic Table**
The Periodic Table arranges all the elements in Periods (rows) and Groups (columns). The colors show some of the major kinds of elements, including metals and transition elements.

What are the noble gases?

Noble gases are the elements in Group 0, on the far right of the Periodic Table. Their outer electron shells have a full complement of electrons. This means they rarely react with other substances. This is why they are sometimes also called inert gases. The noble gases argon and xenon are often used in light bulbs, because the light bulb's filament will get hot in them without burning.

Hydrogen has the lightest and simplest atoms, with just one proton, one neutron and one electron

Group 1 consists of metal elements with just one electron in their outer shells—and so are very reactive

Metals are "electropositive" elements, which means they lose negatively charged electrons easily—which is why they conduct electricity well

The actinides are 15 radioactive elements like radium and plutonium that get their name from actinium

Why are some elements reactive?

Elements are reactive if they readily gain or lose electrons. The further to the left in the table they are, the more reactive they are. Group 1 metals such as sodium and potassium are very reactive.

What is a metal?

Metals are hard, dense, and shiny substances that ring when you hit them with another metal. They also conduct heat and electricity well.

What is a compound?

Compounds are substances made from two or more elements joined together. Every molecule (smallest particle) in a compound is made from the same combination of atoms. Molecules of sodium chloride, for instance, are one sodium atom joined to one chlorine. Compounds have different properties than the elements that make them up. Sodium sputters when put in water; chlorine is a thick green gas. Yet sodium chloride is table salt.

Group 5 is non-metals such as nitrogen at the top, but gets more and more metallic lower down with antimony and bismuth

Group 7 is the halogens—non-metals such as chlorine and iodine

Group 4 includes silicon and carbon, which form more compounds than any other elements

							He helium 2
		B boron 5	C carbon 6	N nitrogen 7	O oxygen 8	F fluorine 9	Ne neon 10
		Al aluminium 13	Si silicon 14	P phosphorus 15	S sulphur 16	Cl chlorine 17	Ar argon 18

Co cobalt 27	Ni nickel 28	Cu copper 29	Zn zinc 30	Ga gallium 31	Ge germanium 32	As arsenic 33	Se selenium 34	Br bromine 35	Kr krypton 36
Rh rhodium 45	Pd palladium 46	Ag silver 47	Cd cadmium 48	In indium 49	Sn tin 50	Sb antimony 51	Te tellurium 52	I iodine 53	Xe xenon 54
Ir iridium 77	Pt platinum 78	Au gold 79	Hg mercury 80	Ti thalium 81	Pb lead 82	Bi bismuth 83	Po polonium 84	At astatine 85	Rn radon 86
Mt meitnerium 109	Uun ununnilium 110	Uuu unununium 111	Uub ununbium 112						

Group 0 is the noble gases, like neon, which have full outer electron shells and are unreactive

Eu europium 63	Gd gadolinium 64	Tb terbium 65	Dy dysprosium 66	Ho holmium 67	Er erbium 68	Tm thulium 69	Yb ytterbium 70
Am americium 95	Cm curium 96	Bk berkelium 97	Cf californium 98	Es einsteinium 99	Fm fermium 100	Md mendelevium 101	No nobelium 102

QUIZ

1 Which two elements is water made from?

2 Is table salt an element?

3 Who discovered the element radium?

4 Diamonds, coal, lead pencils, and racing cars are made from the same element. Which is it?

5 What is the main element in the air besides oxygen?

6 What is the second lightest element?

7 Which has the most protons in its atoms: gold or lead?

8 Krypton is a highly reactive gas: true or false?

9 Chemists can try out new molecules on computer screens: true or false?

Heat and energy

What is heat?

HEAT IS A FORM OF ENERGY—the energy of molecules moving. The faster they move, the hotter it is. When you put your hand over a heater, the warmth you feel is actually an assault by billions of fast-moving air molecules, spurred along by even faster-moving molecules in the heater. We measure how hot something is by its temperature. But temperature is not the same as heat. Heat is the combined energy of all the moving molecules. Temperature is simply a measure of how fast the molecules are moving.

◀ Thermometer
In a thermometer like this, the temperature is shown by how far the liquid in the bulb at the bottom expands and rises up the tube.

▼ Fire
Fire is a chemical reaction in which one substance gets so hot that it combines with oxygen in the air. The reaction releases so much energy that the atoms send out rays of light, making bright, dancing flames.

How does heat move?

Heat moves in three ways: conduction, convection, and radiation. Conduction involves heat spreading from hot areas to cold areas by direct contact, as moving particles knock into one another. Convection occurs when warm air or water rises as it expands and gets lighter. Radiation is heat rays—invisible rays of infrared light.

How is temperature measured?

Temperature is measured with a thermometer. Some thermometers have a metal strip that bends according to how hot it is. Most hold a liquid, such as mercury, in a tube. As the air warms, the liquid expands, and its level rises in the tube. The level of the liquid indicates the temperature.

What are Centigrade and Fahrenheit?

These are two scales for measuring temperature. Centigrade is also called Celsius. Water freezes at 0°C (Centigrade) and 32°F (Fahrenheit). It boils at 100°C and 212°F. To convert from °F to °C, first subtract 32 and divide by nine, and then multiply by five. To change °C to °F, divide by five and multiply by nine, and then add 32.

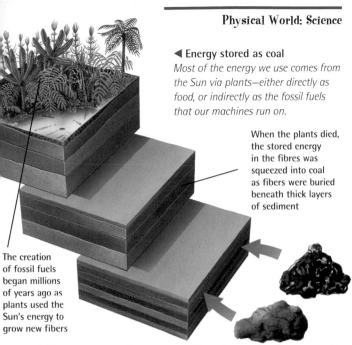

◀ **Energy stored as coal**
Most of the energy we use comes from the Sun via plants—either directly as food, or indirectly as the fossil fuels that our machines run on.

When the plants died, the stored energy in the fibres was squeezed into coal as fibers were buried beneath thick layers of sediment

The creation of fossil fuels began millions of years ago as plants used the Sun's energy to grow new fibers

What is energy?

Energy is the capacity to make things happen or, as scientists put it, "work." It takes many forms. Heat energy boils water. Chemical energy fuels cars and airplanes. Electrical energy drives all kinds of small machines and keeps lights glowing. Most of our energy comes from the Sun, mostly indirectly either from plants or as fossil fuels.

What happens to energy?

Energy can neither be created nor destroyed. When you use energy, you simply convert it from one form to another. When you run, you change the chemical energy of your muscles into heat energy that is lost from the body, and into movement, called "kinetic" energy. When energy is converted, there is always the same amount of energy after as before.

●

What's absolute zero?

Absolute zero is the coldest possible temperature—at which atoms and molecules stop moving altogether. This is 0 on the Kelvin scale, or -459°F (273.15°C).

◀ **Movement to electricity**
Hydroelectric power stations convert the energy of moving water into electrical energy.

QUIZ

1 The highest temperature ever measured, in a nuclear fusion experiment, is about a) 54,000°F b) 900,000°F c) 72 million°F?

2 The highest air temperature recorded, in Death Valley, is a) 98.96°F b) 134.06°F c) 198.32°F?

3 The lowest air temperature ever recorded, in Antarctica, is a) -2.38°F b) -31.9°C c) -128.56°F?

4 What do solar cells do?

5 Energy is a form of mass: true or false?

6 On the Kelvin scale used by scientists, water freezes at 273.15 K: true or false?

7 How much of the world's energy comes from coal a) 12% b) 41% c) 59%?

Forces

What is a force?

A FORCE IS JUST A PUSH OR A PULL. Some forces are invisible, like gravity, which holds us to the ground. Some are visible, like a kick. But they all work by making something go faster, slow down, or change shape.

▲ Isaac Newton
Sir Isaac Newton (1643–1727) was the great 17th century scientist who developed the idea of gravity and other forces.

What did Newton learn from an apple?

According to the great 17th century scientist Sir Isaac Newton, his ideas about the force of gravity came to him as he was sitting under an apple tree. When he saw an apple fall, it occurred to him that the apple was not simply falling, but being pulled to the ground by an invisible force, which he called gravity.

What is gravity?

Gravity is the invisible force of attraction between every bit of matter in the Universe. Its strength depends on the mass of the objects involved and just how far they are apart.

Are mass and weight the same?

No. Mass is the amount of matter in an object. It is the same wherever you measure it. Weight is the force of gravity on an object. It varies with where you measure it.

Are there other forces?

Wherever there is movement there is a force involved, but there are four basic forces that work right down to the level of atoms. These are gravity, electromagnetism, and two "nuclear" forces—forces that act only in the nuclei of atoms.

Tailwings provide a down force to help keep the car stable

Thrust is developed as hot gas expands between the rocket housing and the air

▲ Land speed record breaker
The main obstacle to traveling fast is friction—friction with the ground, friction with the air, and friction between moving parts. To beat the world land speed record, Thrust SSC needed huge rocket motors to develop enough thrust to overcome this force.

Rocket motors provide huge forward thrust

The shape is smooth and streamlined to cut friction with the air— air resistance

► **Strike force**
When a batter hits a ball, the ball shoots off somewhere between the direction of the force of the ball's momentum and the direction of the force of the bat. Just where in between depends on the force of the ball's momentum and the force of the strike. The ball's new direction is called the "resultant" by scientists studying forces.

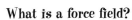

QUIZ

1 What is the force that holds you on the ground?

2 How fast does gravity make things accelerate a) 0.8 inch per second per second b) 32.2 feet per second per second c) 2,894 miles per second per second?

3 What is the force that makes compass needles point to North?

4 What force does a train have to overcome to move fast?

5 All forces act in straight lines: true or false?

6 Who dropped different balls from the Leaning Tower of Pisa in Italy to show they fall at the same rate?

7 Air resistance gets less the faster a car goes: true or false?

What force holds things together?

Nuclear forces hold atomic nuclei together, but electromagnetism holds atoms together, binds atoms to make molecules and binds molecules, to make different substances. When it binds molecules, it is called an intermolecular force.

What is friction?

Friction is the force between two things rubbing together, which may be brake pads on a bicycle wheel or air against an airplane. It tends to slow things down, making them hot as momentum is changed to heat. It is caused by the intermolecular force between the molecules of the two things rubbing.

What is a force field?

A force field is the region over which forces like gravity and electromagnetism have an effect. They are invisible, and the only way of knowing they exist is by the way they move things coming within range. Force fields are often shown as lines with arrows to show the direction and strength of the movement.

How is force measured?

Force is measured in newtons, in honour of Sir Isaac Newton. A newton is the force needed to accelerate 1kg by 1m per second in a second.

► **Take off**
Airplanes stay up because their wings provide a lift force to counteract the force of gravity. The lift comes from the air, which is forced to flow over the wings as the airplane flies forward. To take off, the plane must accelerate until it is going fast enough for the wings to give the lift to beat gravity.

Movement

How do things start to move?

THINGS ONLY MOVE IF FORCED TO MOVE. This is called inertia. The heavier something is, the more inertia it has and the harder it is to start moving. So when something starts to move, there must be a force involved—whether it is visible, like someone pushing, or invisible, like gravity—and the force must be large enough to overcome the inertia. Once things are moving at the same speed and in the same direction, they keep on doing so until another force (typically friction) slows or turns them.

What's the difference between inertia and momentum?

Inertia is the tendency of things to stay still unless forced to move. Momentum is the tendency of moving things to keep moving, unless forced to stop or slow. This is Newton's First Law of Motion.

What is acceleration?

Acceleration is how fast something gains speed. The larger the force and the lighter the object, the greater the acceleration. This is Newton's Second Law of Motion.

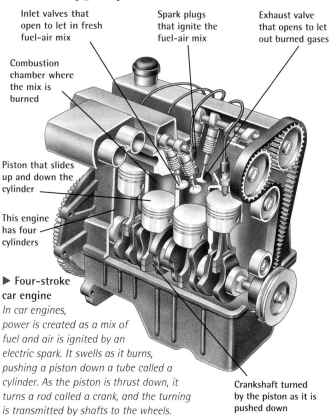

Inlet valves that open to let in fresh fuel-air mix

Spark plugs that ignite the fuel-air mix

Exhaust valve that opens to let out burned gases

Combustion chamber where the mix is burned

Piston that slides up and down the cylinder

This engine has four cylinders

▶ Four-stroke car engine
In car engines, power is created as a mix of fuel and air is ignited by an electric spark. It swells as it burns, pushing a piston down a tube called a cylinder. As the piston is thrust down, it turns a rod called a crank, and the turning is transmitted by shafts to the wheels.

Crankshaft turned by the piston as it is pushed down

The four-stroke sequence

1. Inlet valve opens to let in a dose of fuel drawn in by the descending piston

2. The valve closes and the piston rises, squeezing the fuel as it does

3. The spark ignites the fuel, which swells and thrusts the piston down

4. The piston rises again, pushing burned gases out of the exhaust

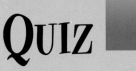

QUIZ

◀ Hydraulic bore

The arms are raised and lowered on this drill by pumping fluid in and out of the tubes that support them. The drill is driven hydraulically, too, to ensure a smooth action.

What is a four-stroke engine?

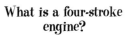

Most car engines are four-stroke engines. This means that each of the pistons goes up and down four times for each power stroke—that is, for every time the piston is thrust down by the burning gases. Most car engines also have at least four cylinders, and each fires in succession, so that one is on its power stroke while the rest are on their idle strokes.

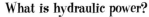

What is hydraulic power?

Fluids like water cannot be squashed. So if you push fluid through a pipe, it will push out of the other end. Hydraulic power uses fluid-filled pipes working like this to drive things smoothly. Hydraulic means water, but most hydraulic systems use oil to avoid rusting.

What is Newton's Third Law of Motion?

That for every action, there is an equal and opposite reaction. This means that whenever something moves, there is a balance of forces pushing the other way. So when you push your feet on the bicycle pedals, the pedals are actually pushing back just as hard.

How do engines work?

Most engines work by burning fuel to make gases that expand rapidly as they get hot. In cars and trains, the hot gases swell inside a chamber, called the combustion chamber, and push against a piston or a turbine (a kind of fan). In jets and rockets, the burning gases swell and push against the whole engine as they shoot out of the back.

▶ Jet engine

A plane's jet engines suck in air through the front to burn with aviation fuel. As it is burned with aviation fuel, it swells so rapidly from the back of the engine that the plane is thrust forward.

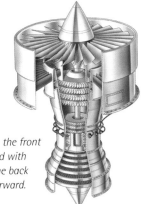

1 Why are racing bicycles made of very light materials?

2 How many Laws of Motion did Sir Isaac Newton find?

3 What are the two major fuels used by car engines?

4 What is the gas that combines with fuel as it burns in a car engine?

5 Why do heavy trucks take longer to stop than cars?

6 Which two scientists invented jet engines?

7 What is the force that slows cars down?

8 Cars are powered by dead shellfish: true or false?

9 What is the world's fastest train?

Water

Why is water special?

THERE ARE MANY REASONS why water is a remarkable substance. But there are two that stand out. First of all, it is the only substance that can be solid, liquid, and gas at everyday temperatures. Second, it has a remarkable capacity for making mild solutions with other substances, so that it can be used to transfer everything from sugar to salt. These two properties above all make water perhaps the most important material of all for life—and make Earth, the only planet known to have an abundance of water, so special.

▲ Floating ship
Ships made of heavy metal float because they trap air inside their hulls. They float at the point where the weight of the ship and air exactly matches the weight of water displaced (pushed out of the way).

▼ How submarines work
Submarines rise to the surface by pumping water out of their buoyancy tanks to lighten them enough to float to the surface. To dive again, they pump water in to their buoyancy tanks to increase their weight enough to sink.

What is water made of?
Water is made of molecules, which are built from two atoms of hydrogen and one of oxygen, bound in a Y-shape. This is why its chemical formula is H_2O. This molecule is said to be "polar," because the oxygen side is a little more negatively charged electrically.

Why is water liquid?
Similar substances like ammonia are gases far below freezing. Water is liquid until 212°F because its polar molecules form strong bonds with each other, as the positively charged end of one molecule is drawn to the negative end of another. These bonds are called hydrogen bonds.

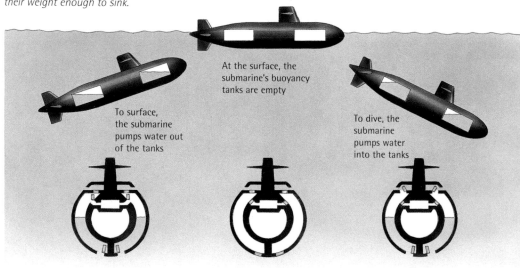

At the surface, the submarine's buoyancy tanks are empty

To surface, the submarine pumps water out of the tanks

To dive, the submarine pumps water into the tanks

▶ Tidal boom
*The rising and
falling of tides in
the sea can generate
electricity as it swishes floating
booms like these back and forth.*

Why don't the bottoms of lakes freeze?

Uniquely, ice is less dense than cold water, so it floats on top of the lake, acting as a blanket and stopping cold water below from freezing. Water is at its densest at 39.2°F. It actually expands when it freezes, which is why water pipes can burst in cold winters, and how water splits rock.

What is water pressure?

Water pressure is the combined push of moving molecules of water. The deeper the water, the greater the pressure.

What is a solution?

When a substance is added to a liquid, various things can happen. If the substance does not mix in at all, and lumps of it float in the liquid, it is a "suspension." If the atoms, ions, and molecules of the substance break up and intermingle with the liquid, it forms a new liquid called a solution. When you dissolve coffee powder in water, you make a solution. Water here is the "solvent" and coffee powder the "solute."

What is a saturated solution?

As you dissolve more of a solid, the solution becomes stronger and stronger until no more will dissolve. The solution is then said to be saturated. If you heat a solution, more will dissolve before it becomes saturated. But if a saturated solution cools down, or is left to evaporate, solute molecules may begin to link and grow into solid crystals.

◀ Sugar solution
Count how many spoonfuls of sugar you can dissolve in cold water or tea. Then count how many you can dissolve in warm water.

QUIZ

1 So much water flows through the Amazon River that it could fill London's St Paul's Cathedral in a) 1 second b) 1 minute c) 1 hour ?

2 How much of the world's surface is covered by water: a) 25% b) 55% c) 70%?

3 How much of the world's water is frozen: a) 2% b) 5% c) 12%?

4 Things float better in salty seawater than freshwater: true or false?

5 Which famous scientist shouted "Eureka!" when he figured out how things float?

Archimedes (287–212 B.C.)
5. The Ancient Greek thinker
4. True!
1. a) 2. c) 3. a)
Answers

337

Electricity

Why does hair get frizzy?

WHEN YOU COMB DRY HAIR, tiny electrons are knocked off the atoms in the comb as it rubs past. The effect is that your hair is coated with these tiny negative electrical charges and so is attracted to anything that has the normal amount of electrons, or less. An electrical charge built up like this is called "static" because it does not move. You could try rubbing a balloon on your sweater to create a static charge on the balloon to stick it to a wall.

What is electric current?

Static electricity does not move. Current electricity does. It is a continuous stream of electrical charge. It only happens when there is a complete, unbroken "circuit" for the current to flow through—typically a loop of copper wire.

What makes lightning flash?

Lightning flashes produce millions of volts of static electricity. Lightning is created when raindrops and ice crystals inside a thundercloud are flung together by strong air currents. They become electrically charged as they gain or lose electrons. Negatively charged particles build up at the base of the cloud. When this charge has built up enough, it discharges as lightning, either flashing within the cloud or forking between the cloud and ground.

▶ **Lightning flashes**

Lightning flashes are sparked by the build-up of huge differences in static electrical charge between the top and bottom of a thundercloud. The flash is the sudden jump of electrons from one place to another to bring the charge back to normal. This can happen within the cloud (sheet lightning), or between the cloud and ground (fork lightning).

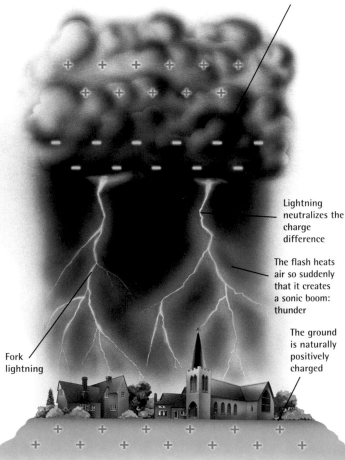

Negative charges build up in the base of the cloud

Lightning neutralizes the charge difference

The flash heats air so suddenly that it creates a sonic boom: thunder

The ground is naturally positively charged

Fork lightning

338

▲ Simple battery

Acid contains both positive and negative particles. When copper and zinc plates are dipped in and connected, pluses are drawn to one, minuses to the other.

How does current flow?

The charge in an electric current is electrons that have broken free from their atoms. None of them move very far, but the current is passed on as they bang into each other like rows of marbles.

How do batteries work?

Batteries work because when certain substances are placed next to each other, there is a difference in charge between them. In the simplest cells, the materials are copper and zinc plates dipped in acid. When a wire between the plates completes the circuit, current flows.

▶ Battery-powered light

In a flashlight the electrical power comes from the charge difference between chemicals in the batteries—typically zinc and carbon. One end of the batteries touches the casing. The other touches the bulb to complete the circuit. The bulb glows because the current meets resistance in the bulb's thin filament.

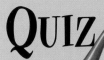

▲ Electric current

Electric current in a wire is passed on by free electrons (tiny blue dots). The electrons are drawn to the positive nuclei of atoms (red).

What is resistance?

Not all substances conduct electric currents equally well. Resistance is a substance's tendency to block the flow of current. A narrow place in the circuit can also be a resistance, and the wire here can get very hot. In light bulbs, a thin section of wire, or "filament," is what glows. A fuse is a thin piece of wire that burns through and breaks the circuit if it gets overloaded.

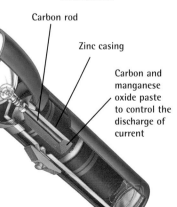

Carbon rod

Zinc casing

Carbon and manganese oxide paste to control the discharge of current

QUIZ

1 The electric current that supplies your house switches direction several times a second: true or false?

2 What two metals are the best conductors of electricity?

3 A volt is a measure of
a) electrical resistance
b) a difference in charge
c) the speed of the current

4 Who invented the battery
a) Volta b) Faraday
c) Maxwell?

5 Which American statesman discovered the electrical nature of lightning?

6 A battery that uses paste rather than acid is called a dry cell: true or false?

7 A good place to stand in a thunderstorm is under a tall tree: true or false?

8 Who discovered the link between electricity and magnetism?

Answers
1. True; 2. Copper and silver; 3. b) 4. a) 5. Benjamin Franklin; 6. True; 7. False: trees attract lightning; 8. Michael Faraday

Electronics

What are electronics?

ELECTRONICS ARE SYSTEMS that control things by switching on and off tiny electrical circuits. The switches are not like light switches on the wall, but work automatically. The simplest are transistors; the most complex are linked together in integrated circuits, silicon chips, and microprocessors. These are the ingenious systems that control everything from kitchen stoves to guided missiles.

▲ **Aircraft flight deck**
The flight deck of a modern aircraft is almost entirely "glass," which means it is full of electronic control screens and displays.

How do electronic systems work?

Inside every electronic device, from TVs to air traffic control systems, there are dozens or even millions of tiny electric circuits continually switching on and off. The operation of the device depends on which circuits are on and which are off. In a computer, each bit of data is directed through a different combination of circuits.

What are transistors?

Transistors are tiny switches made from materials called semiconductors, including germanium and silicon. What makes them special is that their ability to conduct electricity changes quickly as they warm up. Transistors can be used to control an electric current in several ways, including amplifying it (making it bigger) and switching it on and off.

What is a silicon chip?

Dozens or even thousands of tiny transistors can be joined together in a single "integrated circuit." This can be printed onto a tiny sliver of silicon, called a silicon chip. They can be anything from simple circuits for a clock to complex microprocessors for controlling computers.

What are bits in computers?

Since electronic circuits can only be on or off, computers work by using a "binary" system. This codes all data as either 1s or 0s, "ons" or "offs." Each is called a "bit," and bits are grouped together in bytes. This is why a computer's ability to handle data is measured in bytes.

 Internet   Computer   Radio tower   Radio   Satellite dish

 TV   Telephone   Satellite

How do computers remember?

Some computer memory is printed into microcircuits when it is made. This is ROM (read-only memory). RAM (Random-access memory) circuits take new data and instructions. Data is also stored in magnetic patterns on removable discs or in the laser-guided bumps on CDs.

What is a fractal?

In improving computers, scientists have learned much about numbers. Fractals are beautiful patterns generated by the computer from simple repeated mathematical calculations. Since they seem to mimic natural shapes like trees, some believe such shapes were created in a similar way, step by step.

What is virtual reality?

Virtual reality (VR) systems build a picture electronically to give you the illusion of reality. Special eyepieces show a slightly different view to each eye, giving the impression of a real, 3D space. As the view in each changes, it seems you are moving through a real space. Special gloves and other devices to control movement enhance the illusion. VR devices are now used for a wide range of tasks, as well as games. With VR, people can operate a computer-guided device in places where it is far too dangerous or difficult to work themselves, including in wrecks under the sea, inside the body, and many other places.

▼ Telecommunications
The telecommunications systems that now allow virtually instant communication around the world would not be possible without tiny electronic control devices and circuits.

QUIZ

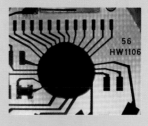

1 **What does CAD stand for: a) Computer-aided Design b) Calculating Arithmetical Device c) Continually-activated Diode?**

2 **The first computer was built by Charles Babbage in the 1830s: true or false?**

3 **Electronic devices can be grown by bacteria: true or false?**

4 **The internet was first developed by the U.S. military: true or false?**

5 **What is the artificial environment created by computers called?**

6 **"Robot" is a Czech word for "forced labour": true or false?**

341

Light

What is light?

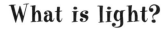

LIGHT IS WHAT YOU SEE THINGS BY. It is a form of radiation sent out by atoms in light sources such as the Sun, stars, and electric lights. There are other kinds of radiation, but light is the only kind your eyes can see. Light always moves in straight lines, and so people talk about light rays, but rays are just the straight path taken by the light.

▲ **Splitting colors**
Daylight and most other lights contain a whole mixture of different wavelengths— different colors—of light. Daylight can be split into a full range of colors, or spectrum, with a triangular chunk of glass called a prism. The prism bends each color of light to a different extent, so each emerges from the prism in a different place.

▼ **Electromagnetic spectrum**
Light is just a small part of a huge range of radiation sent out by atoms. At one end are radio waves, microwaves, and infrared heat radiation. At the other are ultraviolet light (which we can't see), and X-rays and gamma rays.

Does light travel in waves?

In the last century, most scientists thought light did travel in tiny waves fractions of a millimeter long, rather than in bullet-like particles. Now they agree it can be both, and it is best to think of light as vibrating packets of energy.

What are photons?

Photons are almost infinitesimally small particles of light They have no mass, and there are billions of them in a single light beam.

What is a shadow?

Since light travels in straight lines, its path is blocked whenever it meets an obstacle. The shadow is the dark space behind the obstacle.

What happens when light hits things?

When light rays hit a surface, some bounce off. This is called reflection. Some are absorbed by atoms in the surface, warming it very slightly. If the surface is transparent, like glass, some will pass straight through.

Does light change when it hits a surface?

Each kind of atom absorbs a particular wavelength (color) of light. The color of a surface depends on the atoms it contains and so which wavelengths are absorbed and which reflected. A leaf is green because the leaf's atoms soak up all colors but green from sunlight, and you see only the reflected green light.

Radio waves	Microwaves	Infrared	Visible light

◀ Perfect reflection
Mirrors give a clear reflection because light bounces off them at exactly the same angle at which it hits them.

▶ Laser reading
The perfect precision of laser light means it can be used to pick up the tiny pits on the surface of a CD that store the memory of the music. The laser light is bounced into them and the head picks up the reflections from the pits.

How is light bent?
The bending of light rays is called refraction. This happens when they strike a transparent material like glass or water at an angle. The different materials slow the light waves down, so that they move in a sideways direction, like car wheels driving onto sand.

How do mirrors work?
Most mirrors are made of glass, but the back is coated with a shiny metal (called silvering) that perfectly reflects all the light that hits it, at exactly the same angle.

Why is laser light special?
Most light contains a jumbled mix of different wavelengths. Laser light contains only a single wavelength— and what's more, all the waves are traveling perfectly in step. This means the beam can deliver a very concentrated but small burst of energy.

How do fiber optics bend light?
They don't; they simply bounce it again and again down the shiny insides of the long, thin glass fibers they are made from.

Ultraviolet   X-rays   Gamma rays

QUIZ

1 A frosted glass window is
a) opaque b) transparent
c) translucent?

2 Where do the colors of the rainbow come from?

3 Many birds can see ultraviolet light: true or false?

4 The angle that light strikes a mirror is called
a) the angle of reflection
b) the angle of incidence
c) the light angle?

5 Things are the same color in the dark as they are in daylight: true or false?

6 A light bulb works because the pressure of the electric current through its thin filament makes it glow: true or false?

Answers
1. c) 2. Sunlight; 3. True;
4. b) 5. False: they have no color at all in the dark;
6. True.

Sound

What is sound?

SOUND IS VIBRATIONS IN THE AIR. Sometimes you can see the vibration; sometimes you cannot. If you pluck a taut elastic band, you can see the band twang. If you clap your hands, you see nothing. Vibration is there all the same. But it is not only the band or your hands that move. You hear the sound because the air moves, too. As the source of the sound moves, it sets the air molecules moving, too, and so the vibration is transmitted through the air to your ears.

▲ Doppler effect
The sound of a car's engine drops in pitch as it zooms away from you because the sound waves are stretched out behind it.

Can sound travel in a vacuum?

No. Sound can travel through solids and liquids as well as air. In fact, it can travel faster through solids and liquids than air, because their molecules are more closely packed. But there is always complete silence in a vacuum because there is nothing to vibrate.

What are sound waves?

Sound waves are not like waves in the sea, which go up and down. Sound waves move by alternately stretching and squeezing. When a sound is made, air molecules near the sound are squeezed together. They, in turn, jostle up against the molecules next to them—and then are pulled back into place by the molecules behind.

What is the speed of sound?

In air, sound travels about 1,115 feet per second. It travels faster on a hot day.

How do you hear sounds?

You hear because your ears pick up the tiny vibrations in the air made by sounds. Inside the ear is a taut, thin window of skin called the eardrum, which vibrates with the air and rattles three tiny bones called ossicles. The last of them, called the stirrup, rattles farther than the first and amplifies the sound. The stirrup shakes another thin skin, sending waves through a fluid-filled tube called the cochlea, deep inside your head. Ripples in the cochlea trigger sensitive nerve receptors to send signals to your brain.

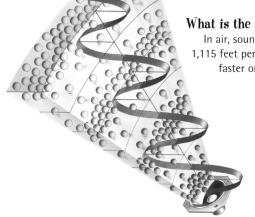

◄ Squeezing the air
When a loudspeaker vibrates with a sound, the vibrations travel out through the air in a series of waves that alternately squeeze the air molecules together and stretch them apart.

QUIZ

▼ The sound barrier
The sound barrier was broken for the first time in 1947 by U.S. test pilot Chuck Yeager flying the specially built Bell X-1.

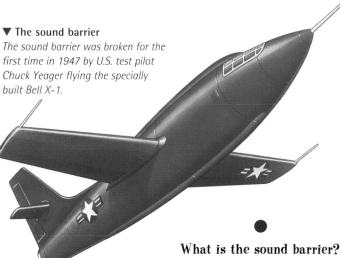

What is the sound barrier?
When a plane starts to fly faster than sound, it breaks the sound barrier. There is no real barrier to break. But as the aircraft travels faster and faster, it squashes the air in front of it, generating a shock wave that is heard as a loud explosive sound called a sonic boom.

What is sound frequency?
Some sounds, like squealing brakes, are high-pitched. Others, like thunder, are low-pitched. The difference is in how frequently the sound waves follow each other. If the waves come in quick succession, the sound is high-pitched. If they are widely separated, the sound is low-pitched. A low sound is 20 Hz, or waves per second. A high sound is 20,000 Hz.

What is an echo?
An echo is sound bouncing back. You don't often hear echoes, because sound only bounces back clearly off smooth, hard surfaces, and in confined spaces. Even in a confined space, the wall must be at least 56 feet away—which is why you usually hear echoes only in large, empty halls.

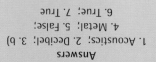

Magnetism

What is magnetism?

MAGNETISM IS AN INVISIBLE FORCE, which acts between iron, steel, and a few other metals. Each magnet has an area around it where it exerts its force power, called its magnetic field. This field gets weaker farther away from the magnet. But if another magnetic material comes closer, the magnet either pulls it closer or pushes it away.

What is a magnetic pole?

Magnetic force is especially strong at the end of each magnet. These two ends are called the poles. One is called the north (or north-seeking) pole, because if the magnet is suspended freely, this pole swings around until it points north. The other is called the south pole. If the opposite poles of two magnets come close, they will be drawn together. If the same poles meet, they will push each other apart.

What is a lodestone?

Long before people learned how to make steel magnets, they found that certain rocks attract or repel each other, and bits of iron. These rocks are called lodestones, and contain iron oxide, which makes them naturally magnetic.

▶ **Magnetic field**
This illustration shows the magnetic field around a simple bar magnet. The lines indicate the direction in which the force works—from turning magnetic materials toward its poles.

Why is the Earth magnetic?

As the Earth spins, the swirling of its iron nickel core turns it into a giant magnet. Like a bar magnet, Earth has two poles, North and South. It is because the Earth is a magnet that small magnets point the same way if left to swivel freely.

How big is Earth's field?

Earth's magnetic field extends far out into space, forming a plum-shaped barrier called the magnetosphere. On the side facing the Sun it stretches out 37,000 feet. On the far side it is blown out four times this far by the solar wind.

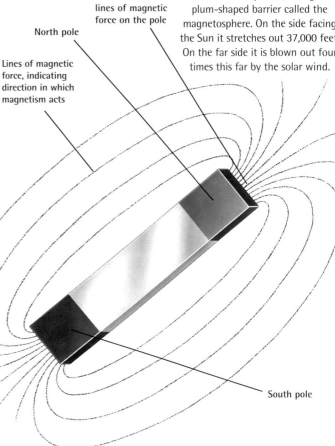

Concentration of lines of magnetic force on the pole

North pole

Lines of magnetic force, indicating direction in which magnetism acts

South pole

◀ Electromagnet
When an electric current is switched on, it creates a magnetic field around the wire. The arrows indicate the direction of the field.

QUIZ

1 **What did sailors use magnets for?**

2 **Iron loses its magnetism above 1,400°F: true or false?**

3 **Every magnet has two poles, no matter what its shape: true or false?**

What are the northern lights?
The northern lights, or *aurora borealis*, are spectacular curtains of light that shimmer in the night sky over the North Pole. They occur because there is a cleft in the magnetosphere above the pole, where lines of magnetic force funnel in. Every now and then, charged particles from the Sun stream in here and cannon into air molecules, making them glow brightly.

What is electromagnetism?
Electricity and magnetism are deeply linked. Every electric current creates a magnetic field around it, and moving a magnet past an electric wire will induce (create) an electric current in it. An electromagnet is a coil of copper wire, which creates a very strong magnetic field when a current is switched through it.

4 **The effects of magnetic attraction are not transmitted between objects: true or false?**

5 **Aluminium is magnetic: true or false?**

6 **The Earth's magnetic North Pole is hundreds of miles from the North Pole: true or false?**

7 **What is the aurora over the South Pole called?**

▼ The Northern Lights
The interaction of solar radiation with the Earth's magnetic field creates spectacular light shows, called aurorae, over the North and South Poles.

Answers
1. To make compasses to find north; 2. True; 3. True; 4. False; 5. False; 6. True; 7. *aurora australis*

Nuclear power

Why is nuclear power huge?

THE ENERGY THAT BINDS TOGETHER the nucleus of an atom is huge, even though the nucleus is minute. In fact, as Einstein showed in 1905 with his theory of special relativity, the particles of the atom can be regarded as pure energy. It is releasing some of this energy from millions of atomic nuclei that allow nuclear power stations to generate so much power from just a few tons of nuclear fuel. It also gives nuclear bombs their terrifying destructive power.

What is nuclear fusion?
Nuclear fusion occurs when nuclear energy is released by fusing, or joining, together small atoms like those of deuterium (a form of hydrogen). Nuclear fusion is the reaction that keeps stars glowing and provides the energy for H-bombs (see *What is an atomic bomb?*) Scientists hope to find a way of harnessing it for power.

▼ A nuclear power station

Inside a nuclear reactor there are fuel rods made from pellets of uranium oxide, separated by spacers. When the station goes on-line, a nuclear fission chain reaction is set up in the fuel rods. This is slowed down by control rods that absorb the neutrons so that heat is produced steadily to make the steam that drives the turbines that generate electricity.

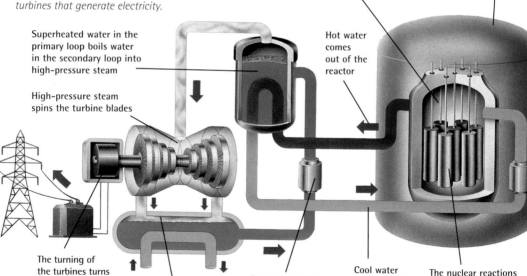

In the reactor vessel, nuclear fission releases huge amounts of heat energy

A containment building houses the reactor vessel, keeping in heat, radioactivity, and other energy

Superheated water in the primary loop boils water in the secondary loop into high-pressure steam

Hot water comes out of the reactor

High-pressure steam spins the turbine blades

The turning of the turbines turns the electricity generator

Steam condenses into liquid water

Pumps keep the water moving around the circuits

Cool water returns to the reactor

The nuclear reactions take place in fuel rods in the reactor core

QUIZ

▶ **Nuclear fission**
Nuclear fission involves firing a neutron (yellow ball) at a nucleus of uranium or plutonium. When the nucleus splits, it fires out more neutrons, which split more nuclei, creating a chain reaction.

What is nuclear fission?

Nuclear fission releases energy by splitting large nuclei such as uranium and plutonium. To split the nuclei, neutrons are fired at it. As they crash into it, they split off more neutrons, which bombard other nuclei, setting off a chain reaction.

What is an atom bomb?

An atomic bomb, or A-bomb, is one of the two main kinds of nuclear weapon. An A-bomb relies on the explosive nuclear fission of uranium-235 or plutonium-239. Hydrogen bombs, also called H-bombs, or thermonuclear weapons, rely on the fusion of hydrogen atoms to create explosions a thousand times bigger.

Who invented the A-bomb?

The first A-bombs were developed in the United States toward the end of World War II by a team led by Robert Oppenheimer (1904–1967). Their first bombs were dropped on Hiroshima and Nagasaki in Japan in 1945 with devastating effect.

What is radioactivity?

The atoms of an element often come in several different forms, or isotopes. Each form has a different number of neutrons in its nucleus, indicated in the name, as in carbon-12 and carbon-14.
The nuclei of some of these isotopes—the ones scientists call radioisotopes—are unstable, and decay (break up). As they break up, they release radiation, consisting of streams of particles called alpha, beta, and gamma rays. This is radioactivity.

What is half-life?

No one can predict when the atomic nucleus will decay. But scientists can predict how long it will take for half the particles in a substance to decay. This is its half-life. Strontium-90 has a half-life of just nine minutes. Uranium-235, on the other hand, has a half-life of 4.5 billion years. Most fall somewhere in between.

1 Exposure to high levels of radioactivity can be fatal: true or false?

2 Which two countries have the biggest stockpile of nuclear weapons?

3 Nuclear power stations do not burn fuel: true or false?

4 Where in Ukraine was there a major accident at a nuclear power station?

5 What is the most devastating accident that can happen to a nuclear reactor?

6 The age of many ancient remains can be dated by their radioactivity: true or false?

7 What do the stars and H-bombs have in common?

Answers
1. True; 2. The United States and Russia; 3. False; 4. Chernobyl; 5. Meltdown; 6. True; 7. Nuclear fusion

Key Facts: Science

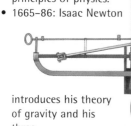

Milestones

- 300 B.C: Greek mathematician Euclid lays down the principles of geometry still used today.
- 250 B.C: Archimedes lays down the basic principles of physics.
- 1665–86: Isaac Newton

introduces his theory of gravity and his three laws of motion.

- 1683: Anton van Leeuwenhoek discovers bacteria.
- 1789: Antoine Lavoisier makes the first list of chemical elements.
- 1804: Richard Trevithick builds the first steam locomotive.
- 1803: John Dalton proposes the atomic theory of matter.
- 1820: Hans Oersted finds that electricity creates a magnetic field.
- 1830: Joseph Henry and Michael Faraday find how electricity can be generated by a magnetic field.
- 1858: Charles Darwin and Alfred Wallace suggest the theory of the evolution of species by natural selection.
- 1860s: Étienne Lenoir builds the first gasoline-engine car.
- 1865: James Clerk Maxwell suggests the idea of electromagnetic fields.
- 1869: Dmitri Mendeléev creates the periodic table of the elements.
- 1897: J.J. Thomson discovers the electron.
- 1900: Max Planck invents quantum theory.
- 1903: Orville and Wilbur Wright make the first powered human aircraft flight.
- 1905: Albert Einstein invents the theory of relativity.
- 1911: Ernest Rutherford discovers the atomic nucleus.
- 1945: The first atomic bomb.
- 1953: Francis Crick and James Watson find the structure of the DNA molecule in every living cell.

Conversions

Conversion factors
To convert, multiply by the number shown

Length
- in to cm   2.54
- ft to m   0.3048
- yd to m   0.9144
- miles to km   1.6093
- cm to in   0.3937
- m to ft   3.2808
- m to yd   1.0936
- km to miles   0.6214

Weight
- oz to g   28.3495
- lb to kg   0.4536
- g to oz   0.0352
- kg to lb   2.2046

Volume
- in^3 to cm^3 (cc)   16.3871
- ft^3 to liters   28.3169
- yd^3 to m^3 0.7646
- fl oz to cm^3 28.4131
- pints to liters   0.5683
- gallons to liters   4.5461
- cm^3 to in^3 0.0610
- liters to ft^3 0.0353
- liters to pints   1.7598
- liters to gallons   0.2200

Fast, slow

Fast phenomonena
- Light   186,282,397 miles per second
- Lightning   up to 31,317 miles per second
- Earth's orbit   66,617 miles per hour (mph)
- Speed of sound in water   4,911 feet per second (fresh water at 77°F)
- Speed of sound in air   1,122 feet per second at 64°F
- Skydiver   621 mph
- Jet stream   up to 435 mph
- Fastest wind speed   317.5 mph
- Tsunami wave   over 497 mph in deep water

Fast machines
- Fastest steam locomotive   126 mph by the *Mallard* in 1934.
- Fastest train   357.2 mph by French TGV in 2007.
- Fastest road car   270 mph by Hennessey Venom GT in 2014.
- Fastest speed on land   763 mph by *Thrust SSC* in 1997.
- Fastest jet plane   2,242 mph by Lockheed SR-71A in 1990.
- Fastest airliner   1,607 mph by Russian Tupolev Tu-144.
- Fastest human flight   24,791 mph by crew of *Apollo 10* spacecraft in 1969.

Go slow
- Fingernails grow at around 0.02 inch a week.
- Toenails grow at about 0.004 inch a week.
- Continents move at about 0.8–3.9 inches a year.
- Snails move at up to 0.005 mph.
- A tortoise moves at 0.17 mph.
- Lichen grows at 0.00000000006 mph.

Loud, soft

Loud noises
- Supernova explosion   210 decibels
- Rocket launch   180 db
- Toy guns   170 db
- Jet taking off at 98 feet   140 db
- Rock concert   130 db
- Racing car   125 db
- Dance club   117 db
- Baby's cry   115 db
- Car horn   110 db
- Chainsaw   100 db
- Thunder   90 db

Quiet sounds
- Ant breathing   less than 0 db
- The quietest we can hear   0 db
- Rustling leaves   10 db
- Quiet whisper   12 db
- Average whisper   20 db
- Conversation   40 db
- Empty theater   45 db
- Loud conversation   60 db
- Niagara Falls   85 db
- Loud snore   87 db
- Heavy traffic   90 db

Key Facts: Science

Number power

Large and small numbers
- Large numbers can have a huge number of digits. There are 17,000,000,000,000,000,000 water molecules in a single drop of water. So scientists often express large numbers in terms of "powers" of 10. This is the number of times you have to multiply 10 by 10 to give the number. So 100 is 10 to the power of 2, which is written 10^2. One thousand is 10 to the power 3, written 10^3, and so on.

- Tiny fractions can be written in the same way—as the number of times you have to divide 10 by 10 to give the fraction. So a hundredth is 10^{-2}. A thousandth is 10^{-3}, and so on.

Millions
- One million is 10 to the power 6, or 10^6.
- Ten million is 10 to the power 7, or 10^7.
- Seven million, or 7×10^6, people live in London, U.K.
- The Sun is 93 million miles or 93×10^6 km away.
- There are just over 31 million or 3.1×10^7 seconds in a year.

Billions
- One billion is 10 to the power 9 or 10^9.

- There are 7 billion or 7×10^9 people in the world.
- There are 100 billion or 1×10^{11} brain cells in your brain.

Trillions
- One trillion is 10 to the power 12 or 10^{12}.
- Your body contains 25 trillion or 2.5×10^{13} red blood cells .
- A swarm of 12.5 trillion or 1.25×10^{13} locusts invaded Nebraska in 1875.

Quadrillions
- One quadrillion is 10 to the power 15, or 10^{15}.
- There are over one quadrillion, or 10^{15}, ants in the world.
- There are about 10 million quadrillion or 10^{22} molecules in a single apple.

Add-ons

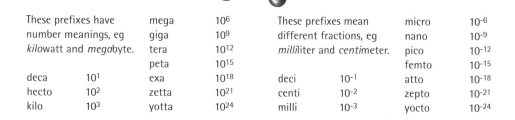

These prefixes have number meanings, eg *kilo*watt and *mega*byte.		mega	10^6	These prefixes mean different fractions, eg *milli*liter and *centi*meter.		micro	10^{-6}
		giga	10^9			nano	10^{-9}
		tera	10^{12}			pico	10^{-12}
		peta	10^{15}			femto	10^{-15}
deca	10^1	exa	10^{18}	deci	10^{-1}	atto	10^{-18}
hecto	10^2	zetta	10^{21}	centi	10^{-2}	zepto	10^{-21}
kilo	10^3	yotta	10^{24}	milli	10^{-3}	yocto	10^{-24}

Cold, hot

Cold and hot points	°C	°F	K
Coldest possible temperature (atoms stop moving)	-273.15	-459.67	0
Coldest temperature achieved in a laboratory	-272.999	-459.399	2
Helium melts	-272.2	-458	3
Outer space	-270	-457	4
Helium boils	-268.9	-452	5
Nitrogen melts	-209.86	-344	67
Coldest weather recorded on Earth	-89.2	-128.6	183.8
Water freezes	0	32	273.15
Butter melts	30	90	300
Human body temperature	37	98.6	310
Hottest weather recorded on Earth	58	136.4	331
Water boils	100	212	373.15
Surface of Venus	480	890	750
Coal fire burns	800	1500	1100
Iron melts	1535	2795	1808
Gas flame burns	1600	3000	1900
Molten lava	1700	3200	2000
Carbon melts	3550	6422	3820
Surface of the Sun	6000	10,000	6000
Center of the Earth	16,000	30,000	16,000
Lightning	30,000	54,000	30,000
Center of a star	100 mill	180 mill	100 mill
Center of an H-bomb	400 mill	700 mill	400 mill

Tiny, big

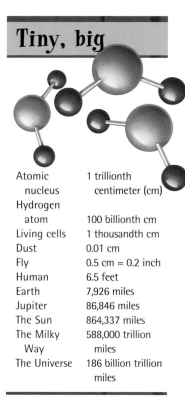

Atomic nucleus	1 trillionth centimeter (cm)
Hydrogen atom	100 billionth cm
Living cells	1 thousandth cm
Dust	0.01 cm
Fly	0.5 cm = 0.2 inch
Human	6.5 feet
Earth	7,926 miles
Jupiter	86,846 miles
The Sun	864,337 miles
The Milky Way	588,000 trillion miles
The Universe	186 billion trillion miles

Light, heavy

Photon	11.7×10^{-63} lb
Oxygen atom	6.6×10^{-26} lb
Ant	2.2×10^{-5} lb
Human	220 lb
Elephant	2.2×10^{4} lb
Blue whale	2.2×10^{5} lb
Oil tanker	2.2×10^{8} lb
The Earth	13×10^{24} lb
The Sun	4.4×10^{30} lb
The Galaxy	4.4×10^{41} lb
The Universe	2.2×10^{51} lb

Key Facts: Space

The planets.

Planet	Diameter (miles)	Av. distance from Sun (million miles)	Rotation period	Length of year	Tilt of axis	Mass, if Earth =1	Brightness
Mercury	3,031	35.98	58.65 days	87.97 dys	0°	0.055	-1.9
Venus	7,520	67.23	243.01 dys	224.7 dys	177.3°	0.815	-4.4
Earth	7,926	93	23.93 hours	365.26 dys	23.45°	1	
Mars	4,217	141.6	24.62 hrs	686.98 dys	25.19°	0.107	-2.0
Jupiter	88,846	483	9.84 hrs	11.86 years	3.1°	317.94	-2.7
Saturn	74,898	887	10.66 hrs	29.46 yrs	26.7°	95.18	+0.7
Uranus	46,539	1,784	17.9 hrs	84.01 yrs	98°	14.53	+5.5
Neptune	30,775	2,794	16.11 hrs	164.79 yrs	28.3°	17.14	+7.8

Milestones

- A.D. 140: Ptolemy devises his model of the motion of the planets and stars.
- 1543: Nicolaus Copernicus shows that the planets revolve around the Sun, not the Earth.
- 1610: Galileo uses a telescope to see things such as the phases of Venus and the moons of Jupiter.
- 1659: Christiaan Huygens discovers the rings of Saturn.
- 1781: William Herschel discovers the planet Uranus.
- 1801: Giuseppi Piazzi discovers Ceres, the first asteroid.
- 1846: John Galle discovers the planet Neptune.
- 1929: Edwin Hubble shows that there are other galaxies beyond our own and that the Universe is expanding.
- 1930: Clyde Tombaugh discovers Pluto.
- 1995: Michael Mayer and Didier Queloz spot a planet circling the star 51 Pegasi.
- 2006: Pluto officially reclassified as a dwarf planet.

The Constellations

Andromeda
Antlia, the Air Pump
Apus, the Bird of Paradise
Aquarius, the Water-Bearer
Aquila, the Eagle
Ara, the Altar
Aries, the Ram
Auriga, the Charioteer
Boötes, the Herdsman
Caelum, the Graving Tool
Camelopardalis, the Giraffe
Cancer, the Crab
Canes Venatici, the Hunting Dogs
Canis Major, the Great Dog
Canis Minor, the Little Dog
Capricornus, the Sea Goat
Carina, the Keel
Cassiopeia
Centaurus, the Centaur
Cepheus
Cetus, the Whale
Chamaeleon, the Chameleon
Circinus, the Compasses
Columba, the Dove
Coma Berenices, Berenice's Hair
Corona Australis, Southern Crown
Corona Borealis, the Northern Crown
Corvus, the Crow
Crater, the Cup
Crux, the Southern Cross
Cygnus, the Swan
Delphinius, the Dolphin
Dorado, the Swordfish
Draco, the Dragon
Equuleus, the Foal

Eridanus
Fornax, the Furnace
Gemini, the Twins
Grus, the Crane
Hercules
Horologium, the Clock
Hydra, the Water Snake
Hydrus, the Little Snake
Indus, the Indian
Lacerta, the Lizard
Leo, the Lion
Leo Minor, the Little Lion
Lepus, the Hair
Libra, the Scales of Justice
Lupus, the Wolf
Lynx, the Lynx
Lyra, the Lyre
Mensa, the Table
Microscopium, the Microscope
Monoceros, the Unicorn
Musca, the Fly
Norma, the Rule
Octans, the Octant
Ophiuchus, the Serpent-Bearer
Orion
Pavo, the Peacock
Pegasus, the Flying Horse
Perseus

Phoenix, the Phoenix
Pictor, the Painter
Pisces, the Fishes
Piscis Austrinus, the Southern Fish
Puppis, the Poop Deck
Pyxis, the Compass
Reticulum, the Net
Sagitta, the Arrow
Sagittarius, the Archer
Scorpius, the Scorpion
Sculptor, the Sculptor
Scutum, the Shield
Serpens, the Serpent
Sextans, the Sextant
Taurus, the Bull
Telescopium, the Telescope
Triangulum, the Triangle
Triangulum Australe, the Southern Triangle
Tucana, the Toucan
Ursa Major, the Great Bear
Ursa Minor, the Little Bear
Vela, the Sails
Virgo, the Virgin
Volans, the Flying Fish
Vulpecula, the Fox

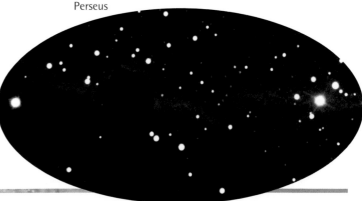

Key Facts: Space

Planets' biggest moons

Earth's moon
- The Moon

Mars's moons
- Phobos
- Deimos

Jupiter's moons
- Ganymede
- Callisto
- Io
- Europa
- Amalthea
- Himalia
- Thebe
- Elara
- Pasiphaë
- Metis
- Carme
- Sinope

- Lysithea
- Ananke
- Adrastea

Saturn's moons
- Titan
- Rhea
- Iapetus
- Dione
- Tethys
- Enceladus
- Mimas
- Hyperion
- Phoebe
- Janus
- Epimetheus
- Prometheus
- Pandora
- Siarnaq
- Helene

Uranus's moons
- Titania
- Oberon
- Umbriel
- Ariel
- Miranda
- Puck
- Sycorax
- Portia
- Juliet
- Belinda
- Cressida
- Caliban
- Rosalind
- Desdemona
- Bianca

Neptune's moons
- Triton
- Proteus
- Nereid
- Larissa
- Galatea
- Despina
- Thalassa
- Naiad
- Halimede
- Neso

Saturn, with 53 named moons, has more moons than any other planet in our Solar System.

Nearest and brightest stars

Nearest stars
- Sun (93 million miles away from Earth)
- Proxima Centauri (4.2 light-years away)
- Alpha Centauri A (4.3 light-years)
- Alpha Centauri B (4.3 light-years)
- Barnard's star (5.9 light-years)
- Wolf 359 (7.6 light-years)
- Lalane 21185 (8.1 light-years)
- Sirius A (8.6 light-years)
- Sirius B (8.6 light-years)
- UV Ceti A (8.9 light-years)

Brightest stars
- Sun (93 million miles away from Earth)
- Sirius A (8.6 light-years away)
- Canopus (200 light-years)
- Alpha Centauri (4.3 light-years)

- Arcturus (36 light-years)
- Vega (26 light-years)
- Capella (42 light-years)
- Rigel (910 light-years)
- Procyon (11 light-years)
- Achernar (85 light-years)

Space exploration

- **1926** The U.S. engineer Robert Goddard designed and launched the first liquid fuel rocket.
- **1942** Wernher von Braun developed the V2 rocket in Nazi Germany.
- **1957** The world's first artificial satellite, the Soviet Union's *Sputnik 1*, was launched.
- **1957** The Russian dog Laika became the first living creature in space aboard *Sputnik 2*.
- **1961** The Soviet cosmonaut Yuri Gagarin became the first man in space aboard *Vostok 1*.
- **1963** The Soviet cosmonaut Valentina Tereshkova became the first woman in space.
- **1966** The Soviet Union's unmanned probe *Lunar 9* landed on the Moon.
- **1969** U.S. astronauts Neil Armstrong and Edwin Aldrin were the first men to walk on the Moon.
- **1972** *Apollo 17* was the sixth and last U.S. manned mission to the Moon.
- **1973** First U.S. space station, *Skylab*, launched.

- **1980** The U.S. *Voyager 1* took the first detailed photos of Saturn's ring systems and discovered six additional moons.
- **1981** The U.S. space shuttle *Columbia*, the world's first reusable spacecraft, was launched.
- **1982** The Soviet probe *Venera 13* sent back color photos of the surface of Venus.
- **1990** The Hubble space telescope was launched.
- **1996** U.S. scientists found evidence in meteor fragments that microbes may have existed on Mars.
- **2000** The first crew arrived on the ISS
- **2011** *Messenger* spacecraft orbits Mercury.

Key Facts: Earth

Highest waterfalls

Mardalsfossen (S)(Norway)	2,425 ft
Tugela Falls (S. Africa)	2,011 ft
Cuquenan Falls (Venez.)	2,001 ft
Sutherland Falls (NZ)	1,903 ft
Ribbon Falls (USA)	1,611 ft
Great Falls (Guyana)	1,601 ft
Mardalsfossen (N)	1,535 ft
Della Falls (Canada)	1,444 ft
Gavarnie Falls (France)	1,385 ft
Skjeggedal Falls (N'way)	1,378 ft
Glass Falls (Brazil)	1,325 ft
Krimml Falls (Austria)	1,312 ft
Trummelbach Falls (Switz)	1,312 ft
Takakkaw Falls (Canada)	1,201 ft
Silver Strand Falls (USA)	1,171 ft
Wallaman Falls (Aus)	1,138 ft
Wollomombi Falls (Aus)	1,099 ft

Angel Falls (Venezuela)	3,212 ft
Yosemite Falls (USA)	2,425 ft

Cities

The world's biggest cities

Tokyo	37,126,000
Seoul	22,547,000
Delhi	22,242,000
Jakarta	26,063,000
Shangai	20,860,000
Karachi	20,711,000
New York	20,464,000
São Paulo	20,186,000
Mexico City	19,463,000
Cairo	17,816,000
Beijing	17,311,000
Mumbai	16,910,000
Moscow	15,512,000
Calcutta	14,374,000
Istanbul	13,576,000
Paris	10,755,000
London	8,586,000

Continents

Asia
Area 17,200,000 sq miles
Population 4.1 billion
Population density
(People per sq mile) 225

Africa
Area 11,600,222 sq miles
Population 1.1 billion
Population density 80

Antarctica
Area 5,400,000 sq miles

North America
Area 9,500,000 sq miles
Population 530,000,000
Population density 59

South America
Area 6,900,000 sq miles
Population 385,000,000
Population density 56

Europe
Area 3,930,000 sq miles
Population 740,000,000
Population density 134

Australia/Oceania
Area 3,300,000 sq miles
Population 36,650,000
Population density 11

Population

The most populous countries

China	1,350,395,000
India	1,236,687,000
USA	313,914,000
Indonesia	246,864,000
Brazil	198,656,000
Pakistan	179,160,000
Nigeria	168,834,000
Bangladesh	154,695,000
Russia	143,533,000
Japan	127,561,000
Mexico	120,847,000
Philippines	96,707,000
Vietnam	88,776,000
Germany	81,890,000

Biggest lakes

Caspian Sea	14,669 sq miles	Lake Winnipeg	9,416 sq miles
Lake Superior	32,526 sq miles	Lake Ontario	7,336 sq miles
Lake Victoria	28,820 sq miles	Lake Balkhash	7,115 sq miles
Lake Huron	24,362 sq miles	Lake Ladoga	6,835 sq miles
Lake Michigan	22,300 sq miles	Lake Onega	3,710 sq miles
Lake Tanganyika	12,650 sq miles	Lake Titicaca	3,200 sq miles
Lake Baikal	12,160 sq miles	Lake Nicaragua	3,100 sq miles
Great Bear Lake	12,096 sq miles	Lake Athabasca	3,063 sq miles
Lake Nyasa	11,150 sq miles	Lake Taymyr	2,699 sq miles
Great Slave Lake	11,030 sq miles	Lake Turkana	2,471 sq miles
Lake Erie	9,966 sq miles	Reindeer Lake	2,444 sq miles

Richest and poorest

The world's richest countries GDP per head in 2013		The world's poorest countries GDP per head in 2013	
	$US	Mozambique	1,262
Qatar	105,000	Ethiopia	1,258
Luxembourg	79,500	Guinea	1,162
Singapore	61,500	Togo	1,146
Norway	56,500	Mali	1,137
Brunei	55,000	Afghanistan	1,072
Hong Kong	53,500	Madagascar	972
United States of America	51,000	Malawi	894
United Arab Emirates	50,000	Niger	853
Switzerland	46,500	Central African Republic	828
Australia	44,000	Eritrea	792
Canada	43,500	Liberia	716
Austria	43,000	Burundi	649

Mountains

The world's highest mountains

Asia	
Everest	29,029 ft
K2	28,251 ft
Kanchenjunga	28,169 ft

South America	
Aconcagua	22,835 ft
Ojos del Salado	22,615 ft
Bonete	22,175 ft

North America	
McKinley	20,321 ft
Logan	19,524 ft
Citlaltépetl	18,488 ft

Africa	
Kilimanjaro	19,341 ft
Kenya	17,060 ft
Margherita Peak	16,761 ft

Europe	
Elbrus	18,510 ft
Dykh Tau	17,070 ft
Shkara	17,037 ft

Australia/Oceania	
Wilhelm	14,793 ft
Cook	12,316 ft
Tasman	11,473 ft

Key Facts: Earth

Major rivers of the world

The world's longest rivers

Nile	4,160 miles
Amazon	4,048 miles
Yangtze	3,964 miles
Mississippi-Missouri-	
Red Rock	3,709 miles
Ob-Irtysh	3,460 miles
Yenesei-Angara	3,449 miles
Yellow	3,395 miles
Congo	2,900 miles
Rio de la Plata-Parana	2,796 miles
Mekong	2,750 miles

Islands

The world's biggest islands

	square miles
Greenland	840,004
New Guinea	303,380
Borneo	288,869
Madagascar	226,924
Baffin (Canada)	194,574
Sumatra (Indonesia)	171,069
Honshu, Japan	87,182
Great Britain	88,787
Victoria (Can)	85,154
Ellesmere (Can)	71,029

Earthquake disasters

Date	Location	death toll
856	Damghan, Iran	200,000
1138	Aleppo, Syria	230,000
1556	Shaanxi, China	830,000
1920	Haiyhan, China	200,000
1923	Kwanto, Japan	144,000
1948	Ashgabat, Turkmenistan	110,000
1976	Tangshan, China	255,000
2004	Sumatra, South Asia	227,000
2010	Haiti, Caribbean	316,000

Sea deeps

The deepest sea trenches
(feet below sea level)

Mariana	35,797
Tonga	35,702
Philippine	34,580
Kuril-Kamchatka	34,449
Kermadec	32,963
Japan	29,528
Puerto Rico	28,232
Yap	27,976
South Sandwich	27,651
Peru-Chile	26,460

Glaciers

The world's longest glaciers

Lambert-Fisher Ice Passage (Antarctica)	320 miles
Petermanns Glacier (Greenland)	124 miles
Hubbard Glacier (N. America)	80 miles
Siachen Glacier (Karakoram, Asia)	47 miles
Skeidarajokull (Iceland)	30 miles
Tasman (New Zealand)	18 miles
Aletsch Gletscher (European Alps)	24 km

Oceans & seas

Oceans	(square miles)
Pacific	60,060,893
Atlantic	29,637,974
Indian	26,469,620
Arctic	5,427,052
Seas	
South China	1,422,787
Caribbean	1,062,939
Mediterranean	969,116
Gulf of Mexico	598,458
Sea of Japan	377,608
East China	290,349
North	220,078
Black	177,993
Baltic	149,035

The world's major deserts

	(square miles)
Antarctic	5,339,573
Arctic	5,300,000
Sahara	3,513,530
Arabian	899,618
Gobi	500,000
Kalahari	347,492
Patagonian	258,688
Great Victoria	249,808
Syrian	200,773
Great Basin	189,962

Weather

The world's sunniest place
is the Eastern Sahara, with
sunshine for over 90% of all
daylight hours.
The world's hottest place
is Dallol, Ethiopia, with an
average temperature of 93°F
in the shade.
The world's driest place is the
Atacama Desert in Chile, with
an annual average of just 0.2
inch of rain.
The world's coldest place is
Vostok in Antarctica, where it
averages -72°F.

Key Facts: Animals

Kingdoms

1. Monerans
Simple single-cell organisms with no nucleus, e.g. bacteria.
2. Protista
Mostly single-cell organisms with a nucleus, e.g. amoebas.
3. Fungi
Multi-celled organisms that feed on living or dead organic matter, e.g. molds.
4. Plantae
Multi-celled organisms such as trees, plants, and grasses.
5. Animalia
Animals—multi-celled organisms that must find food and can move around.

The animal kingdom:
- **Vertebrates**
  Mammals
  Birds
  Amphibians
  Reptiles
  Jawless fish
  Sea squirts
  Sharks and rays
  Bony fish
- **Invertebrates**
  Echinoderms
  Arthropods
  Velvetworms, lampshells, etc.
  Worms of all kinds
  Sponges
  Cnidaria
  Molluscs

Animal classification

Classification of a lion:

Kingdom
Animalia
Multi-celled organisms that cannot make their own food.
Phylum
Chordate
Animals that have a single nerve cord at some stage during their life.
Class
Mammal
Animals that suckle their young on milk and have hair or fur.
Order
Carnivore
Land mammals adapted to hunting.

Family
Cats
Have sharp, retractable front claws.
Genus
Big cats
Includes five species—lions, tigers, leopards, snow leopards, and jaguars.
Species
Lion

Males, females, and babies

Animal	Male	Female	Young
Antelope	Buck	Doe	Kid
Bobcat	Tom	Lioness	Kitten
Buffalo	Bull	Cow	Calf
Camel	Bull	Cow	Calf
Caribou	Stag	Doe	Fawn
Chicken	Rooster	Hen	Chick
Duck	Drake	Duck	Duckling
Goat	Billygoat	Nannygoat	Kid
Goose	Gander	Goose	Gosling
Seal	Bull	Cow	Pup
Swan	Cob	Pen	Cygnet
Weasel	Boar	Cow	Kit

Animal habitats

Freshwater lakes
- otter, water vole, harvest mouse
- reed warbler, heron, kingfisher, marsh harrier, coot
- frogs, toads, newts
- dragonfly, pondskater, waterboatman, mayfly
- stickleback, tench, pike, bream, trout, muskellunge

Tundra and Arctic
- polar bear, Arctic fox, Arctic hare, gray wolf, vole, ermine, lemming, musk ox, caribou
- eagles, grouse, plover, goose, snowy owl
- mosquito

Mountains
- ibex, chamois deer, yak, llama, vicuna, puma, cougar, snow leopard, lynx, chinchilla, marmot
- eagles, condor, lammergeier
- ice worm

Tropical grasslands
- giraffe, zebra, antelope, lion, leopard, cheetah, elephant, water buffalo, mongoose, hyena, jackal
- ostrich, marabou stork, oxpecker, weaver bird, secretary bird, vulture
- Eastern brown snakes, red-bellied snakes
- dung beetle, termite, locust

Temperate grasslands
- saiga antelope, pronghorn antelope, bison, prairie dog, mole rat, coyote, fox
- rhea, guanaco, buzzard
- grass snakes, lizards
- grasshoppers, flies

Tropical forests
- monkeys, leopard, shrew, sloth, coati, opossum, okapi, tamandua, jaguar
- macaws, parrots, toucans, hummingbirds, jacamars
- viper, anaconda, python, tree frogs, iguana, crocodiles, turtles
- morpho butterfly, hunting spider, ants

Temperate forests
- squirrel, skunk, badger, mouse, raccoon, hedgehog, chipmunk, beaver, rabbit, fox, deer, bear, wolf, wild boar
- warbler, robins, woodpeckers, woodcock, jay, owl
- salamanders, slugs
- ants, purple emperor butterfly, moths, beetles, earthworm, snails, centipede

Deserts
- camels, addax, fennec fox, long-eared jackrabbit, kangaroo rat, gundi, jerboa
- roadrunner, hummingbird, vultures, nighthawk, burrowing owl, sand grouse
- spiny lizard, gila monster, rattlesnake, gecko, thorny devil, tortoises
- scorpion, antlion, spiders

Seashore
- anenomes, barnacles, mussles, starfish, crabs, sea cucumber, cockles, lugworm, sea urchin, scallop, limpets
- gulls, tern, gannet, pelican

Oceans
- Surface waters: seal, porpoise, shark, mackerel, jellyfish, turtle, sea horse
- Midocean: squid, octopus, swordfish, hatchet fish, lanternfish, flatfish
- Deep sea: ray, gulper eel, angler fish, giant squid, sperm whale

Key Facts: Animals

Birds

- **The biggest bird**
  The biggest bird is the ostrich, which can grow up to 9 feet tall.
- **The smallest bird**
  The smallest bird is the bee hummingbird, which is just 2.25 inches long.
- **The biggest flying bird**
  The biggest flying bird is the Kori bustard, which can weigh up to 44 lb.
- **The biggest bird of prey**
  The Andean condor can weigh 33 lb or more.
- **The fastest flier**
  The fastest flier is the peregrine falcon, which can fly up to 217 mph.
- **The oldest bird**
  Cocky the cockatoo of the London Zoo was over 80 when he died in 1982.

- **The longest journey**
  An Arctic tern flew 14,000 miles from Russia down through the Atlantic over Africa and the Indian Ocean to Australia.
- **The most time in the air**
  No bird spends more time flying than the sooty tern, which can remain in the air for 3–10 years.
- **The biggest egg**
  The biggest egg is the ostrich egg, which can grow up to 8 inches across.
- **The highest flier**
  The highest flight was by a Ruppell's vulture, which hit a plane at 37,000 ft.
- **The fastest swimmer**
  A gentoo penguin swims up to 17 mph.

Sea creatures

- **The smallest fish**
  The smallest fish is the Marshall Islands goby, which is only 0.6 inches long.
- **The largest fish**
  The largest crab is the Whale shark, which can grow over 12 m long.
- **The fastest fish**
  The fastest fish is the sailfish, which can travel at up to 68 mph.
- **The oldest fish**
  The whale shark can live to over 70 years.
- **The deadliest jellyfish**
  The deadly Australian Sea Wasp can kill a man in just one minute.
- **The noisiest animal**
  The noisiest animal is the blue whale. Its sounds can be detected from as far away as 516 miles.
- **The smallest crab**
  The smallest crab is the pea crab, which really is as small as a pea.
- **The largest turtle**
  The largest turtle is the Pacific leatherback, which grows up to 7 feet long.
- **The longest journey**
  European eels travel 4,660 miles on their spawning migration from the Baltic to the Sargasso Sea.

Mammals

- **The biggest mammal**
  The biggest mammal is the Blue whale, which can grow up to 108 feet long and weigh up to 190 tons.
- **The biggest land mammal**
  The biggest land mammal is the African bush elephant, which can grow up 13 feet tall and weigh up to 12 tons.
- **The tallest mammal**
  The tallest mammal is the giraffe, which can grow over 20 feet tall.
- **The smallest mammal**
  The smallest mammal is the bumblebee bat of Thailand, which weighs under 0.07 ounce.
- **The smallest land mammal**
  The smallest land mammal is the Etruscan shrew, which is under 2 inches long.
- **The fastest-sprinting land mammal**
  The fastest land mammal is the cheetah, which can reach 62 mph for short bursts.
- **The fastest-running land mammal**
  The fastest-running land mammal over a sustained distance is the North American pronghorn antelope, which can keep up 35 mph for nearly 4 miles.
- **The fastest marine mammal**
  The fastest-swimming mammal is the killer whale, which can reach 34 mph.
- **The highest jumper**
  The highest-jumping animals are pumas and leopards, which can jump over 16 ft into trees.
- **The oldest mammal**
  The oldest mammal (apart from humans, of course) is the elephant, which can live over 70 years.

Reptiles

- **The largest reptile**
  The largest reptiles are the crocodiles of Southeast Asia, which can grow up to 16.5 feet in length.
- **The biggest lizard**
  The biggest lizard is the komodo dragon, which grows over 10 feet and has been said to grow to 30 feet.
- **The biggest amphibian**
  The biggest amphibian is the Chinese giant salamander, which is over 3 feet long.
- **The longest snake**
  The longest snake may be the reticulated python, which can grow over 30 feet long.
- **The most poisonous snake**
  The most poisonous snake is the Marine Cobra of the western Pacific.

Insects

- **The heaviest insects**
  The heaviest flying insects are the Goliath beetles of Africa, which weigh up to 0.221 pound.
- **The longest insect**
  The longest insects are stick insects, which can grow up to 16 inches long.
- **The fastest flier**
  The Australian dragonfly can reach 37 mph.
- **The largest butterfly**
  The Queen Alexandra's birdwing of Papua New Guinea can be up to 12 inches across.
- **The loudest insect**
  Male cicadas (like crickets) rub their abdomens so loud they can be heard from 1,312 ft away.

Key Facts: Plants

Plant records

- **The smallest plant**
  The smallest plant is the duckweed Wolffia arrhiza, which has fronds less than 0.04 inch across.
- **The biggest plant**
  The biggest plant is the Giant Sequioa tree called General Sherman in California, which is 272 feet tall and 82 feet around the trunk.
- **The oldest plant**
  The oldest plant is a lichen in Antarctica thought to be more than 10,000 years old.
- **The tallest tree**
  A eucalyptus in Victoria, Australia, is 470 feet tall.

- **The biggest flower**
  The biggest flower is the Rafflesia of Indonesia, which has blooms more than 6.5 feet across.
- **The biggest water plant**
  The biggest water plant is the Amazon water lily, which has leaves more than 6 feet across.
- **The biggest leaves**
  The biggest leaves belong to the raffia palm, which can grow up to 82 feet long.
- **The deepest roots**
  The deepest roots belong to a fig tree growing in South Africa, which has roots down more than 390 feet.

- **The biggest seed**
  The biggest seed is the coco de mer coconut, which weighs up to 44 pounds.
- **The fastest-growing plant**
  The fastest growing plant is the bamboo, which can grow 3.3 feet in a single day.

Plants

1. **Flowering plants, or angiosperms**
   Monocotyledons
   (one leaf sprout, e.g., grasses, cereals, tulips, and daffodils)
   Dicotyledons
   (two leaf sprout, e.g., most deciduous trees, vegetables, and fruits)
2. **Gymnosperms**
   Conifers
   (e.g., spruces, firs, pines, and larches)
   Cycads
   Gingkos
3. **Ferns**
4. **Club mosses**
5. **Horsetails**
6. **Mosses and liverworts**
7. **Algae**
   Red
   Green
   Brown

Fungi

1. Rusts and mildews
2. Molds
3. Sac fungi
4. Club fungi
5. Imperfect fungi
6. Slime molds

Plant environments

Temperate woodlands
Deciduous
- trees such as beeches, birches, hickories, maples, oaks, poplars, and walnuts
- shrubs such as brambles, hawthorn, and honeysuckle
- woodland flowers such as bluebells, primroses, foxgloves, willow herbs and anenomes

Coniferous
- trees such as redwoods, giant sequoias, Douglas firs, cedars, and pines
- small trees such as rowan and hazel
- ferns
- bilberries

Grasslands
- grasses such as tussock, marram, meadow, blue, and rye
- trees and shrubs such as acacia, thorn, baobab, and

rokerboom
- flowers such as vetches, trefoils, orchids, blazing star, worts, and coneflowers

Tropical forests
- trees such as mahoganies, teaks, banyans, and palms
- lichens
- vines and lianas
- epiphytes such as orchids, ferns, tree ferns, and bromeliads
- carnivorous plants such as Venus flytraps and pitcher plants

Lakes and rivers
- reeds, rushes, and papyrus
- sedges
- worts such as bladderwort and fanwort
- water crowfoot
- waterlilies and irises
- water hyacinths

Deserts
- cacti
- creosote bushes, thorn trees, quiver trees, Joshua trees, sagebrush, yuccas, and prickly pear
- window plants and pebble plants
- palm trees
- evening primrose

High mountains
- rowan and dwarf willow, crowberries, and bilberries
- wild flowers such as alpine bluebells, mountain avens, gentian, edelweiss, snowbells, saxifrage, and saussurea
- grasses and mosses

Key Facts: Body

People: tallest, shortest, oldest, youngest

- The tallest man ever was the American Robert Wadlow (b. 1918), who reached a towering 8.9 feet tall.
- The shortest man is Chandra Bahadur Dangi from Nepal, who is just 1.8 feet tall.
- The fattest man ever was American Jon Minnoch, who weighed 1,400 pounds when he died in 1983.
- The lightest human adult ever was the Mexican girl Lucia Xarate, who weighed just 4.7 pounds when she was 17 in 1889.
- There is a woman in Africa who is thought to be 150 years old, but no one can prove it.
- In 1997, French woman Jeanne Calment died aged 122 years and 164 days.
- In 1986, a Japanese man, Shigechiyo Izumi, died aged 120 years and 237 days.
- The most children born at once were decaplets—2 boys and 8 girls born in 1946 in Bacacy, Brazil.
- Mr. and Mrs. Vassileyev, who lived near Moscow in 1782, had 69 of their own children.

Inside the body

- There are over 600 billion cells in your body.
- There are over 200 different types of cell in your body.
- There are 100 billion nerve cells in your brain.
- 14% of your body weight is bone; 40% is muscle.
- You have 206 bones in your body.
- Babies have 270 bones.
- There are 22 bones in your skull.
- There are 33 bones, or vertebrae, in your spine.
- You have 7 pairs of true ribs, 3 false ribs, and 2 floating ribs.
- There are 27 bones in your hand.
- The longest bone is the femur, or thighbone.
- You have 640 muscles in your body.
- The longest muscle is the sartorius on the inside of the thigh.
- The biggest muscle in your body is the gluteus maximus, or buttock.

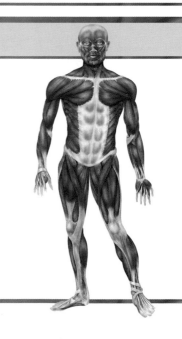

Breath facts

- You will probably take about 600 million breaths if you live to the age of 75.
- Every minute you are alive, you breathe in more than 1.5 gallons of air.
- A normal breath takes in about 1.7 cups of air. A deep breath can take up to 1 gallon.
- On average, you breathe about 13–17 times a minute.
- If you run hard, you may have to breathe up to 80 times a minute.
- Newborn babies breathe about 40 times a minute.
- There are about 300 million little air sacs, or alveoli, in your body.
- Opened out and laid flat, your lungs would cover an area about the size of a tennis court.
- There are over 1,500 miles of airways in your lungs.

Blood count

- Your heart beats 30 million times each year.
- The chambers of the heart each hold about 2.4 cups of blood.
- Pulse rates average 60 to 100 beats a minute.
- Blood travels through the capillaries at 3.3 feet a second.
- There are 37,300 miles of capillaries in your body.
- Capillaries may be just a 0.0004 inch thick.
- Someone who weighs 165 lb has about 1.3 gallons of blood.
- Someone who weighs 77 lb has 2.6 quarts of blood.
- Someone who weighs 165 lb and lives in the high Andes has about 1.6 gallons of blood.
- A microliter of blood holds 4-6 million red blood cells, 5,000–10,000 white blood cells, and 150,000–500,000 platelets. (1 microliter = one-millionth of a quart)
- Blood is 60% plasma.
- Plasma is 90% water.
- There are 13 blood clotting factors, numbers I-XIII.
- There are 4 blood groups: A, O, N, and ABO.
- 85% belong to the blood type Rh (Rhesus) positive. 15% are Rh negative.

Milestones

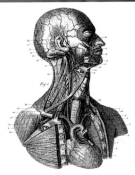

- 1543: Vesalius created his book *De Humani Corporis Fabrica*—which became the basis of modern anatomy.
- 1550: Gabriel Fallopio's close study of the body revealed tiny structures.
- 1590: Santorio Sanctorius created the science of physiology. He also showed how to measure pulse and temperature.
- 1628: William Harvey revealed how the heart circulates blood.
- 1661: Using a microscope, Marcello Malphigi saw tiny blood vessels called capillaries.
- 1798: Edward Jenner showed people could be vaccinated against infectious diseases.
- 1840s: Rudolf Virchow and Jakob Henle found that the body is built up of tissues made of tiny cells.
- 1900: Karl Landsteiner showed that people's blood belongs to different groups.

Index

squirrel 43
St. Bernard 55
stack 150, 290–291
stalactite 173, 292–293
stalagmite 173, 292–293
stamens 186
standard candles 119, 319
stapes 23
star anise 93
stars 105, 112–113, 116–117, 123, 302–303, 312–316, 318–319, 321
static electricity 155, 338
statics 167
stem 24
steppes 202
sternum (see bones)
stethoscope 34
stigma 186
stomach 29, 250
stomata 71
Stone Age 241
stonefish 237
storm surge 132
storms 129, 132
stratosphere 129
strawberry plant 73
strike 146
strirrup (see bones, also stapes)
stromatolites 270
strontium 161
style 186
subatomic particles 174
subduction 135, 140
submarines 336
submillimeter 303
succulents 94, 205
suckers 73
Sudan Desert 288
sugar 191
sugar cane 91
sulfur 106, 141, 175
sulfuric acid 105, 308–309
Sumer 247
Sumeria 248
Sun 102–103, 104, 108–109,

115, 118–119, 123, 130–131, 132,   136, 157, 168, 296–302, 308–   312, 314, 316–319, 346–347
sunflower 90
sunspot 103, 300–301
supercells 133
superforce 320
supergiant stars 314–315
supernova 113, 119, 314–315, 319
superplumes 134
surgery 38–39
suspension (chemical) 337
swallowhole 292–293
swan 60
swells 291
swim bladder 237
synapse 25, 263
syncline 146, 277
system 105, 110–111, 120, 123

T

tadpole 64–65, 232
takin 45
taproot 72, 77
Tasmanian devil 230
taste 23, 260–261
taste bud 260–261
tea 92
tectonic plate 135, 142, 144–145, 272, 275, 277, 279–281
teeth 251
telescope 302–303
television 158
Telstar 306
temperature 330
tephra 142
terminal velocity 167
terminator 299
termite 67
terrier 54
Tertiary Period 137, 269
testicles 26, 265
tetanus 36

Tethys 107
tetracycline 36
TGV 335
thalamus 24
thermometer 170–171, 330
thermosphere 129
thinking 262–263
thorax 66–67
thorny devil 231
thrift 76
Thrust SSC 332
thunder 130
Tibet 224
tidal boom 337
tides 150, 291
tiger 46
timber 194
timber wolf 225
time zones 127
Tiros 1 306
Titan 107, 311
Titanic 287
titanium 39
toad 64–65
toadstools 86
togas 249
tongue 260–261
tor 283
torch 339
Tornado Alley 133
tortoise 63
toucan 212–213
touch 260–261
trabeculae 254
trace fossil 270
trachea 16–17
trajectory 116, 307
transistor 158, 340
Transition metals 176–177
translucent 162
transparent 162
transplant 38
tree rings 188
tree-line 206
trees 78–83, 184–185
tremors 145

Acknowledgments

All photographs from
Miles Kelly Archive